INVENTING THE RENAISSANCE PUTTO

BETTIE ALLISON RAND LECTURES
IN ART HISTORY

Inventing the Renaissance Putto

CHARLES DEMPSEY

The University of North Carolina Press
Chapel Hill & London

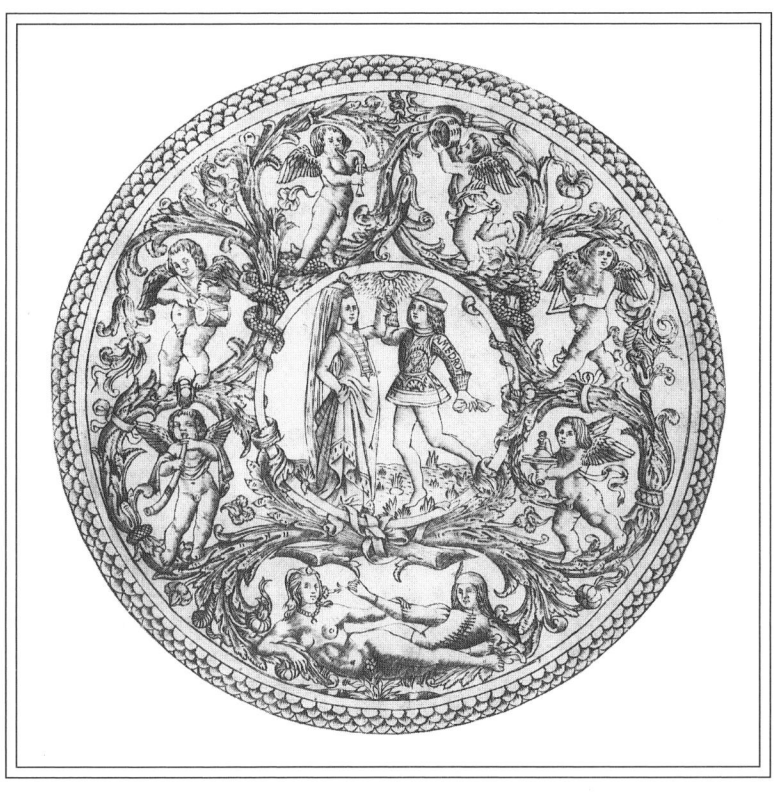

© 2001 The University of North Carolina Press
All rights reserved

Designed by April Leidig-Higgins
Set in Jenson by Keystone Typesetting, Inc.
Manufactured in the United States of America

The paper in this book meets the guidelines for permanence and
durability of the Committee on Production Guidelines for
Book Longevity of the Council on Library Resources.

The publication of books in this series is made possible through
the generous support of William G. Rand in memory of
Bettie Allison Rand.

Library of Congress Cataloging-in-Publication Data
Dempsey, Charles.
Inventing the Renaissance putto / Charles Dempsey.
p. cm.—(Bettie Allison Rand lectures in art history)
Includes bibliographical references and index.
ISBN 0-8078-2616-2 (cloth: alk. paper)
1. Arts, Italian. 2. Arts, Renaissance—Italy. 3. Angels in art.
4. Popular culture—Italy—Influence. I. Title. II. Series.
NX552.AI D455 2001   709'45'09024—DC21   00-051206

05 04 03 02 01   5 4 3 2 1

Frontispiece. Baccio Baldini, *Dancers Encircled in a Wreath
of Music-Making Sprites*, London, British Museum.
(Photograph © The British Museum)

In loving memory of
Betsey Mills Beach Dempsey

CONTENTS

Preface ix

CHAPTER ONE
Donatello and the
Invention of the Putto
1

CHAPTER TWO
Spiritelli d'Amore:
Idle Fancies and Childish Follies
63

CHAPTER THREE
Spirits of the Nightmare:
Botticelli's *Mars and Venus* as a Problem
in Grammatical Interpretation
107

CHAPTER FOUR
Politian's *Stanze per la Giostra
di Giuliano de' Medici*:
Julio's False Dream
147

CHAPTER FIVE
The End of the Masquerade
189

Notes 233

Index 269

PREFACE

THIS BOOK had already been partly written when I received the welcome invitation to deliver the Bettie Alison Rand Lectures at the University of North Carolina at Chapel Hill. In order to adapt the material to the lecture format, I considerably altered and rearranged my text (which I have in part restored and amplified upon), and I gave the lectures under the hastily chosen and rather cumbersome title, "Renaissance and Renovation in Florentine Art: Classical Tradition and Vernacular Expression." This managed simultaneously to offer rather more, but also rather less, than I intended. As the title implied, with its echo of Erwin Panofsky's classic *Renaissance and Renascences in Western Art*, I had hoped (and still do) that my lectures might be seen as contributing to the larger effort to define the Renaissance itself.

There are perennial problems of period definition that gain in intensity from time to time in historical studies, exciting intense interest and debate for a while and then receding again, not because they have been resolved so much as from temporary exhaustion. Yet, whether actively contended or lying passively dormant, such problems can never be far from any scholar's mind. One example is the question of Mannerism, which has been much discussed over the last forty years, but which recently has been relatively muted as scholars have turned their attention to other things. Another is the more complex question of the Renaissance itself, which, despite Panofsky's defense of the concept, has become downright unfashionable even to mention among social and economic historians (and their art-historical epigones), who prefer instead to speak of the Early Modern period. Yet there is no sign that cultural historians of humanism and scholars of literature and the arts are conceding that the concept of the Renaissance can be so easily and definitively eradicated. Nor do I think it likely that it will be. After all, the conviction that a renewal of learning, literature, and the arts occurred during the two and a half centuries ranging from Dante and Petrarch to Politian and Bembo on the one hand, and Giotto and Simone Martini to Raphael and Michelangelo on the other, is one stated from the very inception of that period in the late years of the thirteenth century. So far as the visual arts are concerned, it is one affirmed by Ghiberti in his *Commentarii* and Vasari in his *Vite*. The historical development of the cultural renewal they and many others describe has moreover been filled in—and in the minutest detail—during the passage of nearly half a millennium.

What occurred in that period was the progressive flowering of new linguistic and visual forms of expression that, through mutual interchange—bringing together the new learning with the new literature and art—produced a slowly evolving but measurable change in the ways people perceived the world, and in the very language (whether literary or plastic) they used to describe their experience of it. If in Petrarch and Boccaccio there appear the earliest fruits of the new spirit of humanism, it is, as Eugenio Garin has written, in Politian's *Stanze per la Giostra di Giuliano de'Medici* that for the first time Italian seems to speak in perfect Latin; and, moreover, in his exquisite epicedion on the death of Albiera degli Albizzi that Latin itself seems to speak perfect Italian. Much the same might be said of Mantegna's Latinity in the *Triumph of Caesar*, in which, notwithstanding his learnedly antiquarian and rather dusty *Romanitas*, the artist's performance is also determined by his experience of the contemporary idioms of Squarcione and Donatello, as well as the vernacular *trionfi* enacted for court festivals and jousts. It is certainly true of Botticelli's expression in the *Primavera*, in which, as I have suggested in several earlier studies, a philologically refined classical theme is conceived as a species of vernacular poetry, invoking the shared experiences of the present. This book is intended as an extension of that argument. As Pierre Francastel perceived (and Aby Warburg before him), the *Primavera* is a true "fête mythologique" parallel to the one celebrated in Politian's *Stanze*. In both works of art classical learning appears in a contemporary, vernacular guise. The result for both poetry and painting was the creation, on the one hand, of art of the highest degree of refinement, classically learned and aristocratic in the extreme, and, on the other hand, a new art that was, by mythologizing contemporary experiences as enacted in the public rituals and civic feasts of Florence, at the same time popular and accessible to all. In a deeper sense, as the Renaissance unfolds over the slow evolution of two centuries, we can trace in the development of art and literature, as classical and vernacular cultures become more and more entwined, the progression of a slow but clear alteration in general cultural coloration, deepening like a stain, that amounts to a cultural, and even psychological mutation. For the ways in which human beings see the world, and represent it, and the ways they put their perceptions into language, determines who they are.

Panofsky's *Renaissance and Renascences* came out when I was still a graduate student working under the influence of his inspiring guidance and encouragement, for which I shall always be grateful. The book provoked then, as it still does, great admiration for its learning and warm debate over its powerfully argued central thesis. In retrospect it now appears that Panofsky, in common with most scholars of his generation, did not sufficiently acknowledge the place of vernacular culture in his conception of the Renaissance, which he understood to be an almost literal rebirth, or revival, of the forms of classical antiquity. Hence for him there could be no real Renaissance until classical forms of expression (embodying pathos, in Aristotelian terms) had for the first time been truly united with classical content (or ethos). In his view this union did not occur until the last quarter of the fifteenth century, first becoming manifest precisely in the works of Mantegna (in particular the *Triumph of Caesar*) and Botticelli (notably in *The Birth of Venus*). However, because his formulation did not take into account that Botticelli's paintings (as well as Politian's poetry) represent not a beginning but rather a turning point, and a crucial one, in a long development traceable from Giotto and Simone Martini (and Petrarch) to its completion in the generation of Raphael (and Bembo), the result was a startling, and indeed eccentric, revision, not only of the dating, but also the very concept of the Renaissance. For there never had been a desire for the revival of antiquity as such, for the literal renaissance of a long dead past (as is implied in the nineteenth-century coinage of the word), but rather an intention to renew the present by ennobling and perfecting its own living institutions, and its own forms of artistic and literary expression (as is implied in the fifteenth-century concept of a *renovatio litteris*). Lorenzo de'Medici's famous motto, *Le tems revient*, refers precisely to his own desire to renew vernacular literature and art, in which the experiences of life in the present are expressed by measuring them in relation to, and placing them in rivalry with, the supreme achievements of the great cultures of Italy, both Latin and Tuscan. As he wrote in the letter prefacing the poems gathered together in the *Raccolta Aragonese*, the new flowering of literature he envisaged was conceived not as a rebirth of the past, but as a *renovatio* of the present, in exactly the same sense of the renewal of the world each spring (*renovatio mundi*). In such a way the present found its own place in an evolving history, renewing itself by assimilating and emulating the achievements of the past, and moreover found reliable standards for measuring its own performance by setting this in rivalry with not just one, but both of the great cultures of Italy, as set forth in the traditions of Latin and the vernacular.

Roberti Longhi once wrote that when Primaticcio and Rosso Fiorentino arrived in France they found the forest of Fontainebleau filled with hobgoblins and kobolds, but when they left it was populated instead with nymphs and Satyrs. In fact hobgoblins and Satyrs are cognate beings representing very similar concepts, the former being rooted in popular superstition, and the latter having been refined and even civilized (as Longhi intended to suggest) in classical poetry and literature. These and similar spirits comprise the theme of this book, for which I have adopted the figure of the infant putto as the test case for examining the interaction between vernacular and classical forms of expression in the fifteenth century. I chose the putto because on the one hand the figure is an instance of classical revival, owing its origins in particular to representations of infant *Bacchoi* on second-century Roman sarcophagi, and because on the other hand it embodies a vernacular concept or interpretation of these tiny *genii*, which were commonly identified as *spiritelli*, or sprites. The different meanings and various deployments of the putto in art hence perfectly illuminate the complex interactions between contemporary expression and ancient tradition, nourished by the coming together of the new learning and the new art, that I have outlined above.

In addition, the artistic invention and ornamental deployment of the new figure of the putto-*spiritello*, which owes its existence above all to the genius of Donatello, constitute a prime example of the initial discovery and instantaneously widespread dissemination of what Warburg named a *Pathosformel*, that is, a new expressive archetype. His example was the figure of the "Nymph" with agitated draperies and wind-tossed hair, which he recognized as the expressive essence of the liveliness, and indeed forthrightly sexual energies, latent not only in classical nymphs and goddesses, but also, and especially, in Quattrocento Florentine girls approaching marriageable age, who were moreover called *ninfe* in the vernacular tongue. Another, expressly classical, example—that is to say one in which the pathos of the figure directly expresses its own classical ethos in a way that is certainly not true for the Florentine *Ninfa*, who, whatever may be her relationship to classical poetic and formal prototypes, is in her character (or ethos) very much a creature of the fifteenth century—is provided by the *Laokoon*, only discovered in 1506 and immediately recognized as the *exemplum doloris par excellence*. The recognition of the *Laokoon* as such an exemplum of a particular *Pathosformel* was recently documented in great detail by Sonia Maffei in the appendix of sixteenth-century responses to the statue she attached to Salvatore Settis's recent indispensable study, *Laocoonte: Fama e Stile* (Rome, 1999). Suffice it only to mention Pietro Aretino's identification (followed by Ulisse Aldrovandi) of *Laokoon* as expressive of *il dolore*, and his two sons of the *pathe* of fear (*la paura*) and death (*la morte*); and Aretino's consequent recommendation (followed by Giovanni Andrea Gilio) that the image of *Laokoon* might therefore serve as a model for the agonies of martyrdom. Strictly speaking, Laokoon's younger son expresses the pathos of dying, his head thrown back with parted lips echoing another famous ancient *exemplum moriendi*, the so-called *Alessandro morente*. The *exemplum mortis* proper had already been well established in the previous century on the models of the so-called *letto di Policleto* and the figure of the dead Meleager on numerous Roman sarcophagi.

It is Anthony Colantuono's great merit, as we will see in the following pages, to have identified the infant putto (called *tener* in Latin) as a *Pathosformel* for innocent tenderness. We shall see how his vernacular designation as a volatile *spiritello*, or airy sprite, further suggests the fecklessness and sheer joy of infancy, guileless and as yet unencumbered by any understanding of right and wrong, making of the putto the perfect figuration for all those uncontrollable sensations and irrational physical and mental alterations that constantly arise in the body unbidden, whether induced by a sudden fright, the rhapsodical effects of music, excessive drinking, sexual arousal, or the stunning experience of suddenly falling overwhelmingly in love at first sight. The very name *spiritello*, moreover, which has no real Latin equivalent, also places the infant sprite securely in the company (as any reader of Shakespeare will immediately sense) of such minor demons of the popular imagination as the hobgoblins and fairies that populated the *forêt de Fontainebleau* before Primaticcio and Rosso Fiorentino brought the Renaissance to France. It is this that makes study of the putto in his Quattrocento origins so fruitful. On the one hand the figure exemplifies a classical revival, in form and partially in content; and on the other it also expresses in vernacular terms popular concepts and imaginative experiences. At one and the same time learned and popular, formally sophisticated in the hands of artists and poets like Donatello and Politian, it is also immediately apprehensible in its charm and adaptability, accessible to all. It is, as Eugenio Garin once wrote of Politian's description of a rose, *umanissima*—precisely because of its union of these two terms, traditional and new, aristocratic and popular, learned and familiar, classic and vernacular.

A special case of the *spiritello* is that of the putto who plays the bogey man, concealing his true identity behind a ferocious Silenus-mask or hiding beneath Mars's armor in order to frighten some equally childish companion. The putto thus disguised has the same name in both Latin and the vernacular, a *larva*, and his earliest appearance in art is in plaquettes and manuscript illuminations deriving from Roman jewelry and sarcophagi. The meaning of the figure, as is set out in some detail in this book, is more thoroughly humanist in its foundations than is that of the *spiritello*, but at the same time it announces a theme that is important to the argument of my last three chapters, namely that of masking. These chapters are all devoted to exegesis of the imagery of two works of art, one a painting and the other a poem: Botticelli's *Mars and Venus* in London, the invention for which was devised by the humanist philologist and poet Politian; and Politian's own vernacular poem entitled *Stanze cominciate per la giostra di Giuliano de'Medici*. As works of art each develops parallel ideas directly attributable to a single mind, and as performances each exemplifies the expressive powers latent in what began as a lighthearted humanist *facetia*. The final chapter ends with a consideration of the phenomenon of masking itself—as this appears in the public *mascherate* invented and sponsored by Lorenzo de'Medici, and as the mask provides the hermeneutical crux for interpreting the realities veiled beneath the beautiful fictions of poetry and art in Laurentian Florence.

I AM GRATEFUL to Mary Sturgeon and the Department of the History of Art at the University of North Carolina at Chapel Hill for their invitation to deliver the Bettie Allison Rand Lectures, and for the hospitality they extended to me during my visit. I recall with special pleasure meeting and conversing with many old friends, among them Mary Sturgeon, Mary Pardo, Jaroslav Folda, Helen Hills, all members of the Department of Art History at Chapel Hill, as well as Louise Rice of the Art History Department at Duke University, and Charles Millard, then only just retired as Director of the Ackland Art Museum. I am especially beholden to William Rand, who endowed the Lectures in memory of his wife, and whose personal warmth and hospitality, and that of his family, I remember with particular pleasure. I am grateful to Ann Woodward, Curator of Slides and Photographs for the Department of History of Art at The Johns Hopkins University, for her help in securing photographs and permissions, as well as to Rosemary Trippe and Jane Van Deuren for the work they did in ordering and arranging the illustrative material. Thanks are also due to Elaine Maisner and the staff of the University of North Carolina Press for their work in seeing this book through to its final production. As always, Elizabeth Cropper's support and informed criticism have been invaluable, and are especially appreciated.

The invitation to present these lectures was especially opportune in that it gave me the spur I needed to complete the work I had already begun, and parts of which I had presented in several forums. I am especially grateful to Daniel Arasse for inviting me to discuss some of this material in seminars I gave as a visiting professor at the École des Hautes Études en Sciences Sociales in 1995; and to Marc Fumaroli for his invitation to present several of my arguments in a series of lectures I read as a Visiting Professor at the Collège de France in 1996. The discussions that attended these lectures were valuable in helping to sharpen my arguments, as was the warm and thoughtful questioning I received when I presented some of my material at Yale University in 1998 and as Robert Lehman Lecturer at Emory University in 1999. I am especially grateful to David Quint for the invitation to speak at Yale, and for his abiding interest, acute and informed criticism, and encouragement throughout the course of my work. Special thanks are also due to C. Jean Campbell for her hospitality at Emory, and for her firm and probing criticism; and to Hellmut Wohl, whose generous and careful reading of my manuscript has saved me from several blunders. Some of the material presented in chapter five was the subject of the Josephine Waters Bennett Lecture at the annual meetings of the Renaissance Society of America in 1998, which was then published as "Portraits and Masks in the Art of Lorenzo de'Medici, Botticelli, and Politian's *Stanze per la Giostra*," *Renaissance Quarterly* 52(1999): 1–42. Similarly, parts of my discussion of the putto-*spiritello* were first tested in contributions to two Festschrifts: "Donatello's Spiritelli" in *Ars naturam adiuvans: Festschrift für Matthias Winner zum 11. März 1966*, edited by Victoria von Flemming and Sebastian Schütze (Mainz am Rhein, 1996), 50–61; and "Niccolò di Giovanni's *Spiritelli* in the Chapel of the Blessed Giovanni Orsini in the Cathedral of Trogir," in *Razprave iz Europske Umetnosti za Ksenijo Rosman*, edited by Barbara Jaki (Ljubljana, 1999),

43–55. Finally, some of my arguments concerning the larvate putto were presented at a symposium held at Villa I Tatti on the occasion of the five-hundredth anniversary of Lorenzo de'Medici's death, and published as "Lorenzo's Ombra," in *Lorenzo il Magnifico e il suo mondo* (Convegno internazionale di studi, Firenze, 9–13 giugno 1992), edited by Gian Carlo Garfagnini (Florence, 1994), 341–55.

Villa Spelman
March 2000

INVENTING THE RENAISSANCE PUTTO

CHAPTER ONE

Donatello and the Invention of the Putto

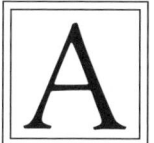FTER THE publication of *Laokoon* in 1766, the great Gotthold Ephraim Lessing became embroiled in a long polemic with Christian Adolf Klotz (1738–1771), then a young professor at the University of Halle, who provoked from him the fifty-seven *Antiquarian Letters*, as well as his famous essay of 1769, *How the Ancients Represented Death*. This had been written in response to Klotz's assertion that Lessing was mistaken in saying that the ancients had not shown Death as a skeleton, citing in refutation many ancient representations of skeletons. Lessing pointed out that he had not said the ancients did not represent skeletons in art, only that for them skeletons did not personify Death; they were rather *larvae*, the spirits of the dead. Lessing was right, but his true polemic did not turn on antiquarian quibbles so much as it did on a mindlessly deployed pedantry. As he wrote, "I would beg [Herr Klotz] to consult his understanding rather more than his memory."[1]

More famous than Lessing's assertion about skeletal *larvae* was his further claim that the winged infant or youth in ancient art did not necessarily denote Amor, but can also designate any of the many possible types of genius, of which the genius of Love is but one. For ancient representations of Death, twin brother to Sleep, he adduced funerary sculptures showing winged infants or youths leaning on reversed torches. One of the best known of these, reproduced by Lessing for the frontispiece to *How the Ancients Represented Death* (Fig. 1), had been engraved by Pietro Santi Bartoli for the sumptuous *Admiranda romanarum antiquitatum* of 1691 (Fig. 2). It derives from a Roman sarcophagus sculptured with the

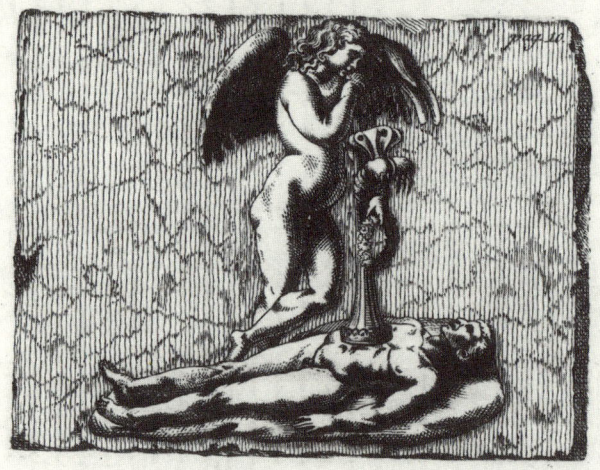

FIGURE I
Anonymous engraver, frontispiece to Gotthold Ephraim Lessing, *Wie die Alten den Tod gebildet*, Berlin, 1769. (Photograph: Special Collections, Milton S. Eisenhower Library, The Johns Hopkins University)

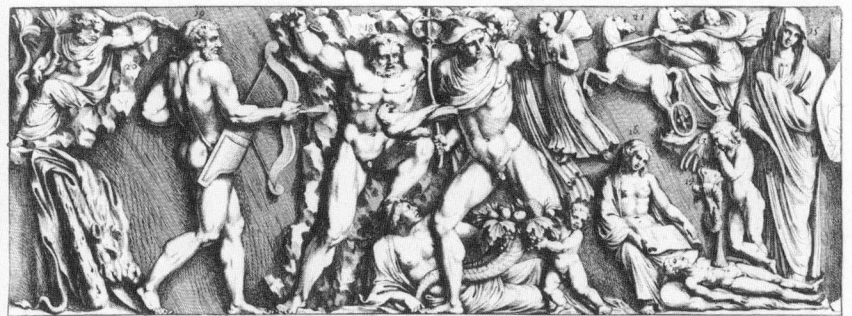

FIGURE 2
Pietro Santi Bartoli, *Roman Sarcophagus with the Myth of Prometheus*. Engraving from Pietro Santi Bartoli and Giovan Pietro Bellori, *Admiranda romanarum antiquitatum*, Rome, 1691 (fol. 67). (Photograph: Special Collections, Milton S. Eisenhower Library, The Johns Hopkins University)

myth of Prometheus, then in the collection of Prince Camillo Pamphili, on which appears a winged youth extinguishing a torch on the breast of a recumbent figure. In the state of scholarship as inherited by Klotz, such a youth could only mean Amor, and this he had documented by drawing up long lists of examples drawn from the entire corpus of antiquarian scholarly books. After all, as Giovanni Pietro Bellori had written in the caption prepared for Bartoli's engraving, it is Love who is shown extinguishing the torch, that is, the affections, in the breast of the dead man:—"Amor facem et affectus in pectore demortui hominis extinguit."[2]

"This figure, says Bellori, is Amor," thundered Lessing in reply, "and I say, this figure is Death!" More precisely, it is the genius of Death, even as a winged youth in antiquity might in a different context represent the genius of Love, or indeed any of the myriad kinds of genius:

> Not every winged boy or youth need be an Amor. Amor and the swarm of his brothers had this form in common with various spiritual beings. How many of the race of genii were shown as boys? And

what had not its genius? Every place, every man, every human social connection, every human occupation from the lowest to the highest, indeed I might say every inanimate thing whose preservation was of consequence, had its genius. Had this not been a wholly unknown matter to Herr Klotz, and others too, he would surely have spared us the greater part of his sugary story of Amor on engraved gems. With the most attentive fingers this great scholar has leafed through all the engraved books searching for this pretty little god, and wherever he saw a naked little boy, there he cried: Amor! Amor! and quickly registered him in his catalogue. I wish much patience to the scrutinizer of these Klotzian Amors. At every moment he will have to eject one from the ranks. But more of this elsewhere.[3]

It is certainly true that by the sixteenth and seventeenth centuries winged infants and youths in art had become universally understood to be representations of love gods, *amorini*, or cupids, and, Lessing to the contrary notwithstanding, this automatic identification still remains in force. An instructive example of its power appears in Albert Gilbert's statue in Piccadilly Circus in London (Fig. 3), commissioned as a memorial to the seventh Earl of Shaftesbury and intended as an allegory, in the words of the Memorial Committee, of "Christian Charity." Nevertheless, the figure has always been known to every Londoner as Eros, and rightly so. This is because Gilbert's attempt to personify Christian Charity in the form of a winged and blindfolded boy archer was nothing more than a blunder on his part, the commission of a true visual malapropism. For, contrary to Ernst Gombrich's adducing of his statue as an example of the elusiveness of iconological meaning, it may well be asked if the figure is not unmistakeable in its meaning, and that it was obtuse of Gilbert to think to convince the British public (much less the denizens of Soho!) that the universally known embodiment of erotic love really stood for Christian Charity.[4]

So firm an identification of the putto with the god of love, however, did not always obtain, either in antiquity itself, when, as Lessing pointed out, the infant could embody various types of spiritual beings all broadly

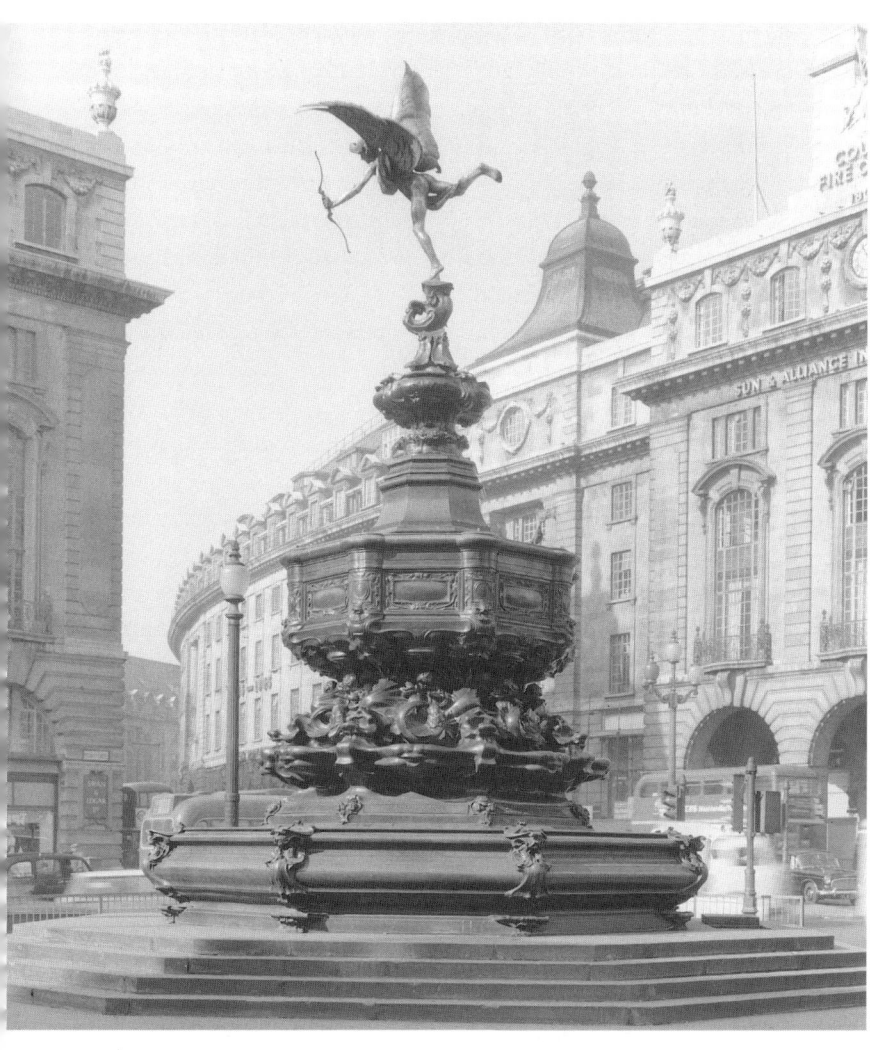

FIGURE 3
Albert Gilbert, *Monument to Anthony Ashley Cooper, Seventh Earl Shaftesbury*, London, Piccadilly Circus. (Photograph: The Conway Library, Courtauld Institute of Art)

denoted by the Latin word *genius*, or at the moment of its definitive revival in the early years of the fifteenth century, when, as we shall see, it was familiarly known in the vernacular as a *spiritello*, a diminutive spirit or sprite. Its artistic origins are as a new form of ornament, and I shall accordingly begin by examining the meaning of the vernacular concept embodied in the *spiritello*, together with the ornamental context in which it most often appears, that of the *festa*; and I shall continue with a consideration of how they transformed, and were in turn transformed by their counterparts in Roman ornament, the genius and the *festa corona*.

A DISTINCTIVE feature of the interior of Amiens cathedral is the rich foliage band adorning the triforium, dating before 1230 (Fig. 4).[5] The decoration is not ancient in style, and it was motivated by the legend of St. Firmin, whose body was discovered in the middle of winter (January 12), at which moment the temperature miraculously rose, so that the trees and flowers blossomed. The miracle was annually commemorated on the day before the feast of the finding of St. Firmin's relics by the appearance of a Green Man (*l'Homme Vert*), played by a beadle dressed in green and wearing a garland of leaves, who distributed foliate garlands to the members of the clergy.[6] The Green Man also appeared on other occasions of great festive significance, such as the visit of the king to Amiens, when the cathedral would be festooned with garlands. He is sculptured in the right tympanum of the west facade, wearing a leafy crown and carrying a flowering branch, following in the path of some members of the clergy bearing the reliquary of St. Firmin (Fig. 5). His attributes of the garland crown and May branch, or *maius*, as well as his very greenness, clearly identify him with the popular festivals of the spring that had been celebrated from time immemorial in the folkloristic traditions of the countryside.[7] The miraculous revival of natural life that attended the finding of St. Firmin's relics is thus celebrated in the permanent feast, or fête, sculptured in the flowering festoons decorating the triforium gallery at Amiens, and in the leaves and buds sprouting from the cathedral's capitals and trefoil windows.

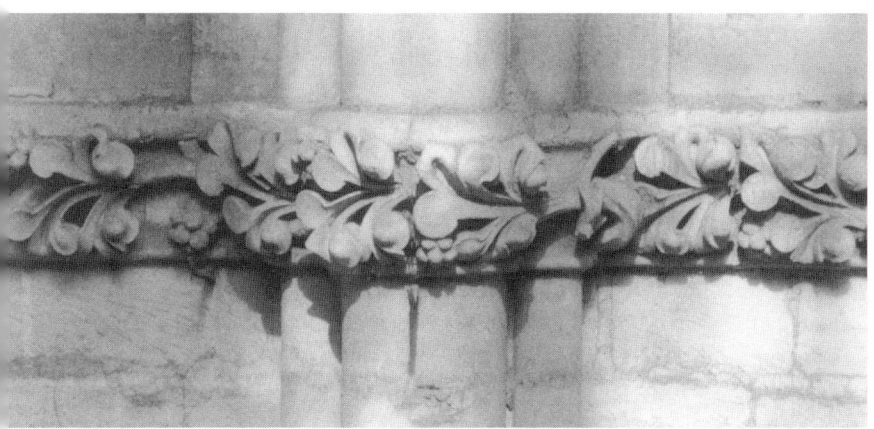

FIGURE 4
Amiens Cathedral, Nave Triforium, foliate relief decoration.
(Photograph by James T. Van Rensselaer)

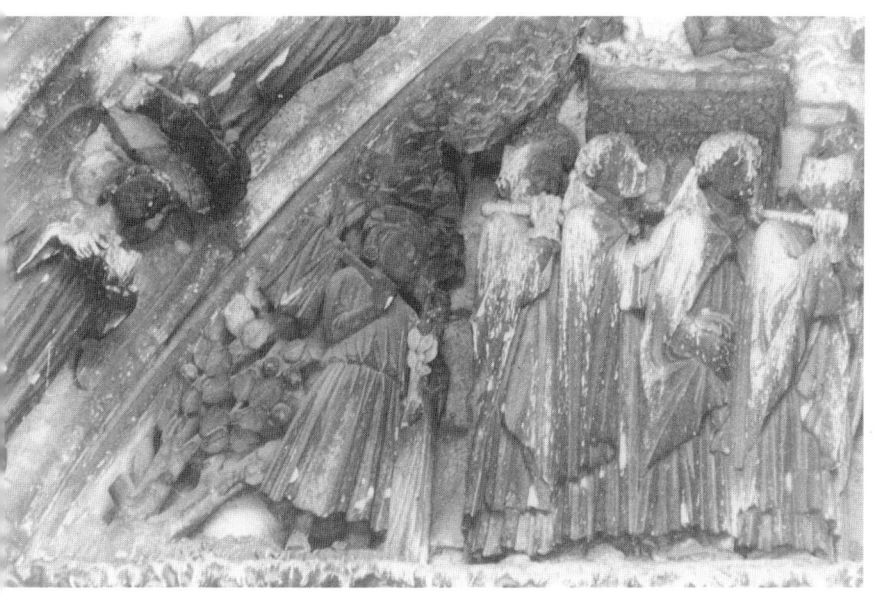

FIGURE 5
Amiens Cathedral, West Facade, North Portal, tympanum relief with
L'homme vert. (Photograph by James T. Van Rensselaer)

In 1453 Maffeo Vallaresso, bishop of Zara in Dalmatia, wrote his friend Ermolao Barbaro the Elder, bishop of Treviso, asking him to send designs for the *feste romane* that had been sculptured by Donatello in Barbaro's palace.[8] About a decade later, we find Filarete describing the main portal of the Medici Bank in Milan (Fig. 6) as decorated with sculptures of various figures, namely "fogliami e spiritegli e feste e l'armi divise."[9] And again, in 1464, we find a note in the *zibaldone* of the Florentine Giovanni Rucellai (1403–1481) describing a *festa* comprising the arms and devices of his family in the boxwood borders of the garden of his villa at Quaracchi, as well as (among much else) topiary *spiritelli coll'archo*.[10] The meaning of *festa* in each instance is not "feast" but "festoon" (*festone*), which is in the etymological sense a decoration for a feast (also a *festa*).[11] Moreover, as Vallaresso's reference to Donatello's *feste romane* testifies, it is a type of festival decoration that is especially associated with ancient Roman forms of ornament. The same usage appears in the extraordinarily detailed contract for building and adorning a chapel dedicated to the Blessed Giovanni Orsini in the Duomo of Trogir, drawn in January of 1468 by the Opera of the Cathedral with Donatello's pupil Niccolò di Giovanni Fiorentino, together with the Albanian architect and sculptor Andrea Alessi. The contract specifies that at the base of the walls of the chapel were to appear seventeen torch-bearing *spiritelli*, or sprites (Fig. 7), save for the part below the statue of Christ, where there were to be instead three *feste romane*; and further on the contract twice calls for other representations of "feste romane de fructi e fo[gl]ie."[12] We may therefore understand the meaning of *festa* to refer to the familiar forms of the Roman garland swag (called a *festa corona* in Latin) that were actually realized in the Orsini Chapel, as well as in Alessi's design for the baptistry (Fig. 8)—that is, a celebratory chain of foliage, fruit, or flowers suspended in swags between supports—often, as in the case of the baptistry, putti or *spiritelli*. We may also understand it to refer to any decorative object capable of being arranged in festoons, as when both Filarete and Giovanni Rucellai refer to *feste* made up of arms and devices (which are also ancient forms of ornament).

As Filarete's description of the *feste romane* adorning the portal of the

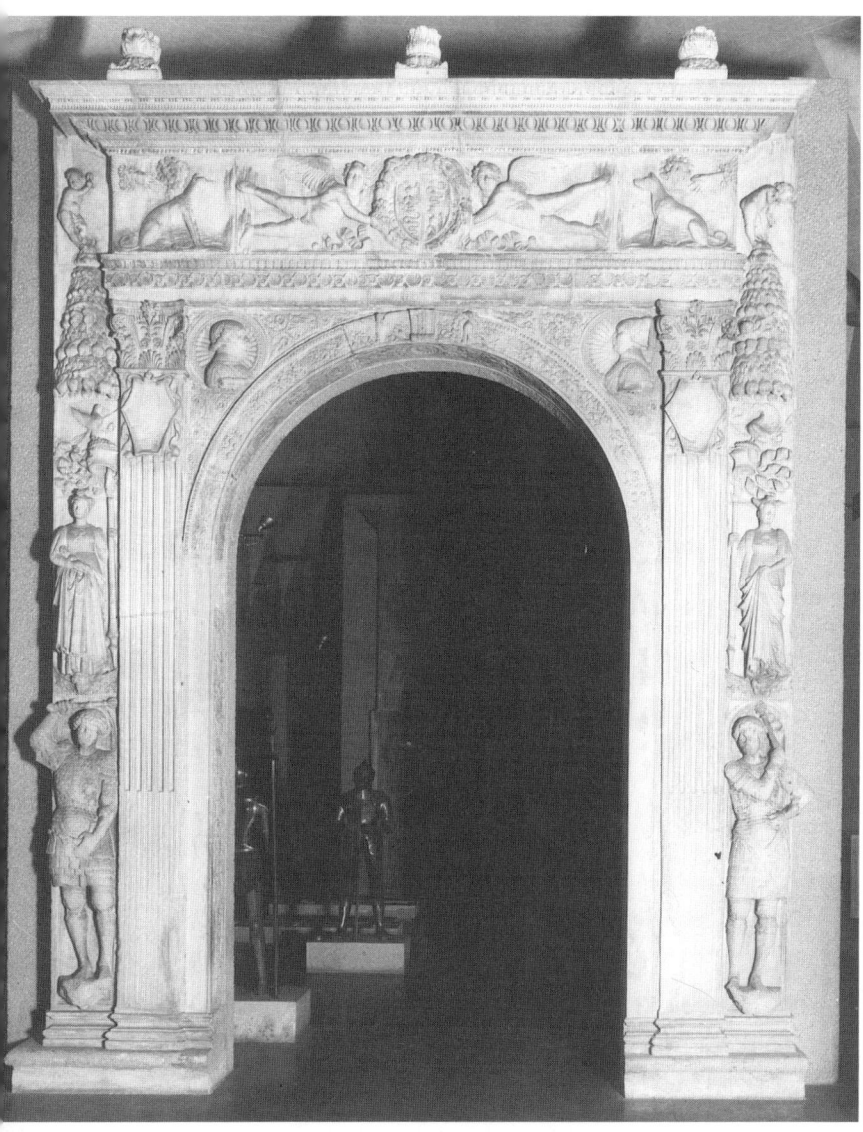

FIGURE 6
Antonio Filarete, facade of the Medici Bank, Milan, Museo Civico.
(Photograph: Milan, Museo Civico)

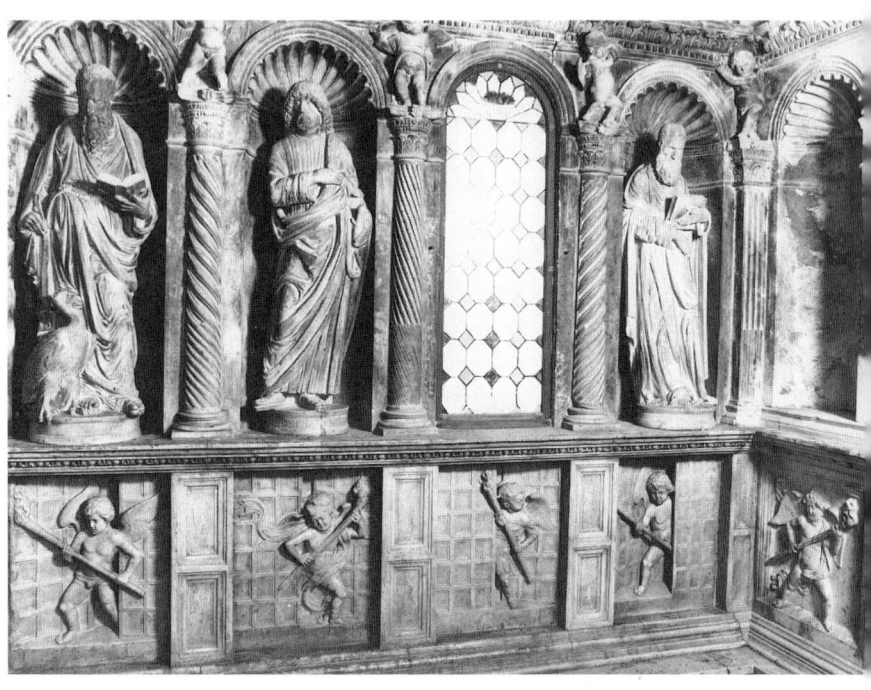

FIGURE 7
Niccolò di Giovanni Fiorentino and Andrea Alessi, *Chapel of the Blessed Giovanni Orsini*, Trogir Cathedral. (Photograph by Živko Bačić)

Medici bank recalls, a row of putti—which he also named as *spiritelli*—bearing garlands of flowers and fruit swinging in loops from their shoulders comprised one of the best known sculptural supports for such festive garlands. The motif gives its name to a familiar type of Roman sarcophagus, known by the classification "garland sarcophagus" (Fig. 9), which makes its appearance in the second century A.D. in the context of Bacchic and seasonal imagery, and the characteristic forms of which were for the first time revived in the Quattrocento, when it appears ubiquitously in art.[13] Garland-bearing putti were virtually unknown to the Italian Middle Ages, making their definitive post-antique reappearance only with Jacopo della Quercia's immortal tomb in San Martino in Lucca for Ilaria del

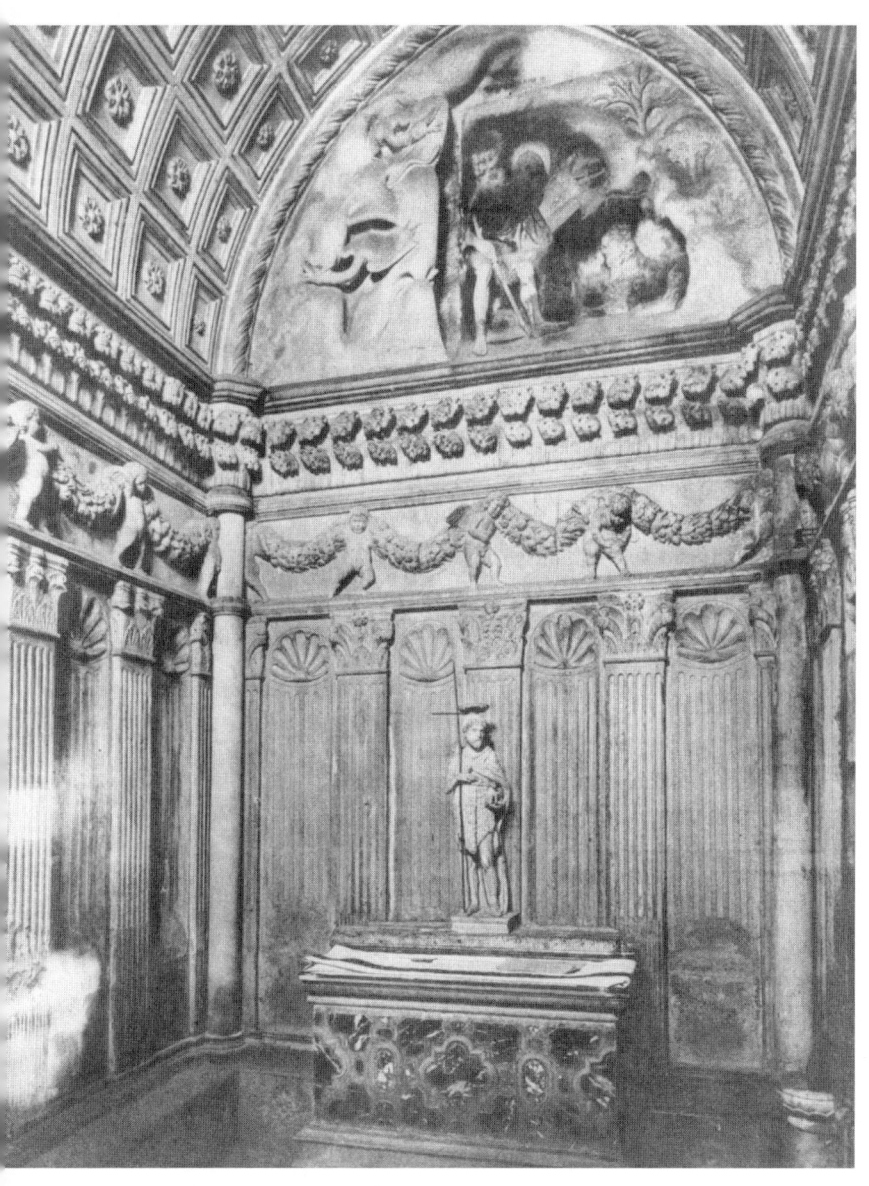

FIGURE 8
Niccolò di Giovanni Fiorentino and Andrea Alessi, Baptistery,
Trogir Cathedral. (Photograph by James T. Van Rensselaer)

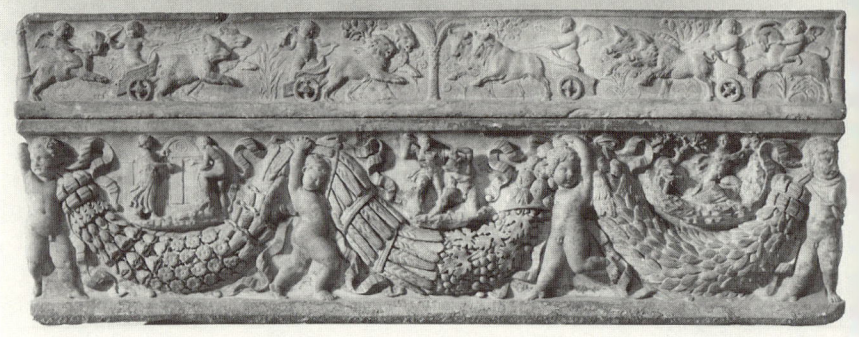

FIGURE 9
Garland Sarcophagus, Roman, second century A.D., New York, Metropolitan Museum of Art. (Photograph: The Metropolitan Museum of Art)

Carretto, who died in childbirth in 1406 (Plate 7).[14] What is more, Quercia's infants are an important part of the central novelty of his conception, since they usurp the place normally reserved for religious images, and do not even appear as infant angels carrying coats of arms or the emblems of Christian salvation. They instead ornament Ilaria's beauty with garlands, *feste romane*, and they do not so much mourn her death in the manner of *pleurants* as celebrate her life. Adolfo Venturi acutely described this celebratory air of Quercia's image, which is enhanced by the sense that, unlike earlier tomb-effigies in the Trecento, Ilaria seems alive:

> Ilaria del Carretto sleeps on her sarcophagus wrapped in an atmosphere of peace. She lies with hands placed one over the other, dressed as for a *festa*, as though prepared for a wedding. *Amorini* with open wings step round the sarcophagus which seems a nuptial bed. They bear festoons of fruit and flowers, garlanding the bed in which the sweet Ilaria dreams. . . . A deceased female had rarely been figured in art: in the Angevin monuments in Naples, Marie de Valois is wrapped in her funeral shroud; Maria di Calabria lies on her death bed; and Maria di Durazzo is presented covered in an arabesque mantle, with the lilied crown, sceptre and globe, as if laid

out in a mortuary chapel. Ilaria del Carretto does not have, like this princess, desiccated and sunken features: Death has respected her beauty and not despoiled her face of its transparent purity. This Christian lady rests in peace, blessed in the sleep of death by the feeling of immortal life. The *genietti* with garlands around the sarcophagus, as in classical urns but without the Bacchic passion of the ancients, ingenuous children instead, form a *corona* [a garland] for her remains.[15]

With the tomb of Ilaria in fact we are confronted with a new concept of ornament, derived specifically from Roman art but at the same time understood and deployed, as we shall see—and as the very words *festa* and *spiritello* indicate—in a vernacular and popular setting, in which context only can it be understood. Venturi was uncertain what to call the garland-bearing infants ornamenting Ilaria's sarcophagus, first calling them *amorini* and then *genietti*. However, neither term agrees with Quattrocento usage. Though nowadays such putti are familiarly called cupids, *amorini*, or *eroti*, the words used to name them in the fifteenth century do not correspond to the classical *eros*, *amor*, or *cupid* (*Amor* and *Cupid* being reserved for the god of love himself). A putto might be generically named in Latin with such formulations as *puer nudus* and *puerulus allatus*; or in the vernacular as *putto*, *puttino*, *bambino*, and even *fanciullino ignudo* (the term used in Donatello's contract of 1429 for the putti on the baptismal font in Siena).[16] Most commonly, however, the putto is called a *spiritello*, or sprite—the word used, as we have seen, by Filarete and in the contract given to Niccolò di Giovanni Fiorentino and Andrea Alessi for the Orsini Chapel in Trogir.[17] *Spiritello* is again the word appearing in Donatello's contract of 1428 for the giddily swirling infants on the Prato pulpit (Fig. 10), as well as for those on the capital that supports it (Fig. 11).[18] In 1432 Cosimo de'Medici paid a painter named Antonio for gilding a *spiritello* placed over a well in the *orticino del pozzo* of the house he shared with his brother in the via Larga, before the Palazzo Medici was built, and Doris Carl has suggested this might be the *idolo di bronzo in su la palla* mentioned in inventories of the *casa vecchia* made in 1503 and 1516. She also noticed the

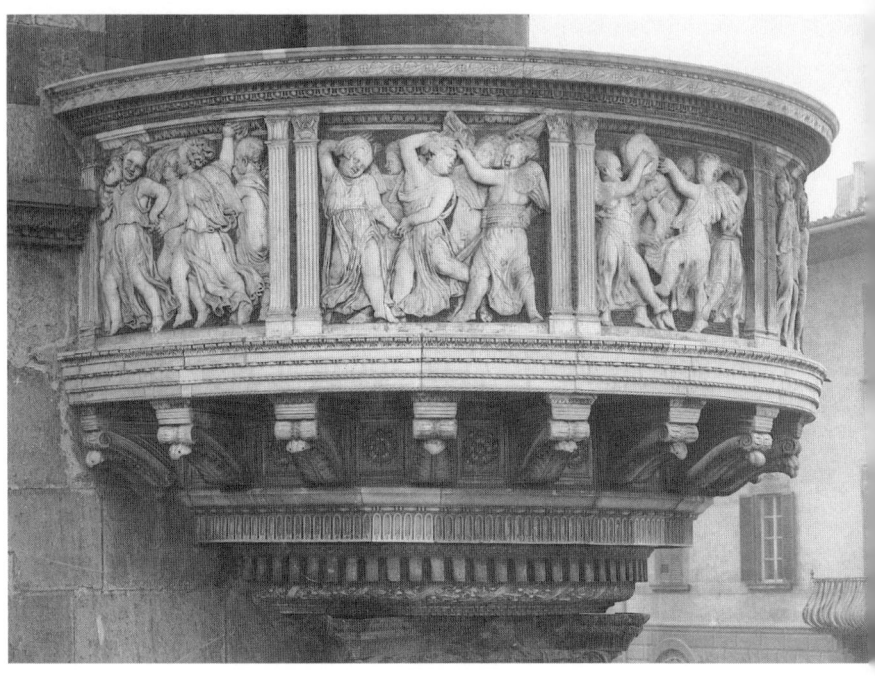

FIGURE 10
Donatello, *Prato Pulpit*, Prato Cathedral. (Photograph: Alinari/Art Resource)

analogy this infant sprite bears to Verrocchio's *Putto with a Dolphin* for the garden of the Medici Villa at Carreggi, for it too was originally placed on a ball over a fountain in such a way that the spurting jets of water made it turn about.[19]

Finally, *spiritello* is the word again used in documents of payment made to Donatello in 1446 for the rushing and dancing putti (*predictis spiritellis*) he sculptured on the Cantoria for the Duomo in Florence (Fig. 12).[20] This is especially notable because the document is in Latin, and *spiritello* is neither Latin nor is it an exact synonym for *genius*. In the absence of such a synonym, the notary found it necessary to adapt the vernacular term into pseudo-Latin, as we also find in a Bolognese contract of 1476 to Taddeo Crivelli for illuminating choir books for San Petronio, requiring him to

THE INVENTION OF THE PUTTO

14

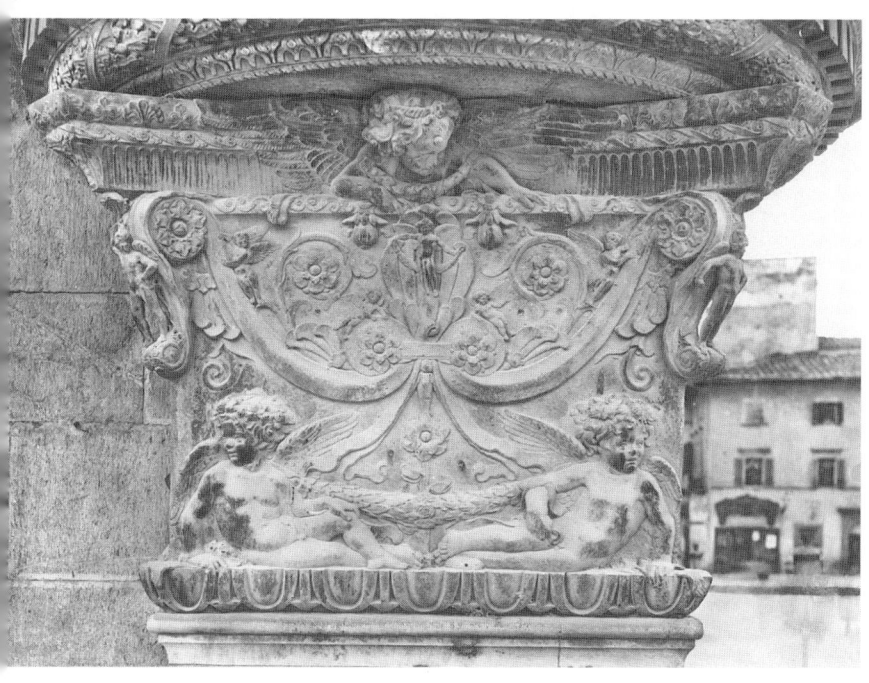

FIGURE II
Donatello, *Capital Supporting Prato Pulpit*, Prato Cathedral.
(Photograph: Alinari/Art Resource)

decorate the bottom margins, "cum animalibus, spiritellis, avibus, et alijs pulcris inventionibus [cfr. Fig. 13]."[21] Moreover, *spirito* and *spiritello* (never *amor*) are the words used to describe genuinely ancient putti, as can be found in Giovanni Rucellai's praise for the "molti spiritegli che navicano" depicted in the mosaics in Santa Costanza in Rome.[22] As early as 1282, for example, we find Ristoro d'Arezzo writing in his *Libro della composizione del Mondo* (in which he praises the beauty of artifacts made from the earth by extolling the wonders of ancient Aretine pottery), that on Etruscan *bucchero* ware can be seen "*spiriti* appearing as nude boys flying through the air carrying swags of all kinds of fruit, and others who are armed and fighting among themselves, and yet others in chariots."[23] In 1430 Nanni di Viterbo, called Fora, wrote to Matteo Strozzi reporting that Donatello himself had

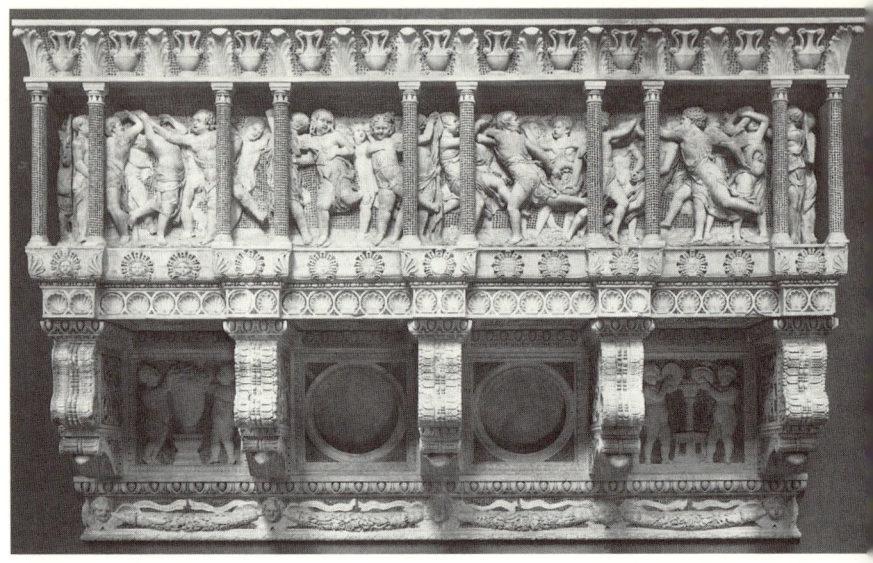

FIGURE 12
Donatello, *Cantoria*, Florence, Museo del Opera del Duomo.
(Photograph: Alinari/Art Resource)

highly praised two ancient sarcophagi in the territories of Lucca and Pisa, the former sculptured with the story of Bacchus and the latter with "ispiritegli" (Fig. 14).[24] And in the inventory of the Medici Palace drawn up at the time of the death of Lorenzo the Magnificent in 1492, several ancient cameos are identified as carved either with *bambini* or *spiritelli* (not *amorini*). One entry describes one of Lorenzo's most important cameos, often reproduced in medals and manuscript illuminations, the imagery of which was reproduced in a sculptured roundel made in Donatello's shop that still adorns the courtyard of the Medici Palace. The cameo, now in Naples (Fig. 15), is by Sostratos and takes as its subject Dionysus in a chariot drawn by Psyches.[25] In the inventory it is described as "a concave-cut cameo set in gold, on which there is a nude figure with a tree behind him and a *bambino* next to the chariot-wheel.... [A] *spiritello* throwing fire [i.e. a flaming torch] is on the chariot-shaft, which is pulled by two figures

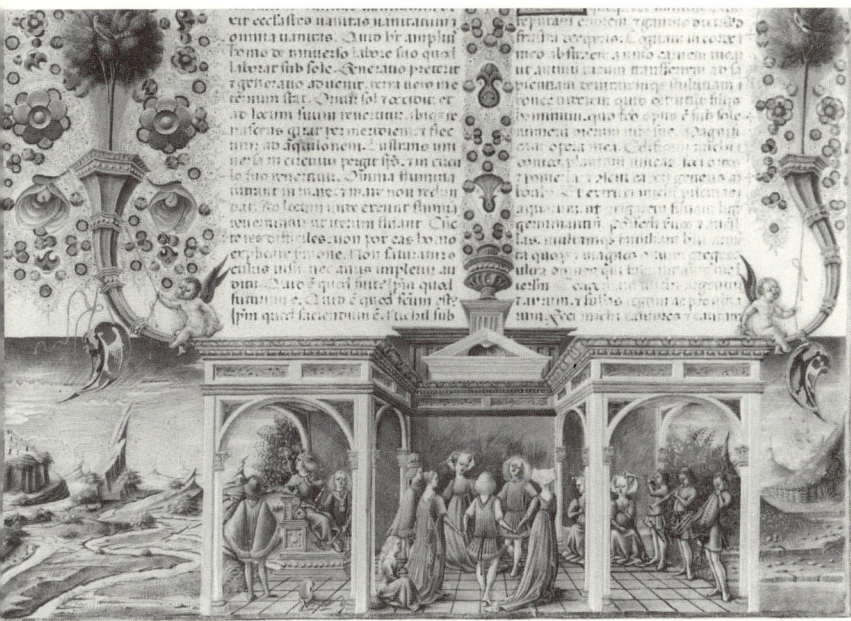

FIGURE 13
Taddeo Crivelli, frontispiece to *Ecclesiastes*, *Bible of Borso d'Este*, Modena, Biblioteca Estense (ms. lat. 442). (Photograph: Biblioteca Estense Universitaria)

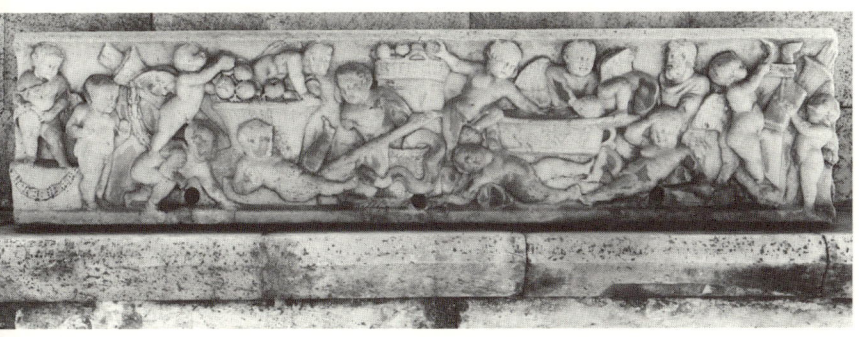

FIGURE 14
Bacchic Sarcophagus, Roman (second century A.D.), Pisa, Campo Santo. (Photograph: Deutschen Archaeologischen Instituts)

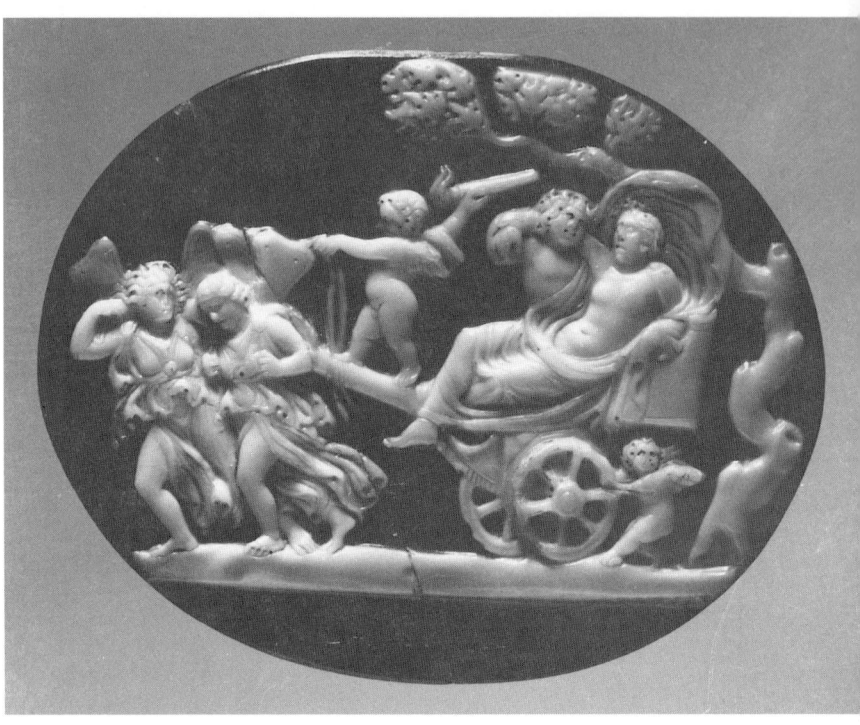

FIGURE 15
Sostratos, *Cameo with Dionysus in Chariot Drawn by Psyches*, first century B.C., Naples, Museo Nazionale. (Photograph: Ministero per i Beni e le Attività Culturali, Soprintendenza Archeologica de Napoli)

who are partly nude and partly veiled."[26] Other ancient cameos with *spiritelli* are also listed, as well as a contemporary table-clock adorned with the Medici arms, "and *spiritegli* enameled on the face which shows the time."[27]

As John Pope-Hennessy and Artur Rosenauer have recently reaffirmed, the earliest post-antique sculptural representations of putti in the round are by Donatello. These are the three bronzes of winged infants, dating to 1429, two playing musical instruments while one airily dances to the sound (Fig. 16), which ornament, instead of the conventional Gothic

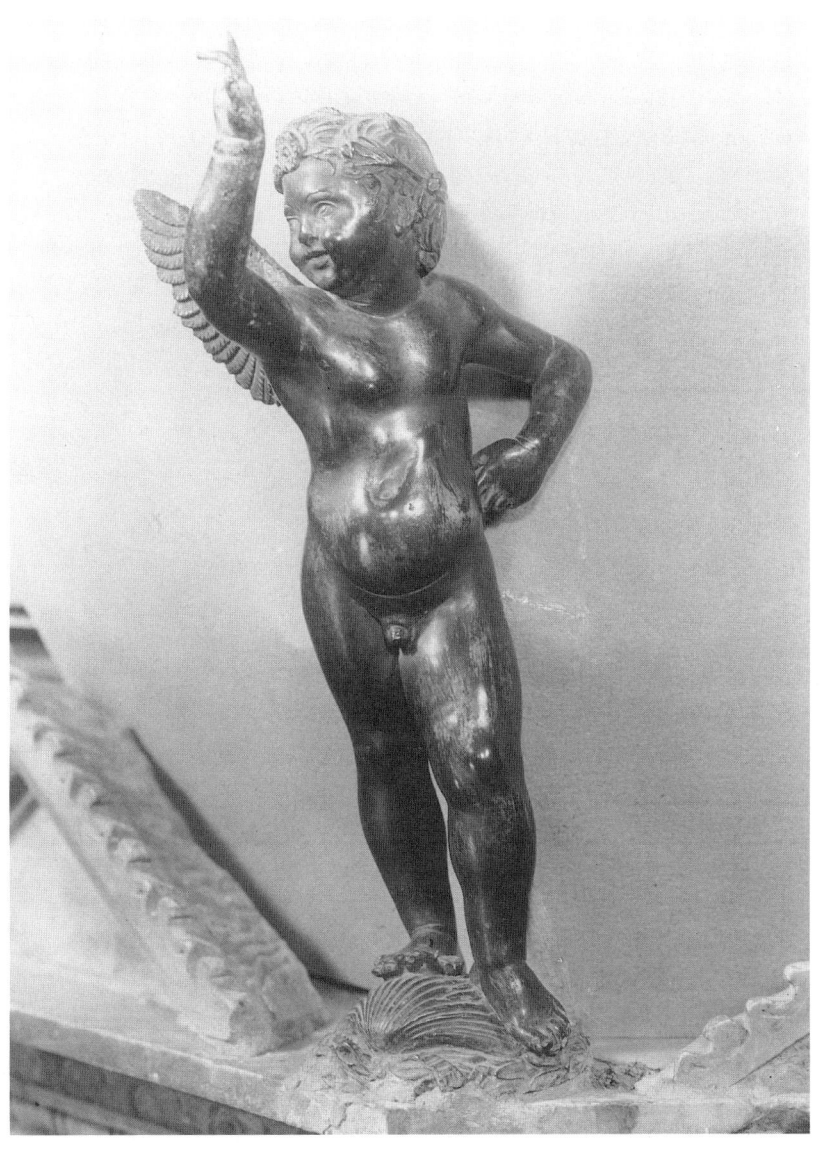

FIGURE 16
Donatello, *Spiritello*, Tabernacle of Baptismal Font, Siena Cathedral.
(Photograph: Alinari/Art Resource)

finials, the tabernacle designed by Jacopo della Quercia for the baptismal font in Siena.[28] Although Donatello's collaboration with Quercia here is without doubt important for the invention of the Renaissance putto, as is the partial precedent of Quercia's tomb of Ilaria del Carretto (Plate 7), nevertheless the new ornamental figure of the fully active putto as seen in the Siena Baptistry—the *spiritello* in all its airy animation and playful volatility—has no precedent and was truly the invention of Donatello. This was, I believe, first pointed out by Eugène Müntz, and it was Wilhelm Bode who then went on to characterize in detail how the mature concept of the putto first found its full expression in Donatello's art, on the basis of which it spread with all but instantaneous rapidity, becoming ubiquitous throughout the Italian peninsula and its adjacent territories. I can do no better than to quote in full Bode's fine paragraph defining the concept and nature of the new Quattrocento putto:

> The putto is at that enchanting age of childhood that is still innocent and without guile, when the consciousness of right and wrong still slumbers, even as unconsciously his growing strength and independence already stir impulses that arouse the mischievous imp within him. . . . Akin to the German brownie, the childrens' good-hearted kobold, the putto is art's authentic goblin, the good spirit of the Quattrocento sculptor's workshop. Summoned into existence by the artist, the putto gives him a hand, helping him and ornamenting his work everywhere. . . . From the cradle to the grave he keeps guard over mankind. He stands and mourns beside the bier [Fig. 17], bedecks the tomb with garlands [Fig. 18] or proclaims the glories of the dead. The putto plays his biggest role in the decoration of churches:—he flutters onto the altars and tabernacles to festoon them with garlands of fruits and flowers, to loop up a curtain or to draw it back; he looks down from some high ledge [Fig. 19], laughing into the abyss with no thought of danger; he scrambles amid the leaves and blossoms of the tendrils twining round the pilasters; he plays with his companions in childish glee, or sings to the lute or mandolin [Fig. 20]. He climbs upon the fountains,

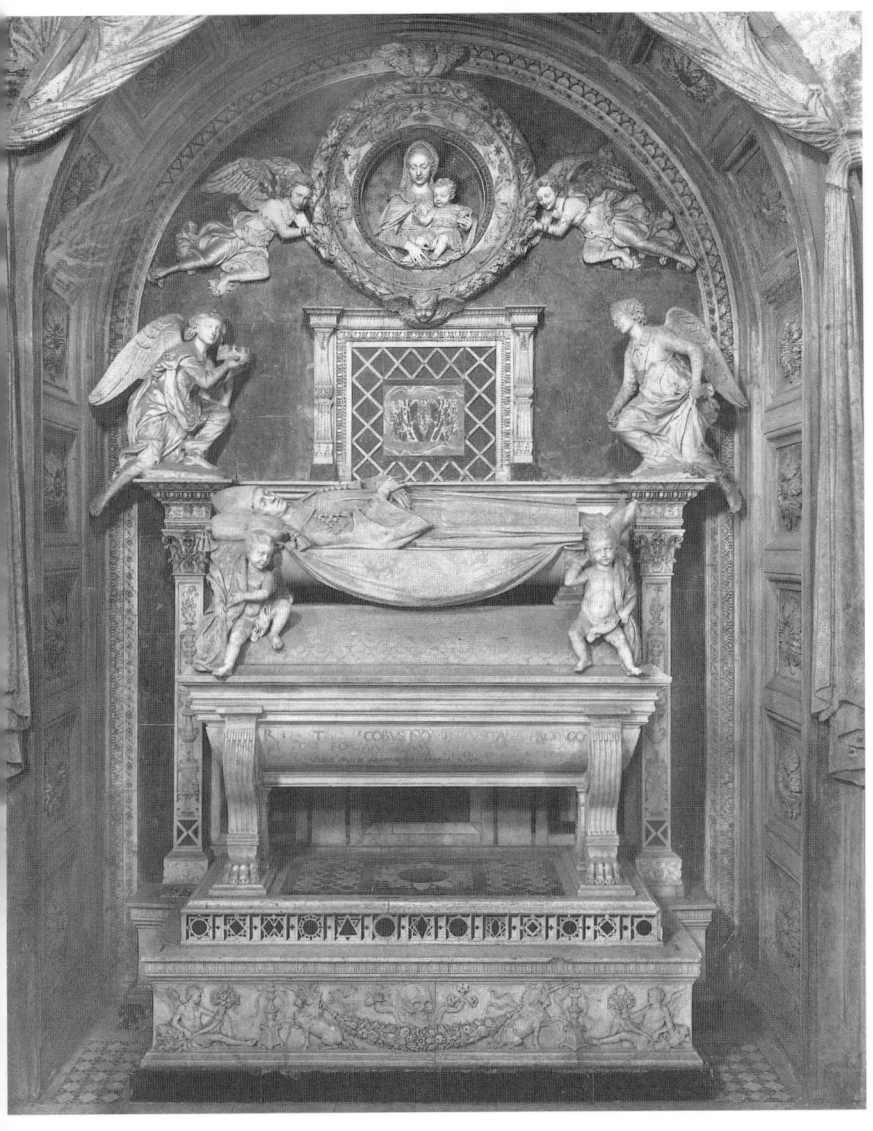

FIGURE 17
Antonio Rosellino, *Tomb of the Cardinal of Portugal*, Florence, San Minato al Monte. (Photograph: Alinari/Art Resource)

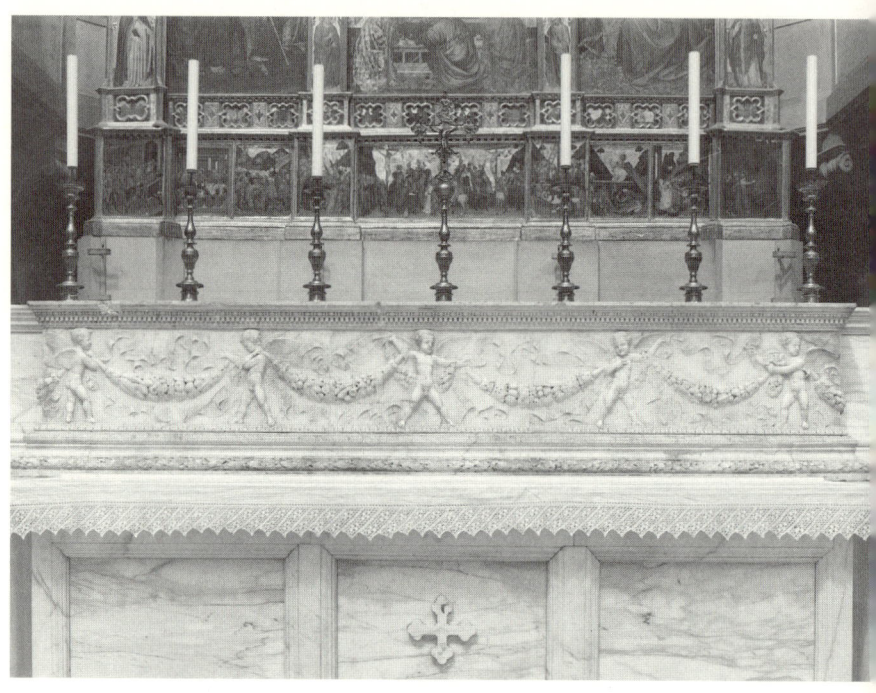

FIGURE 18
Michelozzo, *Tomb of Bartolomeo Aragazzi*, Montepulciano, Cathedral.
Detail, *Spiritelli*. (Photograph: Don Azelio Mariani, Proprietario del
Sepolcro di Montepulciano)

squeezes water through a pipe, pours it from a vase, or he catches a fish who sprays water from its mouth [Plate 4]. Music and dancing are the putto's greatest delight. The putti joyfully dance hand in hand round the pulpits to music played by other putti, or else accompany their playing with a song [see Fig. 10]. With their music and childish games played on the altars and pulpits, putti offer a measure of relief from all the earnest themes taken from the Passion or the lives of the Saints. They set their games in motion on the socles of statues, or in the ornaments adorning the robes of the personages represented [Fig. 21], playfully mimicking and mocking

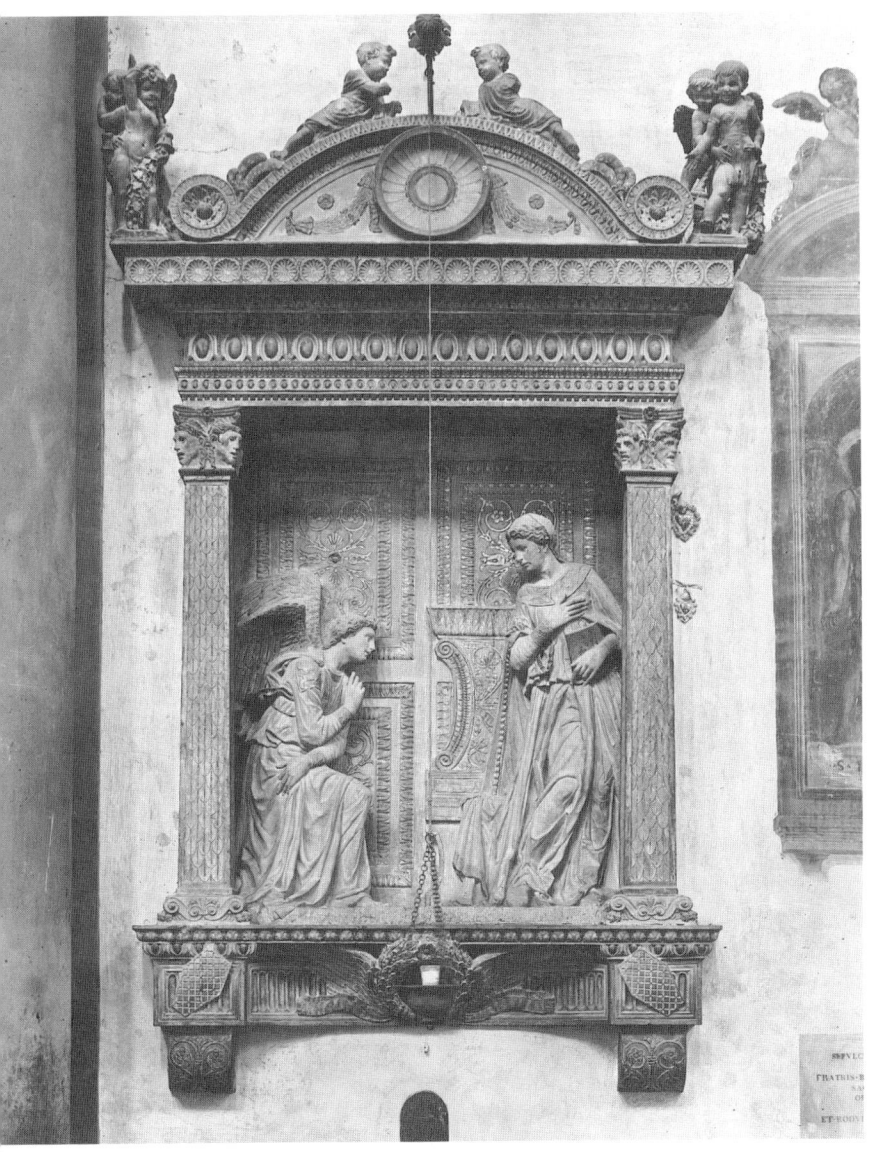

FIGURE 19
Donatello, *Cavalcanti Altar*, Florence, S. Croce.
(Photograph: Alinari/Art Resource)

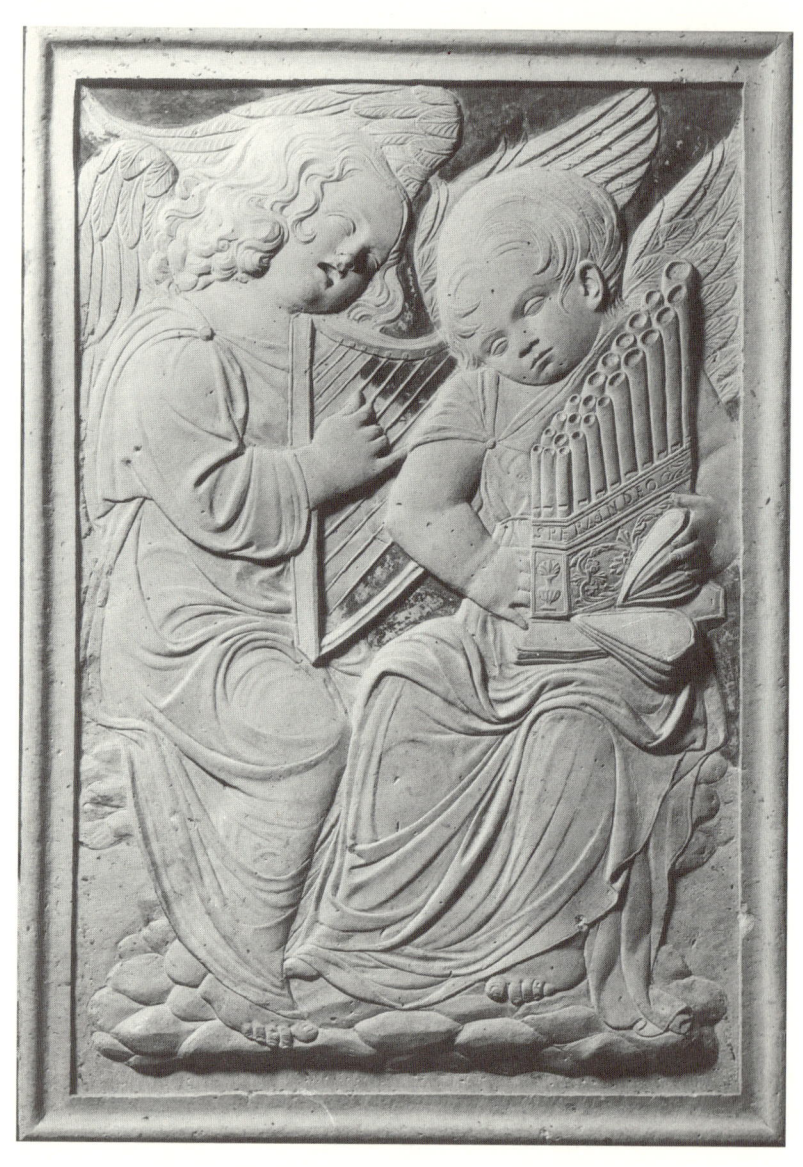

FIGURE 20
Agostino di Duccio, *Spiritelli*, Chapel of the Infant Games, Rimini, Tempio Maletestiano. (Photograph: Alinari/Art Resource)

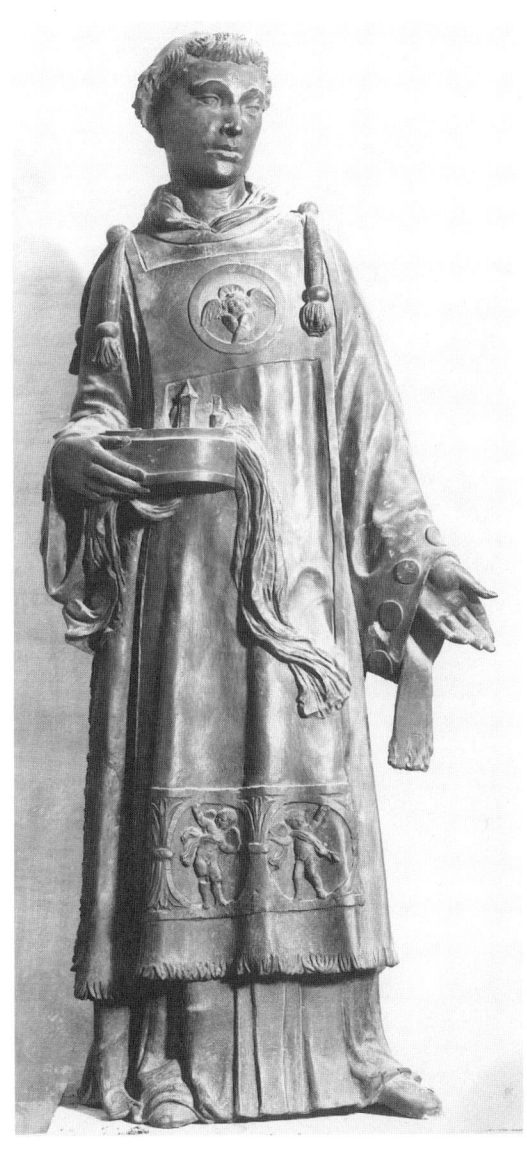

FIGURE 21
Donatello, *St. Daniel*, Padua, Basilica of S. Antonio.
(Photograph: Alinari/Art Resource)

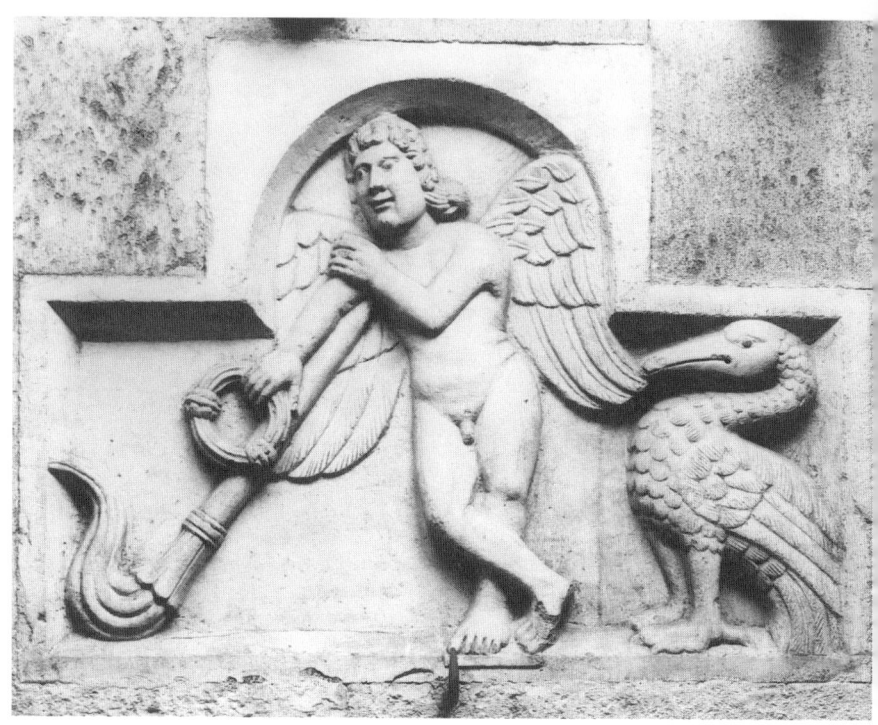

FIGURE 22
Putto with Ibis, Modena Cathedral. (Photograph by James T. Van Rensselaer)

their character and profession. Thus, in the visual arts of the Quattrocento, putti assume a role analogous to that of the less charming, and more coarsely fashioned Satyrs in the Satyr-plays for the tragedies of the classical period of Greek poetry.[29]

Now, to be sure there are precedents in medieval art for the figure of the putto before Donatello. For example, in sculpture they can be found on the façade of the Duomo in Modena (Fig. 22), in the capitals in the cloister of Monreale, the columns of San Domenico in Perugia, and those flanking the portals of the Duomo in Siena. They appear in the door frames of the Palazzo dei Priori in Perugia (Fig. 23), in the vine tendrils

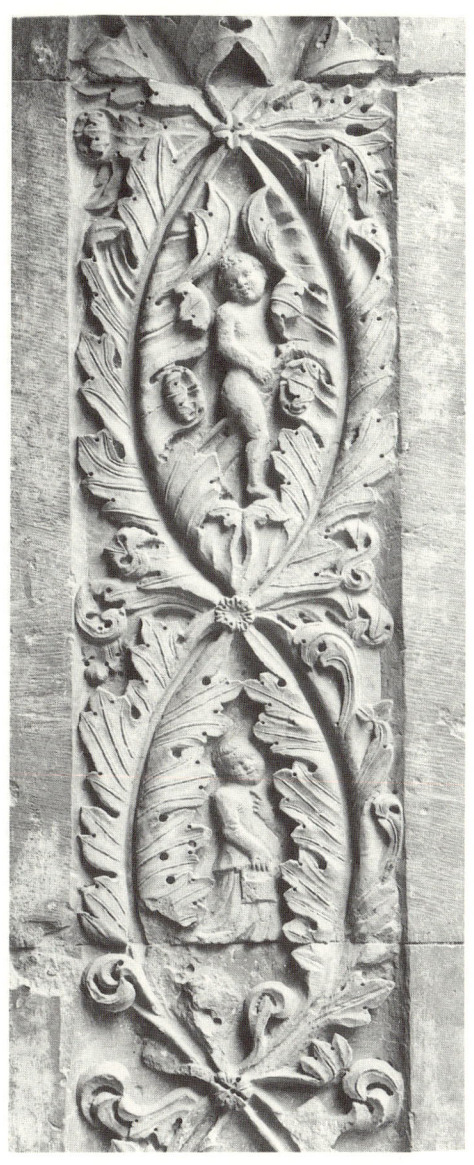

FIGURE 23
Spiritelli, Perugia, Palazzo dei Priori, door jamb. (Photograph: Università degli Studi di Pisa, Dipartimento di Storia delle Arti, 5059)

flanking the north door of the Duomo in Città di Castello (Fig. 24), as well as in the capitals of the baptistry in Pistoia, which are probably by the same master (Fig. 25). They can be seen in Torriti's mosaics in Santa Maria Maggiore (Fig. 26), which derive from the late-antique putti sailing in boats in Santa Costanza that were so admired by Giovanni Rucellai. They appear in the *rinceaux* that frame Cimabue's frescoes in the upper church at Assisi, and in the *Last Supper* from Pietro Lorenzetti's workshop in the lower church (Fig. 27), where they are to be understood as representing pagan idols rather than being only ornamental.[30] Nevertheless, despite their Roman parentage, such examples in their extremely small scale and limited function appear in minor ornamental roles with no special emphasis that distinguishes them from other decorative elements, such as the acanthus leaf, or real and fanciful beasts, or peering grotesque heads. As Bode wrote, they tend not only to be tucked away in door jambs, capitals, and frames as marginal decorations, but also are relatively static, conceived in the manner of other ornaments likewise borrowed directly from Roman art: his examples were the vase and the palmetto. What had begun, in Panofsky's words, as a "decorative adaptation" was decisively transformed in the hands of Donatello into spirited pictorial animation.

Certainly implicated in the emergence of the putto from its rare and secondary decorative function into a more conspicuous celebratory role at the beginning of the Quattrocento are two well-known Roman ornamental types. The first, the putto supporting a swag of *feste romane*, we might call the *reggifestone*, or garland-bearing type, which we have already seen in its original adaptation for the tomb of Ilaria del Carretto (1406–10; Plate 7), and which appears ubiquitously thereafter, as in Michelozzo's Aragazzi Tomb in Montepulciano (1427–38; see Fig. 18), and in the wooden *spiritelli* later sculptured by the shop of Giuliano da Maiano in the Sacrestia delle Messe in the Duomo of Florence (1465–68; Fig. 28).[31] A second type of ornamental putto we might name the *reggistemma*, the shield- or plaque-bearing type, according to which two symmetrically disposed infants, flying horizontally with legs parted as though to balance them in their flight, carry a plaque variously decorated with a coat of arms, a device, or

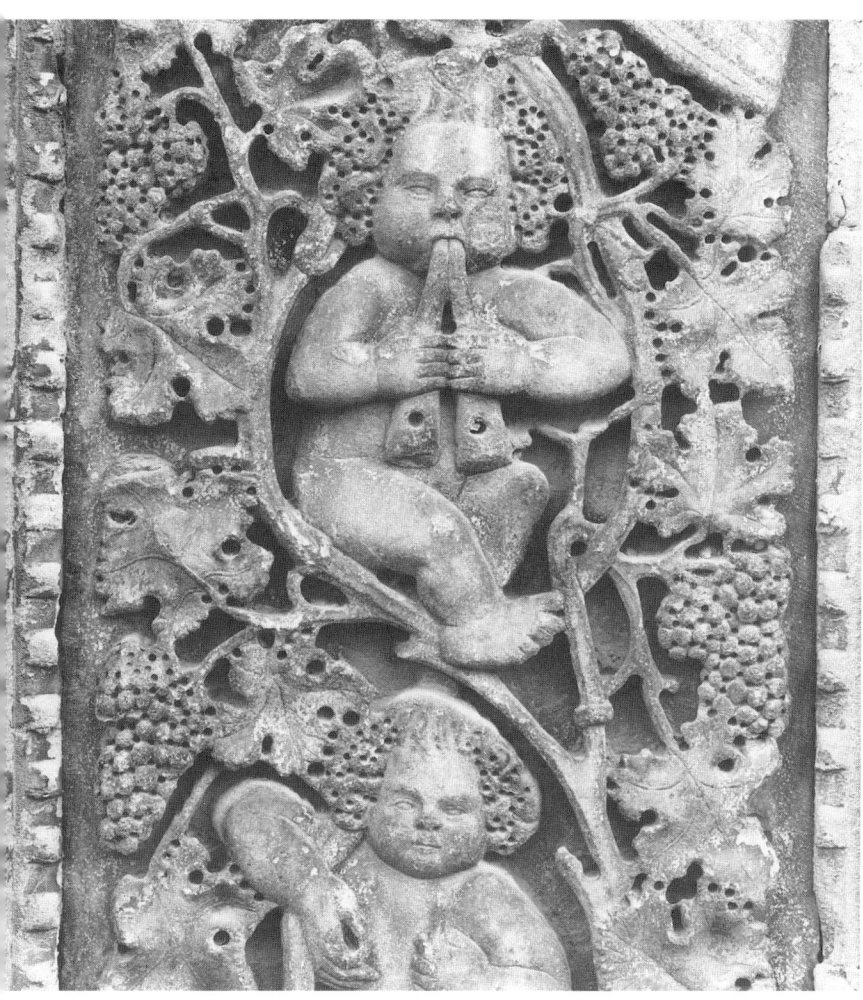

FIGURE 24
Spiritelli, Città di Castello Cathedral, door jamb. (Photograph: Università degli Studi di Pisa, Dipartimento di Storia delle Arti, 5073)

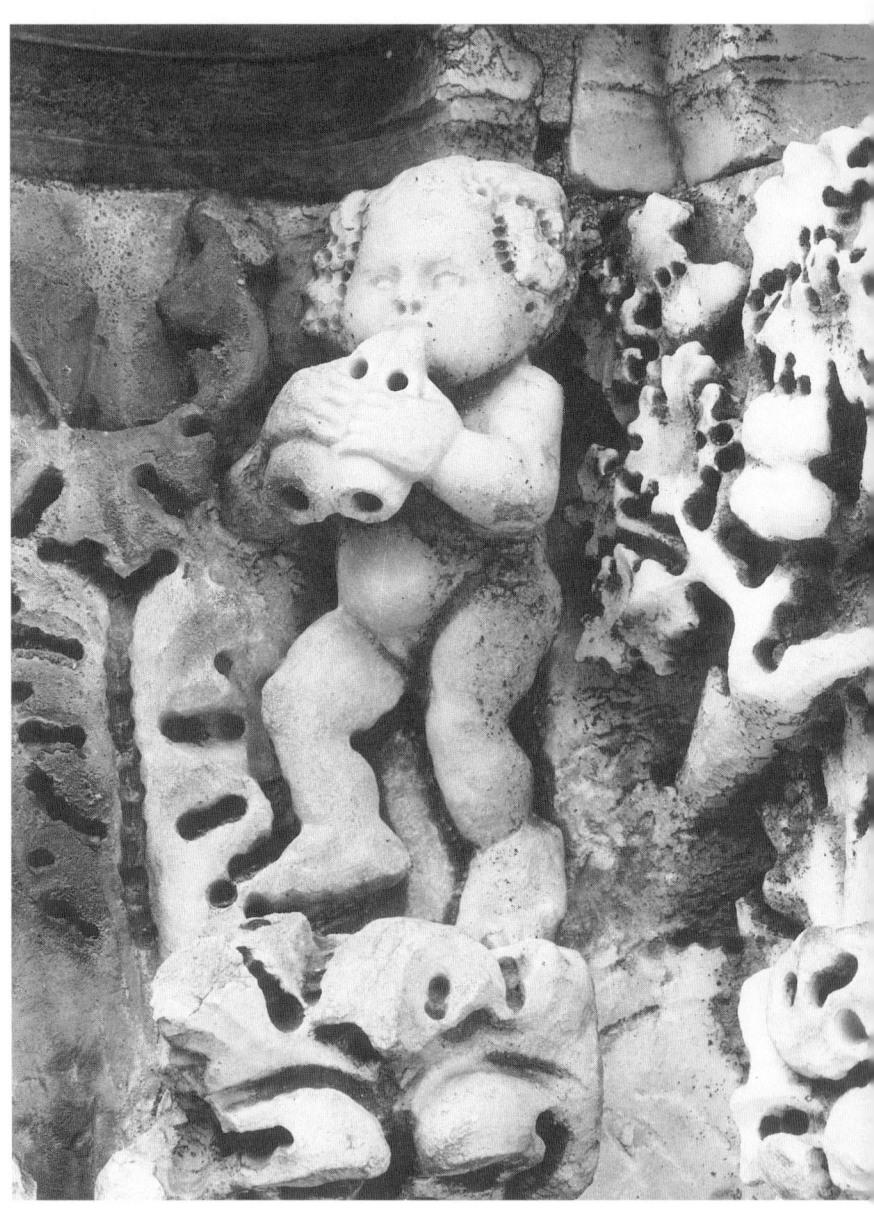

FIGURE 25
Spiritello, Pistoia, Baptistery, capital. (Photograph: Università degli Studi di Pisa, Dipartimento di Storia delle Arti, 5084)

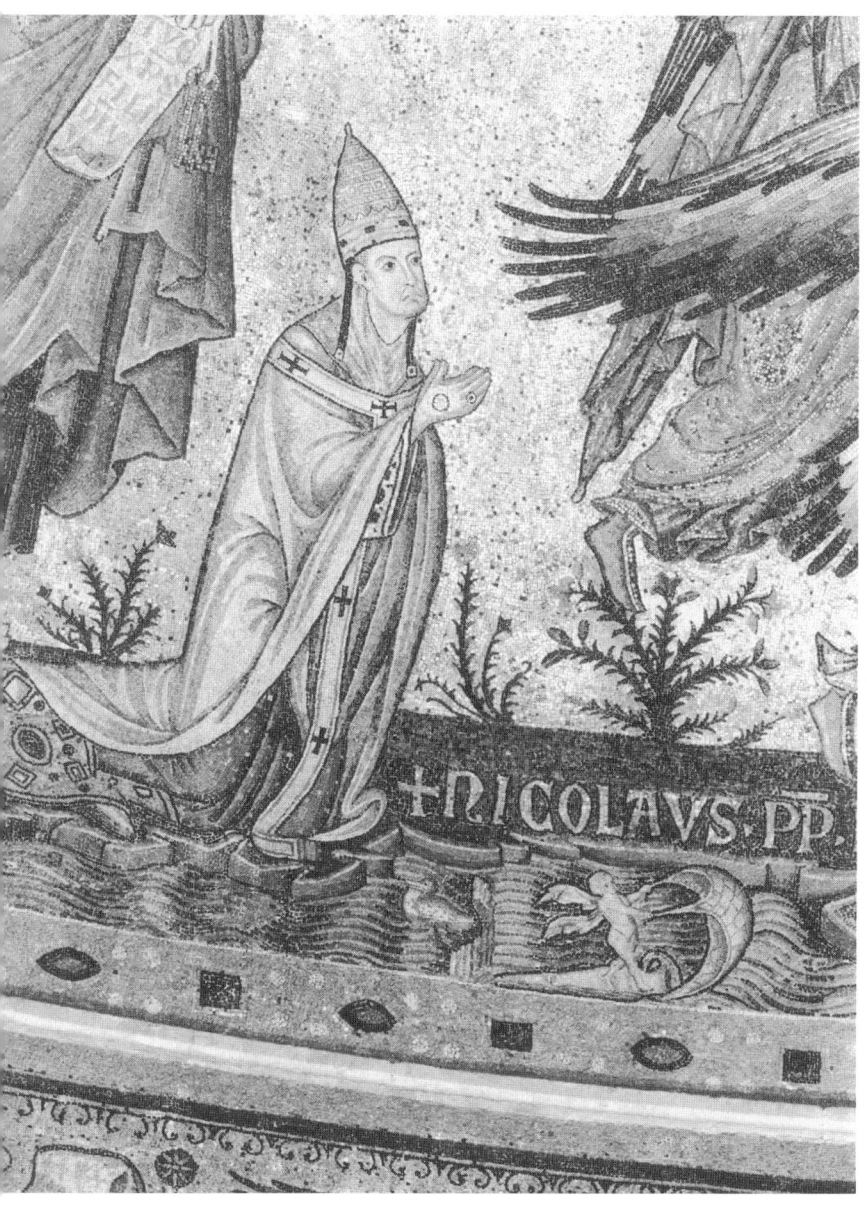

FIGURE 26
Spiritello, Rome, Sta. Maria Maggiore, apse mosaic.
(Photograph by James T. Van Rensselaer)

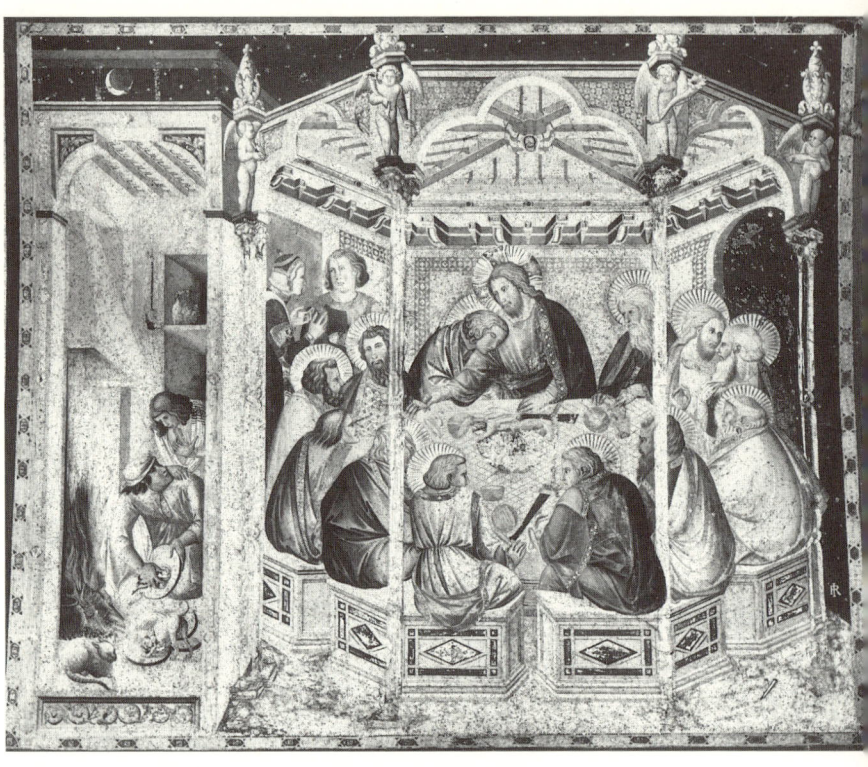

FIGURE 27
Pietro Lorenzetti, *Last Supper*, Assisi, San Francesco, Lower Church.
(Photograph: Scala/Art Resource)

often an inscription. A very early example of this type, which also derives from Roman sarcophagi, appears in the *Triumph of Death* recently attributed to Buffalmacco in the Camposanto in Pisa (ca. 1350; Fig. 29); and a characteristic example can be seen on the tomb of Nofri Strozzi by Niccolò di Pietro Lamberti in the church of Santa Trinità in Florence (1421; Fig. 30).

Examples of both types can be found in Donatello's art, one being the two *putti reggistemma* he designed for the St. Louis tabernacle of Orsanmichele. But the origin of the true Quattrocento putto, who plays an

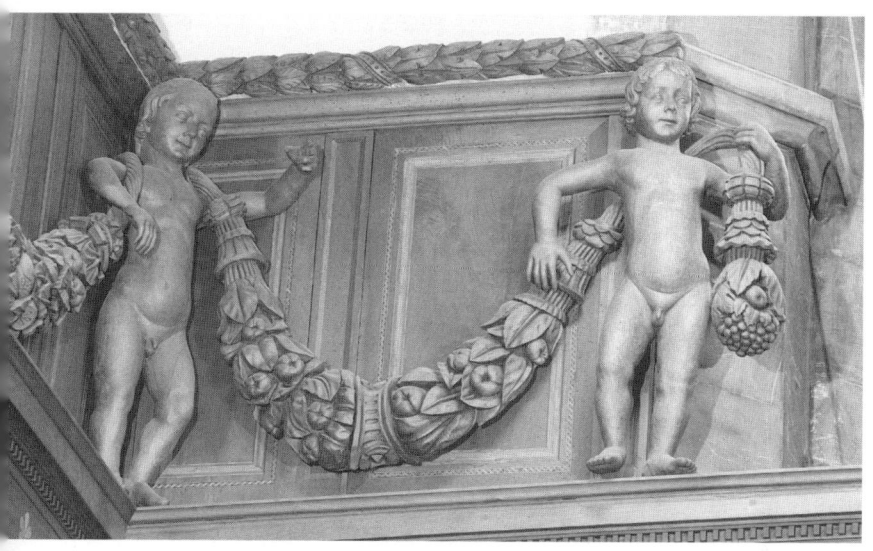

FIGURE 28
Giuliano da Maiano, *Spiritelli*, Florence Cathedral, Sacrestia delle Messe.
(Photograph by Nicolò Orsi Battaglini)

independently celebratory role and is endowed with a distinct, appealingly childish personality of his own, entailed something more complex than the simple assimilation and redeployment of familiar antique ornamental motifs. It derived not only from a deeper study and understanding of ancient sculpture itself, and from an increased artistic mastery of the infant's natural and affective deportment, but also from the translation of both ancient culture and natural experience into the readily accessible vocabulary and syntactical visual forms of vernacular expression. In contrast to the volatile and infinitely active new putto invented by Donatello—a true *spiritello*, or airy sprite—even the tiny infants sculptured by Quercia for Ilaria del Carretto's tomb seem heavy and static. It is doubtless true that the tomb of Ilaria greatly fired the young Donatello's imagination, and no doubt the decorations by Lamberti and others of the Porta della Mandorla of the Duomo in Florence, completed in the first decade of the fifteenth century, also set an important precedent (Fig. 31).[32] In the

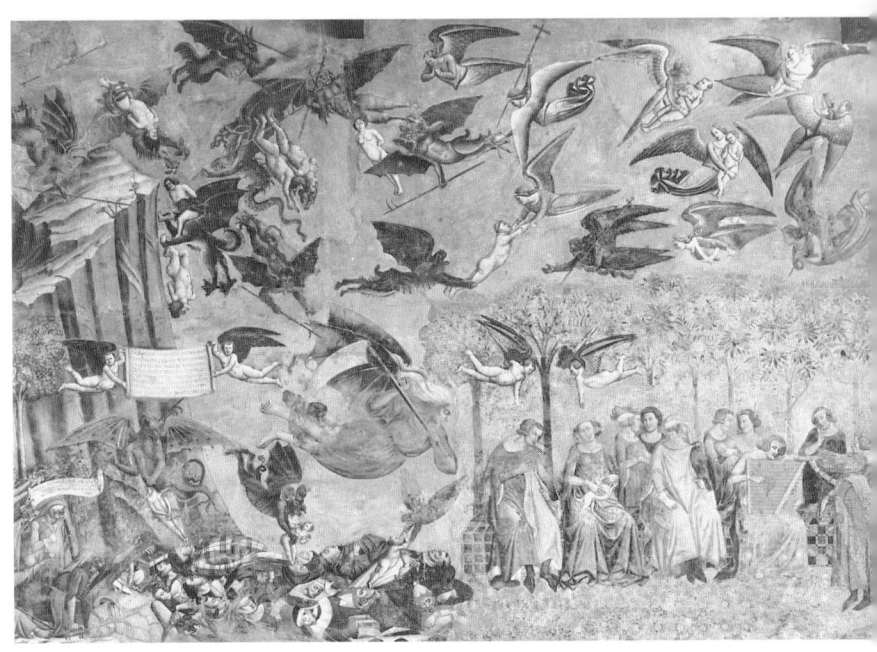

FIGURE 29
Buffalmacco, *Triumph of Death*, Pisa, Camposanto. Detail, *Spiritelli*.
(Photograph: Foto Marburg/Art Resource)

door frame of the Porta della Mandorla, putti may be seen with musical instruments, pouring water or wine from ewers, or frolicking in the foliage. Like their easily recognized antecedents in Pistoia and Città di Castello, however, they are small in scale, set within the margin of the door frame, and they are discretely framed by, rather than clambering about in, the *rinceaux* that define the ornamental structure of the frame. Moreover, like the tomb of Ilaria, they derive directly from the vocabulary of ancient ornament rather than constitute truly new inventions. Bode was hence perfectly right to see that the true origin of the Quattrocento putto—which might be characterized as the embodiment of a new concept of ornament in action—derives from Donatello himself.

The distinction between the static and active uses of the putto in orna-

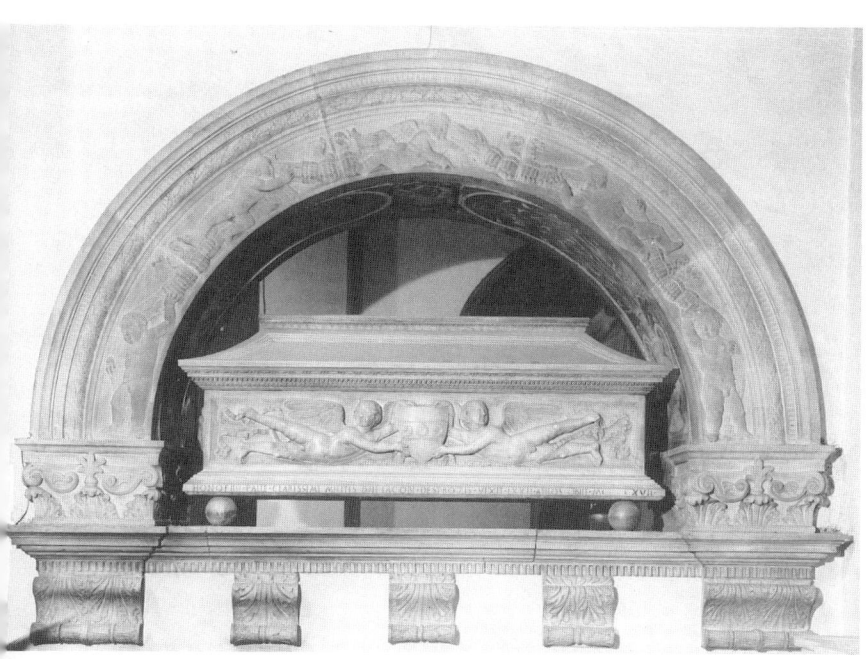

FIGURE 30
Niccolò di Pietro Lamberti, *Tomb of Nofri Strozzi*, Florence, Sta. Trinità.
(Photograph: by Nicolò Orsi Battaglini)

mentation may be illustrated by a comparison of the *spiritelli* bearing *feste romane* on the tomb of Ilaria del Carretto, dating to about 1410 (Plate 7), with the garland-carrying putti standing on top of the frame of Donatello's Cavalcanti *Annunciation* in Santa Croce, dating some twenty or so years later (Fig. 32, Plate 2; see also Fig. 19). Though it is perhaps true, in the overwrought phrase of Marcel Reymond, that the infants on Ilaria's tomb may be imagined as "the spirits of the Renaissance carrying Gothic art to its grave"[33] (and they are *spiritelli* in fact), it is also true that by contrast to Quercia's putti, Donatello's sprites function in a way that is simultaneously more independent of the principal theme of his relief, and also more interactive with it.

They first of all have an independent interest because they act a part.

THE INVENTION OF THE PUTTO

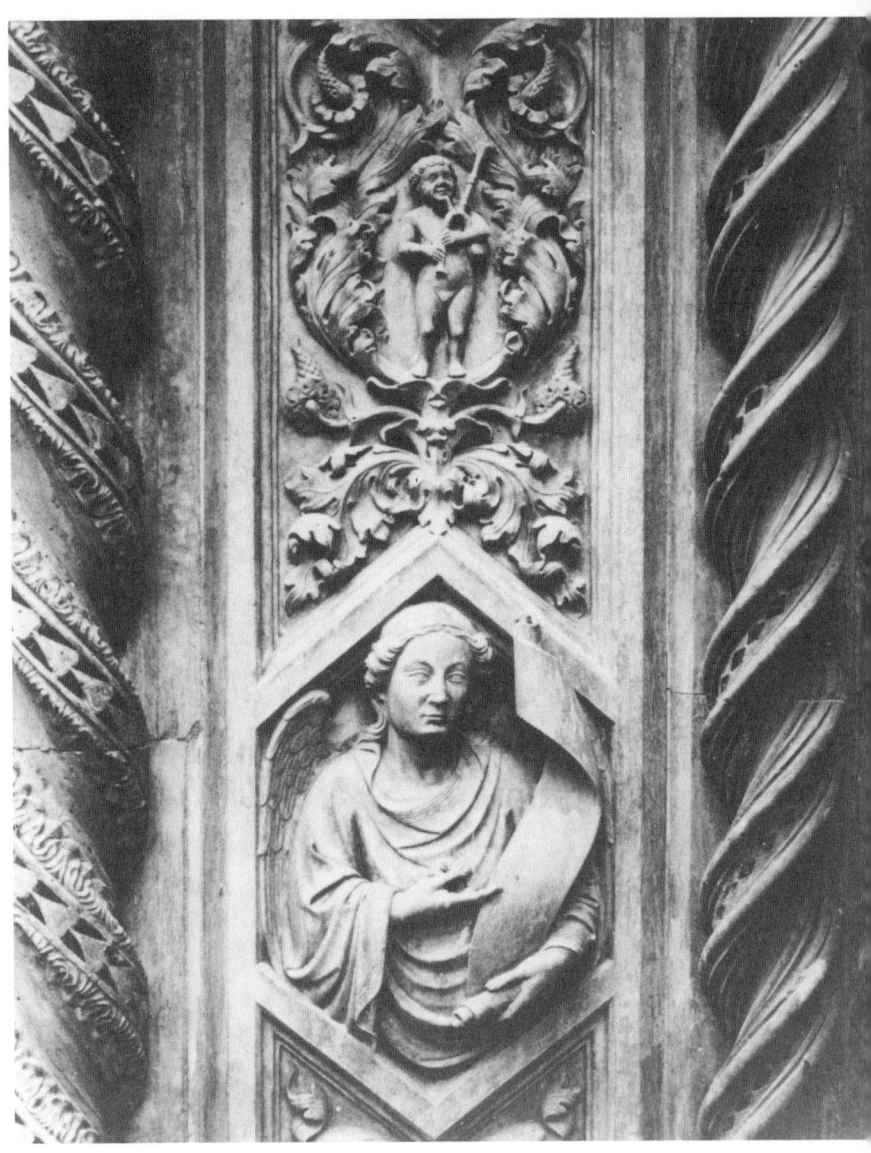

FIGURE 31
Jacopo di Pietro Guidi, *Porta della Mandorla*, Florence Cathedral, door jamb.
Detail, *Spiritello*. (Photograph: Alinari/Art Resource)

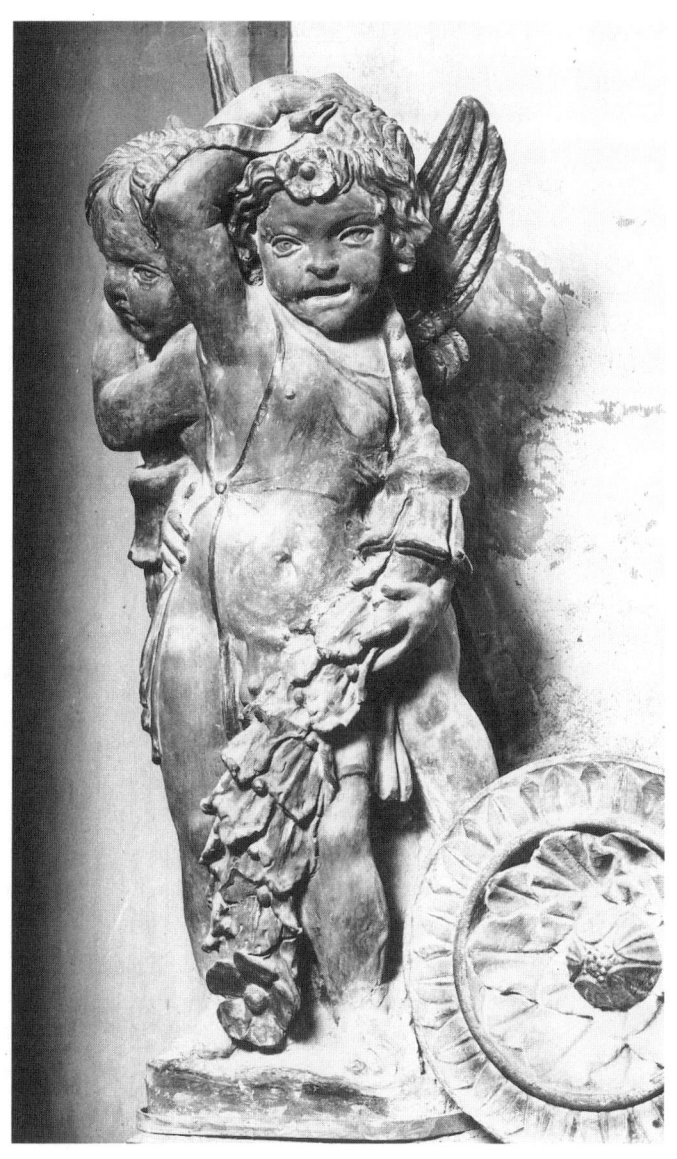

FIGURE 32
Donatello, *Cavalcanti Altar*, Florence, Sta. Croce. Detail, *Garland-bearing Putto*.
(Photograph: Alinari / Art Resource)

They are *putti reggifestone*, but instead of holding up their *feste* in celebration of the Annunciate Virgin as they ought, they have let them drop unceremoniously from their shoulders as they teeter off-balance on the very edge of the high cornice of the tabernacle. Accordingly, as Vasari wrote of the two pairs, one on each side of the frame, it appears that "for fear of the height [*per paura dell'altezza*], one clasps the other in his embrace so as to reassure one other."[34] They thus have an anecdotal function, arousing the spectator's interest and amusement by playing out a light-hearted little drama that is independent of the seriousness of the principal theme of the Annunciation. It is to this idea that Pontormo appealed when he adapted Donatello's frightened putti in an early idea for his fresco of *Vertumnus and Pomona* at Poggio a Caiano (Fig. 34), which is also set above a cornice high over the floor.[35] Secondly, however, Donatello's putti also interact with his principle theme, for, as Vasari writes in the very next sentence, he "showed great art and ingenuity in the figure of the Virgin, who, frightened by the unexpected appearance of the Angel [*impaurita dall'improvviso apparire dell'Angelo*], timidly and sweetly adjusts her person into an honorable reverence, and turns with beautiful grace toward him who salutes her."[36] In other words, the Virgin has been startled, and, suddenly taken by a spirit of fright, she recoils; but she at once recovers herself and, mastering her sudden fear, in the very same movement turns and bows reverently to the announcing Angel (Fig. 33).[37] The sudden rush of fright that has momentarily shocked her, causing her to start back, is acted out by the infants on the frame above her, who mischievously push each other to the brink and look down from the precipice, just for the thrill of it. They mirror the surging spirit of fear that has momentarily taken hold of her, they enact it on a different scale and in a different context, and they communicate it viscerally to the viewer, who looks with alarm at small infants giddily trying to balance themselves many meters above the floor. They also arouse amusement because of their infantile cleverness—their cuteness—and they indicate the essential childishness of startled fright, which mature and upright people, and certainly the Virgin, can at once bring under control. In another sense, however, they literally objectify the rush of fear she feels. They personify the pneumatic spirits of startled

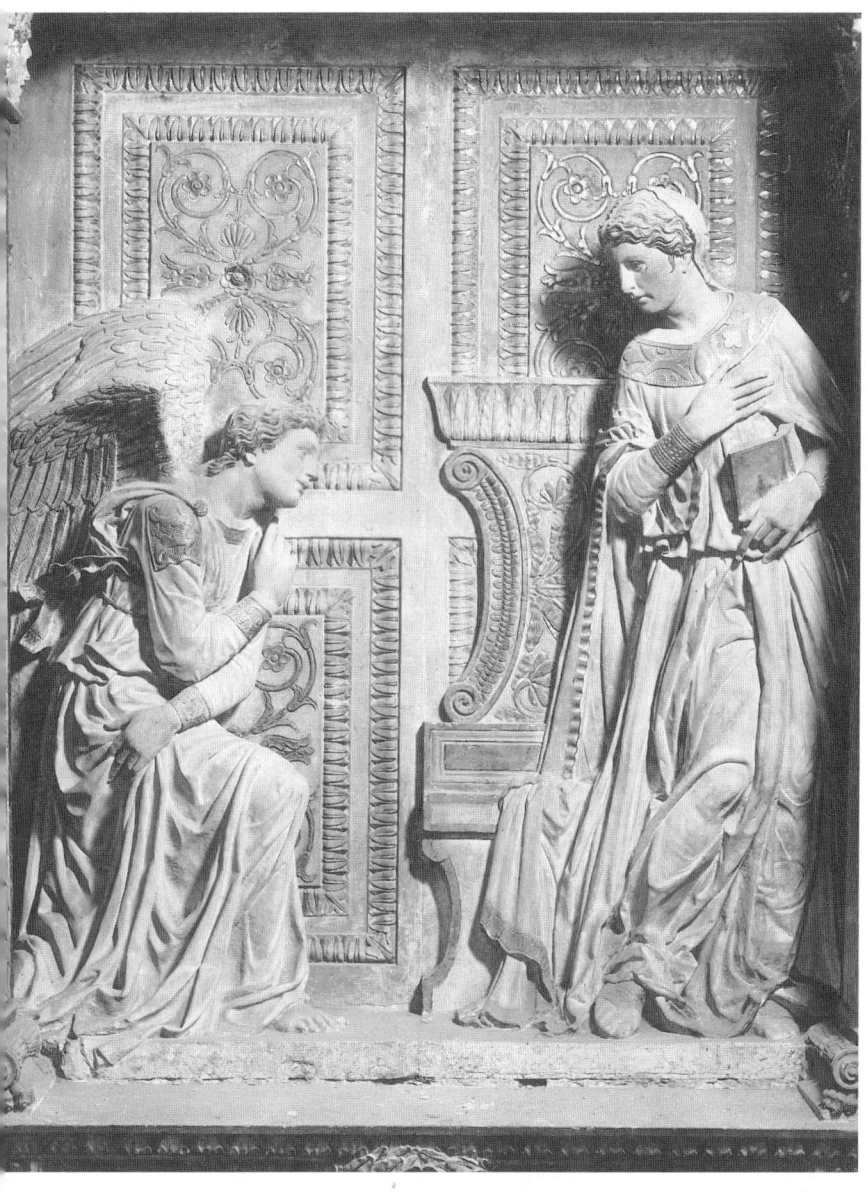

FIGURE 33
Donatello, *Cavalcanti Altar*, Florence, Sta. Croce. Detail, *Annunciation*.
(Photograph: Alinari/Art Resource)

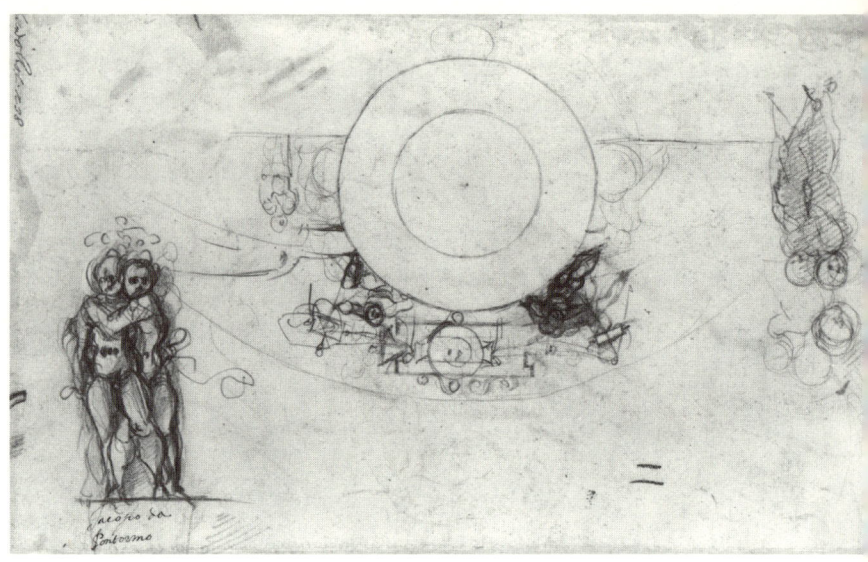

FIGURE 34
Jacopo da Pontormo, *Preparatory Drawing for Vertumnus and Pomona*, Florence, Uffizi, Gabinetto degli Stampe e Disegni. (Photograph: Soprintendenza per i Beni Artisitici e Storici delle Provincie di Firenze, Pistoia e Prato)

fright that can suddenly rise and course like an electric shock through the nerves, causing the heart to beat faster and one's hair to stand on end.

What exactly is a *spiritello*? Although, as Lessing pointed out, in Latin the spirit of Love is one kind of genius, not all the many species of genius are Loves. The same is true of the *spiritello*, which has many species and which, as we have already indicated, is not synonymous with the Latin *genius*. *Spiritello* is the diminutive of *spirito*, the root meaning of which refers to a movement of air, whether by the action of a breeze or by the act of breathing itself. Benvenuto Cellini, for example, in an interesting passage, reproaches the French bronze founders because "non gli avete dati tanti spiriti da basso, ch'el vento possa girare."[38] He is referring to air vents (*sfiatatoi*), but it is significant that he does not use the word *aria* but rather refers to the active spirits agitating the air, visible in eddies of wind, as well as of fire, visible in shimmering heat waves, the latter being commonly called *fuochi fatui* (*feux-follets*) in popular superstition, referring to the playful actions of the minor demons, for the most part benign, that animate the fire. *Spiritus* translates the Greek *pneuma*, which also means wind, breath, a spiritual being (such as the Holy Ghost), or even an angel (such as the ministering angel-*pneuma* referred to by St. Paul in the Epistle to the Hebrews, 13–14). Accordingly, the enchanting angelic spirits playing upon musical instruments sculptured by Donatello and his shop for the high altar of the Basilica of the Santo in Padua (1447–50)—which are in fact named as *angeli* in the documents—are conceived, as their infantile state indicates, as airily diminutive *spiritelli* (Fig. 35).[39] Spirit is the breath of life animating the human organism, departing from it at death (when the body gives up the ghost). Before this moment the manifold lesser spirits attending to the life of the body gradually weaken, and in the process of death precede the soul in abandoning the organism. In life, spirits drawn in from the air are mixed with blood in the veins and arteries, through which they transmit life-sustaining nutriments, as well as sensations that enter involuntarily through the sensory organs and stimulate the passions. These basic physiological tenets, ultimately derived from Aristotle and the Greek pneumatic school of medicine (especially as transmitted by Galen) are fundamental to Medieval and Renaissance thinking in natural philosophy and medicine, and they indeed continued to be held long after William Harvey's crucial discovery of the circulation of blood in the first quarter of the seventeenth century.[40] They provide the "scientific" basis for Charles Le Brun's *conférence* on the passions, delivered to the Académie Royale de Peinture et de Sculpture as late as 1668, as well as René Bary's even later *Méthode pour bien prononcer un discours* of 1679. Read as a diagnostic account of the effects produced by fear in the body, Bary's words, drawing as they do (and as we shall see) on traditions transmitted unbroken from Medieval and Renaissance medical thought, would have been perfectly comprehensible to an attentive contemporary viewer (such as Vasari) of the sequence of actions Donatello portrayed in the Virgin in the Cavalcanti altar—from the onset of startled

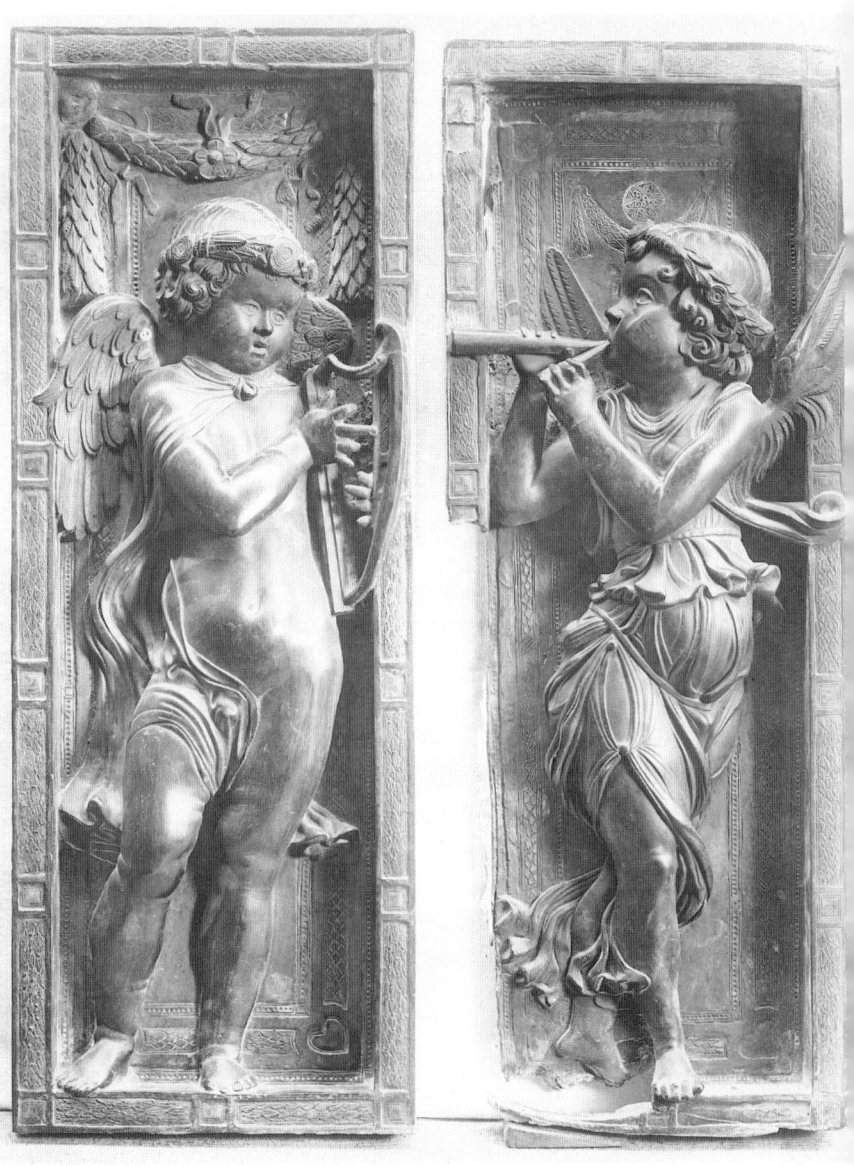

FIGURE 35
Donatello, *High Altar*, Padua, Basilica of S. Antonio. Detail, *Music-making Angel-Spiritelli*. (Photograph: Alinari/Art Resource)

fright that leaves her speechless, to her immediate mastery of her fear and with it the recovery of her spirits, and her turning to the Angel and responding to his salutation:

> When Fear is aroused by the presence of something terrifying it has a feeble and hesitant voice, because the fright has drawn the spirits [*esprits*] from the circumference [of the body] to the center, overwhelms the heart, and the heart thus overwhelmed being almost suffocated, the speaker is so alarmed that he remains speechless.[41]

In the thematics of love poetry, the movements of spirit can be virtually synonymous with an active force (*virtù attiva*) that impels the involuntary heaving of the breast that produces a lover's sigh; and accordingly Dante writes in the *Vita nuova* that a *spiritel d'amore* "is a breath of Love [*spiramento d'Amore*] that brings out the desires of love with it, and it is moved by so gentle a cause as that pleaded by the eyes of the lady who has demonstrated such compassion."[42] As pneumatic substances, such spirits are not merely allegorical. They have real material and physiological existence. Spirits are characterized by their invisibility, lightness, and extreme volatility. Although having physical existence, they are highly rarefied, and in the medical and philosophical thought of the Middle Ages and Renaissance they are conceived as active powers that are the source of all the body's functions, transmitting nutriment, sensory data, and even emotions in airy movement through the tubes of the arteries, veins, and nerves.

Such *spiriti* are of three main types: (1) natural spirits, which are seated in the liver and expand pneumatically through the body by way of the veins, and which provide for nutrition by transmitting the life-supporting essences contained in water, meat, and the fruits of the earth; (2) vital spirits, dependent upon the former, which reside in the heart and spread through the arteries, maintaining life by attending to pulse and respiration; and (3) animal spirits (the most rarefied of all), which are sited in the brain and rush through the nerves connected to the organs of sense, from which they receive external data communicated by *spiriti sensitivi*. Among these sensitive spirits are the *spiriti del viso* and the *spiriti del suono*, the spirits of sight and sound. In the *Vita nuova* Dante writes of how the *spiritelli del viso* lament because they have been overwhelmed by the stunning beauty of Beatrice; and he describes an actual physiological disorder when he tells of his responses upon first setting eyes upon her:

> At that moment I say truly that the vital spirit, which resides in the most secret chambers of the heart, began to tremble so strongly that it made itself felt most horribly in the smallest beats of my pulse; and trembling it spoke these words: "*Ecce deus fortior me, qui veniens dominabitur michi.*" At that moment the animal spirit, which dwells in that high chamber to which all the sensitive spirits carry their perceptions, began to marvel greatly, and speaking especially to the spirits of sight it said these words: "*Apparuit iam beatitudo vestra.*" At that moment the natural spirit, which resides in that part that ministers to our nutriment, began to weep, and weeping spoke these words: "*Heu miser, quia frequenter impeditus ero deinceps!*" From that moment forward I say that Love ruled over my soul."[43]

In the literature of love the effect of the poet's first gazing into the eyes of his lady is almost invariably expressed in terms of a similar physiological response provoked by a sudden and unexpected movement of the spirits, producing sensations that are unwilled and beyond immediate rational control. Lorenzo de'Medici, for example, when describing his own response to the spirit of love flashing from his lady's eyes and entering through his own in a rush to his heart (in his *Comento de' miei sonetti*, inspired by the example of the *Vita nuova*), follows a tradition of similar physiological descriptions widely diffused throughout the poetry of the *Stil novo*. The fear he feels differs in no way from the physiological effects of fear as described by René Bary in the passage quoted above. Looking into his lady's eyes for the first time, Lorenzo writes that his timid heart was seized by fright, not knowing whether the love it sensed was true or not, thus causing the vital spirits to flee from his face and rush back through his arteries in order to lend assistance to his wildly beating heart. His face was drained of blood, becoming cold, pallid, and lifeless, and the vital spirits clustered round his heart generated such heat as almost to suffocate themselves, making breathing difficult. "But then," Lorenzo adds, "gazing again upon her face, it seemed to me that so many were the signs of compassion there that my heart put its fear to one side and regained some of its ardor; and because of this the vital spirits returned to the place whence they had fled, and with them there returned that valor and color which had earlier been lost."[44]

From a physiological point of view, a sudden spurt of fright that is instantly mastered, such as Lorenzo describes, is in all respects identical to the momentary surge of fear affecting the Virgin described by Vasari when writing of the expressive effects of Donatello's Cavalcanti *Annunciation*. There we see enacted in immediate succession the Virgin's initial startled fright at the sudden sensible appearance of the Archangel in her tiny chamber—caused by the *spiriti visivi*, the spirits entering her eyes and transmitted by her vital and animal spirits in a pneumatic surge through her arteries and nerves to her heart and brain—and her instantaneous recovery of intellectual self-control, so that in the very moment of flinching recoil she is able to turn and bow to the heavenly messenger. Although we would attribute the Virgin's involuntary recoil to the chemical effects of a surge of adrenalin, Vasari would have said it is caused by an airy rush of spirits. The *spiritelli* Donatello showed teetering uncertainly on the frame above her personify those very spirits that transmit the surge of fright she experiences, even as they also represent the childish fears of which she is thoroughly the mistress.

The *spiriti sensitivi* are of many kinds, and make themselves felt in the form of random impulses—whether startlement, sudden erotic arousal, panicky terrors, drunken giddiness, or wonderment that makes the hairs on the back of the neck stand on end—all of which seem to invade the body unbidden, as though by the force of some external stimulus. They produce sensations *all'improvviso*, impelling involuntary responses, not produced by an act of reason or the will but "as the spirit moves." Donatello's *spiritelli* for the Prato pulpit (Fig. 36; see also Fig. 10), so named in the contract of 1428, as well as the dancing sprites on the Siena baptismal font (see Fig. 16), are neither celestial (they have no haloes) nor infernal, neither angels (as in the Padua altar) nor devils, but the essences of a pure

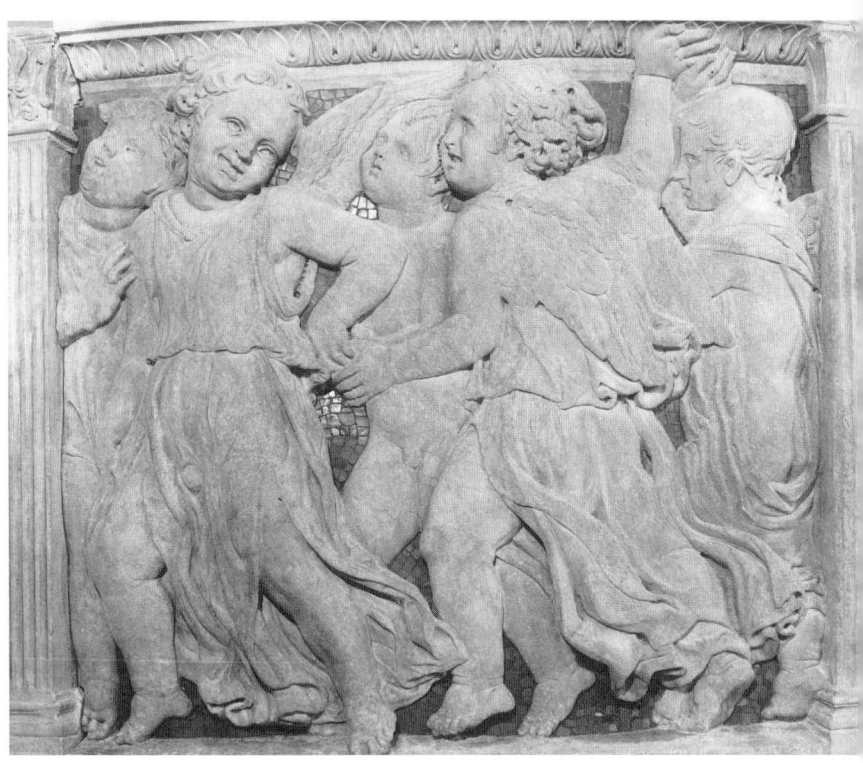

FIGURE 36
Donatello, *Spiritelli*, Prato Pulpit, Prato Cathedral.
(Photograph by Nicolò Orsi Battaglini)

and irresistible sensation of innocent joy that makes the pulse beat faster. Each of them dances or plays a musical instrument, and embodies what Dante calls the *"spirito sensibile* that receives sound," whether produced by the rhythmic sounds of music itself or by what Dante in another place calls the *vocale spirto*, the harmonious words of the sermons preached from the pulpit at the time of the display of the Madonna's girdle, Prato's most sacred relic.[45] Donatello's *spiritelli* for the Cantoria of the cathedral of Florence (also named as such in the documents), on the other hand, certainly personify the sensible spirits carried by the rhythms and melo-

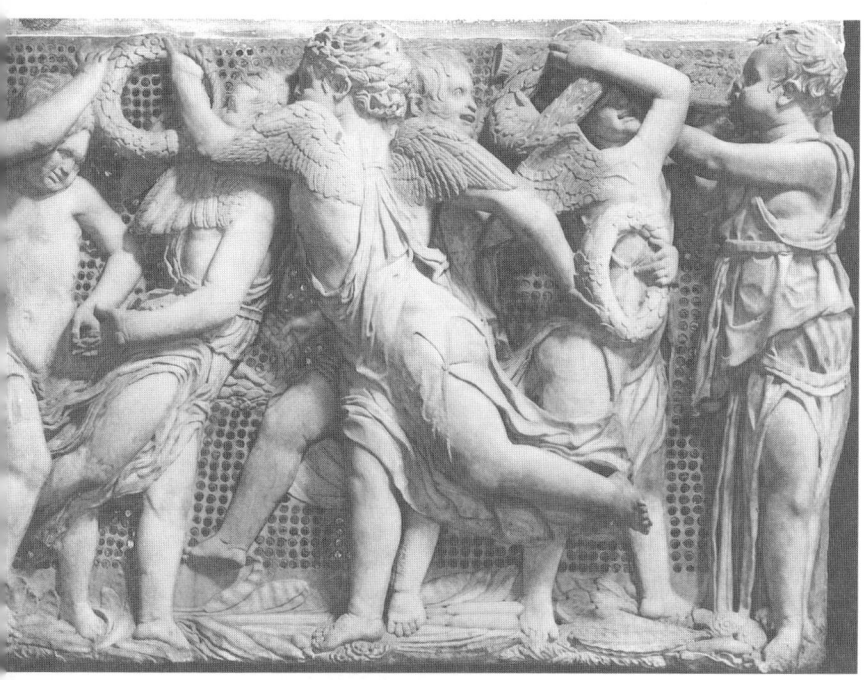

FIGURE 37
Donatello, *Cantoria*, Florence, Museo del Opera del Duomo. Detail, *Spiritelli del Suono*. (Photograph: Alinari/Art Resource)

dies of the music, which enter through the ear, quicken the heartbeat, and involuntarily stir the soul (Fig. 37; see also Fig. 12). The rhythmic airs of the music are given visible form in the sprites dancing in an endless chain, and are perpetually enacted in the ebb and flow of their interlaced movements around and about the two planes of the small stage established by Donatello along the front of the Cantoria.

The genius of Donatello's artistic invention of the true putto, the diminutive embodiment of any and all such varied airy *spiritelli* in innocent action, derives from its great charm and adaptability, so that we are not only enchanted by the infantile figures, brimming with the spirit of life (of which they are the very essences), but must also respond to the figure and

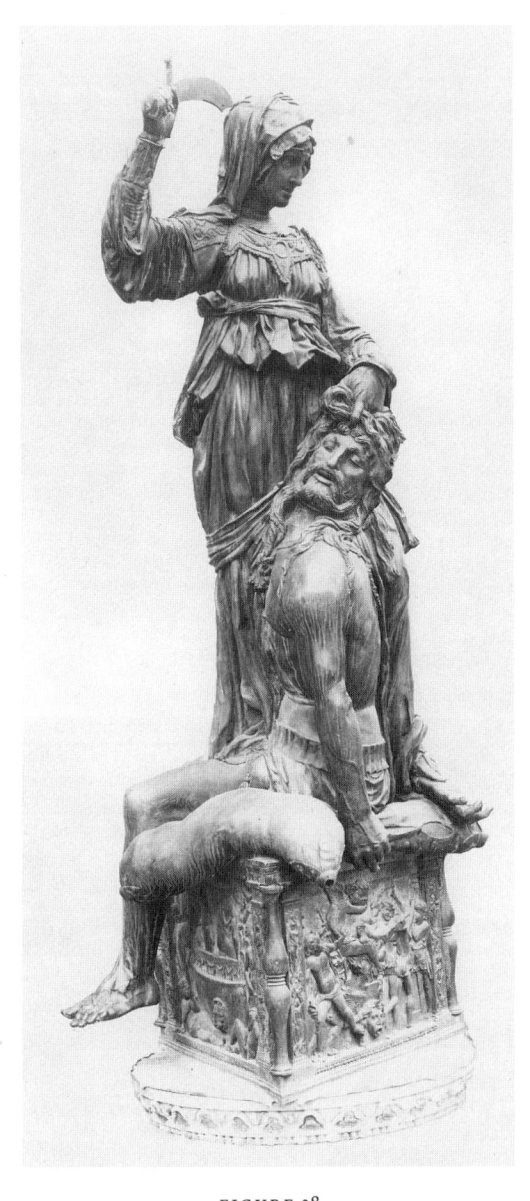

FIGURE 38
Donatello, *Judith and Holofernes*, Florence, Palazzo Vecchio.
(Photograph: Brogi/Art Resource)

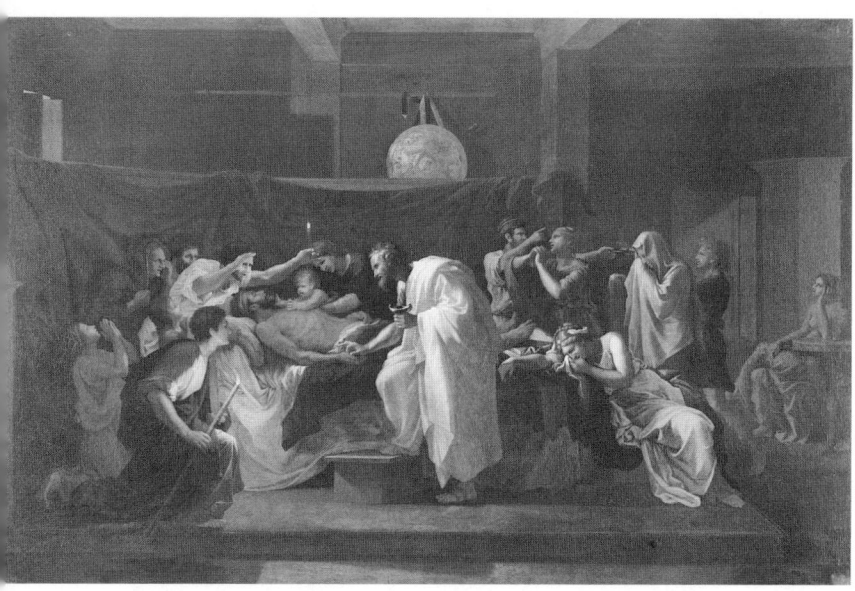

FIGURE 39
Nicolas Poussin, *Extreme Unction*, Duke of Sutherland Collection,
on Loan to the National of Scotland, Edinburgh.
(Photograph: National Gallery of Scotland)

its function as an ornament in action. The *spiritello* is not merely the static embellishment to some other scene, but a participant in its larger meaning, and even an independent bearer of meaning itself. Because of its iconographic fluidity, and because of its almost infinite capacity for multiplication, the sprite embodies an almost musical purity and directness of expression.

Such a union of expressive with narrative effects is highly typical of the sculpture of Donatello and his followers. Vasari writes of the *Judith and Holofernes* (Fig. 38), for example, that the effects of sleep and the grape can clearly be seen in the air of Holofernes, and that at the same time one can see "death in his extremities, which have lost their spirits and appear cold and drooping."[46] In 1672 Bellori wrote much the same of the dying man in Poussin's *Extreme Unction* (Fig. 39), saying that as the spirits abandon his

THE INVENTION OF THE PUTTO

body one can see the pallor of death in his most extreme members, "and particularly in the feet, which are the first to die."⁴⁷ Medically speaking, the departure of the *spiriti vitali* from Holofernes's extremities marks the initial stage of the death of the body, which is caused by the final expelling of those vital spirits, concluding with his giving up of the ghost. A remarkable representation of the vital spirits appears in the sculptures for the Orsini Chapel in Trogir by Niccolò di Giovanni Fiorentino, a student of Donatello's, to which we have already referred (see Fig. 7). The high basement of the chapel is lined with a series of classical tomb doors, all of them slightly ajar, from each of which emerges after long confinement— exactly as the commissioning document of 1468 had specified—"a *spiritello* bearing a torch in hand." As they escape from the darkness to which they had been banished at the death of the Blessed Giovanni Orsini, some of the *spiritelli vitali* blink in the blinding light (Fig. 40), and one blows on his nearly extinct torch to bring the flame to life (Fig. 41). And, while Christ, his Evangelists, and Apostles gather silently round, and as God the Father bursts into the chapel through an opening in the vault, these life-spirits all rush forward to reanimate the body of the Blessed Giovanni, who lies in an *arca* in the center of the chapel in hopes of the resurrection.⁴⁸

As with the ultimate death of the body, gradual dimming and loss of eyesight or hearing is caused by a weakening or departure of those animal spirits that convey the sensations of sight and sound. Natural spirits, which attend to nutriment, are at the foundation of the chain of life, being the basis for sustained life in the organism, and hence for continuous life in the world itself. The *reggifestone* putto who bears his *feste romane* laden with fruits embodies even as he celebrates in plastic form the life-supporting spirits contained in the fruits of the earth, the source of all life in nature. Such garland-bearing sprites may appear in generic ornamental contexts, in permanent festival celebration atop some altar railing or cornice, as we see in Giuliano da Maiano's *spiritelli* with garlands (see Fig. 28) that adorn the Sacrestia delle Messe in the Duomo of Florence (named in the commission of 1468 as "the garland with *spiritelli* to be placed over the cupboards").⁴⁹ They may appear as the initial stage for some expanding concept of life extending from the earth to the heavens, as in Agostino di

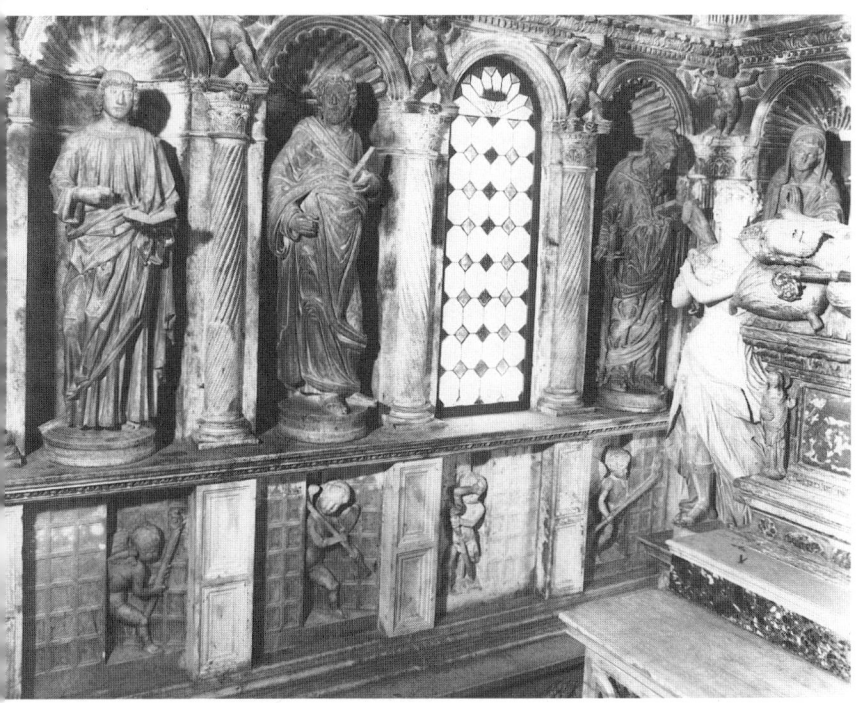

FIGURE 40
Niccolò di Giovanni Fiorentino, *Chapel of the Blessed Giovanni Orsini*,
Trogir Cathedral. (Photograph by Živko Bačić)

Duccio's column bases for the Chapel of the Planets in the Tempio Malatestiano in Rimini (Fig. 42), dating from about a decade earlier, where *spiritelli* bearing *feste romane* guard wicker baskets bursting with grapes that seem to be crushed by the weight of the piers they support, squeezing the nourishing juices from them.[50] Or they may appear on tomb sculpture, acting as *pleurants* mourning the extinction of natural life even as they personify and celebrate the principle of life itself, as in Jacopo della Quercia's tomb of Ilaria del Carretto in Lucca or Michelozzo's tomb of Bartolomeo Aragazzi in Montepulciano (see Plate 7 and Fig. 18). Similarly, Verrocchio's famous fountain sculpture of the *Putto with a Dolphin* (unpoetically described as a *bambino di bronzo* by the sculptor's brother

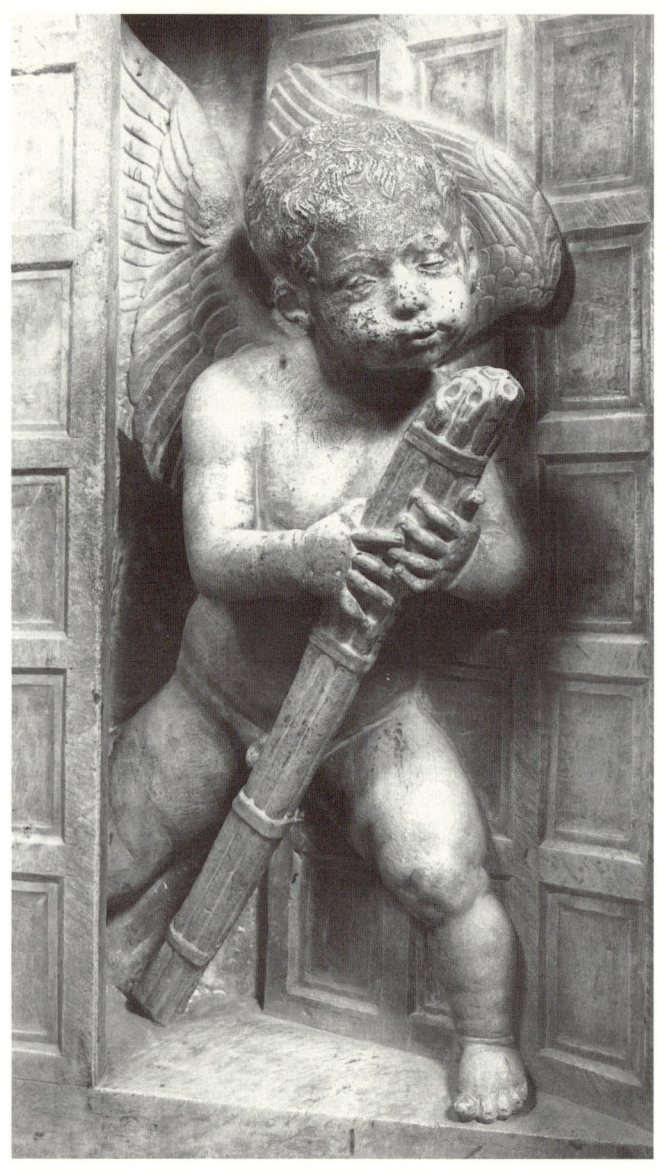

FIGURE 41
Niccolò di Giovanni Fiorentino, *Chapel of the Blessed Giovanni Orsini*, Trogir Cathedral. Detail, *Spiritello Blowing on Torch*. (Photograph by Živko Bačić)

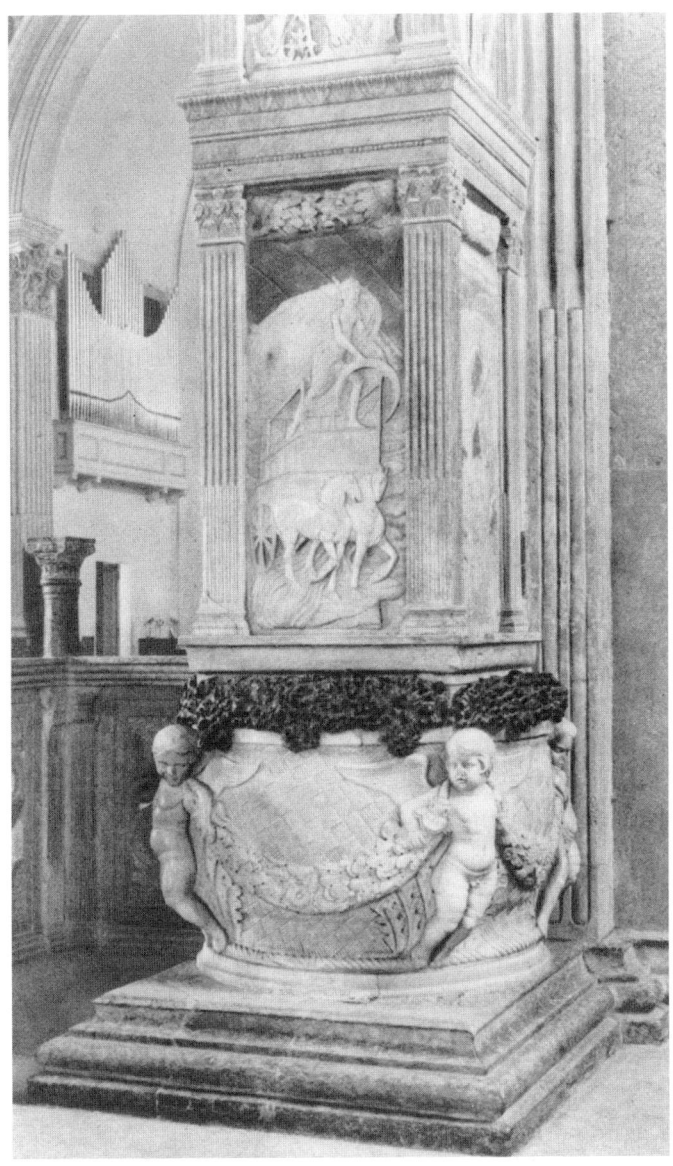

FIGURE 42
Agostino di Duccio, *Spiritelli Trampling Grapes*, Chapel of the Planets, column base, Rimini, Tempio Malatestiano. (Photograph: Alinari/Art Resource)

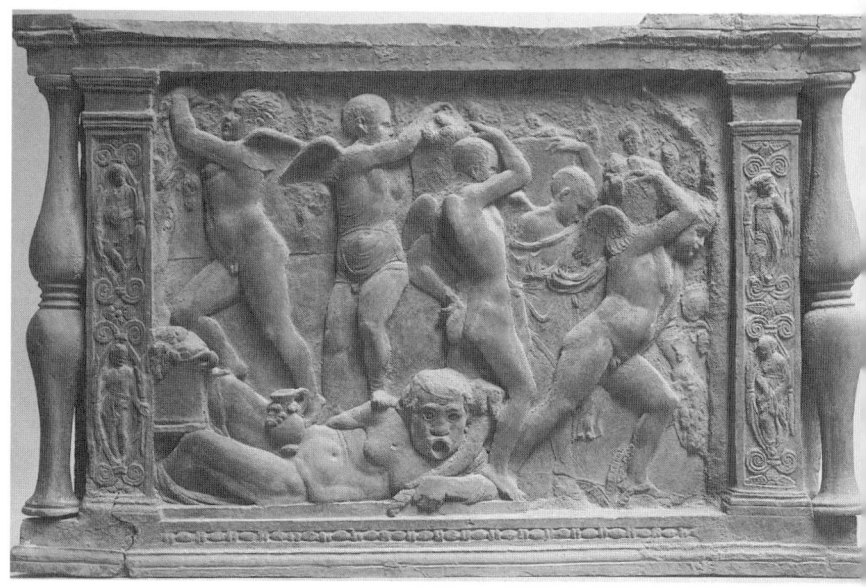

FIGURE 43
Donatello, *Judith and Holofernes*, Florence, Palazzo Vecchio. Detail from base, *Spiritelli Gathering Grapes*. (Photograph: Alinari/Art Resource)

Tommaso in the list he drew up in 1496 of works for which he claimed the Medici still owed payment) is a water sprite, the natural spirit of the mobile and laughing waters (Plate 4).[51] Piero Adorno is not the first to respond to the infant's lively animation, writing that "One can readily imagine what great luminosity it must have had when it was immersed in the open air of the garden at Careggi, with the shifting breezes changing the direction of the falling water on its bronze surface."[52] Like his close cousin, the *spirito naturale* of the fruits of the earth personified by the vine- and fruit-bearing putto, he is the nourishing natural spirit of animated life contained in the randomly jetting water, not merely its signifier but its expressive essence. Whatever the particular context, the natural spirits personified by these garland-bearing and aquatic infants perpetually celebrate the sweetness and sheer joy of mortal existence at its purest and simplest.

THE INVENTION OF THE PUTTO

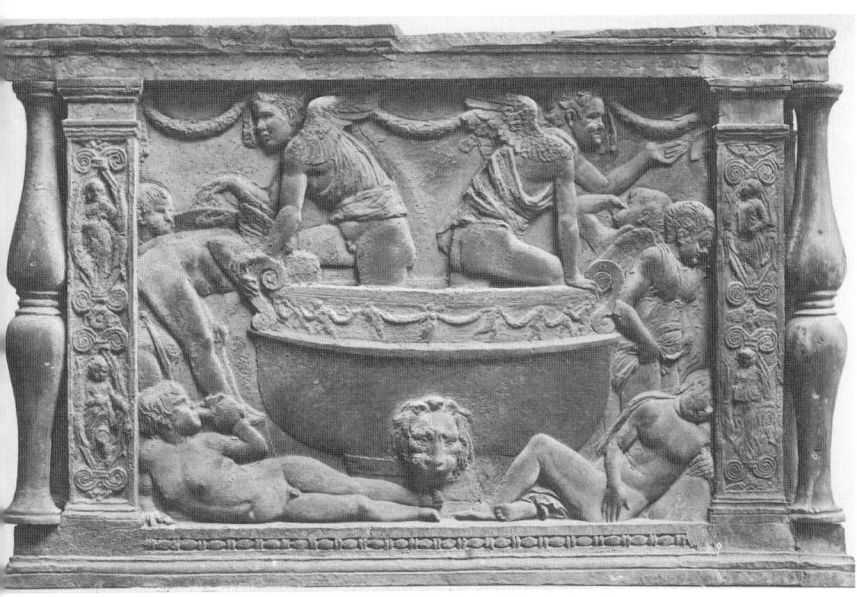

FIGURE 44
Donatello, *Judith and Holofernes*, Florence, Palazzo Vecchio. Detail from base,
Spiritelli Treading the Grape. (Photograph: Alinari/Art Resource)

The natural spirits of the earth's fruits may also ferment, however, and the spirits living in the grape can invade and take possession of the mind and body, producing progressive sensations of merriment, giddiness, loss of judgment, nausea, and ultimately narcotic sleep. When Othello's lieutenant Cassio is dismissed for drunkenness he bewails his fate by cursing the demon sprite that has overwhelmed his senses: "O thou invisible spirit of wine, if thou hast no name to be called by, let us call thee devil!"[53] It was with the spirits of the winepress that Judith brought Holofernes to his end, and Donatello represented these *spiritelli del vino* in the three incomparable bronze reliefs on the base of the statue of *Judith and Holofernes* (Figs. 43, 44, and 45). The reliefs are in part derived from the Roman sarcophagus in Pisa (see Fig. 14), which Nanni di Viterbo in his letter of 1430 said Donatello had praised for its *spiritelli*, referring to the drunken infants treading the grape.[54] As late as 1499 a similar relief (Fig. 46) was

THE INVENTION OF THE PUTTO

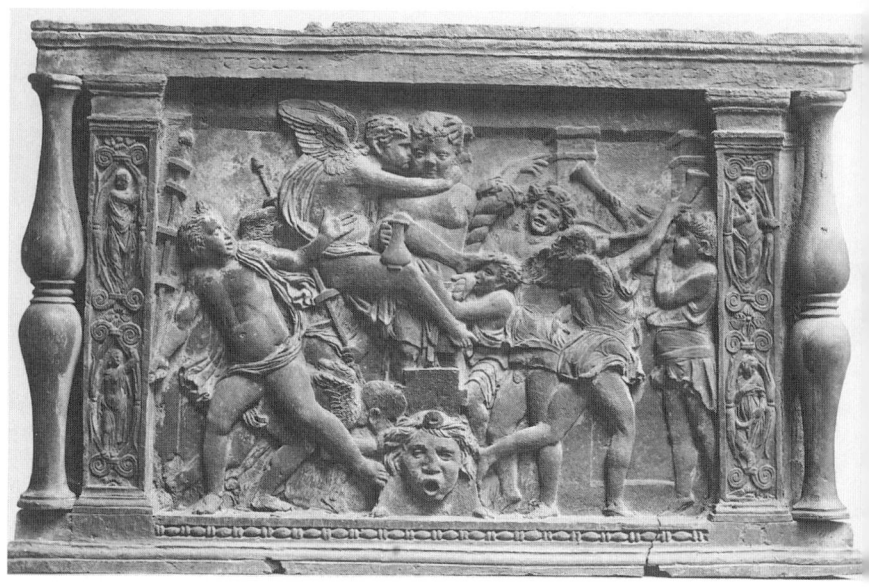

FIGURE 45
Donatello, *Judith and Holofernes*, Florence, Palazzo Vecchio. Detail from base, *Spiritelli Reveling*. (Photograph: Alinari/Art Resource)

described by Francesco Colonna in the *Hypnerotomachia Polifili* in terms that, save for the presence of the infant Bacchus, might as easily describe Donatello's reliefs for the base of the *Judith and Holofernes*:

> Some beautiful nude *spiritelli* with laughing faces were climbing on top of a pergola. There they were plucking the hanging and swollen mature grape clusters. Some were cleverly offering them in baskets to the divine spirit [Bacchus], and he, placidly taking notice, was receiving them. Some were lying alone, supine upon the greensward, provoked to sweet sleep by the juice of the grape. Others were applying themselves intently to the labors of the mustulent Autumn.[55]

Donatello's bronze reliefs for the base of the *Judith and Holofernes*, rather than comprising the subject of his sculpture, instead function, as do the terracotta *spiritelli* on the frame of the Cavalcanti *Annunciation*, as a kind of

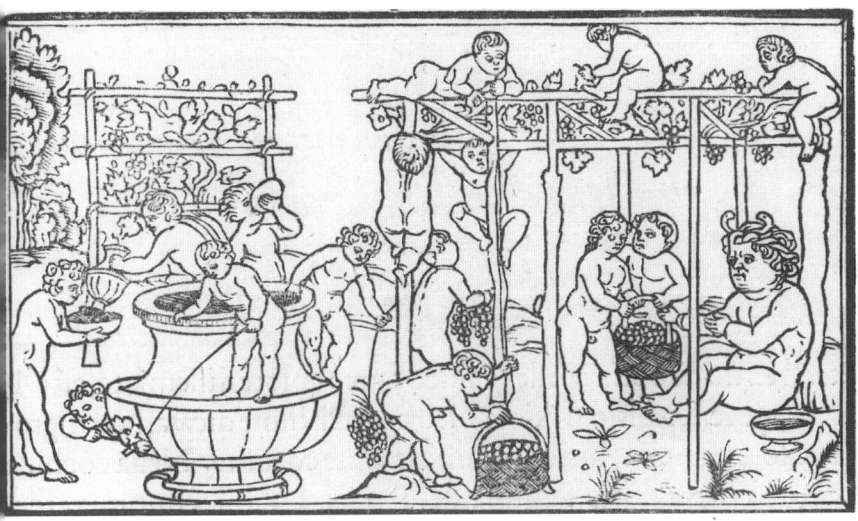

FIGURE 46
Spiritelli Harvesting the Grape, woodcut from Francesco Colonna, *Hypnerotomachia Polifili*, Venice, 1499, George Peabody Library, The Johns Hopkins University (fol. L4r). (Photograph by James T. Van Rensselaer)

ornament in action that comments upon and enlarges his main theme. In the first of them, five *spiritelli del vino* harvest the ripe grapes suspended from the trees and carry the clusters away in baskets. A sixth, a drinking pot in one hand and a cornucopia bursting with grapes in the other, lies in a drunken stupor on the ground. His belly is gluttonously swollen with wine, his face distorted by nausea, and the grotesque child vomits in the direction of the viewer—in an effect that would originally have been even more vivid, since the statue was designed as a fountain, and a hole is drilled in the sprite's mouth from out of which a jet of liquid would have spewed forth. In the second relief, two *spiritelli*, having cinched up their tunics so that they are naked from the waist down, tread the grapes while others drink, urinate, and lie prostrate in drunken oblivion. The imagery of the third relief, placed at the front of the pedestal supporting the *Judith and Holofernes*, in the most prominent position, is the most complex. Here we see *spiritelli* blowing horns and dancing in giddy revel at the right. Another flees away in terror to the left. He seems to carry a child's windmill (the vanes of which, like drunken fancies, spin uncontrollably with every passing breeze). The same sprite who appeared in the first relief, still carrying his drinking pot and cornucopia, stands in the center, where he is embraced and kissed by another *spiritello*. Below them an infant bends down and, mirroring their action, bestows a kiss upon a mask affixed to a stone block, its mouth fitted with a water spout. The empty mask (*larva*) signifies a deluded fancy of the sort drink can induce—a *folletto*, or empty folly, a mere scarecrow used to frighten small children and animals—and the relief thus summarizes Holofernes's fate and its cause. The *spiritelli del vino* act out the delirious sensations of drunken revelry that they produce: the exaggerated noises of music pounding in the brain; the unsteady swirling and dancing of the head; and the onset of incontinence, nausea, startled hallucinations, and lustful impulses, all finally ending in narcotic oblivion.

Spiritelli also adorn Judith's dress, two of them supporting a roundel at her breast, and two pairs at each of her shoulders who dance to either side of vases filled with poppies, indicative of the narcotic effects of the wine with which she has defeated Holofernes. The same attributes also adorn Donatello's so-called *Attis-Amorino*, the earliest fully independent bronze statue with a pagan theme that survives from the Renaissance, and one that is doubly misnamed, being neither Attis nor an *amorino* (Fig. 47). It is a *spiritello*, and, as Janson realized, without much doubt a wine-spirit, given that its attributes predominantly derive from Bacchic imagery.[56] The child wears a poppy on his forehead, and pods filled with sleep-inducing poppyseeds adorn his peasant's belt, which is assuredly non-classical. Nor are the open-fronted leather trouser-legs suspended from his belt classical. They are instead, as Reymond was the first to point out long ago, a form of chaps, or protective leggings, worn by workmen and by peasants in the field together with loincloths or some other undergarment to protect their legs from abrasions.[57] The writhing Bacchic snake—an image ubiquitous in Bacchic sarcophagi, including the one with drunken putti in Pisa (see Fig. 14) and the adaptation of the type in the *Hypnerotomachia* (see Fig. 46)—coils through the soles of his sandals and

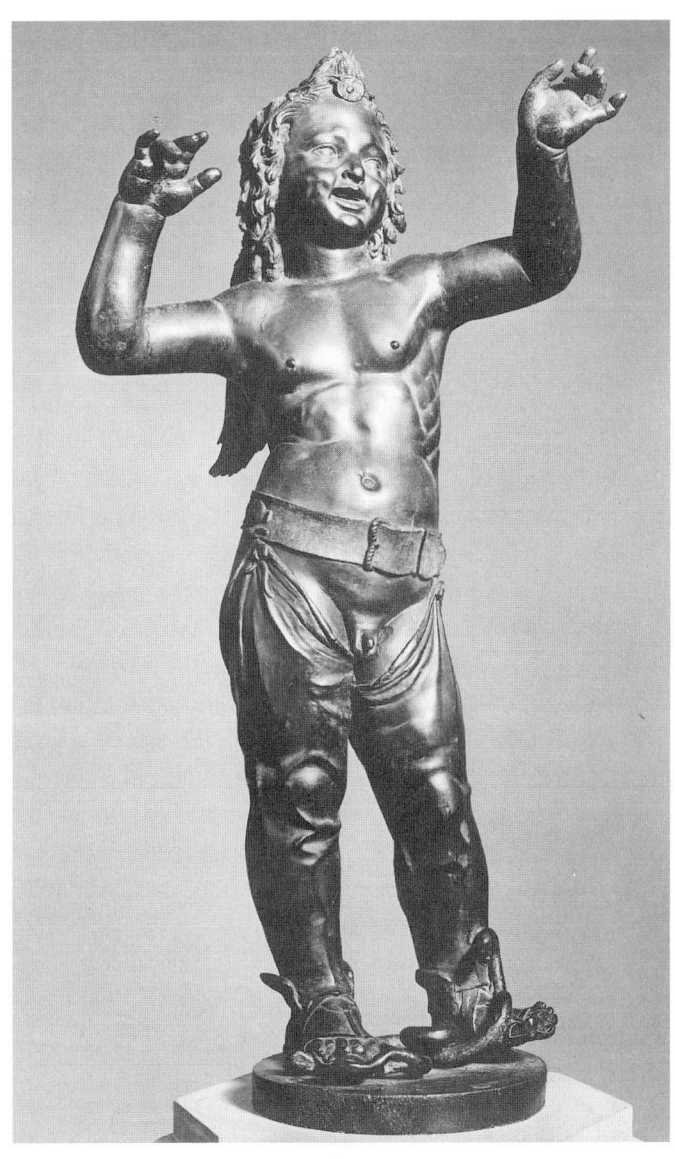

FIGURE 47
Donatello, *Wine Spirit* (so-called *Attis-Amorino*), Florence, Museo del Bargello.
(Photograph: Brogi/Art Resource)

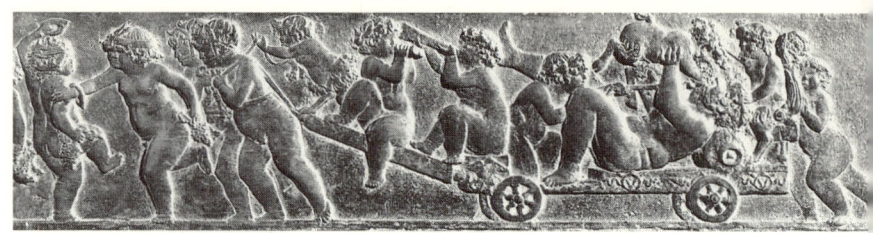

FIGURE 48
Bertoldo di Giovanni, *Bacchic Procession*, Florence, Museo del Bargello.
(Photograph by Nicolò Orsi Battaglini)

around his toes. His ribald nature is indicated by his saucy smile (which it is not far-fetched to sense as rubicund), as well as by his lack of loincloth and his Satyr's tail, contributing to this *spiritello* the attributes not only of a winged *eros* but also of the *Satyriscus*, the sensual spirit (and often demon) of lustful phantasms, whose meaning and attributes we shall be examining in a later chapter. Both are commonplace in ancient Bacchic imagery. Indeed, Bertoldo's exquisite relief in the Bargello (the theme of which the *Hypnerotomachia* woodcut merely varies), which shows the infant Bacchus in a cart pulled in the train of the merrily tripping *spiritelli del vino*, also includes two *Satyrisci*. One stands on the wagon-pole pulled by two little sprites, whom he reins to his bidding, and the other is drunkenly dandled aloft by the infant god (Fig. 48).[58] Donatello's wine-spirit, however, though his Satyr's tail and immodest self-exposure indicate the erotic thrills that wine can spark in the drinker, is also more rarefied than the unalloyed *Satyriscus*, in keeping with his true nature as a *spiritello*. The wings on his back and those attached to his sandals are there, not as the attributes of Mercury or Cupid, but in order to indicate his airiness and extreme volatility.

Such multiplicity (and simplicity) of expressive possibility was not to last. By the sixteenth century the putto, that most characteristic of Italian artistic forms, had begun to acquire a more limited, but still powerful meaning, becoming identified as one of the myriad little brothers of Cupid, as Politian refers to them in the *Stanze per la Giostra di Giuliano de' Medici*. Putti are called *erotes* or *amores* in antiquity, and in the *Stanze* they are alternatively named *spiritelli* and, with more exact Latinity, *piccioletti Amori*. Partly as a consequence of Politian's poetic and linguistic authority, by the early years of the next century putti had come to be generally called *eroti, amori, cupidi*, or by diminutives drawn from them. But that is the subject of the next chapter.

CHAPTER TWO

Spiritelli d'Amore

Idle Fancies and Childish Follies

IN THE FIRST chapter we examined the ornamental function and various meanings inherent in Donatello's revival and reinvention of the putto, called a *spiritello* in the vernacular tongue. Such infant sprites can personify any of those many different impulses that affect the body without conscious bidding, unwilled by the intellect. These impulses and sensations are caused by volatile, airy spirits that enter the body through such sensory organs as the eyes (receiving the *spiriti del viso*) or ears (receiving the *spiriti del suono*). They are then transmitted by the body's own natural, vital, and animal spirits in a pneumatic rush through the tubes of the veins, arteries, and nerves to the liver, heart, and brain. They provoke sensations like the surge of fright causing the hair to stand on end, musical ecstasy, sudden sexual arousal, or the involuntary heaving of a lover's sigh. Putti can also personify the nourishing, life-supporting spirits contained in the fruits of the earth, as in the swag-bearing *spiritelli* carved on the tomb of Ilaria del Carretto (Plate 7). Then again, they may embody the intoxicating spirits of the fermented grape, as we find illustrated by the bibulous infants appearing on the ancient relief portrayed in the *Hypnerotomachia Polifili* (see Fig. 46), and on the base of Donatello's *Judith and Holofernes* (see Figs. 43, 44, and 45), where they act out all the effects and symptoms of the luxurious drunkenness that overwhelmed the Philistine general and brought him to his shameful end. Moreover, even though the infant *spiritello* in his very name and nature speaks in the vernacular tongue, Donatello's adaptation of the Bacchic putti shown on Roman sarcophagi such as the one in

Pisa (see Fig. 14) also indicates an interpretation, and a pretty good one, of their Latin meaning.

Both the earliest and most common appearances of the putto in ancient art appear on Bacchic sarcophagi, from which Jacopo della Quercia derived the *reggifestone*, or garland-bearing type for his tomb of Ilaria, where the figures represent the natural spirits contained in the nourishing fruits of the earth. The sarcophagus in Pisa that Donatello had praised and also imitated for the base of his *Judith and Holofernes* belongs to one of the most familiar types of Roman sarcophagus, from which the woodcut in Colonna's *Hypnerotomachia* also derives. This is the Dionysiac sarcophagus (together with its cognate, the Season sarcophagus), on which putti, sometimes with wings and sometimes without, do not appear as *erotes* but instead as infantile *Bacchoi* who celebrate, often drunkenly, a revelry (or *thiasos*) in honor of Dionysus.[1] They inhabit a kind of Bacchants' paradise, replete with imagery of the garden, and in particular imagery of the autumnal *Vindemia*, or vintage, including swags heavily laden with fruits (the source of the putto *reggisfestone*) in honor of Bacchus as the god of vegetal regeneration. The symbolism of the Bacchic *Vindemia* is founded in the red blood of the newly pressed vine, and this symbolic equivalence was early adopted in Christian exegesis, taking as its point of departure Christ's well-known parable, "I am the vine" as interpreted by such early Church fathers as Clement of Alexandria, who wrote of "the grape trampled for our salvation, the blood of the vine."[2] It further informs visual interpretations of the parable in early Christian art, as we find, for example, in the sarcophagus of the Three Good Shepherds in the Museo Pio Cristiano in the Vatican (Lateran 181). On the ends of this sarcophagus, in common with that of Junius Bassus, appear putti harvesting grapes, wheat, and olives, in reference to the resurrection as adumbrated in the annually renewing cycle of life in nature. The front shows three shepherds (the familiar type for Christ as the Good Shepherd) standing in a vineyard teeming with infants who clamber among the grape clusters (Fig. 49).[3] The meaning of the image differs not at all from that of Lorenzo Lotto's frescoes of *Christ the Vine* in the Suardi Oratory in Trescore (Fig. 50), in which we see the vine that grows from

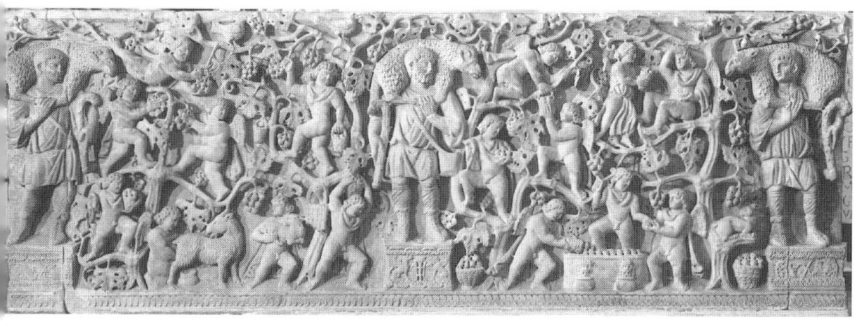

FIGURE 49
Sarcophagus of the Good Shepherds, Vatican, Museo Pio Christiano.
(Photograph: Monumenti Musei e Gallerie Pontificie, Città del Vaticano)

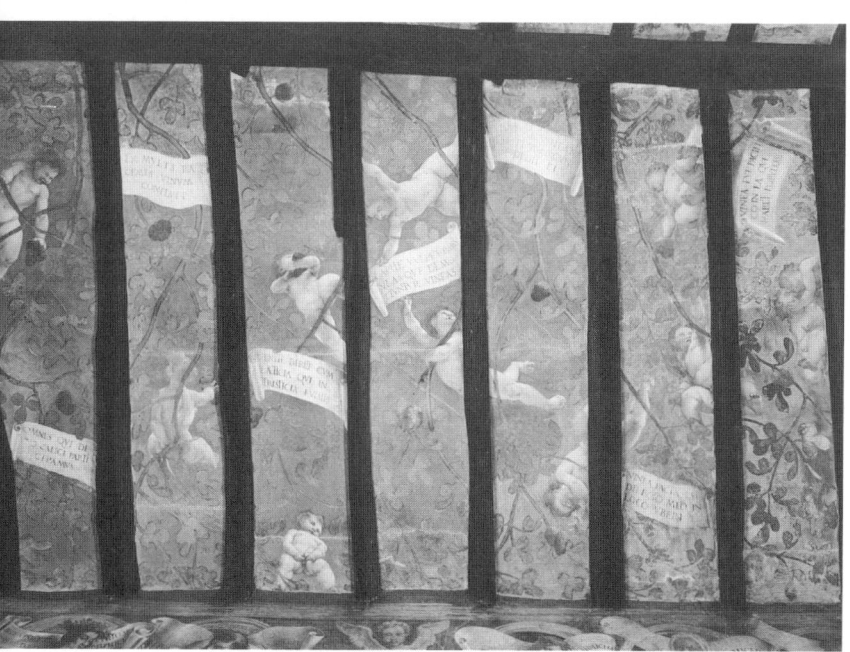

FIGURE 50
Lorenzo Lotto, *Spirits of the Vine*, Trescore, Suardi Oratory.
(Photograph: Edizioni Bolis srl)

Christ's hands spreading upward across the beams supporting the ceiling to form a trellis filled with grape clusters swarming with *spiritelli*. Both derive from Christ's words in John 15.5, "Ego sum vitis, vos palmites" (referring by paronomasia to the speech recorded just before in John 11.25, "Ego sum resurrectio et vita"), and both constitute a reference to the idea of Christ, of whose vine we are the branches, in union with whom we acquire the fruits of eternal life.[4] And in both the spirits of renewed life symbolized by the grape racemes are overtly expressed by the infant putti, whether interpreted as *spiritelli*, *genii*, or as the souls of Dionysian initiates.

In fact, the present-day understanding of the infant *Bacchoi* on Roman Dionysiac sarcophagi as the souls of Dionysian initiates is not really so far removed from the Renaissance interpretation of them as infant *spiritelli*. The vernacular meaning of *spirito* of course encompasses that of the soul, even though *spiritello* refers not so much to the human soul as it does to the natural spirit (*pneuma*) animating the vine itself, whether with regard to its nourishing substance or to its inebriative powers. And as such, Quattrocento identification of the infant *Bacchoi* on Roman sarcophagi as *spiritelli* follows Virgil's second *Georgic*, verses 362–96, where the poet writes of the care of the new vine. All editors have noted that in this passage Virgil is making use of personification, notably through the meaning deeply embedded in the Latin word *tener*, which as an adjective carries the meaning of delicate or tender, but as a noun refers to an infant in the first age of life.[5] Virgil writes:

> Ac dum prima novis adolescit frondibus aetas,
> parcendum teneris, et dum se laetus ad auras
> palmes agit laxis per purum immissus habenis,
> ipsa acie nondum falcis temptanda, sed uncis
> carpendae manibus frondes interque legendae.
> inde ubi iam validis amplexae stirpibus ulmos
> exierint, tum stringe comas, tum bracchia tonde
> (ante reformidant ferrum), tum denique dura
> exerce imperia et ramos compesce fluentis.

(And when in their infancy [*prima aetas*] the new leaves bud [*adolescit*], you must spare the tender child [*parcendum teneris*], and while the shoot pushes joyfully towards the sky, racing through the breezes with loosened reins, do not yet attack the plants with the knife's edge, but with bent fingers pluck the leaves and trim at random. Later, after their stout stems have clasped the elms, then clip their hair, then crop their arms (before they fear the blade), and then impose discipline and check the straggling branches.)

There immediately follows the famous passage in which Virgil warns that while the vine leaves are tender sheep and cattle must be fenced out, and especially the sharp-toothed goat, whose crime against Bacchus by attacking the tiny shoots is punished by being sacrificed to the god of the vine. An invention by Raphael based on this passage is recorded in an engraving by the Master of the Die (Fig. 51), which shows the tender infants fighting the goat, who tramples one into the ground while others attempt to hobble him with a cord, beat him off with sticks, and frighten him with the childish pounding of their tom-toms. Their infantile efforts to distract and frighten the goat are ingenious inventions based on Virgil's statement that wooden masks—*oscilla*—are hung on the trees and vines to turn in the breeze—oscillate—functioning as scarecrows to keep the goats at bay. The same passage was given an elegant interpretation in a sculptural relief by François Duquesnoy (Fig. 52), as well as in two paintings by his friend Nicolas Poussin (Figs. 53 and 54). They all date to around 1626, when the two artists shared rooms together, and when, as their biographers report, they first established the proportions of the *putto moderno*, or tender infant, embodying the perfect *tenerezza* of a baby in the first year of life (precisely Virgil's *tener* in *prima aetas*).[6] Duquesnoy's and Poussin's interpretations of the second *Georgic* were prompted by an iconographic reading of the imagery on a Roman sarcophagus in the collection of the Marchese Vincenzo Giustiniani, on which appear winged putti who clamber about in baskets of fruit while one hides behind a mask and startles another (Fig. 55). Duquesnoy's relief shows several tender infants trying to wrest the goat away from the vine while two try to frighten it, one

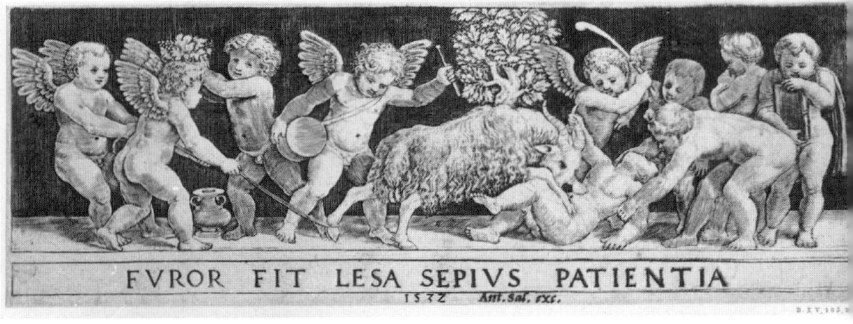

FIGURE 51
Master of the Die, *Tender Sprites Attacking a Goat*, engraving, London, British Museum (Bartsch 15.205.29). (Photograph © The British Museum)

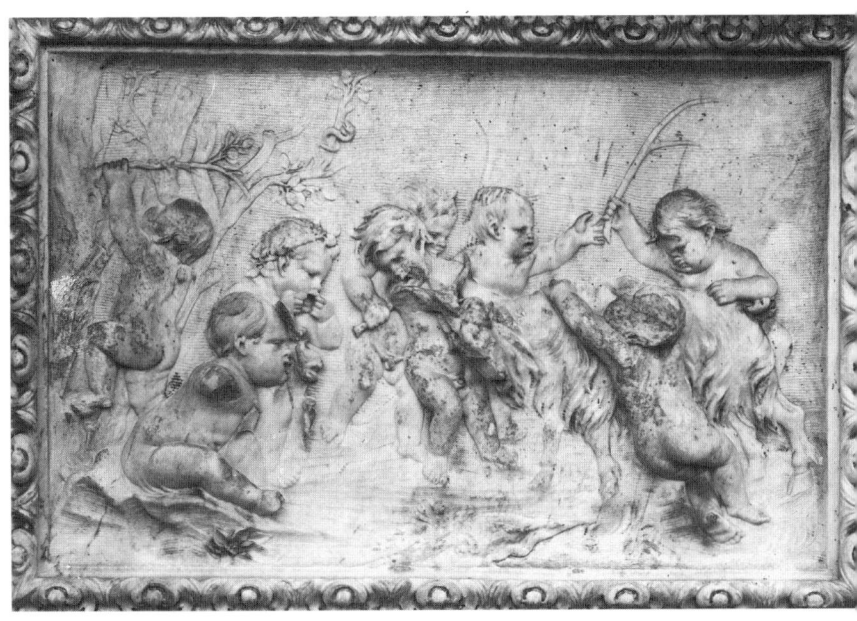

FIGURE 52
François Duquesnoy, *Infant Bacchanal with Larvate Putto and Goat*, Rome, Galleria Doria Pamphili. (Photograph: Fototeca Nazionale, Roma)

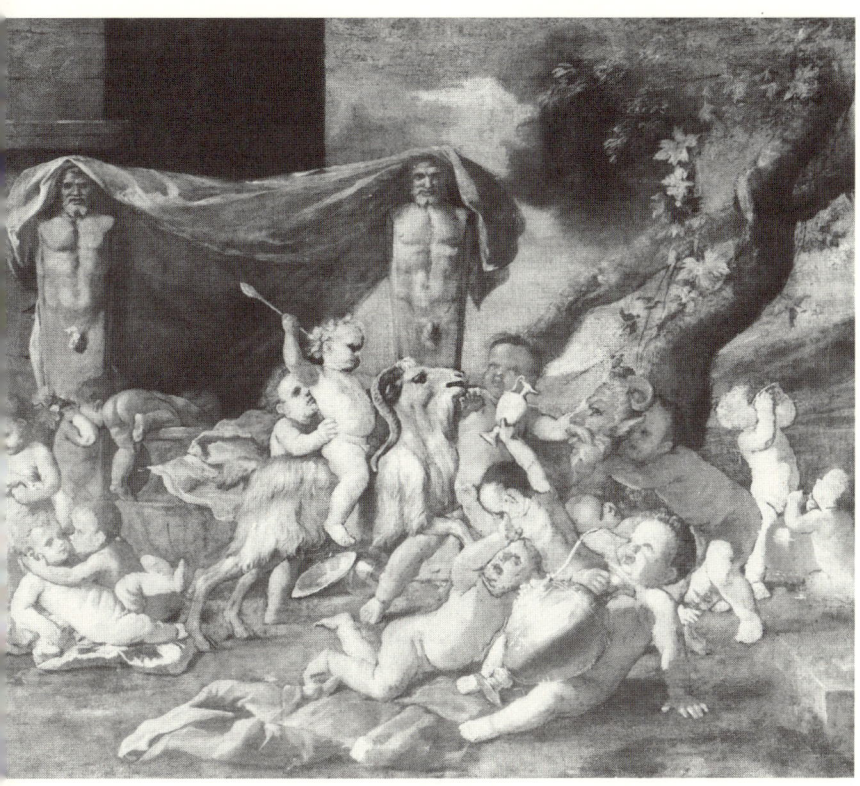

FIGURE 53
Nicolas Poussin, *Infant Bacchanal with Goat and Larvate Putto*, Rome, Galleria Nazionale d'Arte Antica. (Photograph: Archivio Fotografico Soprintendenza Beni Artistici e Storici di Roma)

putting his hands to his mouth to make a face, the second waving a mask (now broken) that dissembles his childish helplessness. In Poussin's painting the tender *genii* of the vine (Virgil's *teneri*, or what Donatello would have called *spiritelli*) fall headlong in flight before the advance of the goat, which one rides in mock triumph. A second hides behind the mask, which he oscillates in the goat's face in an attempt to frighten it. In the companion painting Poussin showed the defeated goat harnessed to a child's triumphal chariot in which the masks are piled up.

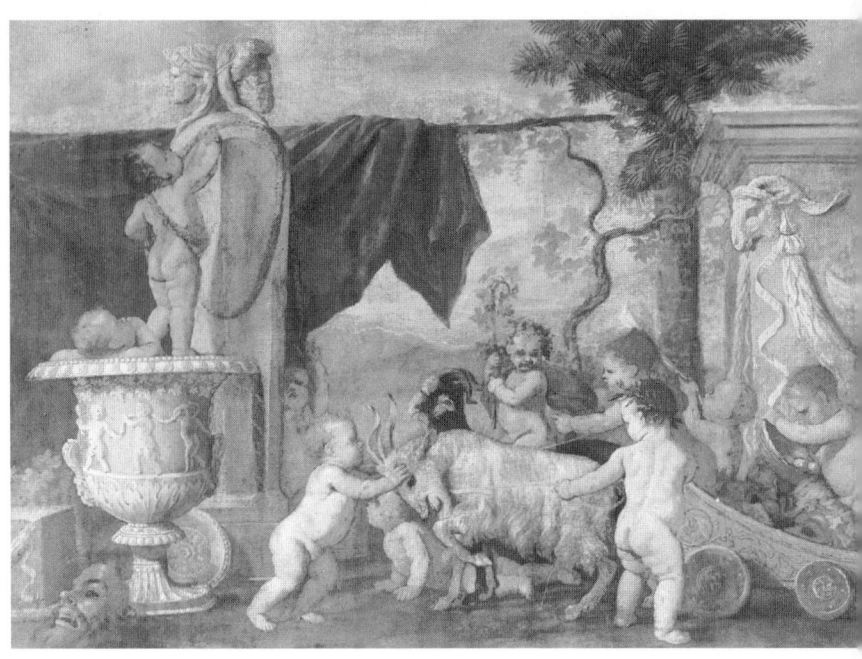

FIGURE 54
Nicolas Poussin, *Infant Bacchanal with Chariot and Masks*, Rome, Galleria Nazionale d'arte Antica. (Photograph: Archivio Fotografico Soprintendenza Beni Artistici e Storici di Roma)

The Quattrocento interpretation of the infant *Bacchoi* on ancient Dionysiac sarcophagi as *spiritelli*, and in particular as the nourishing, natural spirits of life in nature, whether as the life-supporting essences of the vine, fruits, grains, or olives, thus finds support in classical literature and art, as well as in early Christianity. As we saw in the last chapter, Verrocchio's *Putto with a Dolphin*, named as the *bambino di bronzo* in the list of his works for the Medici drawn up by his brother Tommaso after the Medici expulsion in 1494, is similarly a nourishing water sprite, the benign natural spirit animating the waters jetting from the fountain at Carreggi for which the statue was designed.[7] A second item in Tommaso's list, however, introduces us to the subject of this chapter, which is the *spiritello d'amore*,

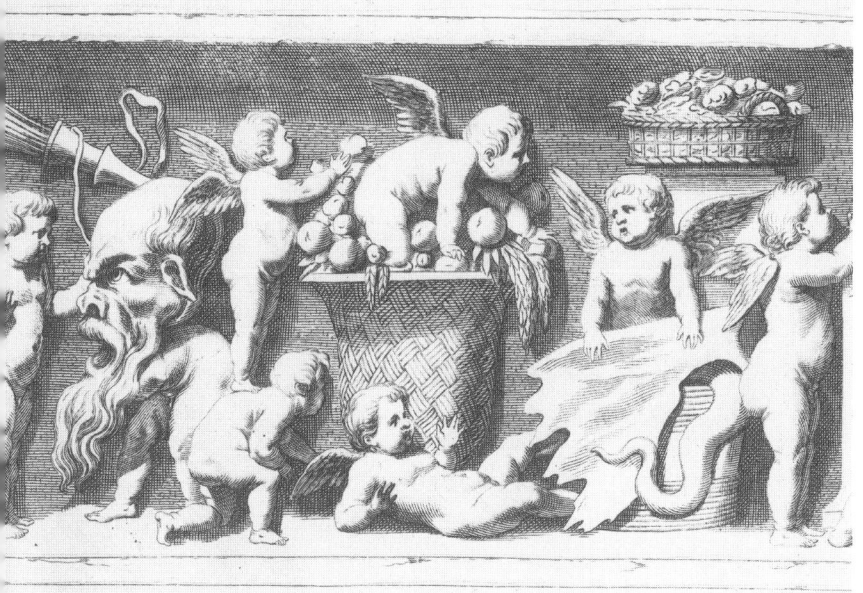

FIGURE 55
Larvate Eros, detail from an engraving of a Bacchic sarcophagus in the
Galleria Giustiniana, Rome, 1627 (book 2, plate 128).
(Photograph by James T. Van Rensselaer)

or vernacular cousin to the classical *eros*. He cites a *spiritello* painted on a standard that Verrocchio had made for the joust won by Lorenzo de'Medici's brother Giuliano in 1475 (*uno stendardo chon uno spiritello per la giostra di Giuliano*).[8] It has been suggested that this was the standard carried, not by Giuliano himself (who in fact bore a banner painted with the image of Pallas by Botticelli), but by Giovanni di Papi Morelli, whose ensign was thus described by an anonymous witness:

> Giovanni di Papi Morelli carried in his hand a red lance, to which was attached a standard of crimson taffeta that was fringed all around. At the top was a winged *spiritello* with a bow at his shoulder,

and a quiver. In his hand was a vase filled with flowers of various colors, which he was tossing into the lap of a nymph with intertwined tresses, who wore a white dress shaded with gold. She was seated on a rock at the edge of a meadow adorned with various flowers, and she had tied a jousting shield to an olive tree that was in the meadow. She was holding the traces of the shield in her hand, and flowers were bursting forth everywhere from those that the *spiritello* had thrown at her.[9]

This passage in turn has been associated with a drawing for a jousting banner by Verrocchio in the Uffizi, which David Brown has recently argued had the finishing touches added by his pupil Leonardo da Vinci (Fig. 56).[10] The drawing is triangular, in the shape of such a banner, and it shows a nymph sleeping on a rocky ledge, upon which she has placed her quiver as a pillow. She has gathered flowers into her lap, and at the left is a stalk of the tall cereal grass known as millet (*Panicum miliaceum*). As she sleeps, a winged *spiritello* furtively emerges from behind the rock and steals an arrow from her quiver. However, there are important differences between Verrocchio's image and the one that was painted on Morelli's standard. In the banner the action of the flower-tossing *spiritello* instead calls to mind an image, unrelated to Giuliano's joust, in Lorenzo Lotto's much later and enigmatically evocative painting in the National Gallery in Washington, where we see an *eros* scattering rose petals from a cloud down into the lap of a nymph sleeping in a grassy meadow (Fig. 57). Although it might be argued that Verrocchio's drawing (which is certainly for a jousting banner) is a first thought for the banner carried by Morelli, it is not in the present state of knowledge possible to identify it with an actual banner made for Giuliano's or any other joust. Nevertheless, the concept of the *spiritello d'amore* depicted thereon, which in part defines the idea of love to which some young knight had pledged his honor in a joust, substantially overlaps that of the ancient *eros* and its vernacular derivative the *amorino*. It is especially familiar in the jousts, civic festivals, and popular imagery of the fifteenth century, and it is this that interests us now.

Thus, in his "La giostra di Lorenzo de'Medici" the poet Luigi Pulci de-

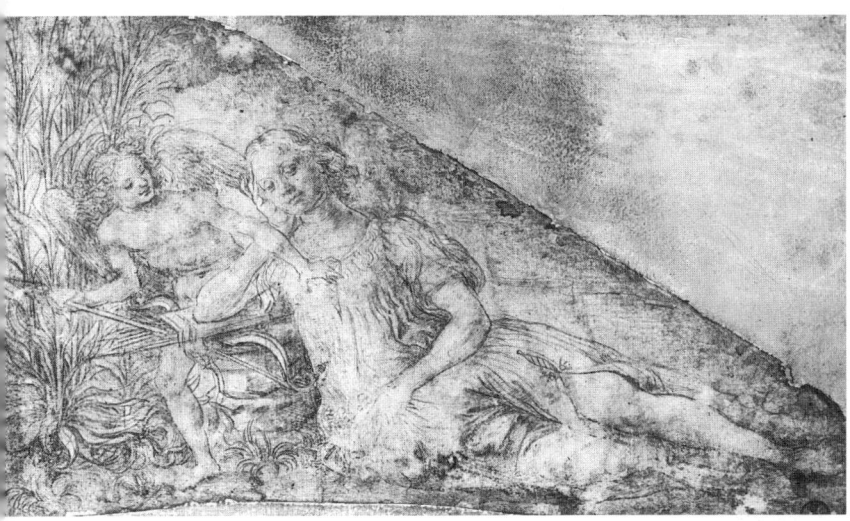

FIGURE 56
Andrea del Verrocchio (and Leonardo da Vinci?), *Nymph and Spiritello*, drawing, Florence, Uffizi, Gabinetto degli Stampe e Disegni. (Photograph: Gabinetto Fotografico Soprintendenza Beni Artistici e Storici di Firenze)

scribes a standard painted with a *spiritello* carried by Salvestro Benci in the earlier joust won by Lorenzo de'Medici in 1469. In addition, on Salvestro's helmet there was a nude woman covered by a veil ("una donna ignuda con un velo atraverso," in the words of an anonymous witness), perhaps, as Pulci suggests, to indicate that Salvestro wished to keep his meaning hidden:[11]

> In the meantime a great noise was raised, and all the people shouted, "She's veiled!" Behold the armed Salvestro Benci appears, and, as a gentle heart that never hides the truth, he did not carry a woman on his standard, so beautiful and light, but a *spiritello* instead. And yet, on the crest of his helmet there is a maid, which I would not know how to interpret other than to think our Salvestro made sport of her in this way so as to drive the people crazy.

Again we find references to *spiritelli* in an anonymous poetic description—"di sapore canterino," in Rossella Bessi's words, "tasting of the street

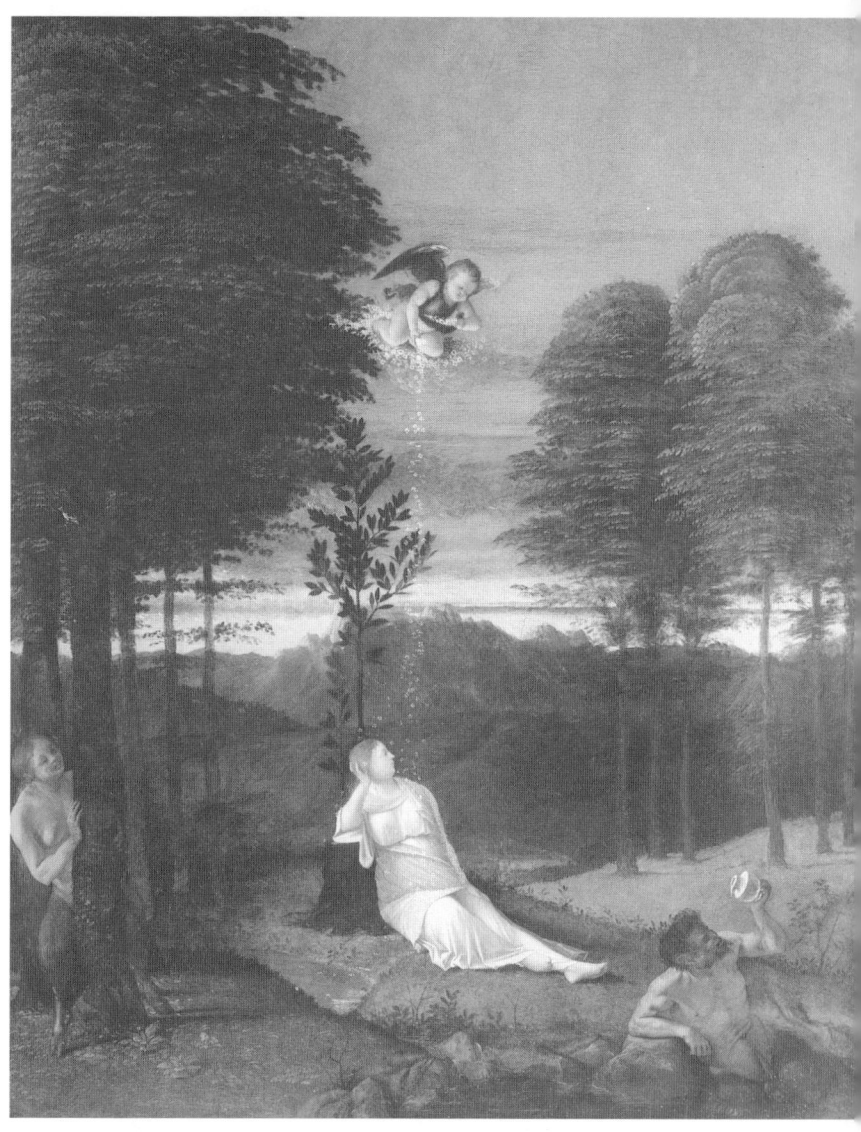

FIGURE 57
Lorenzo Lotto, *Sleeping Nymph*, Washington, National Gallery of Art.
(Photograph © Board of Trustees, National Gallery of Art)

singer"—of a triumphal car (called by the Florentines a *trionfo*, or *edificio*) that was built as part of the sumptuous celebrations arranged for the visit to Florence in the spring of 1459 of Pope Pius II and the fifteen-year-old Galeazzo Maria Sforza, son of the Duke of Milan. The festivities began on Sunday with a joust in the piazza of Santa Spirito, followed the next day with a dance in the Mercato Nuovo. On Tuesday afternoon there was an animal hunt (*caccia*) in the piazza of the Signoria, and the celebrations came to a close in the evening with a parade of the Triumph of Love, led by the ten-year-old Lorenzo the Magnificent, which passed from San Marco down the via Larga past the Medici Palace, where it was witnessed by the distinguished guests, ending at the baptistry. The poem, which describes the float in astonishingly matter-of-fact terms, is preserved in a manuscript entitled *Terze rime in praise of Cosimo de'Medici, his sons, and of the Honors done in the year 1458 [s.f.] for the son of the Duke of Milan and the pope on the occasion of their coming to Florence*:[12]

> The Triumphal Car was made in this form. It had four sides, each of which was graduated upwards according to due measure. It stood on four wheels, each finely balanced for rolling along, and if someone moved but one of them, they all turned. Now I want to tell of the loveliness of its composition on every side, and how greatly lustrous, lively, and worthy a thing it is. Each side is five *braccia* high from the bottom, and is decorated with so many ornaments that it seems impossible to me that it could ever be made. There are many things worked in silver and gold, with so many enamels and pieces of glass crystal that one can see oneself reflected in it as in a mirror. It shines like the sun on all sides, and up at the summit, in the four corners, there are four singular *spiritelli*. In the midst of them are three diamonds [a Medici device] which have at their points a large golden ball [the Medici *palla*] and all of the diamonds are gilded in gold. The *spiritelli* hover above every feastmaker, each has a torch in his hand, and they are naked with wings at their shoulders. The torch was made of silver scales and threw forth a flame of immense fire— please understand, real flame and fire. The Triumph is filled every-

where on all sides with so much fire and so many flames that the highest element seems but a negligible thing. He to whom Venus is the mamma was standing on top of the ball, upright, not bending so much as an inch. With the blindfold over his eyes, carrying the bow in his hand and the quiver at his side, he appears cruel, and was treating those in his path without humanity, with his two great wings and all his body naked.

The characteristic imagery of such triumphs is well known, not only from written accounts, but also from many depictions of it in all artistic media, including tapestries, manuscript illuminations, engravings and paintings, especially for *cassoni* and *deschi da parto*. One Florentine *desco da parto* in the Galleria Sabauda in Turin (1450–1460), for example, shows Cupid standing at the top of his triumphal chariot together with trumpet-blowing *spiritelli* at each of the four corners (Fig. 58). Another of about the same date in the Victoria and Albert Museum also shows the winged and nude god of love at the summit of his triumphal car, bow and flaming arrow in hand, while *spiritelli* at each of the four corners shoot flaming arrows out over the heads of the subdued lovers following in Cupid's path (Fig. 59). Baccio Baldini's fine-manner engraving of the *Triumph of Love* (Fig. 60), dating sometime around 1475, shows blindfolded Love on a ball of flame supported by four cornucopias belching flames from their mouths, much in the manner of the *trionfo* we have seen vividly described by the anonymous rhymester in his account of the celebrations of 1459. Jacopo del Sellaio's even later *Triumph of Love* in the Museo Bandini in Fiesole (after 1480) again shows Cupid above a flaming cauldron, and four gilded *spiritelli* with flaming torches at the corners (Plate 3). Sellaio's painting is also of particular interest because the participants in the triumph no longer wear fashionable contemporary dress but instead appear in the painted costumes of a true Laurentian *mascherata* (and indeed one nymph in Sellaio's adjacent *Triumph of Chastity* wears a white dress painted with blue cornflowers that is virtually identical to the painted costume worn by Flora in Botticelli's *Birth of Venus*).[13] All these examples faithfully respond to the appearances of actual *trionfi* built for civic parades in Florence.

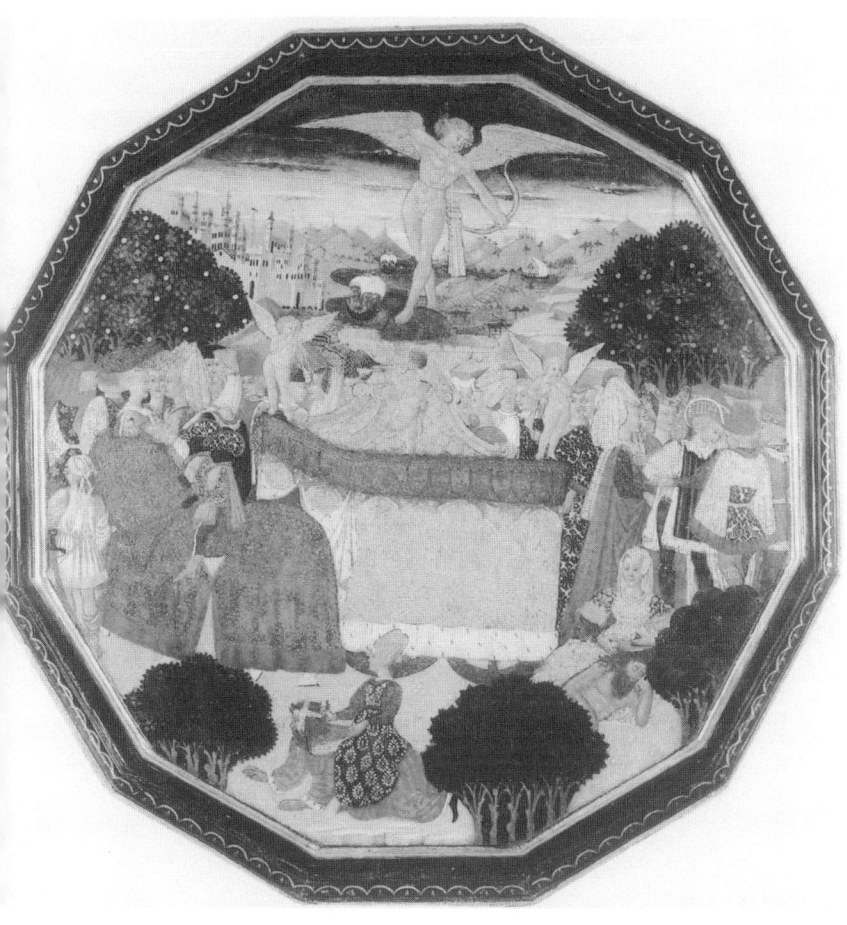

FIGURE 58
The Triumph of Love, Florentine *Desco da parto*, Turin, Galleria Sabauda.
(Photograph: Alinari / Art Resource)

However, lest the courtly and amorous character of painted representations such as these give the impression that the actual triumphs were celebrated in an atmosphere of dignified peace and restraint, we may turn to the accounts given by two eyewitnesses of the *armeggeria* with a Triumph of Love that was arranged during Carnival of 1464 by Bartolomeo

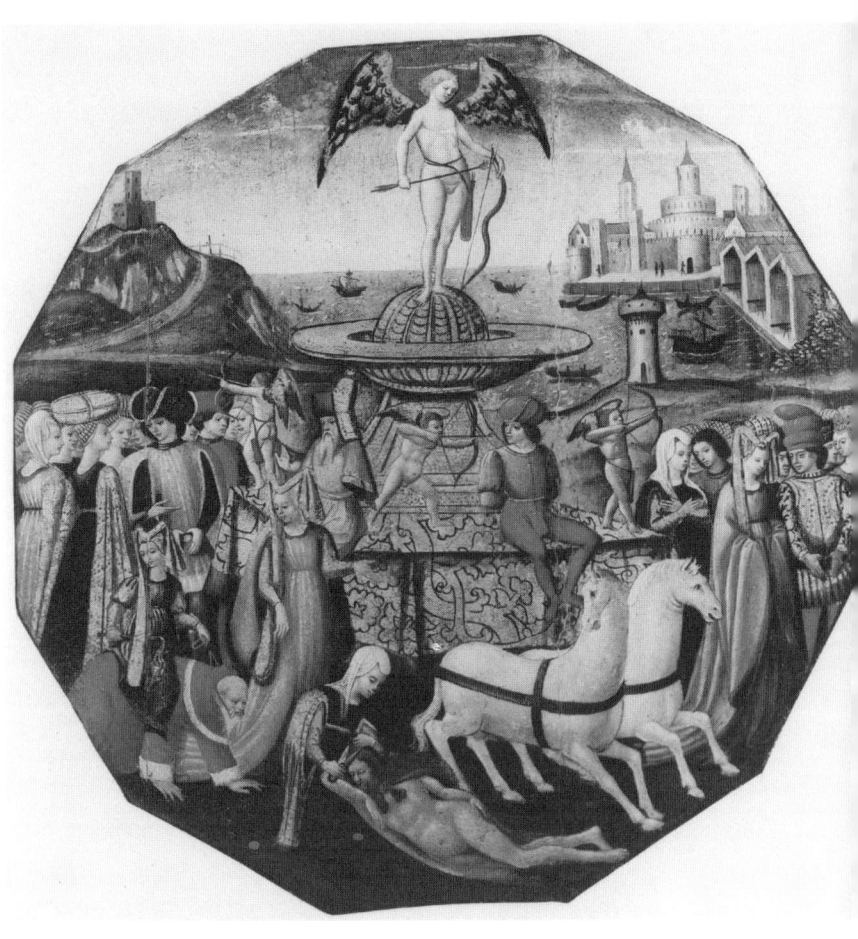

FIGURE 59
The Triumph of Love, Florentine *Desco da parto*, London, Victoria and Albert Museum. (Photograph by James T. Van Rensselaer)

Benci in honor of Marietta degli Strozzi, only five years after the celebration of the Florentine visits of Pius II and Galeazzo Maria Sforza. The *armeggeria* is described in detail by Filippo di Lorenzo Lapaccini in a poem in *terza rima*, and again by the anonymous writer of a manuscript *notizia* under the heading: "Report of the festival held on the night of Carnival for

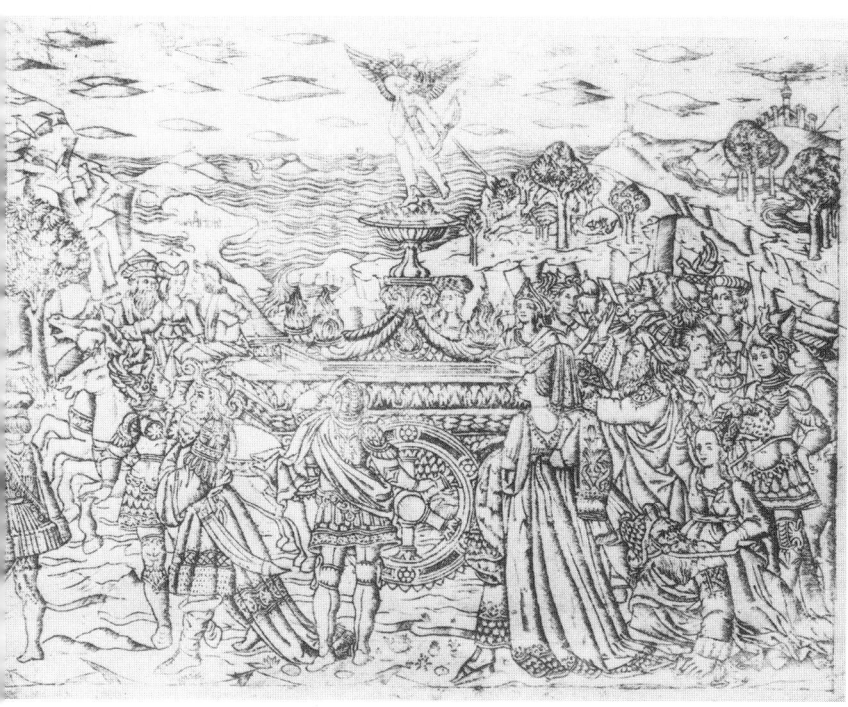

FIGURE 60
Baccio Baldini, *The Triumph of Love*, engraving, Vienna, Staatliche
Graphische Sammlung Albertina (Hind A.I.18).
(Photograph by James T. Van Rensselaer)

a lady who was the daughter of Lorenzo di Messer Palla degli Strozzi, organized by Bartolomeo Benci as the inammorato of the said lady."[14] Before the *armeggeria* took place the Signoria had issued a ban announcing that no one was to ride in the streets save those taking part, and that should anyone of whatsoever status or condition be accidentally injured or killed no action would be taken.[15] Having declared themselves the subjects of Love, and following in the train of Love's triumphal car, Bartolomeo and a cavalcade of eight other noble youths from his *brigata*, each accompanied by about forty shield-bearers and torch-bearing supporters in livery, paraded in full armor through the streets of Florence to the house of Marietta. As the lord and captain of the company, Bartolomeo adopted the title *Signore Amante* (the *inammorato*) and wore Love's wings on his back, thus virtually identifying himself with the god of Love. He was himself attended by fifteen young nobles attired in crimson satin lined with ermine and about a hundred and fifty young men in his colors embroidered with silver falcons. The *trionfo*, that is, Love's triumphal car, was twenty *braccia* high, had a flaming, bleeding heart at its summit, and was swarming with *"spiritelli d'amore,* bows in hand."[16] The chariot itself was surrounded by a host of other *amanti*, men and women who were also Love's subjects, accompanied by blaring trumpeters and flute-players and who loudly shouted and sang the praises of all-conquering Love, their verses punctuated by bellows of *Amore, Amor*. When each knight in turn arrived at the piazza where the Strozzi houses were located, he stood upright in the saddle, spurred his horse to a gallop and gradually lowered his lance until it struck the ground and broke into splinters before the window where Marietta sat between four lighted torches. After this knightly ritual was completed, so Lapaccini writes:

> The Triumph was positioned in the piazza opposite the window where the said lady was seated: and the Lord of the Festival [Bartolomeo Benci] detached his wings and threw them onto the triumphal car; and it had been arranged so that at that moment fire should be set to the said triumphal car; and so it burned, and with such great shouting and thundering that the noise rose even to the stars. And the rockets that had been placed within were so artfully managed that it appeared that the *spiritelli d'amore*, which were on the said Triumph, shot arrows from the bows which they had in their hands; and thus ignited by the air, they flew near to the lady herself. One arrow indeed flew into the house of the said lady, so that it was said that one had entered into her heart, as a sign of her compassion for the said lover. This done, the aforesaid *Signore Amante* withdrew with all his company, and in order not to turn his back upon his lady he made his horse continue to walk backwards until he could no longer behold her. And when they had departed from her, they went

to break lances before the houses of the ladies of each of the Lord's eight aforenamed companions.[17]

In this case (as in the *Triumph of Love* painted by Sellaio) the *spiritelli* were clearly sculptured images, perhaps made of wax, but they could also be played by living boys, as we find in Vasari's life of the Florentine carpenter and engineer Lo Cecca (famous as the designer of the *nuvole* that were the centerpieces for the Ascension plays in the church of the Carmine).[18] The Florentines were famous for their skill with fireworks, and it was Lo Cecca, in the words of Filippo Beroaldo that *Florentinus quidam machinator egregius et mechanicae artis scientissimus*, who built the ingenious and spectacular fireworks display in Bologna for the marriage of Annibale Bentivoglio and Lucrezia d'Este in 1487.[19] Be that as it may, Vasari writes that it was he who contrived the means for representing giants and giantesses in festival pageants by designing a method for guiding heavily costumed and highly skilled stiltwalkers about, together with "*spiritelli*, who differed from the giants because no additions were made to their own forms, and yet they walked ahead on stilts five or six *braccia* high in such a way that they truly appeared to be actual spirits."[20]

As Richard Trexler has written, the form, content, and the dominant passion of such pseudo-feudal rituals were deeply rooted in the conventions of chivalry and courtly love, and one of the primary purposes of the *armeggeria*, as well as the public dance (*balla*) and the joust (*giostra*) that generally succeeded it, was the presentation of an "erotic and lovable male" who was worthy not only of the love of a lady, but also the idea of love that was represented in her. This idea simultaneously incorporated into itself the glory, fame, and triumphant honor of the youth and his lady, as well as of his family and hers, the *brigata* he led, and finally that of the whole of the city itself.[21] Such rituals had a long history in Florence. Giovanni Villani writing in his *Chronicle*, for example, said that, "In the year 1283, for the festival of San Giovanni in the month of June . . . they made a company and *brigata* of a thousand men and more, all of whom were dressed in white robes and followed a *Signore* called *Amore*; and this *brigata* had no other purpose than the making of amusements, games, and dances for the ladies, knights and other people, going about their way with trumpets and diverse instruments."[22] As the *Signore* of the *armeggeria* of 1464, Bartolomeo Benci had merely followed age-old custom in adopting the chivalric title *Amante*. By wearing wings attached to his armor he moreover symbolically identified himself as the *Signore* called *Amore*, hence meaning to indicate that the love he offered by following the *trionfo* with a burning heart to Marietta's window was true. And Marietta too played a courtly and symbolic role, that of Lady Love—not in the guise of Venus so much as in that of the French *Dame Amour* or the German *Frau Minne*.

Moreover, it is significant that the clamorous ceremony enacted before Marietta Strozzi's window, even though the imagery of Love's triumphal car leading a train of courtly and knightly lovers would inevitably have recalled Petrarch's *Trionfi* to any Florentine, nevertheless hearkens back to an older tradition, and much more closely resembles thirteenth- and fourteenth-century chivalric contests, including jousting, staged before a Castle of Love. The theme can be found in the *Roman de la rose*, for example, and Roland Patavin writes that in 1214 a festival took place in Treviso for which a Castle of Love was built that was defended by women in the ramparts, who rained flowers, fruit and perfumes down upon their knightly lover-assailants.[23] A public festival organized around a *Castello d'Amore* is also recorded in Bologna, and the imagery of the castle of love (though in a more peaceful setting) can also be found, virtually contemporary with Bartolomeo Benci's *armeggeria*, in Baccio Baldini's fine-manner engraving of *Venus* from the series of the planets (Fig. 61). Here women (one of whom holds the lover's wreath familiar from dozens of late-medieval images) toss bouquets from the balcony of their palazzo-fortress, which in the first state (Fig. 62) is inscribed *Omnia vincit Amor*, while a lady on the meadow below awards a youth with the lover's wreath. The scheme is well known from earlier representations, especially among French ivories of the fourteenth century. One group of ivories, for example, shows knights storming the Castle of Love in order to claim the hands of their vanquished ladies, who sometimes lean over the wall to bestow the lover's crown on some ascending gallant, and sometimes coquettishly seek to defend themselves by tossing flowers down on their besieging lovers

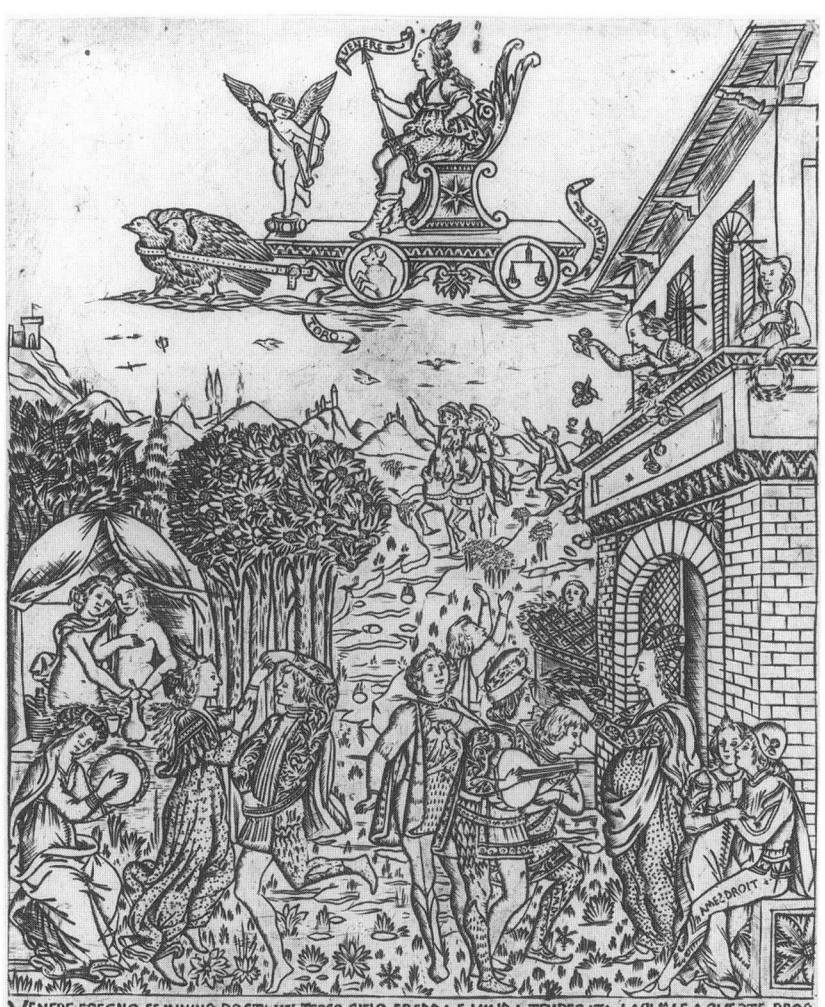

FIGURE 61
Baccio Baldini, *The Planet Venus*, engraving, London, British Museum
(Hind A.III.5,b, second state). (Photograph © The British Museum)

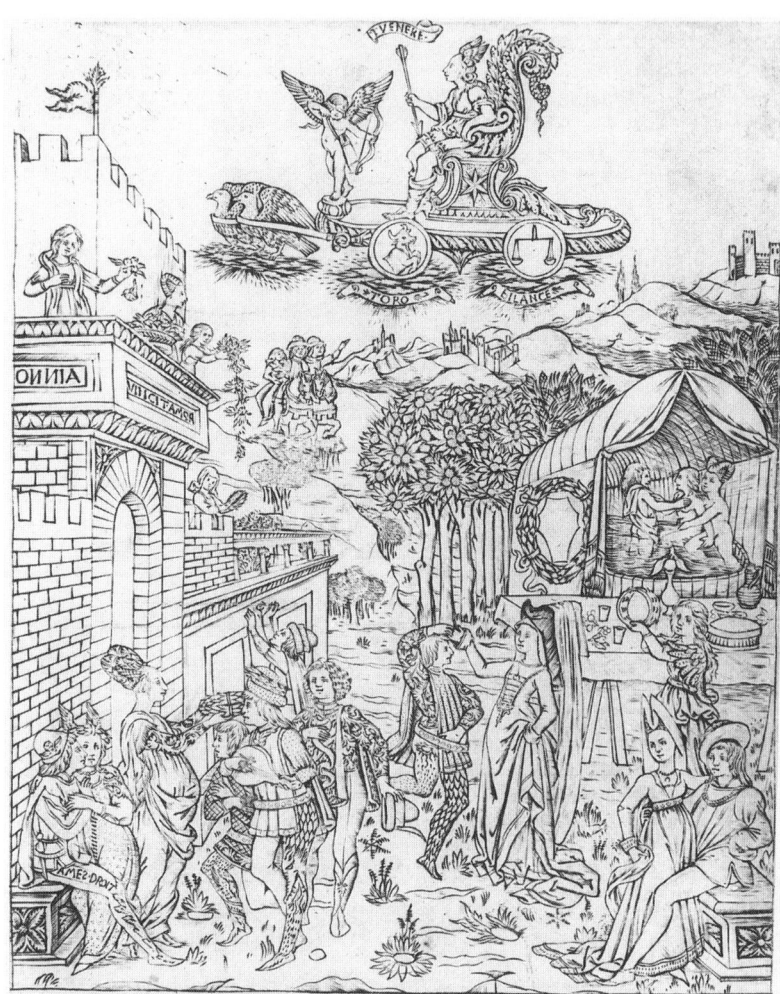

FIGURE 62
Baccio Baldini, *The Planet Venus*, engraving, London, British Museum
(Hind A.III.5,a, first state). (Photograph © The British Museum)

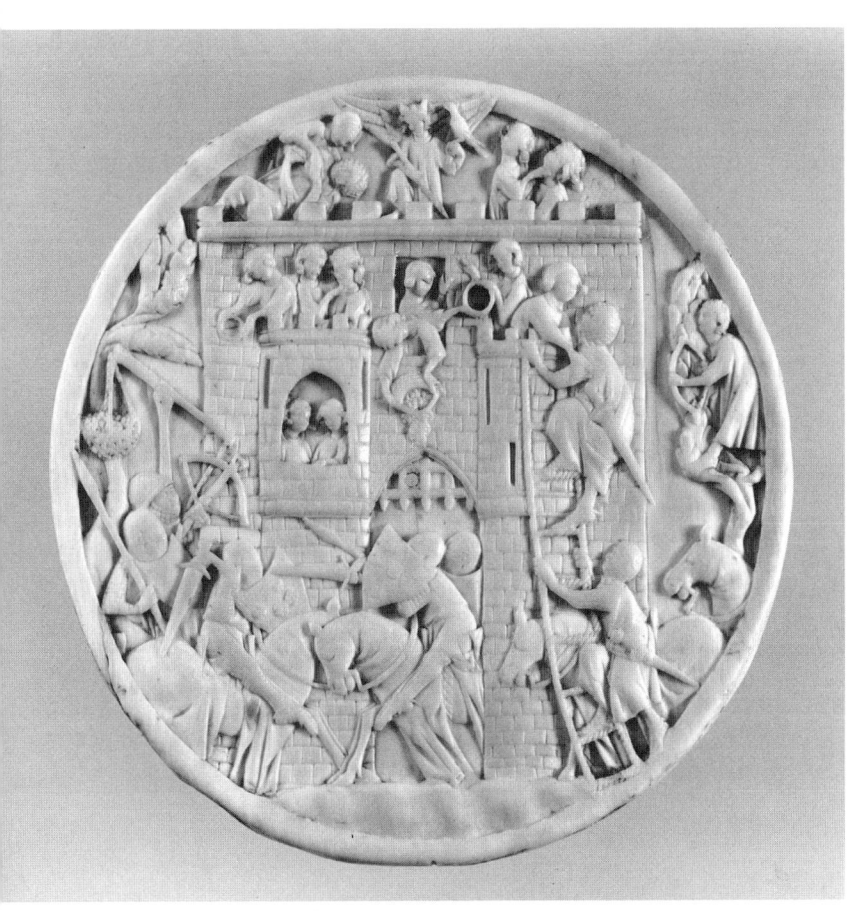

FIGURE 63
The Battle for the Castle of Love, ivory mirror case (fourteenth century), Baltimore, The Walters Art Gallery. (Photograph: The Walters Art Gallery)

(Fig. 63).[24] A related group of ivories shows the knights jousting with flowering branches or with blunted lances before a castle presided over by Love, in the battlements and at the windows of which their besieged ladies show themselves (Plate 8).[25] In Bartolomeo Benci's *armeggeria*, Marietta at her palace window occupied the place of the beseiged lady in her castle, and the ritual splintering of the spears by dashing them to the ground

IDLE FANCIES AND CHILDISH FOLLIES

under her window is nothing more than a symbolic representation (by then traditional) of the breaking of lances in actual passages of arms during the joust. Moreover, the symbolism of the Castle, or Fortress of Love (the *Minneburg*), whereby the heart of the lady is compared to a fortress that the *amante* must conquer, is well understood; and it was certainly understood by the anonymous author of the *notizia* of Benci's *armeggeria* when he wrote that one the flaming arrows shot by the *spiritelli d'amore* had penetrated the window of Marietta's house, indicating that it had entered the lady's heart, filling her with compassionate feelings for Bartolomeo, and hence signifying her surrender.

Just what are these *spiritelli d'amore*? The answer may seem so obvious as to make the question seem hardly worth the asking, so widespread and familiar is the image of the winged and nude infant, or putto, in art. They are the myriad little brothers of Cupid, as Politian refers to them in the *Stanze per la Giostra di Giuliano de'Medici*, and as Cartari was to write in the following century.[26] They are called *erotes* or *amores* in antiquity, and in Italian *i piccioletti Amori*, as Politian names them in the *Stanze* with more exact Latinity than would be the word *spiritelli*, a word he nevertheless twice uses as synonymous with *amori*.[27] By the sixteenth century they are almost invariably called *eroti, amori, cupidi*, or by diminutives drawn from them. That the concepts of the *spiritello d'amore* and *eros* do considerably overlap, moreover, we have already seen from the imagery of the Florentine jousts and *armeggerie*, as well as from the inventory of the contents of the Medici Palace drawn up after the death of Lorenzo the Magnificent in 1492, in which genuinely ancient *erotes* are not named as such, but are called *spiritelli* instead.[28] Nevertheless, *spiritelli d'amore* are no more ancient than are their various cognate *spiritelli*, nor, as we have seen, are they strictly synonymous with *erotes* or *amores*. Their meaning rather derives from vernacular usage, and in particular from the poetic and chivalric traditions that inform the imagery of those jousts and *armeggerie* which we have up to this point been examining.

Nevertheless, the closest vernacular parallel to the ancient *eros* is indeed the *spiritello d'amore*, especially insofar as its effects can be identified with that sudden, overwhelming passion produced in the heart by the sight of a lady, or by a pneumatic surge of erotic sensations. However, the concepts embodied in the *spiritello d'amore*, as I have already suggested through the passages quoted from Dante in the first chapter, are more complex and interesting, nor are they by any means uniformly synonymous with the classical *eros*. In the *Vita nuova* Dante, as we have seen, calls such a spirit a *spiramento d'Amore*, a breath of Love; and in the same passage, commenting upon the following sonnet ("Gentil pensero che parla di vui"), he further writes that it can appear as a random thought, a *pensiero*:

> Gentil pensero che parla di vui
> sen vene a dimorar meco sovente,
> e ragiona d'amor sì dolcemente,
> che face consentir lo core in lui.
> L'anima dice al cor: "Chi è costui,
> che vene a consolar la nostra mente,
> ed è la sua vertù tanto possente,
> ch'altro penser non lascia star con nui?"
> Ei le risponde: "Oi anima pensosa,
> questi è uno spiritel novo d'amore,
> che reca innanzi me li suoi desiri;
> e la sua vita, e tutto 'l suo valore,
> mosse de li occhi di quella pietosa
> che si turbava de' nostri martiri."²⁹

(A gentle thought that speaks of you comes often to dwell with me, and it reasons so sweetly of love as to make the heart consent to it. The soul says to the heart: "Who is this who comes to console our mind, and who has such strength as not to let any other thought remain with us?" He answers her: "O pensive soul, this is a new little spirit of love [*uno spiritel novo d'amore*] that brings its desires before me; and its life and all its power came from the eyes of that compassionate lady who was troubled by our suffering.")

This *spiritello d'amore* is the same as that *gentil pensiero* with which the sonnet begins, and in his commentary Dante refers to this as only one among the many such random notions swirling about in the "battaglia de' pensieri" raging within his head. Here the *pensiero* in favor of the *donna* Philosophy attempts to gain the ascendancy over those that favor Beatrice, and for this reason Dante writes that he calls it *gentile* only insofar as it speaks of a noble lady, who in other respects he considers vile. Dante later returned to this theme in the "Convivio," however, this time succumbing to the loving blandishments of Philosophy. In his commentary to the *canzone* "Voi che 'ntendendo" he tells how, some ten years later, the same *spiritello* returned to him:

> "Tu non se' morta, ma se' ismarrita,
>   anima nostra, che sì ti lamenti,"
>   dice uno spiritel d'amor gentile;
> "ché quella bella donna che tu senti,
>   ha transmutata in tanto la tua vita,
>   che n'hai paura, sì se' fatta vile!
> Mira quant'ell'è pietosa e umile,
>   saggia e cortese ne la sua grandezza,
>   e pensa di chiamarla donna, omai!"[30]

("You are not dead but only bewildered, you, our soul, who lament so much"—thus speaks a noble little spirit of love [*spiritel d'amor gentile*]—"for that beautiful lady whose power you feel has so greatly transformed your life that you are frightened, so base have you become! See how compassionate and humble she is, how wise and courteous in her greatness, and think to call her your lady from now on.")

In the commentary Dante explains the source of his bewilderment and confusion, which has put him in a state of fright, by citing Boethius's *De consolatione philosophiae* (2, par. 1): "No sudden alteration in the state of things occurs without some disturbance to the soul." He declares that the new *pensiero* that has provoked his fear, causing his own sudden alteration and perturbation of soul, is called a *spiritello d'amore* in order to indicate his own inclination toward that very thought.[31] His fright is caused by his sudden attraction to a new lady laying claim to his love, which had previously been given to Beatrice. And further on Dante adds that by this particular *spiritello d'amore* "is meant a *pensiero* that arose from my study; and so it should be understood that, so far as this allegory is concerned, *amore* always means that particular study, which means the application of a mind enamored of something to that thing . . . and I say and affirm that the lady of whom I was enamored after my first love was the most beautiful and most highly honorable daughter of the lord of the universe, to whom Pythagoras gave the name Philosophy."[32]

A *spiritello* can be understood simply as a random thought or feeling, one that suddenly arises and moves the mind, perhaps in the form of an idle fancy or perhaps as a sudden insight. It is itself neutral, being neither necessarily true nor false, and it strikes one unexpectedly, as though from an outside agency rather than through the reasoning process itself. In contrast to such a random thought, a *spiritello d'amore*, as Dante indicates, is an idea or course of study to which one feels a personal inclination and attachment, even though this does not mean that it should be followed. Dante's inner turmoil, caused by the conflict of ideas represented by Beatrice on the one hand and the lady Philosophy on the other, is quite serious, as Tennyson understood when he wrote in "In Memoriam" (102) of "two spirits of a diverse love" who have "striven half a day," contending for "loving masterdom." In the *Vita nuova* Dante resisted the *spiritello d'amore* that urged him toward Philosophy and away from Beatrice, but in the "Convivio" he follows his own inclination and accepts it. What is more, the random thought that convinces him is sent by Philosophy herself, into whose eyes he has gazed, and who *all'improvviso* causes there suddenly to flash into his mind a recollection of the maxim from Boethius that seems to explain his perturbation to him. The unbidden *spiritello* that flashes from her eyes is already sure of the victory, as Dante is well aware, writing: "when already he says *anima nostra*, he shows himself the familiar of it."[33]

Such thoughts of love of course can also be nothing more than mere distractions, idle notions, and they can even be carnal in nature, as in Boccaccio's *Fiammetta*, when the almost insanely jealous Fiammetta listens to the playing of music and thinks of her lover Panfilo: "The pleasant sounds caused every unconscious *spiritello d'amore* to revive within me and brought my mind back to the happy times:"—the times, that is, of her adulterous raptures.[34] However, the characterization by Dante of *spiritelli d'amore* as random *pensieri* arising from the pursuit of one's studies, of which one is by definition enamored, finds an especially appropriate and charming application in the field of manuscript illumination in the later fifteenth century, when the new forms of humanist decoration begin to gain ascendancy over the older twisting vine-leaf (*bianchi girari*) decorative systems. Not surprisingly, the putto begins to play a more pronounced role in such ornaments (as we have seen from Taddeo Crivelli's being asked to paint *spiritelli* in the choir books for San Petronio in Bologna; and see Fig. 13), assuming something of the function of the grotesque figures and fabulous animals of late-medieval manuscript production. They appear especially often in the decorative function of putti *reggistemma*, providing heraldic support for the devices and coats-of-arms identifying the owners of manuscripts, but they can also assume other roles. Often they merely clamber about in the vegetal decorations framing the margins of the title pages of such manuscripts. Or sometimes, as in Attavante's frontispiece to Plotinus's *Enneads*, dedicated to Lorenzo the Magnificent (Fig. 64), we find them seated among the flowers beneath the owner's device, tapping on little drums or rattling a tambourine, enacting the thousand little distracting fancies that invade the reader's thoughts as his attention wanders from his studies and he daydreams over the pages.[35] They may, as in the same manuscript, perch themselves on fanciful portraits of the ancient philosophers, diverting the mind to idle speculations about the appearances of Plotinus and Plato, or they may, as in the title page illuminated by an anonymous Neapolitan to Agathius's *De bello gothorum*, hold up ancient coins that turn the thoughts *all'improvviso* to the true images and inscriptions of the Caesars (Fig. 65).[36] Occasionally they may even embody spontanteous flashes of real philological insight, as we find in an image of battling *spiritelli* painted by the Paduan scribe and illuminator Bartolomeo Sanvito on the title page to Suetonius's *Lives of the Caesars* (Fig. 66, Plate 5).[37]

When Dante wrote of a *spiritello d'amore* arising from the "battaglia de'pensieri" raging within him, he was invoking a topos for describing the

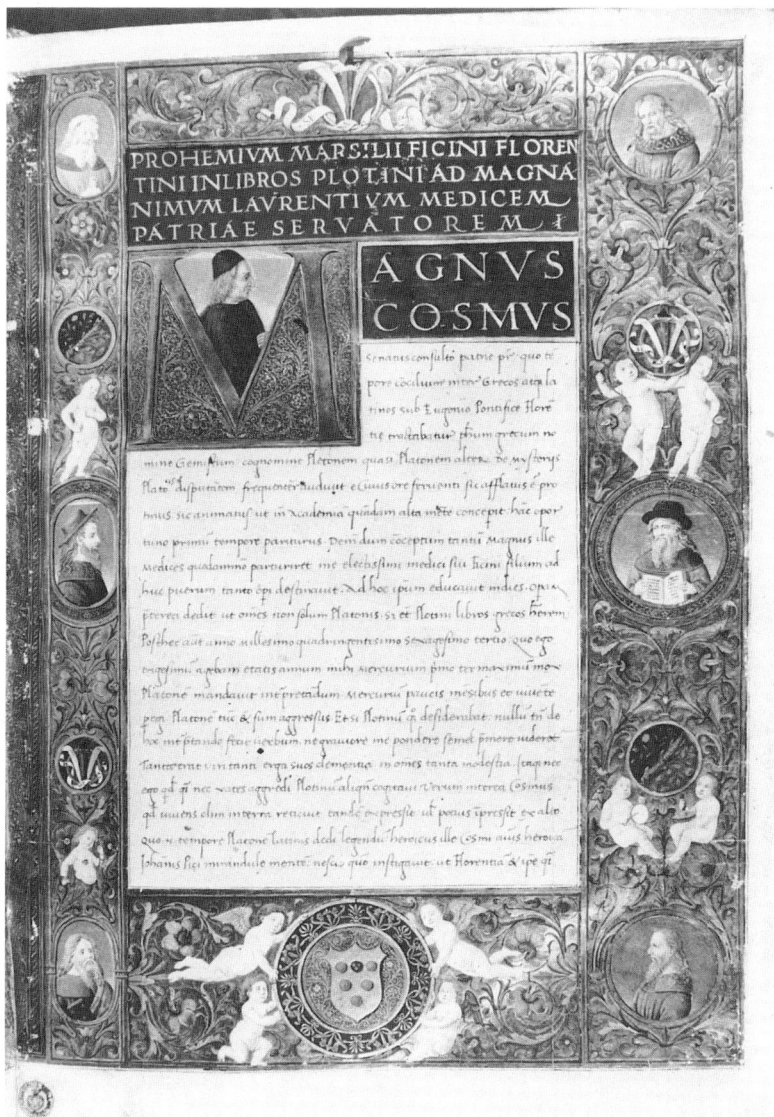

FIGURE 64
Frontispiece to Plotinus, *Enneads*, translated by Marsilio Ficino, Florence, Biblioteca Medicea Laurenziana (ms. Laur. Plut. 82.10). (Photograph: Ministero per i beni e le attività culturali)

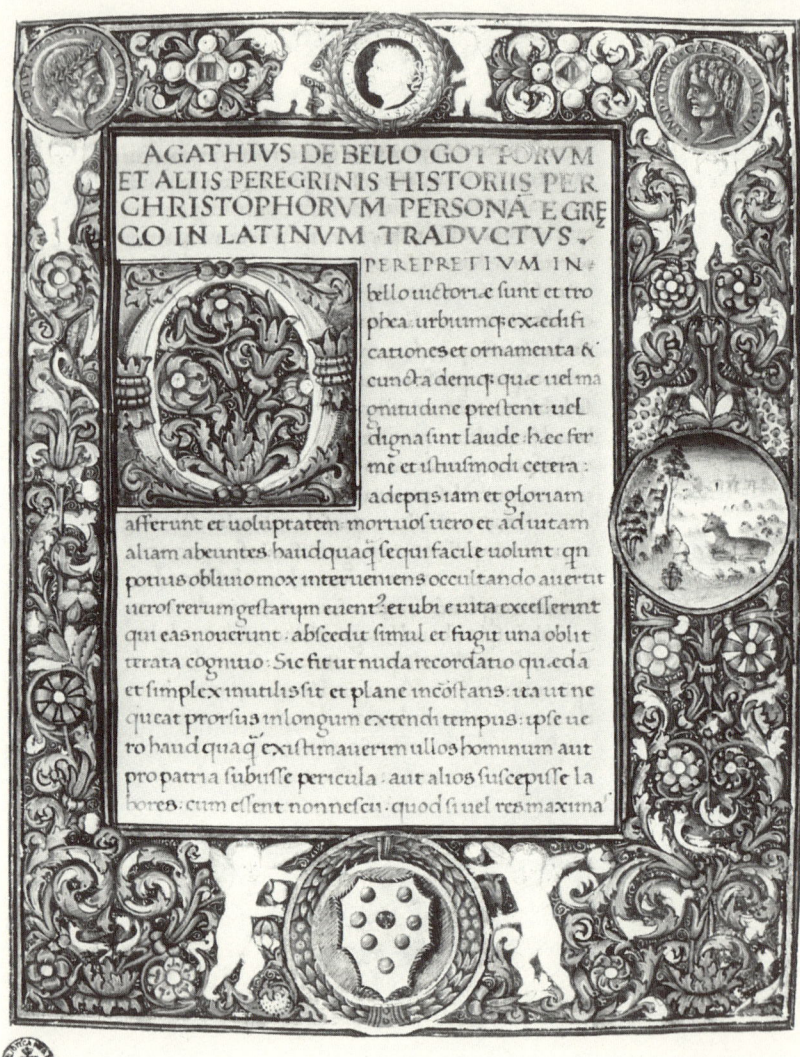

FIGURE 65
Frontispiece to Agathius, *De bello gothorum*, Florence, Biblioteca Medicea Laurenziana (ms. Laur. Plut. 68.23). (Photograph: Ministero per i beni e le attività culturali)

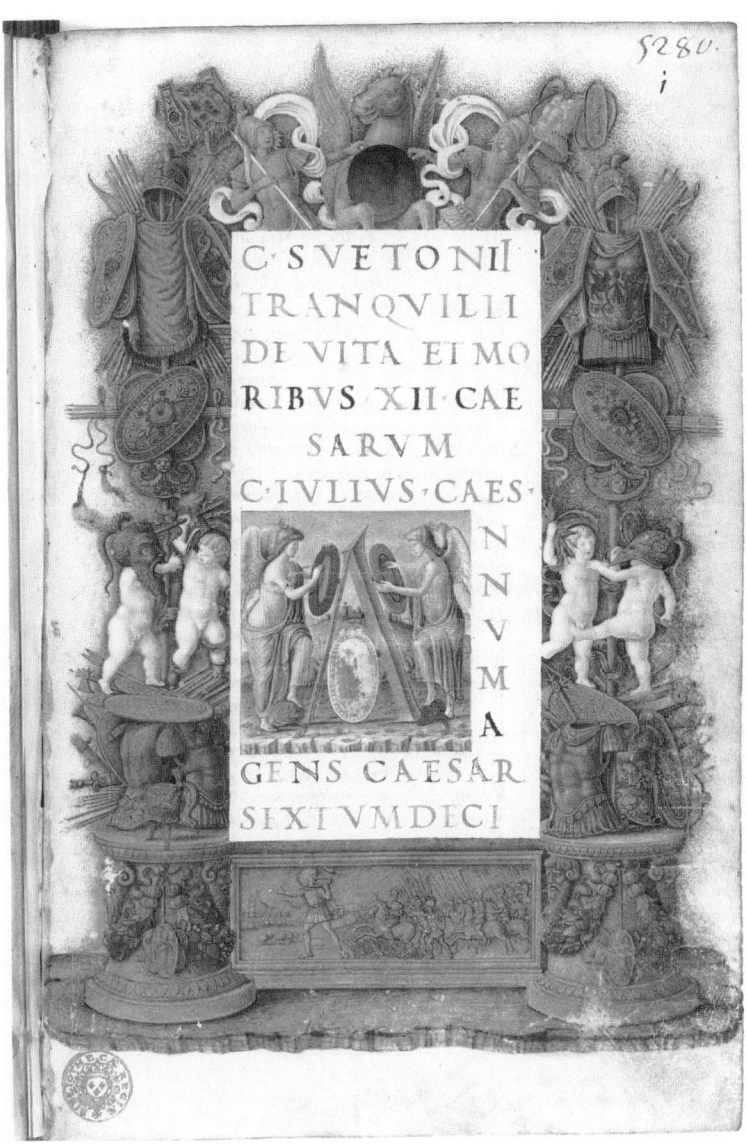

FIGURE 66
Bartolomeo Sanvito, frontispiece to Suetonius, *Lives of the Caesars*, Paris, Bibliothèque Nationale (ms. lat. 5814, fol. 1). Detail, *Larvate Erotes Battling*.
(Photograph: Cliché Bibliothèque Nationale de France, Paris)

lover's condition. And in Sanvito's title page to the *Lives of the Caesars* we see on the right-hand side of the page two such battling *pensieri d'amore* in childish mock-combat. One *spiritello* shakes Jupiter's thunderbolt at the other, who hides his head inside Mars's helmet with its horsehair plume. On the left-hand side of the page appears a pendant pair of battling *spiritelli*, one wearing a Silenus-mask for a helmet and putting his childish foe to panicky flight by thrusting his hand through the mouth of the mask and wiggling his fingers. We have seen how Dante was distracted from loving thoughts of the beatitude that is Beatrice by a new *spiritello d'amore* flashing from the eyes of the lady Philosophy. Sanvito's putti are not so serious. They are rather the childish follies, or empty daydreams, that fill the scholar's mind as he prepares to read of the great exploits and amorous scandals of the Caesars, diverting him from serious study and crowding his brain with distracting fancies, erotic musings perhaps; or perhaps causing there to flash into his mind (as Boethius's maxim had spontaneously flashed into Dante's) Lucian's criticism of historians who write lengthy and rhetorically brilliant introductions, "so that you expect what follows to be marvelous to hear," only to follow with a work "so tiny and so undistinguished that it resembles a child, like an *eros* you may have seen playing and putting on a huge mask of Hercules or a Titan."[38]

However, in writing of a "battaglia de'pensieri" Dante not only refers to a battle between different images presented to the imagination by the spirits of diverse loves, fantasies that then may be accepted or driven out as the heart or mind desires, but also bases himself on the same physiological concepts of *pneuma*, described in the last chapter, that structured his description of his own bodily turmoil when he first beheld Beatrice. For him, as for Cavalcanti, the workings of the imagination derive, in part from the notion of *pneuma* as the vehicle of the soul, and in part from medical theories of the influxes of spirit into the body. The mechanism of the imagination, or *fantasia*, as described both in late-medieval medical treatises and in natural philosophy (and Dante was especially influenced by Albertus Magnus), is driven by what Synesius in *De insomniis* called the *phantastikòn pneuma*, or *spiritus phantasticus*, a rarefied spirit situated at the most extreme point of the *anima sensitiva*.[39] The *spirito fantastico* receives through the mediation of sight the images of objects, as well as forms and apparitions seen in dreams, and its workings help to explain many otherwise inexplicable phenomena, among them images of the dead in dreams, or the appearance of demons (of which *spiritelli d'amore* are a minor genre). The same theory of the imagination also explains the genesis of love, and indeed, as Giorgio Agamben is the most recent to point out, it is not possible to understand the conventions of love set forth in the poetry of the Troubadours and the poets of the Dolce stil novo without taking into account the concept of love as essentially an imaginative process.[40] The object of love is not an exterior being so much as it is an internal image, a phantasm impressed (like the image of the poet's lady etched or imprinted on his heart) by the action of some *spirito fantastico*, which is but another name for a *spiritello d'amore*. Love itself is an imaginative faculty, and indeed the highest one. The various images transmitted into the lover's imagination by contending desires, personified in Sanvito's *facetia* of battling *spiritelli d'amore*, may in themselves be true or false, noble or trivial, divine revelations or demon-inspired, leading to bliss or to destruction depending upon which is chosen. But once a true imagining of love has been chosen, all others are driven out; or rather, as Cavalcanti writes in a famous sonnet that Agamben has called "a true and proper translation into pneumatic terminology of the phantasmatic psychology of love," these rudely contending *spiritelli* are ennobled. Like Dante's description of first seeing Beatrice, discussed in the last chapter, the sonnet begins with the *spirito visivo* striking through the eyes and stirring an animal spirit in the brain, impressing it with the image of the lady; and from this there arises a true spirit of love (*spirito d'amare*) which makes every other *spiritello* noble:

> Pegli occhi fere un spirito sottile,
> Che fa 'n la mente spirito destare,
> Dal qual si move spirito d'amare,
> Ch'ogn'altro spiritello fa gentile.[41]

(A subtle spirit strikes through the eyes and awakens a spirit in the mind, from which a spirit of love is moved that makes every other *spiritello* noble.)

Sanvito's depiction of the battle between as yet ignoble *spiritelli d'amore* in his frontispiece to Suetonius is especially interesting, however, because it also embodies a true humanist *facetia*, and hence provides a striking example of the interaction between classical learning and vernacular traditions. The motif in particular of the untamed *spiritello d'amore* hiding his own infantile and quite harmless nature behind a frightening, but in its very nature merely empty, imagining of a Silenus-mask recurs in a second frontispiece by Sanvito, to Eusebius's *Ecclesiastical History* (Fig. 67). Here we see three infants, the central one wearing the Silenus-mask and playing the bogey man, from whom the other two flee in terror, one stumbling in his headlong flight and falling to his knees. The caprice is highly Alexandrian in spirit, in the manner of the Greek epigrams in the Palatine Anthology so much beloved by the humanists, and is partly derived from an invention by Mantegna preserved in a drawing in the Louvre (Fig. 68).[42] The drawing, which is a fine contemporary copy, shows two masked putti, the central one poking his hand through the mouth of a Silenus-mask, together with two fleeing infants, one of whom has fallen to his knees and reaches back as if to scratch the frightening face that menaces him. Mantegna's invention is described in the eleventh book, written at some time after 1491, of Iacopo Sannazaro's *Arcadia*. There the poet writes of the prizes offered at some funeral games, one of which was a maplewood bowl painted with various scenes by none other than Mantegna:

> Ergasto at once ordained the prizes for whomever wished to take part in the wrestling, offering to give the victor a beautiful maplewood vase painted with many things by the hand of the Paduan Mantegna, an artificer more cunning and ingenious than all the others. . . . Not far from [a female Satyr nursing her child] can be seen two infants, also nude, who, having donned two horrible faces to mask themselves, were thrusting their little hands through the mouths of the masks in order to frighten two others who were in front of them; one of these turns back in his flight and was shouting out with fear, while the other, having already fallen to the ground,

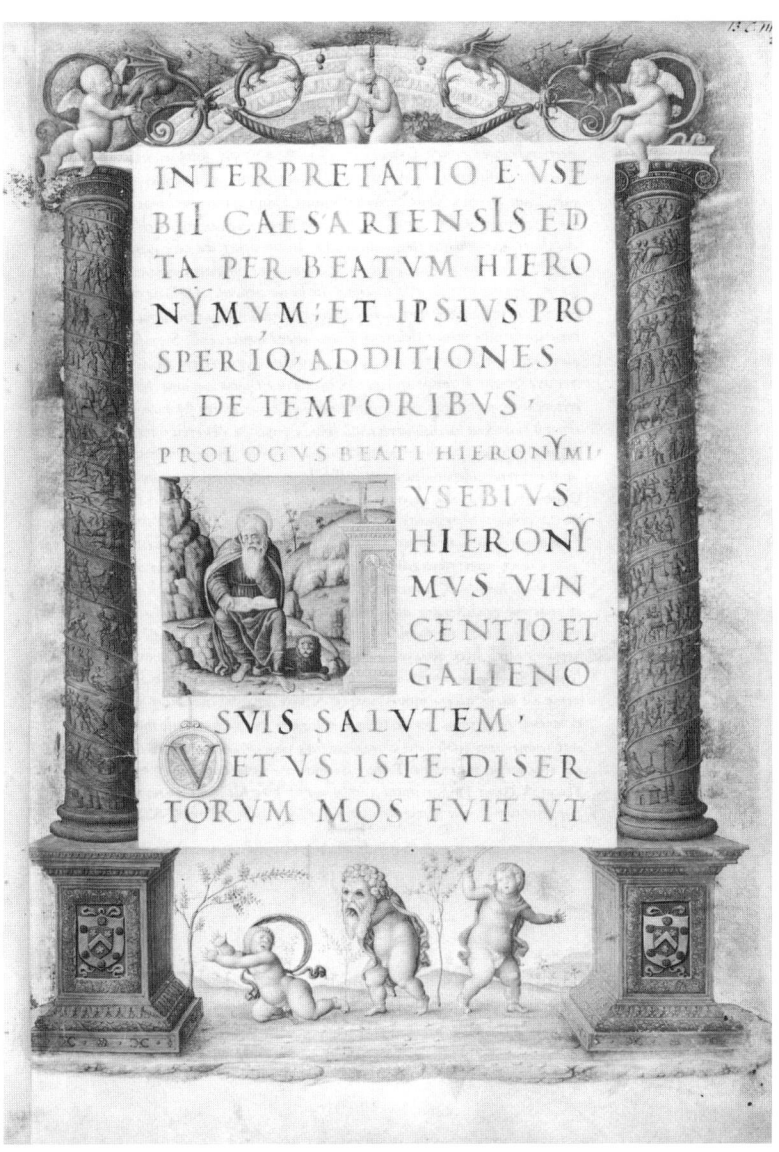

FIGURE 67
Bartolomeo Sanvito, frontispiece to Eusebius, *Ecclesiastical History*, London, British Library (ms. Royal 14C.III, fol. 2). Detail, *Larvate Eros Frightening Two Companions*. (Photograph: The British Library)

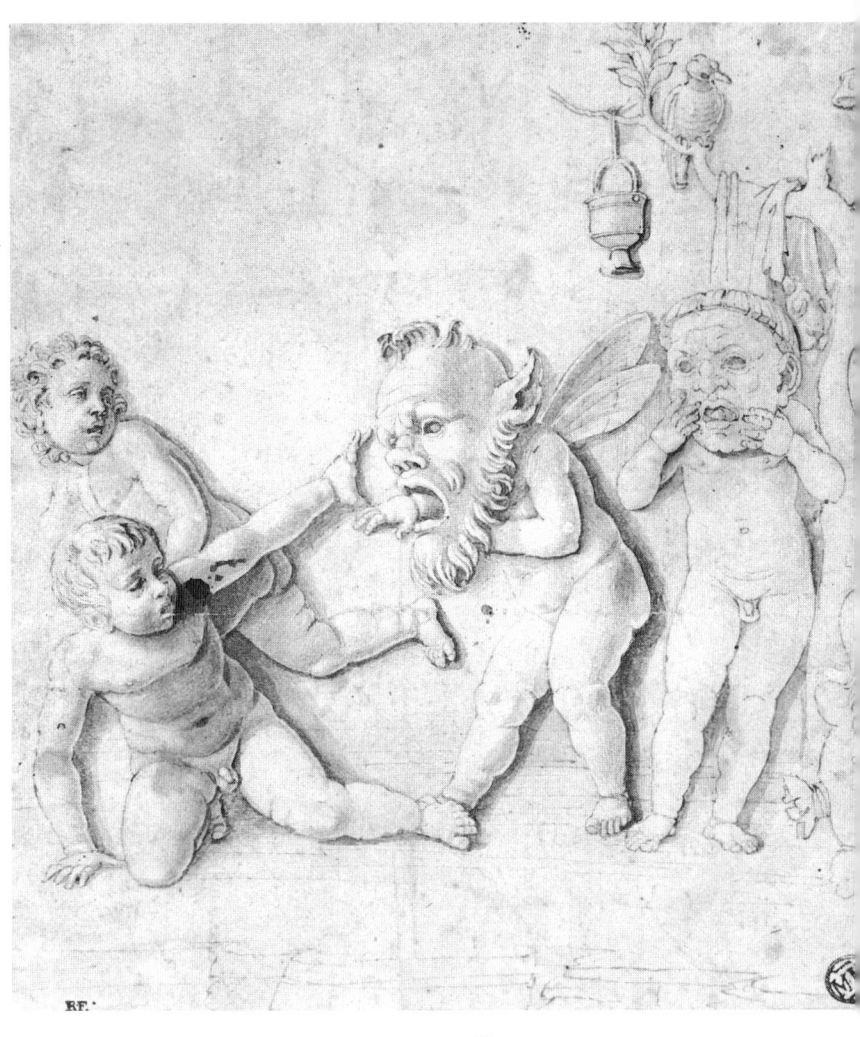

FIGURE 68
Copy after Andrea Mantegna, *Larvate Erotes Frightening Two Companions*, drawing, Paris, Louvre, Cabinet des Dessins. (Photograph © Réunion des Musées Nationaux)

was weeping and, being unable to help himself in any other way, was extending his hand to give the thing a scratch."[43]

The visual origin of this humanist *facetia* of masked infants playing the bogeyman, inflicting their companions with childish frights, is antique, and can be traced in Roman relief sculpture on sarcophagi (see Fig. 55), as well as on gems, where it is fairly common.[44] Despite the Paduan origins of Mantegna and Sanvito, however, its revival is Roman. The first known appearance of the motif occurs on the terracotta matrix for a bronze plaquette that was found in 1876 together with a medal of the Venetian pope Paul II, dated 1465, in an earthen *salvadenai* placed in the foundation walls of the Palazzo Venezia in Rome (Fig. 69), though not before many bronze casts of it had been made (Fig. 70).[45] Undoubtedly the plaquette, which certainly dates before the death of Paul II in 1471 and shows winged *erotes* at play, one frightening another by covering his face with the Silenus-mask, derives from a Roman sarcophagus or an antique gem in the pope's collection. The size and importance of Paul II's collection of ancient gems surpassed even Lorenzo de'Medici's (who acquired a number of gems from the pope's collection after his death), and for this reason Paul II has been recognized as the primary impetus behind the creation of the very earliest Renaissance plaquettes—of which the Palazzo Venezia matrix is a precious example.

Bronze plaquettes were one of the most fertile of all media for transmitting ancient imagery and themes to artists and decorators throughout Italy, and indeed the whole of Europe, and it has long been recognized that much of their imagery derives from that of ancient gems, of which many early plaquettes were conceived as reproductions.[46] Indeed, as Eckhard Leuschner has recently documented, the theme of the masked putto enjoyed a long and remarkable afterlife.[47] We have already taken note of the tender sprites portrayed in Poussin's and Duquesnoy's so-called *Infant Bacchanales* (see Figs. 52, 53, and 54), both elegant interpretations of the theme founded in Virgil's *Georgics*, whereby the infants mask themselves as harmless scarecrows childishly trying to frighten away the sharp-hoofed goat. We also saw the same Virgilian theme treated a century earlier by the

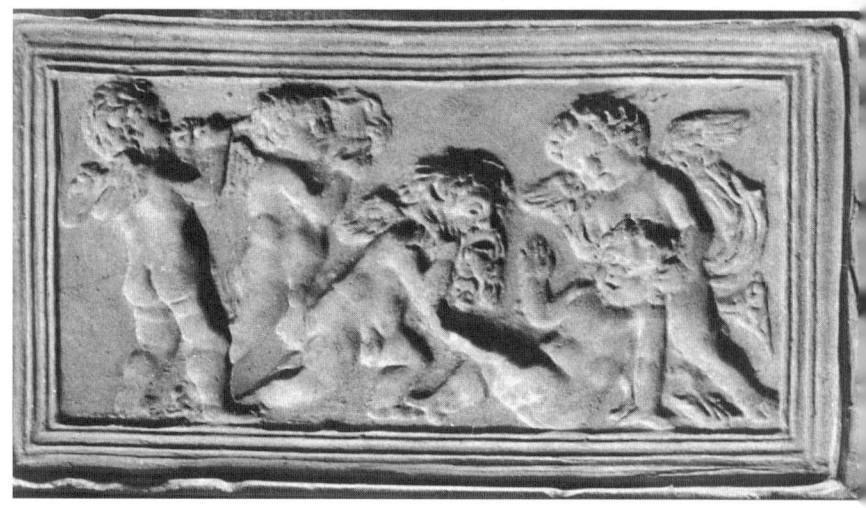

FIGURE 69
Larvate Erotes Frightening a Companion, terracotta matrix for a plaquette, Rome, Museo del Palazzo Venezia. (Photograph: Soprintendenza per i Beni Artistici e Storici di Roma)

Master of the Die (see Fig. 51), who again returned to the subject of the goat tamed by *spiritelli* in a second engraving (Fig. 71). This shows a goat ridden in a mock military triumph by the infants, one of whom turns the *oscillum*, or mask, against his childish playmates in order to frighten them. The sprite is in fact doubly masked, not only by the mask (or *larva*) itself, but also by the lion-skin he wears, and hence the foolish child masquerades as the formidable hero Hercules. This differs in no way from Sanvito's sprites masquerading as Jupiter, Silenus, and as Mars hiding beneath the war god's helmet. The dangers they threaten are not real—they are infantile and without substance. This last image was adapted by Botticelli for his *Mars and Venus* in the National Gallery in London (Plate 1), the subject of the next chapter, in which an infant *paniscus* masks himself with Mars's helmet. As we shall see, Botticelli's adaptation of the *larva* of Mars's essentially empty helmet evokes Valerius Flaccus's description of the empty

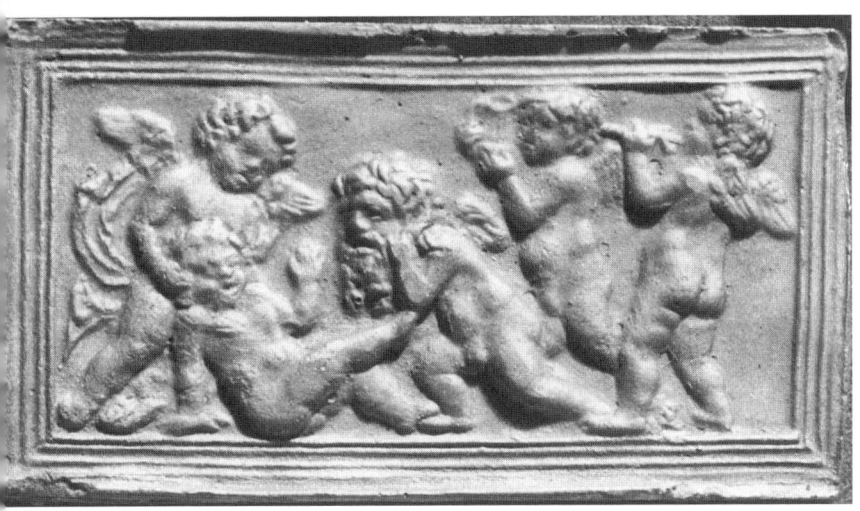

FIGURE 70
Larvate Erotes Frightening a Companion, bronze plaquette, Washington, National Gallery of Art, Widener Collection (Inv. 1942.9.190, A-1512). (Photograph: National Gallery of Art)

panics that can seize whole armies at the sight of Mars's uninhabited helmet alone (*talesque metus non Martia cassis . . . sparserit*: "not the helmet of Mars spreads such terror"). And it also recalls, in a more lighthearted vein, Politian's recounting of the following joke in his *Detti piacevoli*, compiled between the summers of 1477 and 1478. Politian's *facetia*, which in its turn sounds very much like one from a lost comedy by Lucius Afranius recorded by the third-century grammarian Nonius Marcellus (*pertimuistis cassam terriculam adversari*: "you are terrified by the bugbear helmet of your foe"), was made by Braccio Martelli at the expense of Renato de'Pazzi, a youth given over more to *otio humanitatis* than to *furor bellicus*:

> Braccio Martelli, volendo mostrare che Rinato de'Pazzi era pauroso, non avendo egli voluto giostrare ad una giostra ordinata, disse che lo faceva perchè egli avea paura nell'elmo solo.

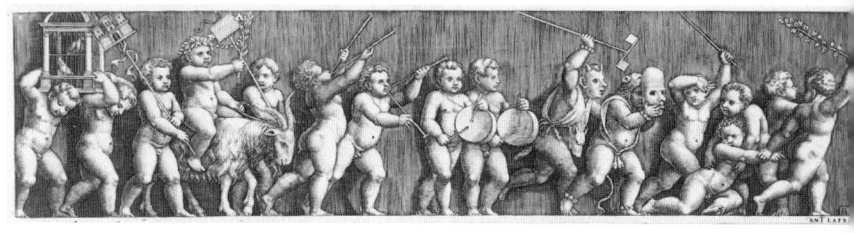

FIGURE 71
Master of the Die, *Procession of Putti with Goat and Masked Infant*, New York, The Metropolitan Museum of Art, engraving, (Bartsch 15.209.36.), The Elisha Whittelsey Collection, The Elisha Whittelsey Fund, 1949 (49.97.335). (Photograph: The Metropolitan Museum of Art)

(Braccio Martelli, wanting to show that Renato de'Pazzi was frightened, since he had not wished to take part in a joust that had been proclaimed, said he did so because he was scared of the helmet all by itself.)[48]

The humanist *facetia* of *eros*, the true classical antecedent to the *spiritello d'amore*, provoking childish frissons by hiding in the helmet of Mars or playing the bogeyman with the Satyr-mask in order to inflict his companions with infantile frights, allows a precious insight into an initial moment in the refining of a vernacular concept through reference to the antique, and in a way that transforms both. For the new image is neither precisely identical in meaning to its Italian antecedent in the *spiritello*, nor to the ancient *eros*, but rather combines both. The origin of *eros* playing the bogeyman, in other words, is uniquely a product of Renaissance humanist and artistic culture.

The panics this harmlessly masked *spiritello d'amore* represents and acts out were defined by Erasmus in the *Adagia* (following Politian's explanation of the meaning of "panic terrors" in the *Miscellanea*), in which he wrote that *panikós* in Greek refers to "empty frights that arise without true cause."[49] And in his comment to the adage *Metum inanem metuisti* ("you fear only empty fear"), he added that the Greeks called such empty panic "a *mormolykeion* or mask, similar to a *larva* or wicked genius used to terrify children" (*nam mormolykeion Graecis persona est, larvae aut malo genio similis, qua pueros territant quidam*)."⁵⁰ In the same passage Erasmus translates Basilius Athenaeus's use of the Greek *mormolykeia* as *terriculamenta*, empty notions, or bugbears (*sane vehementer essem puer, si talibus terriculamentis expaverescem*).⁵¹ Politian translated the same word as *terriculis*, and cited Apuleius's *De deo Socratis* for authority in identifying such *larvae* as a species of minor demon, a bugbear or spook, that induces "empty preoccupations in good men, but can be harmful to bad" (*inane terriculamentum bonis hominibus, ceterum malis noxium*).⁵² In English the concept survives in such usages as "Aunt Sally's taken a notion," she's "come down with the vapors," and "something's bugging her." It refers to idle notions (*pensieri*) that induce empty and obsessive panics. Virtuous and sensible people can put such worries aside, but if adhered to, real damage can result. Like *mormolykeion* in Greek, the word *larva* in Latin and in the Italian vernacular means "mask" as well as "ghost," "bugbear," or "phantasm" (and hence the English "larvate," meaning "masked," and "larval," meaning "panicked," as in a "larval fright"). Accordingly, Benedetto Varchi, in explicating Giovanni della Casa's sonnet on *Cura*—Care, which Edmund Spenser calls the mother of turbulent dreams—wrote of the poet's description of Jealousy afflicting him with *nuove larve* that such "*larve* are faces and forms, which here signify new and various suspicions that constantly generate further unrest . . . for, as you know, the word *larvae* in Latin means, aside from what we call masks, souls condemned by their iniquities, or what we commonly call *ombre* [spirits, or ghosts], although here it means various fantastic images and apparitions."⁵³ Varchi's reference to *larve* as the souls of the iniquitous again follows Apuleius's *De deo Socratis*, and was already well established in the vernacular imagination and tongue. It finds remarkably precocious visual application in Nicola Pisano's representation of a masked putto, or *larva*, as one of the demons tormenting the damned in his sculpture of the *Last Judgment* for the baptismal font in Pisa, dating to around 1260 (Fig. 72).⁵⁴

However, such small sprites, as Apuleius affirms, are only capable of harming the wicked, but are powerless against the good, who are well armed by philosophy and religion. Plato in the *Phaedrus* calls the fear of

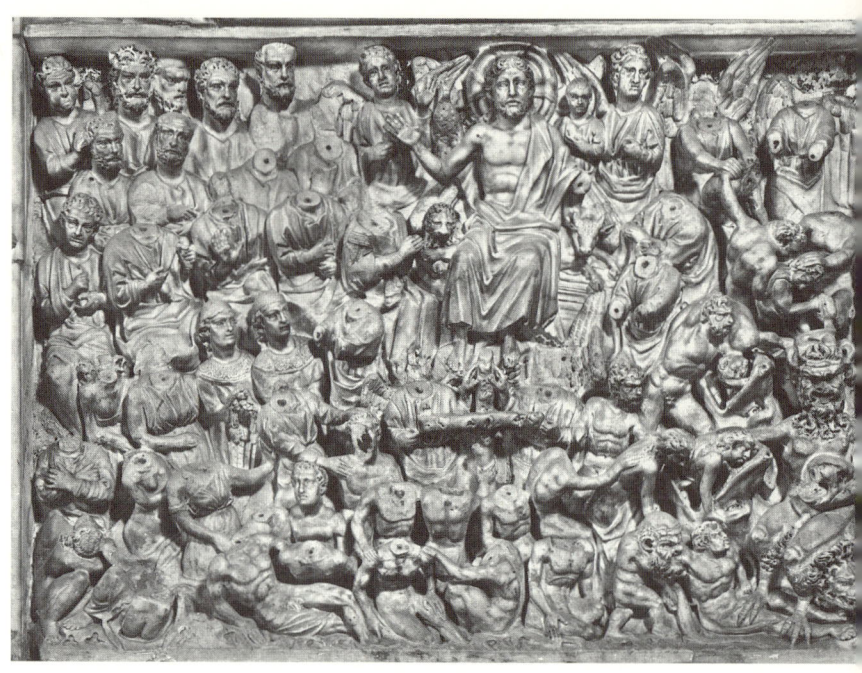

FIGURE 72
Nicola Pisano and assistants, *Last Judgment*, Pisa, Baptistery.
(Photograph: Alinari/Art Resource)

Death only a *mormolykeion*, an empty *terriculum* or scarecrow.[55] Accordingly, the sculptor Andrea Riccio in his series of bronze reliefs for the Della Torre tomb in Verona (now in the Louvre), represented in the panel showing the funeral of the famous physician the motif of the larvate *spiritello* terrifying his infant companion, in order to indicate that the fear of death is only a bugbear (Fig. 73).[56] Similarly, Aristophanes in the *Achanians* calls the brightly burnished armor of Lamachus an empty bogey, a *Mormon*.[57] Like Mars's terrifying helmet inhabited only by harmless *spiritelli* painted in Sanvito's frontispiece to Suetonius (see Fig. 66), and like the toy thunderbolts rattled by his playmate, Lamachus's armor alone is empty stage display, an infant's scarecrow capable only of frightening other children.

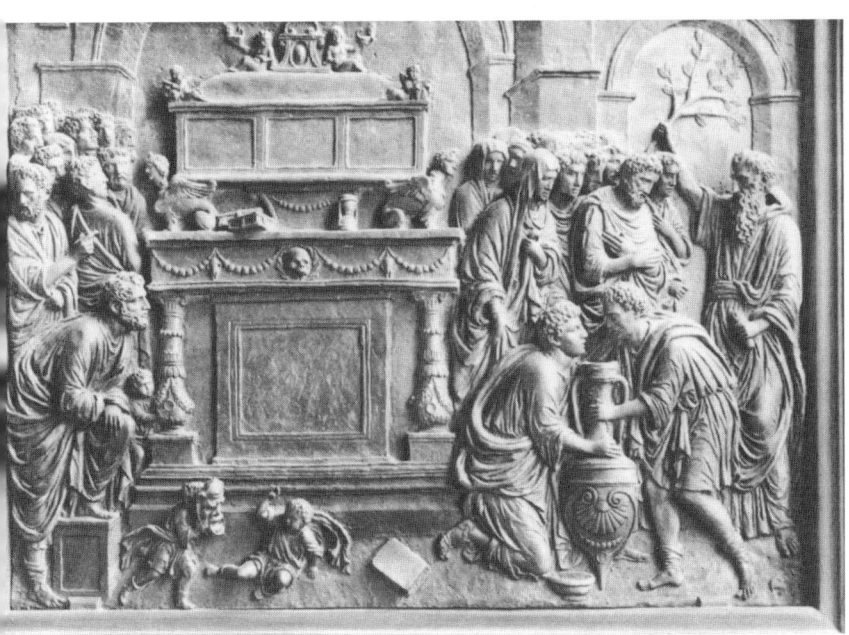

FIGURE 73
Andrea Riccio, *The Funeral of Gerolamo della Torre*, bronze relief, Paris, Louvre.
(Photograph by James T. Van Rensselaer)

In the broadest sense, as Dante indicated in his discussion of the *spiritello d'amore*, the masked, or larvate *eros* denotes all those conflicting and deceptive panics and desires to which the human heart is always prey, whether appearing as an infantile obsession (as in Ralph Waldo Emerson's "A foolish consistency is the hobgoblin of little minds"), an obsessive fear of death, or as Dante's taking a sudden notion to abandon Beatrice for Philosophy. Accordingly Politian, in the *Stanze per la Giostra di Giuliano de'Medici* (to which we shall return in Chapter 4), described a swarm of *ardenti spiritelli* coursing through the arteries of sleeping Florentine youths, inflaming them to enter the joust, followed by a second swarm of false dreams hidden behind their masks, *sogni drento alle lor larve*, sent by Venus to confuse the young Julio in sleep.[58] And in 1555 the poet Ronsard described, in a form by then canonical, how such tiny demons conceal their true forms behind false masks, "que soudain nostre jouë en craingant devient blesme:"

> En ce poinct les DAIMONS masquez de vaines feintes
> Donnent aux coeurs humains de merveilleuses craintes:
> Toute forme & couleur, ce pendant qu'il est jour,
> Puis les rebaille à ceux qui de nature peuvent
> En eux les reçevoir, & qui propres se treuvent:
> Tout ainsi les Daimons font leur masqueres voir
> A nostre fantasie, apte à les reçevoir:
> Puis nostre fantasie à l'Esprit les rapporte
> De la mesme façon & de la mesme sorte
> Qu'elle les imagine, ou dormant, ou veillent:
> Et lors une grand' peur va noz coeurs assaillant,
> Le poil nous dresse au chef, & du front goutte-à-goutte
> Jusqes à noz talons la sueur nous degoutte.[59]

(At this point the demons, masked by empty fictions, bring marvelous frights to human hearts: for even as the Air slowly takes and receives every form and color during the daytime, and then gives them back to those persons who by their nature are able to receive them within themselves and who find them their own, so all the Demons in this way make their masquerades appear to our fantasy, so apt to receive them: then our fantasy carries them to the soul in the same appearance and the same manner that it imagines them whether in sleeping or in waking: and then a great fear assails our hearts, the hair rises on our head, and sweat, falling drop by drop from our forehead, bathes us all the way down to our heels.)

In the next chapter we shall see how the humanist *concetto* of infantile frights becomes adapted to the expression of Botticelli's *Mars and Venus*, now in the National Gallery in London.

CHAPTER THREE

Spirits of the Nightmare

Botticelli's *Mars and Venus* as a Problem
in Grammatical Interpretation

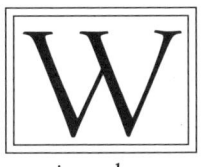HEN Paul Oskar Kristeller wrote in 1955 that "The most characteristic and pervasive aspect of the Italian Renaissance in the field of learning is the humanist movement," he was giving voice to what was in its time a universal consensus.[1] Less consensus existed, however, regarding the extent and nature of humanism and humanist activities themselves. It is partly in consequence of this ongoing disagreement that the values of humanism have continued to be open to misunderstanding and misrepresentation, and that accordingly the very concept of the Renaissance has been eroded by a renewed skepticism arising especially from within the ranks of the social historians, many of whom have abandoned the term "Renaissance" altogether, preferring to speak of "Early Modern" Italian and European history. Paradoxically, this tendency has been encouraged by Kristeller's legitimate concern to set the phenomenon of humanism within its proper professional boundaries, treating the humanists as representatives of a particular class of society. As a tendency, it may fruitfully be compared to the view consistently set forth throughout the writings of Eugenio Garin, which argue the interconnectedness of humanist thought, reaching through to all spheres of cultural activity and making its effects felt at many levels of society. Of special importance to the new culture of humanism, Garin has written, was "the convergence of art—and what art!—and science, of theories and techniques, and behind it all the return of the ancients—the reading of the venerated books and the reading of things: *esperienze e ragionamenti*, as Machiavelli would say in his incompara-

ble way. The divorce between letters, sciences and arts is pure fantasizing by the ill-equipped and sanctimonious historians of today."[2]

By "humanism" Kristeller was of course not referring to the various popular and philosophical doctrines that have been given this name since the time of the Renaissance itself, whether or not appearing as an insistence on the humanity of Christ, as a form of Jamesian pragmatism, as the existentialism of Sartre, or simply as a more or less fully defined notion of the primacy of "human" values. Central to his purpose was to strip the historical phenomenon of Italian Renaissance humanism of such later notional accretions, all of them by and large foreign to it. His concern was further to distinguish humanism as clearly as possible from other aspects of Renaissance culture that are equally characteristic of the period, such as contemporary developments in natural philosophy, vernacular literature, and the arts, all of which may have been affected by the work of the humanists but which are not necessarily to be identified with humanism itself. In so doing he pointed to the fact that the professional foundation for humanist activity lay in the schools and universities in the area of study known as the *studia humanitatis*, the subjects of which were grammar, rhetoric, poetry, history, and moral philosophy; and to the fact that the vast majority of humanists were professionally employed either as secretaries of princes and city governments or as teachers of grammar and rhetoric at the secondary schools and universities.

The reading of the Latin and Greek authors lay at the heart of humanist activity, and it was the genius of the humanists as scholars that they extended the concept and practice of such reading and interpretation into something much more closely resembling modern philology than the practice of the medieval grammarians. From their foundation in the new philology, in the study and criticism of ancient texts, the humanists extended their activities and influence into other spheres of cultural and intellectual activity, such as medicine, mathematics, theology, vernacular literature and the arts. The texts they chose for study were not limited to the curriculum of the *studia humanitatis*, but comprised all the written remains of antiquity. It is this fact that endows humanism with its special cultural significance and that is also the source of disagreement about its nature and influence. If Kristeller's salutary attempt to locate the professional foundations of humanism historically were to be taken too literally, then humanism might be understood (and is in danger of being understood) as merely one academic discipline among many, and not as a cultural phenomenon of the greatest importance. That humanism became such a phenomenon is founded in the claim by the humanists that it was their business to expound upon and to interpret any kind of writing whatsoever, whether in their own areas of poetry, rhetoric, and history, or in the fields of philosophy, theology, medicine, or the law. So far as the arts are concerned, one of the most characteristic works of humanism is Alberti's *De architectura*, written around 1450 and first published in 1486 with a dedication to Lorenzo de'Medici and an introduction by Politian, in which the architectural terms and vocabulary of the ancients as transmitted in corrupt form by Vitruvius are rigorously tested against the standards of a purer Latinity with the intention of elevating both criticism and the practice of architecture.[3]

A remarkable statement of the humanist position exists from the pen of Politian himself, and appears in his well known essay entitled *Lamia—The Witch, or Vampire*—which was written to be read as the introductory lecture to his course on the *Prior Analytics* of Aristotle at the Studio Fiorentino in 1492–93.[4] The *lamiae* to which Politian's title refers are popular bugbears, those purveyors of fantasy and delusion who accuse him, a teacher of grammar, of pretending to be a philosopher by presuming to lecture on Aristotle:

Some of them, seeing me by chance in the street, and pretending not to know me, stop and inspect me up and down as though they were shoppers at a stall; and at length, turning aside and nodding among themselves, they whisper to one another—"Why it is Politian, Politian himself, that humbug who now all at once presents himself as a philosopher"—and having said this they fly off, like wasps who have left their sting [*quasi vespae dimisso aculeo*].[5]

Politian, however, denies, and he denies vigorously that he is a philosopher. He is a teacher of grammar, a scholiast, and it is precisely because of this that he may interpret Aristotle:

> I profess myself an interpreter of Aristotle—whether good or bad is not for me to say. But I certainly profess to be an interpreter, and I do not profess to be a philosopher. And if I were also the interpeter of a king, would you have me think myself a king because of it? Or do you think that Donatus and Servius among us, or Aristarchus and Zenodotus among the Greeks, because they interpret the poets therefore profess to be poets? And is not Philoponus, the disciple of Ammonius and co-disciple of Simplicius, an excellent interpreter of Aristotle? Yet none calls him a philosopher, while everyone calls him *grammaticus*—a grammarian. And what if not grammarians were Xenocritus of Cos, or the Alexandrians Antigonus and Didymus, or Aristarchus, the most famous of them all? Yet all of them, as Erotian says, interpreted the books of Hippocrates, and other works on medicine too, which are listed by Galen; but one does not call them physicians because of this. For it is the business of grammarians to investigate and comment upon writers of every kind, poets, historians, orators, philosophers, medical authorities, and legal experts. Our own age, so little conversant with the ways of antiquity, constrains the grammarian within too tight a circle, and yet among the ancients this class of men possessed such authority that only they were made the censors and judges of all kinds of writing. Because of this the grammarian was also called *criticus*. And Quintilian writes that grammarians not only obelized corrupt passages but also whole books that seemed apocryphal, expelling them like illegitimate children from the family; and indeed they even ordained which authors should be added to the canon and which struck from it. For the Greek word *grammaticus* is the same as *litteratus* in Latin. It is we who have confined this name to the drudges who teach the trivium in the infant schools. Nowadays *litterati* would have the same cause for complaint as did the flutist Antigenides, who could scarcely bear to

hear the players in funeral processions called flutists. *Litterati* may likewise be offended that the name *grammaticus* is now given to those who only teach the first elements. Such as these the Greeks did not call *grammatici*, but *grammatistae*; nor did the Romans call them *litterati*, but *litteratores*.[6]

Politian's concept of *grammaticus*, embracing and defined by the notions of scholiast, interpreter, *litteratus*, and critic, characterizes Politian as a humanist. It is virtually identical to A. E. Housman's concept of the literary critic, the subject of his inaugural lecture as professor of Latin at Cambridge in 1911, when he made his famous (and notorious) remark that, while the number of artists arising on the face of the earth was relatively plentiful, the appearance of a true critic was rather less common than returns of Halley's comet.[7] By a "literary critic" Housman meant a philologist in the same sense that Politian defined a humanist grammarian. Moreover, for Politian the power of philological reasoning entitled the humanist to an especially privileged position. Thus, in the *Panepistemon* he classified his own profession of letters neither under the active nor the contemplative intellects, but claimed it as a function of the rational (or deliberative) intellect. Literary production and criticism, in other words, were neither arts nor sciences, but instead a species of linguistic dialectic, and in consequence of this, linguistic analysis precedes the study and appropriation of particular texts and areas of study by the various experts and cultivators of different fields of knowledge. It was this that allowed the humanist to claim priority in treating, not only the particular subjects proper to the *studia humanitatis* itself, but also the entirety of human knowledge and culture.[8]

The problem of grammatical interpretation to which the title of this chapter refers is thus to be taken at face value, for it is essential that we keep the philological foundation to humanist thought clearly in mind when we come to examine its influence on the living expressions of poetry and its sister art of painting in the Renaissance. The particular interpretive problem I want to take up in this chapter is that of Botticelli's painting in London entitled *Mars and Venus* (Plate 1). The painting is not mentioned by Vasari, and we know nothing of its existence before it was purchased in Florence by Alexander Barker at some moment around 1868. Insofar as it presents us with an interpretation in visual form of a subject taken from ancient letters, it clearly bears the imprint of humanist learning upon its conception and invention. And insofar as Venus is shown wearing a contemporary Florentine *camicia da giorno* while infant Satyrs play with Mars's equally contemporary armor, which includes a jousting lance and a Renaissance sallet, or helmet, beneath which one of the *Satyrisci* masks his true nature, we again encounter the fusion of classical themes with vernacular experience in the conception and expression of Botticelli's painting.[9]

To begin with the infant *Satyrisci*, notably the one masked in Mars's sallet and his companion hiding himself inside the god's cuirass, we have seen in the last chapter that such masked infants denote *larve*, or sudden little panicky distractions that fill the mind with confused and empty notions, diverting it from serious business. Such idle diversions were enacted by the infant *spiritelli* shown in Bartolomeo Sanvito's frontispiece to Suetonius's *Lives of the Caesars* (see Fig. 66), one of them wielding toy thunderbolts, inducing in the reader's mind childish daydreams of Jovian majesty, while the other plays out an empty fantasy of military prowess by masquerading behind Mars's horsehair-plumed helmet. As we saw in the engraving by the Master of the Die (see Fig. 71), in which one sprite appears masked as Hercules, such larvate infants represent empty threats. They are only childish hobgoblins hiding their true natures behind fright masks, scarecrows used to frighten other children. The mask pretends to cover something tremendous and terrifying, but which is really nothing, as we see in the hilarious *spiritello* sculptured by Pierino da Vinci for a fountain (Fig. 74). The laughing sprite uses a grotesque Satyr-mask as a *cache-sexe*, through the mouth of which, in Vasari's words, "gettasse acqua dal membro virile," a tiny arc of water belying the implied potency of his hidden member.[10] Such an empty *larva*, or *mormolykeion* in Greek, is also shown on the Veroli casket, an ivory box of Byzantine manufacture from the early eleventh century made to hold ladies' toiletries (Fig. 75), on which we see an infant *eros* hidden behind a mask, attempting to shock

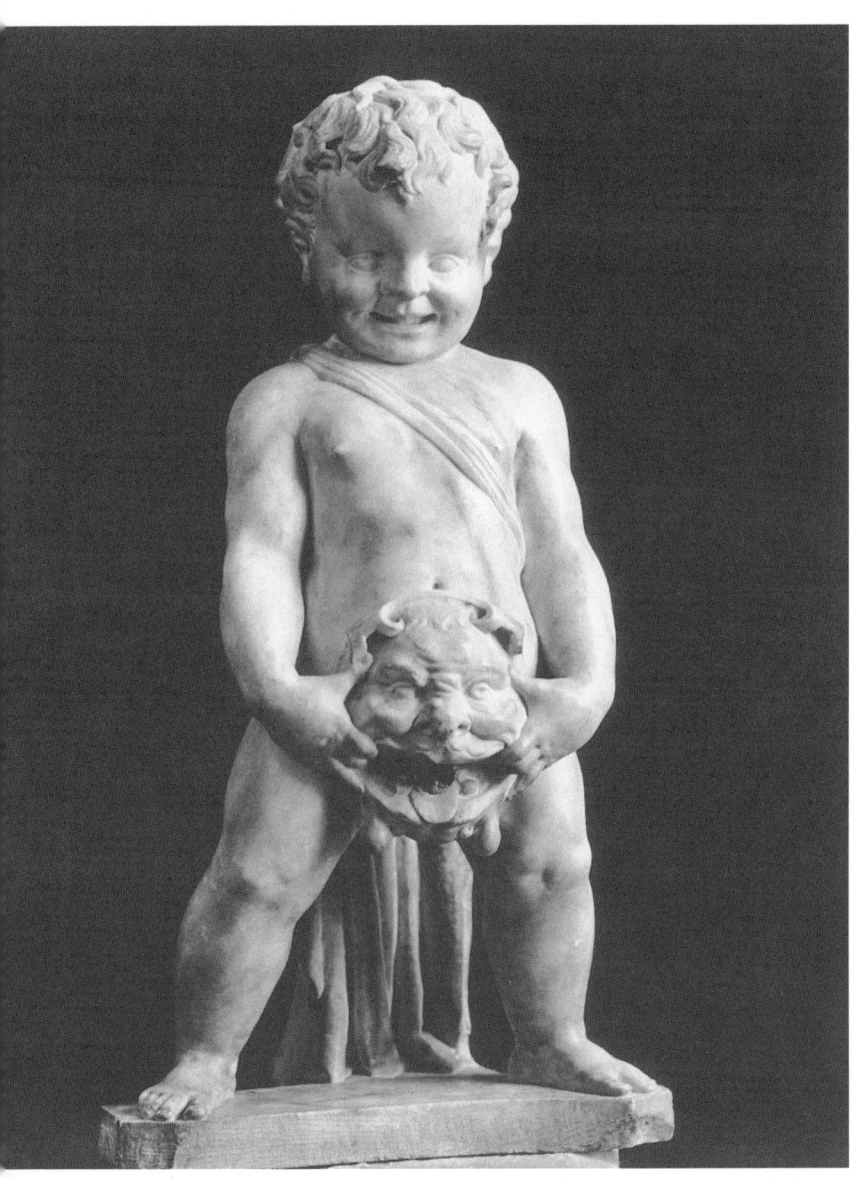

FIGURE 74
Pierino da Vinci, *Puer Mingens*, Arezzo, Museo Civico.
(Photograph: Alinari/Art Resource)

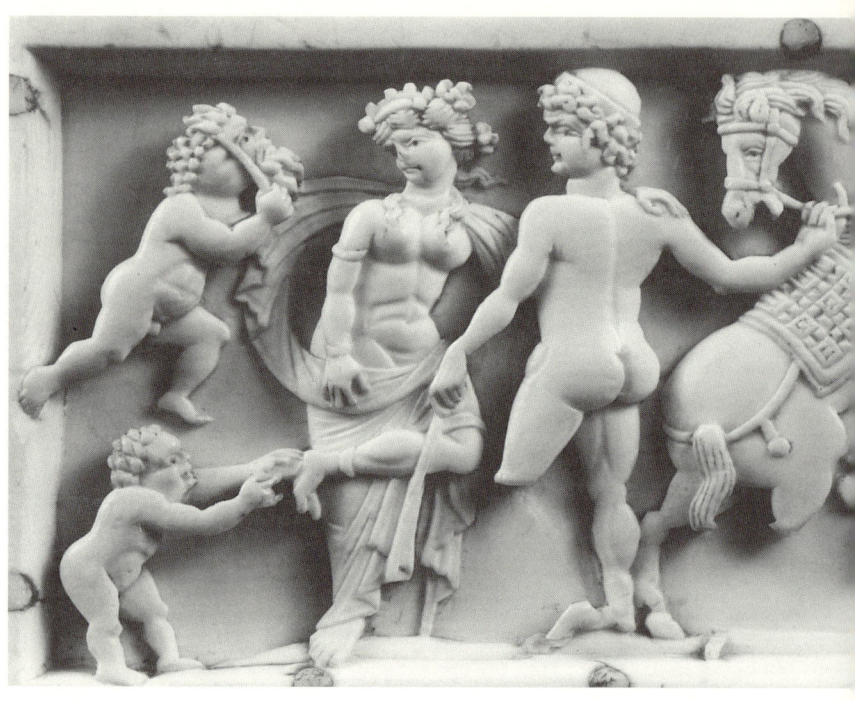

FIGURE 75
Veroli Casket, Byzantine ivory, London, Victoria and Albert Museum. Detail, *Mormolykeion Startling Two Lovers*. (Photograph: Victoria and Albert Museum/Art Resource)

Mars and Venus with a sudden (and harmless) erotic charge.[11] Similarly, Botticelli's infant *Satyrisci*, who as earth sprites are cousins to the airy *spiritello*, disguise their essentially harmless nature by masking themselves within Mars's empty armor, and pretending to threaten him with his own jousting weapons. Is it possible that Mars, like Renato de'Pazzi in Politian's joke, can be afraid of the empty helmet all by itself?

In the present state of scholarship only two things may be assumed as known regarding the subject of Botticelli's painting, and both point to the same conclusion: that the classical concept of empty panic terrors, or *mormolykeia*, which is best understood in relation to connotations inherent in the psychological notion of small, obsessive phobias, is indeed central to Botticelli's theme. What is known also points inescapably to the conclusion that the thought of Politian is fundamental to Botticelli's invention. My initial intent, therefore, is to append some scholia to what can fairly be accepted as known about the painting, and on this basis attempt an interpretation of Botticelli's imagery. To approach a painting in this way, from the point of view of the grammarian, may at first seem perverse to our own age, *parum perita rerum veterum*, which is more used to insisting upon the quite obvious differences between verbal and visual forms of expression. Yet on historical grounds I believe that we are obliged to adopt this approach. Moreover, the results will have surprising critical implications in that the methods of humanist grammar can change the ways in which we actually see and experience Botticelli's painting.

EVER SINCE Giovanni Rosini in 1841 drew attention to the similarities existing between the description of Venus Anadyomene in the "Homeric Hymn to Aphrodite," Politian's description of Venus rising from the sea in the *Stanze per la Giostra di Giuliano de'Medici*, and the imagery of Botticelli's painting known as the *Birth of Venus*, scholars have often and rightly drawn analogies between the imagery of Botticelli's mythological paintings (his poetic *favole*) and the poetry and philological writings of Politian.[12] Such analogies are unquestionably to the point, and have been of great value in helping us to understand the context and potential significance of Botticelli's inventions. Only recently, however, has it proven possible to establish a connection between a particular image made by Botticelli and a particular subject treated by Politian that is so specific as virtually to eliminate any other avenue of interpretation.

The path to this precious discovery was cleared by Panofsky, who showed that the imagery of Correggio's fresco of the god Pan trumpeting on a conch shell (Fig. 76), one of sixteen enigmatic *grisailles* decorating a chamber in the abbatial apartments of the Convent of San Paolo in Parma, was uniquely determined in the whole of ancient and medieval literature by information supplied only by two Greek scholiasts to Aratus's

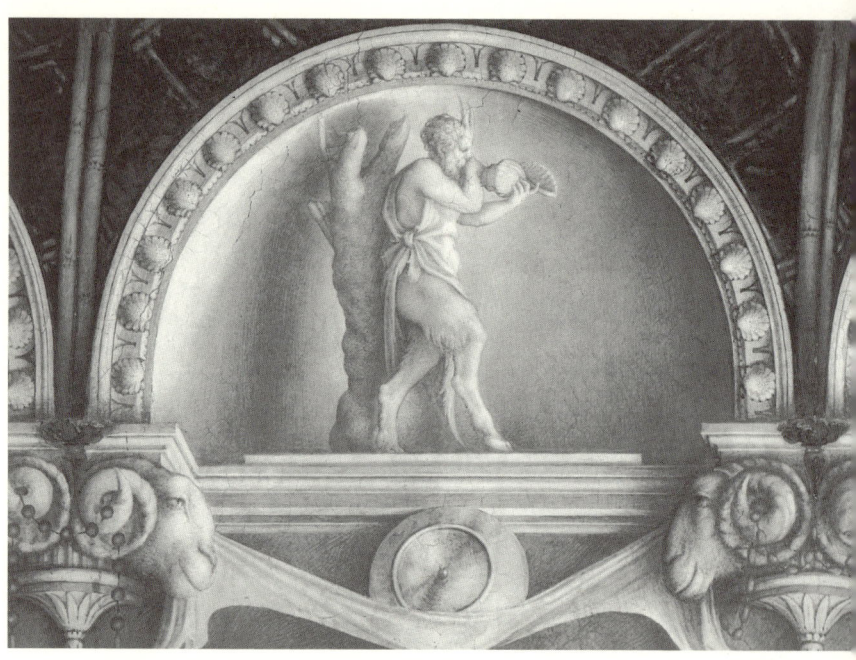

FIGURE 76
Correggio, *Pan with the Conch Shell (Panic Terror)*, Parma, Camera di San Paolo.
(Photograph: Ministero per i Beni e le Attività Culturali, Soprintendenza per
i Beni Artistici e Storici de Parma e Piacenza)

Phaenomena, namely the pseudo-Theon and the pseudo-Eratosthenes.[13] The first comment, ascribed to the famous mathematician Theon of Alexandria, reports that when Pan fought with Jupiter against the Titans he found a conch shell by the sea, and when he blew through it the resultant reverberating sound afflicted the Titans with an overwhelming terror, known ever after as "panic" from the name of Pan himself, causing them to flee the scene of battle.[14] The second scholium, attributed to Eratosthenes, gives essentially the same information, but with the important addition that Pan armed his companions (i.e., the Satyrs, Fauns, and other minor gods of the woods and fields) with the conch-shell trumpet.[15]

Accordingly, Panofsky was able to show that Correggio's image of Pan was intended to denote the concept of "panic terrors," even though he was at a loss to explain how the artist could have gained access to this obscurely located information, since so far as he knew neither the scholia nor their contents had as yet been published.

The discovery specifically linking Botticelli with Politian, precisely on the basis of these two scholia to Aratus, was made by Vladimir Juřen, who began by observing that the Greek texts had in fact been published by Aldus as early as 1499, and so would have been easily available to Correggio's humanist advisors in Parma.[16] Juřen further pointed out that the information about Pan and the conch-shell trumpet was even more readily accessible in Politian's celebrated *Miscellanea*, first published in 1489, the twenty-eighth chapter of which is entitled *Panici terrores qui vocentur, eoque locupletissimi citati testes*.[17] In that chapter Politian writes that Hyginus and the scholiasts to Aratus (Theon, Eratosthenes, and Germanicus) all report that Pan was the first, at the time Jupiter fought against the Titans, to have filled the enemy with panic terrors; and Politian further adds that Theon, "the interpreter of the poet Aratus, says that the god Pan fought against the Titans, and that he was the first, having espied that twisted and cone-shaped shell called *cochlos* in Greek, to have used it as a trumpet; and having done this and in the meantime armed himself and his comrades with a supply of them, they put the Titans to flight with that sound coming from everywhere which is called *Panicós*."[18] Politian's chapter on panic terrors became the basis, not only for Correggio's fresco, but also for Erasmus's essays on three adages (*Panicus casus*, *Multa in bella inania*, and *Metum inanem metuisti*) collected in his *Adagiorum chiliades* and published in the first edition of 1508; and it later was adapted as the foundation for Alciati's emblem *In subitum terrorem*, published in his *Emblematum liber* of 1531 (Fig. 77).[19] Before the publication of the *Miscellanea* in 1489, Politian was the only person who knew the complete etymology and meaning of the Greek word *panikós*. Juřen therefore concluded that Botticelli's depiction of a *paniscus* trumpeting on a conch shell in the *Mars and Venus*—which most scholars have agreed in dating to about 1483, some six years or

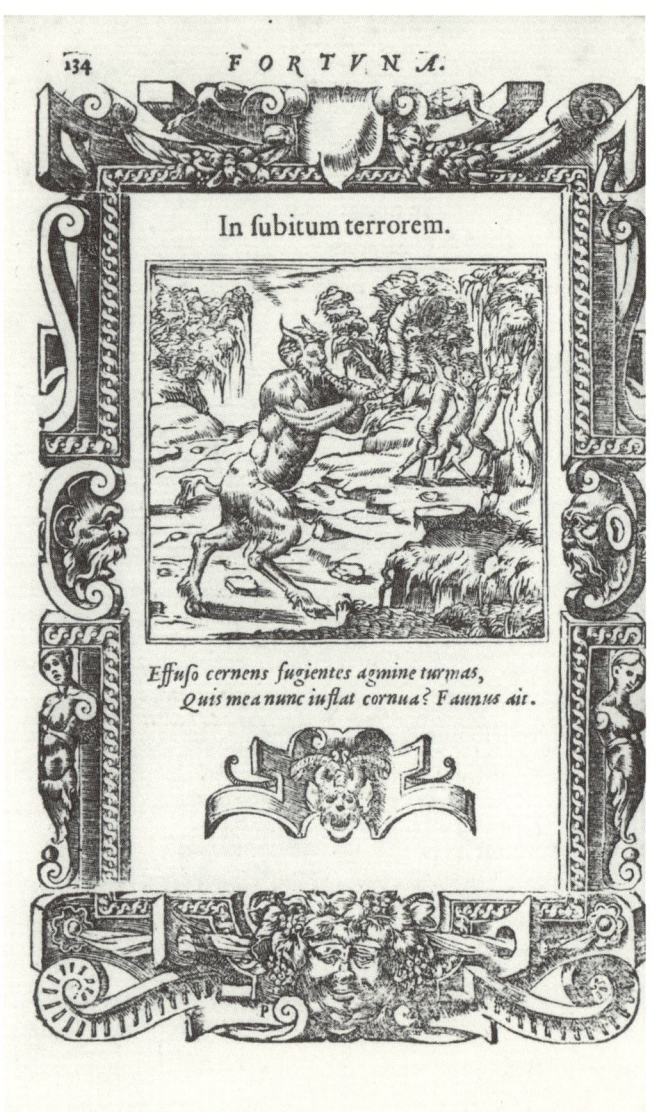

FIGURE 77
In subitum terrorem, from Andrea Alciati, *Emblematum liber*,
1542 or later. (Photograph: The John Work Garrett Library
of The Johns Hopkins University)

so earlier than the publication of the *Miscellanea*—must depend upon Politian's own particular knowledge and understanding of the origin and meaning of the image.

This observation is fundamental. Since the Greek scholiasts to Aratus are unique in giving the conch shell as an attribute to Pan and his woodland companions, the information they provide and Politian's explanation and understanding of it must be assumed as facts about Botticelli's painting, even though there are many who have been perplexed by the artist's representation of *panisci* instead of Pan himself, and unsure of how the concept "panic terrors" applies to the apparently erotic, and even playful tone of the picture.[20] The fact is there, however, and cannot be explained away. Furthermore, it is one that bears a remarkable correspondence with the only other fact that may be assumed as known regarding the *Mars and Venus*. Count Plunkett noticed almost a century ago that Lucian's famous description of an ancient painting by Aëtion entitled the *Marriage of Alexander and Roxana* (adapted in a famous design by Raphael, for which see Fig. 78) must certainly have played a part in Botticelli's conception. In Aëtion's painting of the coming together in marriage of Alexander the Great with his first bride Roxana, the daughter of the satrap Oxyartes and the most beautiful woman in Persia, infant Loves—*erotes*—were represented playing in the armor of Alexander, and Lucian's description of their activities is in certain particulars identical to those of Botticelli's *panisci*.[21] No one has ever been able to explain why Botticelli chose not to adopt Aëtion's principal subject of the story of Alexander and Roxana for his painting (as he did when he painted the *Calumny* after Lucian's description of Apelles's picture on this theme), or why he changed Lucian's *erotes* into *panisci*, but everyone has agreed that the resemblance of their actions to Lucian's description is too close to be fortuitous. The relevant passage from Lucian is this:

> In another part of the picture *erotes* play in the armor of Alexander. Two of them carry his spear, like porters hefting a heavy beam. . . . Another has entered into his breastplate, which lies face upwards, and like someone in ambush will terrify [*os phobéseien*] those who happen to come within his grasp.[22]

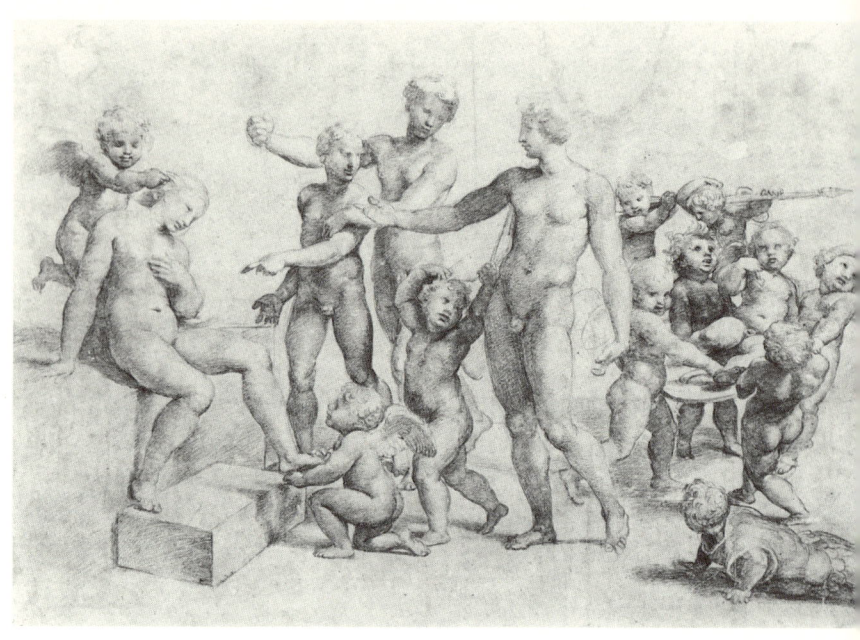

FIGURE 78
Raphael, *The Marriage of Alexander and Roxana*, drawing, Vienna, Staatliche Graphische Sammlung Albertina. (Photograph: Graphische Sammlung Albertina)

The word used by Lucian for "terrify" is *phobéo*—which could just as well be translated as "put into a panic fright." Hence, just as the *paniscus* with the conch shell denotes *panikós*, so his brother within Mars's cuirass denotes *phóbos*, and *pánikoi phóboi*, "panic terrors," are exactly what Politian set out to explain in the *Miscellanea*. We have thus isolated a concept central to Botticelli's invention, namely "panic terrors," and in a way that explains why Lucian's *ekphrasis* contributes to that invention. The concept of "panics" also points toward an explanation of why Lucian's *erotes* were changed to *panisci*—for we already know that *panisci* as the companions of Pan directly denote the idea of "panic" terrors, while *erotes* innocently playing in discarded martial weapons and concealing themselves within an empty helmet or cuirass are more benign, denoting idle distractions, and often childishly erotic *frissons*. What is more, the concepts of fright denoted in the *Mars and Venus* are Greek. For this reason the *Satyrisci* who mask themselves in Mars's helmet and breastplate are best named as *mormolykeía* in Greek, rather than using the synonymous *larvae* in Latin, or *larve* in the vernacular. And, as we have already seen, like *panikós* and *phóbos*, *mormolykeion* also denotes an idea of fear, that of an empty or merely childish fright.

At this point the necessity for what Politian would have called "grammatical" investigation and interpretation arises, for to understand Botticelli's invention we must understand the meaning and application of the Greek word *panikós*, for which no exact vernacular derivative existed when the *Mars and Venus* was painted. As Juřen noted, Politian began compiling the hundred chapters of the *Miscellanea* from about the year 1480, when he was made professor of rhetoric and poetry at the Studio Fiorentino, his purpose being, on the model of the *Attic Nights* of Aulus Gellius, to assemble reliable interpretations regarding various philological puzzles.[23] One such puzzle was the etymology and applications of the word *panikós*, which had been forgotten during the middle ages in the West, and for which no identical parallel existed in other languages. The Italian *panico* and the French *panique* are new coinages of the late fifteenth or early sixteenth centuries that directly derive from Politian's explication of the Greek word, from which both are formed, while the English "panic" and German *panisch* are both later derivations from the Greek via the French, the latter not appearing earlier than the eighteenth century.[24] Moreover, *panicos* is not Latin, but a transliteration of the Greek word employed by Politian for convenience, classical Latin using adjectives like *exterritus*, *pavidus*, *terrificus*, and *lymphaticus* to characterize the *pavor*, *metus*, or *terror* induced by Pan. For this reason *Pan Terrificus* is the Latin epithet for Pan as the god of irresistible, and overwhelming, panic terrors. Since there is no Latin word expressing "panic" that is related etymologically to Pan himself, Hyginus, for example, in a passage cited by Politian, did not attempt to translate the Greek word from the scholiasts to Aratus when he wrote that "Eratosthenes reports that they say [Pan] was the first, when Jupiter fought against the Titans, to have instilled the fear that is called *panikós* in the enemy."²⁵ Cicero also used the Greek word in a letter to Atticus, to which Politian refers, and he used it again in the following letter to Tiro, which Politian directly quotes:

> And yet our friend Atticus, because he once noticed I was upset by panic [*panikois*], always thinks the same of me, nor does he see with what safeguards of philosophy I am hedged round; and, on my oath, he is so timid himself that he causes general alarums and confusions [*thorybopoiei*].²⁶

In sum, at the time Botticelli painted the *Mars and Venus* only Politian knew the story of Pan and the conch-shell trumpet, and so too did only he know the full meaning, derivation, and usages of the Greek word *panikós*. His intention was to explain that meaning in the twenty-eighth chapter of the *Miscellanea*.

Politian defines panic terrors, taking Cicero's two letters, Hyginus, and the scholiasts to Aratus as his points of departure, as sudden terrors, alarmed and tumultuous confusions (*repentini terrores et consternationes*), mad, possessive fears (*lymphatici metus*, called *nympholeptós* by the Greeks) that turn the limbs to water. They are empty and without apparent cause, and hence irrevocable, since panic terrors are neither rational nor even comprehensible, sweeping away not only the reason but also the mind itself (*inrevocabiles, ut non ratione modo, sed mente etiam careant*). Politian's particular authority for this definition derives from two scholiasts, one to Euripides's *Medea* and the other to Synesius's *De providentia*. Where Euripides describes the kind of epileptic frenzy that grips Medea as something sent by Pan or some other god, the scholiast refers his meaning to *pánika deímata*, "panic terrors," which he names the sudden and confused fears sent by the god Pan.²⁷ And when Synesius describes the panicky tumults (*pánikoi thoryboi*) that can overwhelm entire armies, his scholiast adds that panic terrors suddenly strike men, armies, and herds of horses with no apparent cause at all, causing them to stampede or rush to headlong flight; and he goes on to say that the same sudden rush of terror used to strike those who heard the women, filled with the spirit of Pan, while they were celebrating the god's rites.[28] To this Politian adds that the Byzantine writer Nicetas Choniates also refers in one of his *Orationes* to a *panicorum phantasmatum* (*phantásmatos panikós* in Nicetas's text), an empty vision or nightmare that incites terrors.[29] He then concludes by showing (with reference to Nonnus, Valerius Flaccus, Zosimus's *History*, and the Theocritean *Syrinx*) that because of this power Pan, who is also called *belliger*, is a god of war. The maddening sound of his lash, the reverberating echo of his trumpet, or his deafening voice alone can create such insane fear that, in the words of Valerius Flaccus in his "Argonautica," "not the helmet of Mars, not the locks of the Furies, not the baleful Gorgon on high can spread such terror, nor rout an army with so many ghostly apparitions." We are again reminded of Renato de'Pazzi, who declined to joust because "egli avea paura nell'elmo solo." The passage from the "Argonautica" merits quoting in full:

> Ut notis adlapsa vadis, dant aethere longo
> signa tubae, vox et mediis emissa tenebris
> "hostis habet portus, soliti rediere Pelasgi."
> rupta quies; deus ancipitem lymphaverat urbem,
> Mygdoniae Pan iussa ferens saevissima matris,
> Pan nemorum bellique potens, quem lucis ab horis
> antra tenent; patet ad medias per devia noctes
> saetigerum latus et torvae coma sibila frontis.
> vox omnes super una tubas, qua conus et enses,
> qua trepidis auriga rotis nocturnaque muris
> claustra cadunt; talesque metus non Martia cassis
> Eumenidumque comae, non tristis ab aethere Gorgo
> sparserit aut tantis aciem raptaverit umbris.
> ludus est illa deo, pavidum praesepibus aufert
> cum pecus et profugi sternunt dumeta iuvenci.[30]

(As the Argo rode into the familiar shallows, trumpets sounded the alarm far through the air, and a voice cried out in the midst of the darkness: "The enemy has seized the harbor, our old foes the Pelasgians have returned." Men's rest was broken. The god Pan struck the doubting city with insane terror, Pan following the savage commands of the Mygdonian mother, Pan lord of the woodlands and of war, whom the caves shelter in the daylight hours, and whose hairy flank is seen around midnight in lonely places, and the rustling leafage of his fierce brow. His voice alone sounds louder than all trumpets, and at that sound fall helm and sword, the charioteer from his trembling car, and locks from the gates of the walls by night; not the helmet of Mars, not the locks of the Fates, not the baleful Gorgon on high can spread such terror, nor rout an army with so many ghostly apparitions. It is sport to the god when he drives the terrified flocks from their pens, and the steers trample the thickets in their flight.)

The sources drawn upon by Politian characterize Pan both as a god of the woods and fields, and as a god of war (*Pan nemorum bellique potens*). It was to his demonic powers that the ancients attributed on the one hand those sudden and aboriginal terrors that overtake men when lost in the woods, terrors intensified by the strange sounds emanating from the dark interiors of the woods, caves, and hills, empty terrors that also attack herds of animals by night, causing them to stampede. The same powers on the other hand characterize Pan's prowess in war, for with them he put to panic flight not only the Titans but also the Persians at Marathon, the hordes of Brennus at Delphi, and Hannibal before the gates of Rome.[31] And it is because of the irresistible power of *Pan belliger* in war, initiated by his triumph over the Titans, that Luca Signorelli included a triumphal arch among the various attributes of Pan in his otherwise Arcadian vision of the god's kingdom in the *Realm of Pan*, formerly in Berlin (Fig. 79), which was painted about a decade after Botticelli's *Mars and Venus*, and at least in this detail also depends upon Politian's philological knowledge.

Though it may at first occur to us to wonder why Botticelli painted *panisci* rather than Pan himself as emblematic of panic terrors, from the philological point of view his having done so was well founded, for Politian was perfectly right in citing the report of pseudo-Eratosthenes that

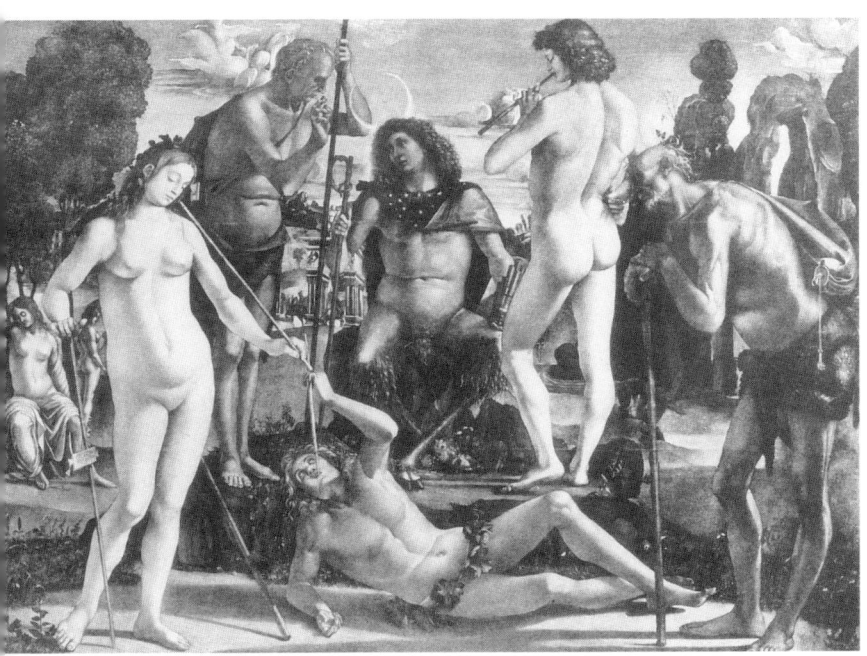

FIGURE 79
Luca Signorelli, *The Realm of Pan*, formerly Berlin, Kaisermuseum.
(Photograph: Giraudon/Art Resource)

Pan is not the only god who incites panics. Dionysus of Halicarnassus writes that it was Faunus who spread terror among the armies at the battle of the Arsian wood—"for the Romans attribute panics to this demon; and whatever *phantásmata* come to men's sight, now in one shape and now in another, inspiring terror, or whatever demonic voices come to their ears to disturb them are the work, they say, of this god."[32] On this basis (and not for metrical reasons, as Panofsky thought) Alciati endowed Faunus, not Pan, with the panic-inducing trumpet in his emblem for "Sudden Terror" (see Fig. 77).[33] Livy, on the other hand, attributes the panic terrors of the same battle to phantasms produced by Sylvanus.[34] Plutarch writes in *Numa* that Picus and Faunus "took a multitude of forms and changed their natures, offering to the eyes strange and terrifying apparitions [*phás-*

mata kaì phoberà];"[35] and it is indeed to Pan's power to invoke frightening phantasms that Signorelli also alludes in the *Realm of Pan*, where among Pan's attributes we see the image of clouds forming themselves into the threatening shape of armed horsemen. And in the *Moralia* Plutarch adds that the Pans and Satyrs who lived in the region of Chemnis in Egypt were the first to tell of the murder of Osiris by Typhon, "and so, even to this day, the sudden confusion and consternation of a crowd is called a panic."[36] In fact all the forest demons who are the companions of Pan have the power to provoke panic terror, as we already know from Politian's citation of the pseudo-Eratosthenes's report that Pan armed his cohorts with the conch-shell trumpet so that together they might put the Titans to panic flight. Accordingly, Lilio Gregorio Giraldi in his chapter "De daemonibus" in the *De deis gentium* of 1548, named as chthonic, or terrestrial demons (following Artemidorus and Hippocrates) Satyrs, *Satyrisci*, Pans, *Panisci*, Sylvans, Sileni, Fauns, female Fauns, *Fatui*, *Fatuae*, Nymphs, *Ephialtae* and *Hyphialtae* (i.e. *Incubi* and *Succubi*), together with all the spirits of the woods and fields. "These creatures," he wrote, "assaulted men with those bugbears [*terriculamenta*] which are called nympholeptic [*nymphóleptoi*] by the Greeks and *lymphatici* by the Romans, from which arise the panic terrors also induced by Pan."[37] And hence Ronsard, in his poem "Les daimons," written in 1555, described the same demons, "Incubes, Larves, Lares, Lemurs, Penates et Succubes,"

> Qui resveillent les coeurs des hommes sommeilans,
> Et donnent grand' frayeur à ceux qui sont veillans, [vv. 236–38]
> ...
> Les uns aucunefois se transforment en Fées,
> En Dryades des bois, en Nymphes et Napées
> En Faunes, en Sylvains, en Satyres et Pans,
> Qui ont le corps pelu, marqueté comme fans, [vv. 331–34]

(Who awaken the hearts of sleeping men, and bring great terror to those who are awake. . . . Sometimes they transform themselves into fairies, or woodland Dryads, Nymphs and Napaeans, into Fauns, Sylvans, Satyrs, and Pans with their hairy bodies, spotted like fawns.)

and ended his poem (though like Cicero he has always himself been immune to such panic terrors) with a prayer to God to keep them far from him:

> O SEIGNEUR eternal, en qui seul gist ma foi,
> Pour l'honneur de ton nom, de grace, donne moy,
> Donne moy que jamais je ne trouve en ma voye
> Ces paniques terreurs, mais ô SEIGNEUR, envoye
> Loin de la Chrestienté, dans le pays des Turcz,
> Ces Larves, ces Daimons, ces Lares et Lemurs.[38] [vv.421–26]

(O eternal Lord, in whom only my faith lies, for the honor of thy name grant me this, grant me that I may never find in my path these Panic Terrors, but, O Lord, banish to the land of the Turks, far from Christianity, all these *Larvae* and Demons, these Lares and *Lemures*.)

All these examples serve to show that Botticelli's depiction of *panisci*, instead of Pan, as the cause of panic terrors is not in itself a problem, but has classical warrant. Nonetheless, it is at first perplexing to try to reconcile their actions with Politian's characterization of the meaning of "panic terrors," especially as the preponderance of the classical texts cited in his commentary emphasizes collective panics and tumults, animal stampedes and military disorder and rout, rather than individual possessive frights. Botticelli's *panisci* are not assailing herds of animals by night, nor (though they might be described, tongue in cheek, as *belligeri*, or at least *armigeri*), are they putting armies to confused and tumultuous flight. They instead swarm about a youthful Mars who has shed his armor and lies upon his back in troubled slumber, brow furrowed, as if between waking and deep sleep. One *paniscus* assaults his rest by sounding in his ear the panic-inducing, reverberating blast of the conch-shell trumpet. A second has entered Mars's discarded breastplate so that, "like someone in ambush," he may leap out and frighten him. Two others, one of them masking his face in Mars's empty helmet, have taken up his lance and appear to be using it to prod the tree trunk against which the god's head is rested. A wasps' nest is within the hollow of the tree trunk, and as the *panisci* poke his lance against the trunk a few wasps begin to swarm around its entrance, just next to the sleeping god's head. We can well imagine, with the sudden blare of the conch shell in one ear and the angry buzzing of the aroused wasps in the other, that Mars will awaken in a state of tumultuous consternation and fright—in other words, in a panic terror.

But the quality of that terror, even though the use of the helmet as a fright-mask by one of the *panisci* inevitably recalls Politian's citation of Valerius Flaccus invoking the terrors that the sight of Mars's helmet all by itself can inspire ("talesque metus non Martia cassis . . . sparserit"), is certainly different from the insane fear that strikes armies. It rather brings to mind the childish fears provoked by Lamachus's empty armor, not to mention Renato de'Pazzi's being afraid of only a helmet. The *paniscus* masking himself in Mars's sallet threatens the sleeping god with his own helmet and jousting lance. The fearsome Mars, *semper timendus, timet*, and is affrighted by the phantasm of his own arms, the instruments of his very manliness, seeming to be turned against him.[39] The helmeted *paniscus* is merely an empty *terriculum*, a bogey, and the *paniscus* trumpeting on the conch shell denotes only an empty panic. In other words, the frights with which Botticelli is concerned are not the tremendous fears which overwhelm entire armies, that *metus terrificus* sent by the fully grown Pan, but are instead something smaller (as the infant *panisci* indicate). They are the little demon-induced imaginings that imprint their illusions on the *spiritus phantasticus* and constantly afflict the soul with panicky confusions. They are merely the hobgoblin fantasies that torment an uneasy soul, allowing it no rest, assailing it, in Politian's words, with *phantasmata panicorum*, empty apparitions or specters. Cicero had been immune to such panicky illusions because, as he explained in his letter to Tiro, he was safeguarded on all sides by philosophy. Not so Botticelli's restlessly sleeping Mars, who is literally assailed by the demons of the turbulent dreams that haunt his sleep—for *phantasmata* are the visions of the nightmare.

Phantasma is in fact a species of the dream. We also know from Politian's definition of empty *phantasmata panicorum* as bringing with them *lymphatici metus*, as well as from Giraldi's characterization of such terrors as *lymphatici* and nympholeptic, that these are the demons of the spiritually or psychologically possessed. The question of Botticelli's Mars is, then, what are the illusory demons that possess him? What panic terrors grip his imagination in sleep? What is it that obsesses his spirit, the bogey that literally "bugs" him?

In the *Panepistemon* Politian defines *phantasma* as a type of dream induced by psychological or physical disturbances, which manifests itself in the common dream or the nightmare: "*Phantasma* occurs in *insomnium*, which Cicero calls *visum*, and in *Ephialtes*, which is called *Incubus* in Latin."[40] His particular sources are Artemidorus's *Oneirocritica*, the most important treatise on the interpretation of dreams surviving from antiquity, and Macrobius's commentary to Cicero's *Somnium Scipionis*, in its turn the most influential source for the development of the literary dream vision.[41] Macrobius, who himself follows Artemidorus's listing of the forms of true and false dreams, distinguishes five species of the dream. These are: (1) *óneiros*, or *somnium*; (2) *órama*, or *visio*; (3) *chrematismós*, or *oraculum*; (4) *enúpnion*, or *insomnium*; and (5) *phántasma*, or *visum*. The first three, the allegorical dream, the prophetic vision, and the oracular dream, are significant dreams and useful in divination, or foretelling the future. The last two, the common dream and the apparition (which Artemidorus considers within a single type), are instead the products of physical or psychological disturbance, and have no prophetic significance.[42]

We need not linger over the distinctions between these species of the dream, but it is useful to give a few examples of their appearance in art. Raphael's *St. Cecilia*, for example, in common with thousands of paintings depicting saintly revelations, shows the saint rapt by a true prophetic *visio* of heaven (Fig. 80). His *Dream of the Knight* (Fig. 81), on the other hand, the imagery of which derives from the *Somnium Scipionis*, presents us with an allegorical dream, or *somnium*. The same is true of the anonymous woodcut of *Hercules at the Crossroad* for Sebastian Brant's *Narrenschiff* (Fig. 82), which shows Hercules asleep in knight's armor contemplating the figures appearing to him (as the text indicates) in a *somnium*. Lucas Cranach's *Judgement of Paris* (Fig. 83), on the other hand, just as clearly represents a false *visum*. Cranach treated this subject, which, like the story of Mars and Venus, derives from ancient mythology, on numerous occasions, and in

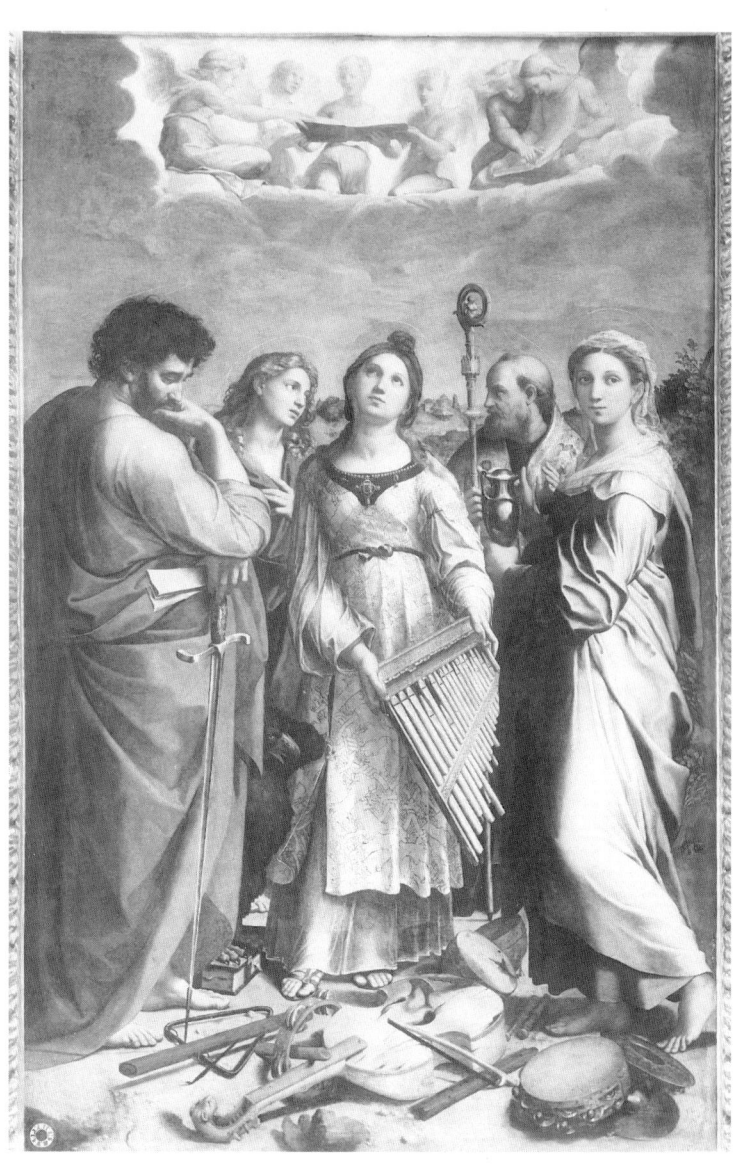

FIGURE 80
Raphael, *St. Cecilia*, Bologna, Pinacoteca.
(Photograph: Alinari/Art Resource)

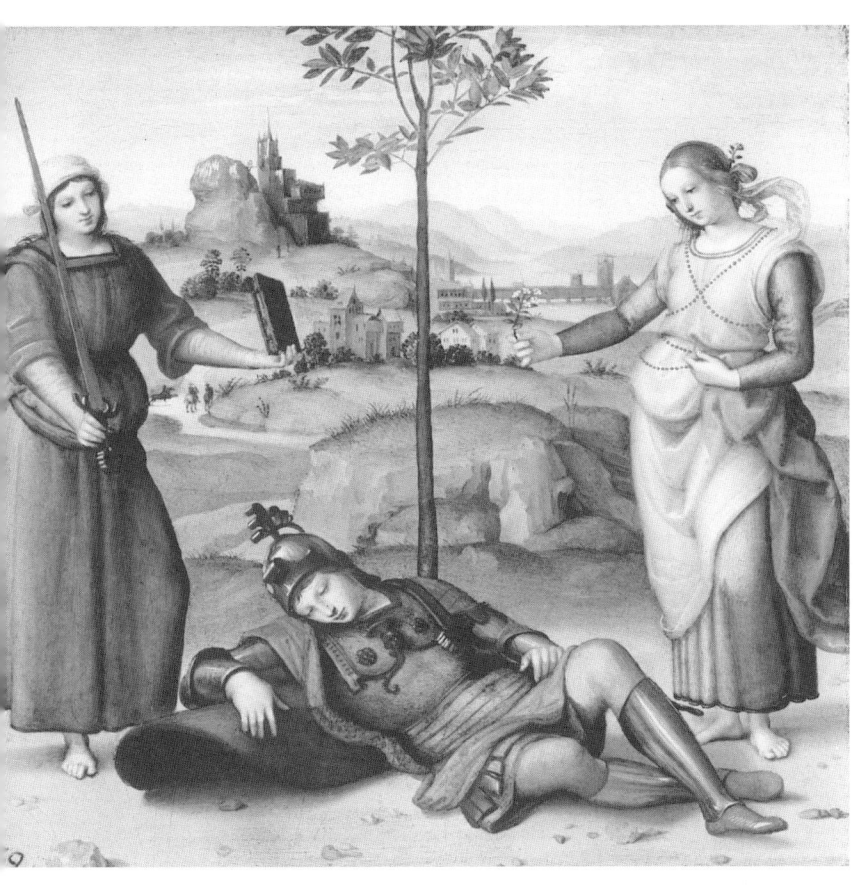

FIGURE 81
Raphael, *The Dream of the Knight*, London, National Gallery.
(Photograph © National Gallery)

these paintings followed the account given by Guido delle Colonne in his romance of the *Historiae destructionis Troiae*. In Guido's tale the three goddesses appeared to Paris in a dream one day at noon (*in ipso sompno meo mirabilem visionem*, as Paris later describes it) after he had been led away from his hunting companions by a deer and left alone in the forest, where he fell into exhausted sleep under a tree.[43] Given the disastrous consequences of Paris's choice, his dream was interpreted as having been the

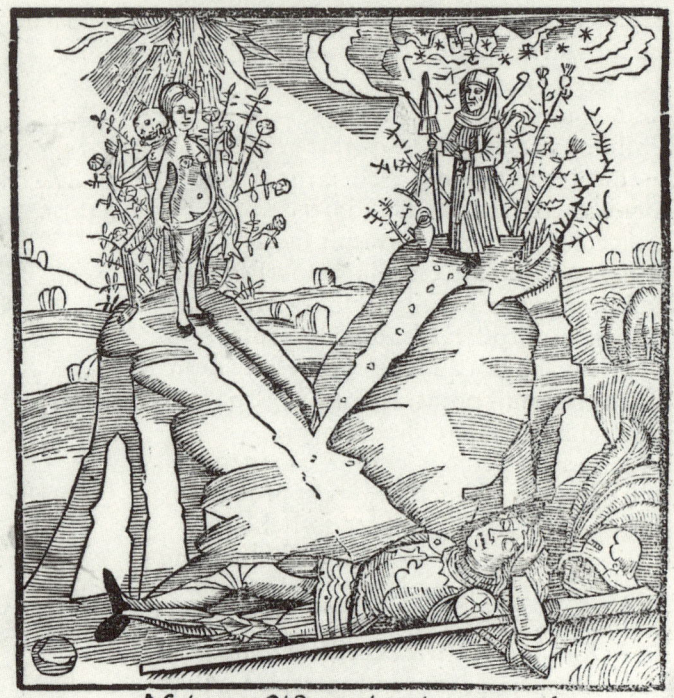

FIGURE 82
Hercules at the Crossroads, from Sebastian Brant, *Narrenschiff*, Basel, 1497.
(Photograph: Special Collections, Milton S. Eisenhower Library)

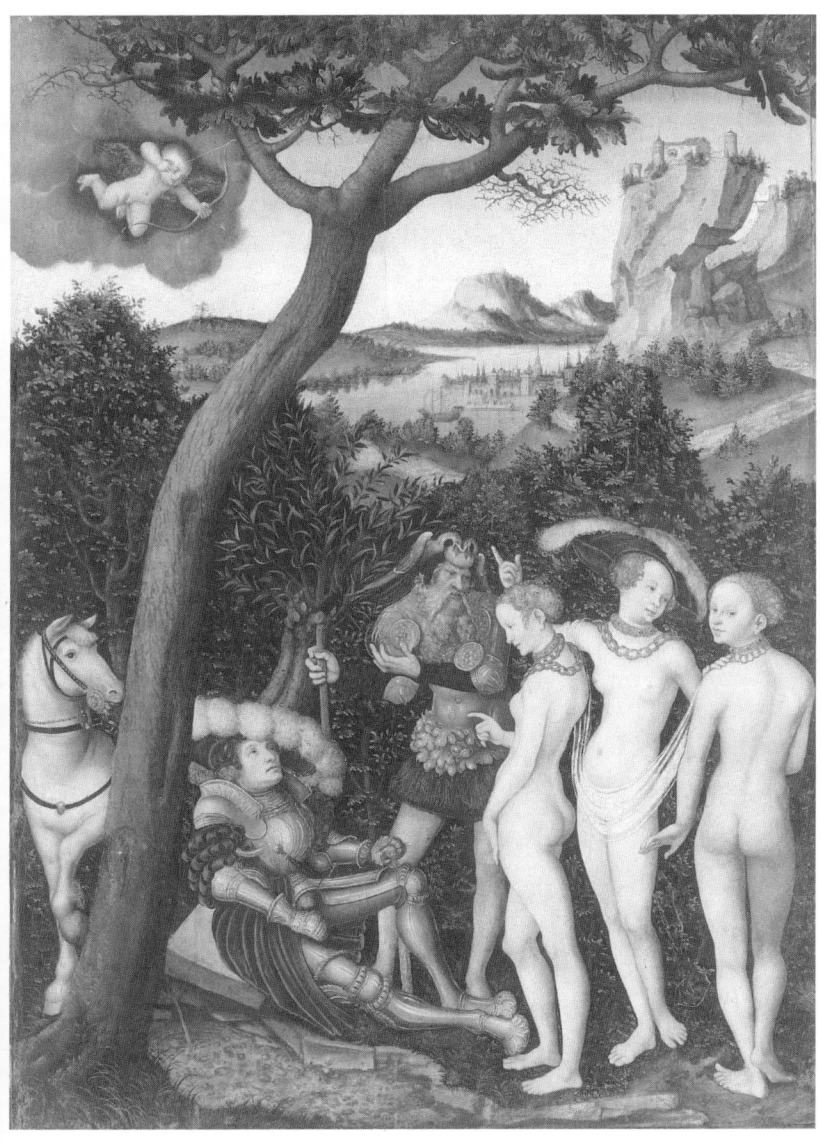

FIGURE 83
Lucas Cranach, *The Judgement of Paris*, New York, The Metropolitan Museum of Art, Rogers Fund (1928, 28.221). (Photograph: The Metropolitan Museum of Art)

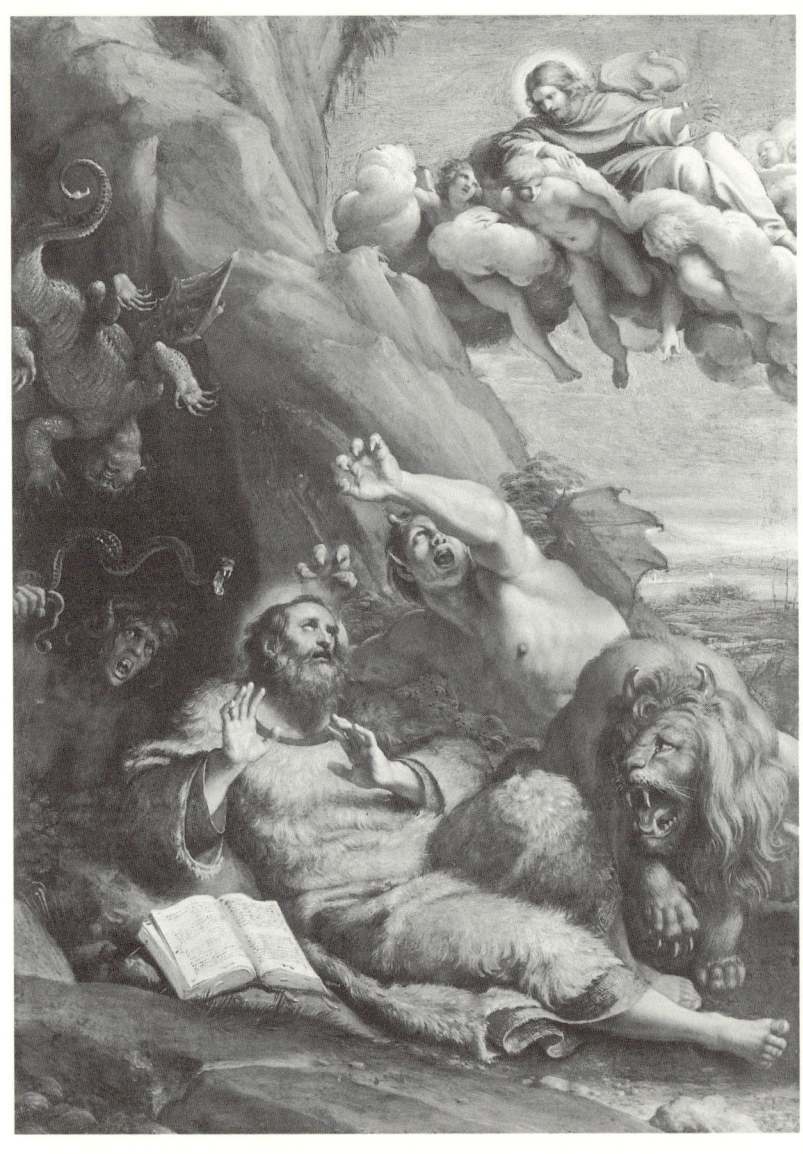

FIGURE 84
Annibale Carracci, *The Temptation of St. Anthony*, London, National Gallery.
(Photograph © National Gallery)

result of demonic intervention, a false vision produced by *lamiae*, or deluding demons appearing in the form of the three goddesses. Accordingly, Giovanni Francesco Pico della Mirandola mentions Paris's judgment in his *Praenotiones* and *Strix* (cited extensively by his friend Giraldi for the chapter "De demonibus, geniis, laribus, caeterisque, ac de Pane, Themide, et Lamiis" in the *De deis gentium*) as an instance of "how easily the demon deceived Paris by assuming the shape of the three goddesses" and thus brought about the Trojan war.[44] In Annibale Carracci's *Temptation of St. Anthony*, painted early in the next century (Fig. 84), there is similarly shown a nightmare *visum* in the Satyr-like demons who torment the saint in his desert refuge, signifying the life of the flesh that continues to haunt him; at the same time, however, Annibale also showed the true *visio* of Christ appearing in the heaven above and behind them, upon which the saint's gaze is fixed steadfastly, and from which the false phantasms themselves recoil in terror. Botticelli's Mars, his spiritual unease vividly indicated by the light that unnaturally strikes his face from below (an extraordinarily precocious use of light effects in order to express psychological condition), his brow furrowed in troubled slumber, as if between waking and deep sleep, and assaulted by demon *panisci*, or *incubi*, also suffers the *visum* of the nightmare.

Of the *visum*, or *phantasma*, Macrobius writes the following:

> The last two [species of dream], *insomnium* and *visum*, are not worth interpreting since they have no prophetic significance. Apparitions may be caused by mental or physical distress, or anxiety about the future: the patient experiences in dreams vexations similar to those that disturb him during the day. As examples of the mental variety, we might mention the lover who dreams of possessing his sweetheart or of losing her. . . . Since these dreams and others like them arise from some condition or disturbance that irritates a man during the day and consequently disturbs him when he falls asleep, they flee when he awakes and vanish into thin air. . . . Virgil, in describing the passion of love, the concerns of which are always accompanied by nightmares, says, "Often the great valor of Aeneas rushes back to

SPIRITS OF THE NIGHTMARE

Dido's heart, and often his glorious ancestry; his looks and his words cling fast within her bosom, and care withholds calm rest from her limbs." And a moment later, "Anna, my sister, what dreams grip me with terrors!" ["*Anna, soror, quae me insomnia terrent!*"]. *Phantasma* is in fact an appearance that occurs between waking and deep sleep, in those first mists of sleep when one still believes oneself to be awake and has just fallen asleep, and which seems to be forcing itself in as wandering spectres of different size, shape or temper, either joyful or disturbing. *Ephialtes* is of this type, which popular belief holds to rush in upon people in sleep and to weigh on them heavily, oppressing them severely.[45]

Ephialtes, which we have already encountered in Politian's *Panepistemon*, is the Greek for *incubus*, or the nightmare. It is also the name given to demons of the nightmare, chief among whom is Pan, one of whose epithets, as Giraldi notes, was Ephialtes.[46] Pan is especially dangerous at noon, when there is the greatest likelihood that he may attack and possess the sleeper with disorienting and frightening phantasms.[47] Giraldi further notes that the ancient physicians characterized the nightmare as a kind of sickness (*morbus*) that afflicts the half-asleep (*semisomnes*), which is why Macrobius in the passage just quoted refers to a "patient" suffering from the apparitions of *insomnium* and *visum*. Macrobius also stresses the often-observed erotic sensations that attend visions of the nightmare (the passions of love are *always* accompanied, he writes, by nightmares), together with shortness of breath and a feeling of suffocation produced by the feeling of a great weight pressing down upon the chest (hence *incubus*).[48] Nightmares are produced by a continuing psychological preoccupation with what most consumes the dreamer's sensual being during the day. Thus it was that Giraldi reports that *ephialtae* and *hyphialtae*, or *incubi* and *succubi*, were numbered by the ancients among the nymphs and Satyrs and other woodland followers of Pan.[49]

The most famous and influential testimony to this is from St. Augustine's *City of God*: "The story is well known, and corroborated by many people either from their own experience or from the accounts given by others of indubitably good faith who have had the experience, that Sylvans and Pans, who are commonly called *Incubi*, often misbehaved toward women and succeeded in their lustful desire to have intercourse with them."[50] The same is repeated by Isidore of Seville, and St. Jerome's commentary to Isaiah identifies such demons as *phantasmata*, going on to say of the prophet's words, *Pilosi saltabunt ibi*—translated in the King James version as "Satyrs shall dance there"—that the *Pilosi* are "*Incubi*, Satyrs, or the ghosts of famous men, which some people call *fauni ficarii*, or fig fauns."[51] Fig fauns are especially pernicious nightmare demons, known for their attacks upon horses and animals of the field, causing them to stampede, and also upon men, and their name perhaps derives from the indecent meaning of fig.[52] That two of Botticelli's ithyphallic *panisci* conspicuously make obscene gestures with their tongues (one looking collusively over his shoulder toward Venus) suggests that they may indeed be *fauni ficarii*, especially since the one lying concealed in Mars's breastplate seems to clutch a green fig in one hand. Of such creatures Isidore adds the following to Jerome's account: "*Pilosi* (whom the Greeks call *Panitae*) are called *Incubi* or *Inui* by the Romans, from *ineundo passim cum animalibus*, while *incubi* are so named from *incumbendo*, lying upon, that is lustfully raping."[53] *Inuus* is in fact the oldest of all Latin names for the nightmare, and is also the oldest and most familiar epithet for Pan, as well as for Faunus, who is often identified with Pan.[54] And finally, Politian himself cites, in his commentary to Statius's *Sylvae*, the passage in St. Jerome's *Life of Paul the Hermit* in which the story is told of the Satyr who appeared to torment St. Anthony but was forced to admit that he was merely "a mortal being and one of those inhabitants of the desert whom the Gentiles, deluded by various forms of error, worship under the names of Fauns, Satyrs, and *Incubi*."[55]

The theme of Botticelli's *Mars and Venus* can accordingly be defined as a nightmare of sexual obsession and domination, of a soul possessed and tormented, not just by erotic fantasies, but by the demons of Mars's own moral confusion, his preoccupation with luxuriousness and venery. By definition the nightmares that disturb his sleep cannot denote anything positive or true. What is more, Botticelli's conception, precisely by virtue

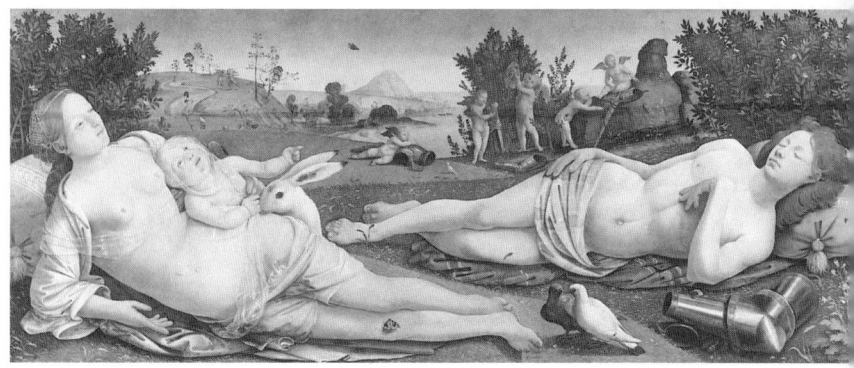

FIGURE 85
Piero di Cosimo, *Mars and Venus*, Berlin, Staatliche Museen zu Berlin-Preußischer Kulturbesitz Gemäldegalerie. (Photograph by Jörg P. Anders)

of giving his nightmare terrors the form of *panisci*, differs fundamentally from Aëtion's use of *erotes* as figures for the sudden thrill of sexual arousal. Mars is tormented by real demons, while Aëtion's Alexander, as described by Lucian, is merely attended by startling *erotes* who play everywhere within his armor. They personify the pneumatic surge of sexual desire aroused by the *spiritelli d'amore* within him, and allegorize the anticipation felt by the great warrior-king as he gazes upon his bride being disrobed by *eros* for the nuptial bed, while other *erotes* "lift his spear like a heavy beam." The theme of the startling (and scarifying) thrill of such erotic arousal plays a part in Piero di Cosimo's painting of *Mars and Venus* in Berlin (Fig. 85), which without question derives both from Lucian and from Botticelli's painting (not least because the story of Mars and Venus again substitutes for Lucian's description of Alexander and Roxana). Like Botticelli, Piero depicts Mars asleep in a meadow, but unlike him he retained Lucian's motif of *erotes* playing in Mars's armor. An awake and alert Venus reclines in the foreground opposite and to the front of him, a rabbit at her side and another *eros* cradled in her arm. The infant, his head partly covered by her sheer scarf in which he has playfully entangled himself, recoils violently backward, and with one hand points in the direction of Mars and his little brothers in the background. At one time the picture was owned by none other than Vasari, who describes it in the following manner:

> [Piero di Cosimo] also painted a picture where there is a naked Venus with Mars equally so, who sleeps undressed and naked on a meadow filled with flowers; and around them are diverse Loves, who one here and one there carry away Mars's sallet, armguards, and other armaments. There is a stand of myrtle and a Cupid who is afraid of a rabbit [*un Cupido che ha paura d'un coniglio*]; and so too there are Venus's doves and other amorous things. This painting is in Florence in the house of Giorgio Vasari, kept by him in memory of this master because he always found his caprices pleasing.[56]

It is a moot point whether Vasari is correct in identifying the rabbit, rather than the *erotes* playing with Mars's armor in the background, as the source of the infant Cupid's fright, but he is certainly right in indicating thereby its childishness. It has also been pointed out that the rabbit is a well-known symbol for insatiable sexual appetites, thus suggesting the content of Mars's dream of Venus. It has further been argued that Piero di Cosimo's painting turns upon a pun established between the rabbit (*cuniculus*), resting his head against Venus's thigh, and the goddess's *cunnus*, thus suggesting both the erotic thrill of Mars's dream and its attendant apprehension, as acted out by the frightened *eros* in Venus's lap.[57] Be that as it may, Botticelli's translation of Lucian's *eros* into a *paniscus*, or true nightmare spirit, is owing to the philological genius of Politian. The airy *spiritello d'amore* facetiously denotes the startling thrill of sudden erotic arousal. The chthonic *paniscus*, or earth *daimon*, denotes sexual obsession, and the torments of lust.

At this point our grammatical analysis of Botticelli's image of "panic terrors" suggests a radical and startling alteration of the way in which the *Mars and Venus* has actually been seen. When the picture was painted at some moment in the 1480s the subject of Mars and Venus was not yet familiar in Renaissance painting, but even so an interpretation of it in a genially erotic spirit has seemed naturally to follow upon the nature of the subject itself, as well as the spirit in which it was later treated in art.[58]

SPIRITS OF THE NIGHTMARE

There are good reasons for such a view. The domination of the young and lovesick knight (for so might Mars be described, since his armor, sallet, and jousting lance are not ancient but of the fifteenth century) by a woman of stunning beauty (coiffed and dressed in equally contemporary fashion) is clearly based as a nonetheless classical subject in Lucretius's famous description in the *De rerum natura* of Mars's surrender to the peaceful powers of Venus.[59] Lucretius's stirring invocation to Venus, praying her to disarm *Mavors armipotens*, to subdue the spirit of war through the power of love in order that the Romans might enjoy peace, is the *locus classicus* that is the cardinal point of departure for all Renaissance interpretations of the subject, whether in literature or in painting.[60] The unique manuscript of the *De rerum natura* had been found by Poggio Bracciolini at St. Gall in 1417, and the material of Lucretius's invocation to Venus indeed plays an important part in the inventions for two other paintings by Botticelli, the *Primavera* and *Birth of Venus*.[61] It is also well known that the ancients took the union of the two gods as an emblem not only of peace but also marriage because of the power of Love and Beauty to conquer strife and nourish procreation. Lucian's description of Aëtion's *Marriage of Alexander and Roxana* is itself based upon the metaphorical equation of Alexander and Roxana with Mars and Venus, showing Alexander as the very spirit of martial valor, as Mars disarmed by beauty and love, and Roxana in the role of Venus attended by *erotes* who strip Alexander's armor from him for use in their childish games.[62] Because of this it has reasonably been suggested that Botticelli's *Mars and Venus* may refer to an actual wedding; and the attractive hypothesis has further been put forward that the wasps, or *vespe*, swarming around Mars's head may be a punning reference to the name of one of the families in that putative wedding, the Vespucci, whose coats of arms bore the insignia of the wasps.[63]

Botticelli's painting does not represent a moment of amorous bliss, however, much less, as has often been claimed, the happy post-coital slumber of Mars. The god is not surrounded by benign images of erotic love, Lucianic *erotes*, but instead by malevolent nightmare *panisci* that can express no true idea of love, nor even effective sexuality. They are obscene in name and nature, both ithyphallic and tongue-spearing, and as such

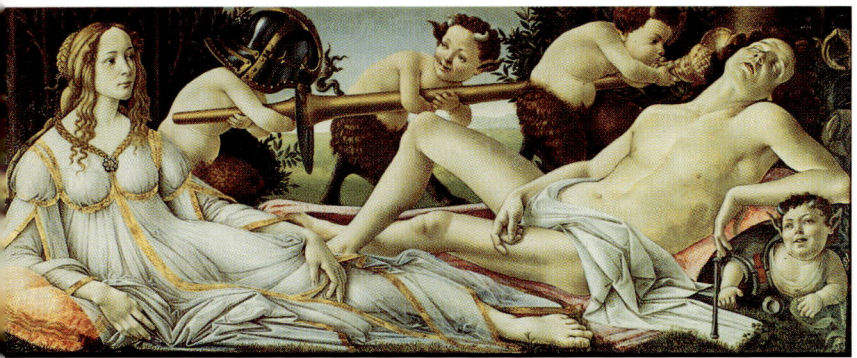

PLATE 1
Sandro Botticelli, *Mars and Venus*, London, National Gallery.
(Photograph: Art Resource)

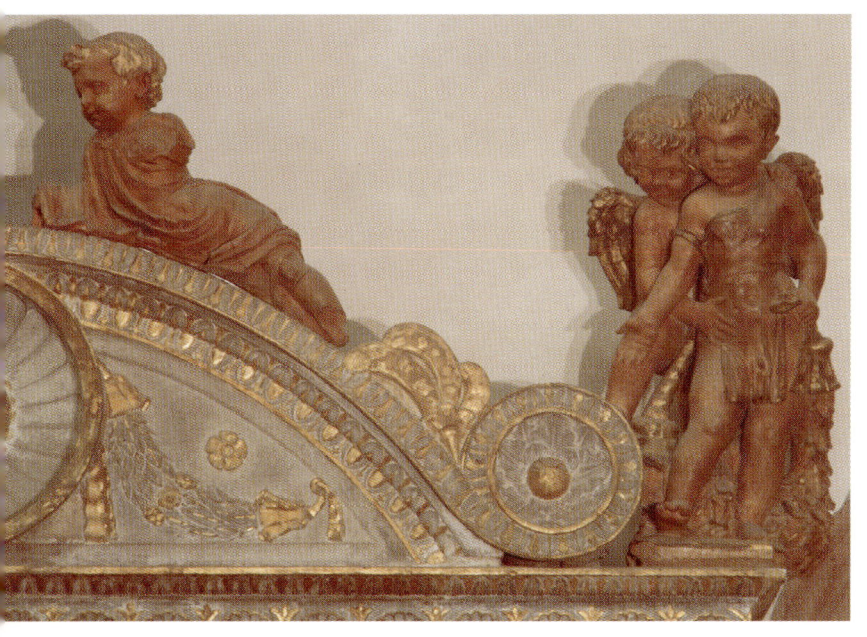

PLATE 2
Donatello, *Cavalcanti Altar*, Florence, S. Croce. Detail, *Garland-bearing Putto*.
(Photograph by Nicolò Orsi Battaglini)

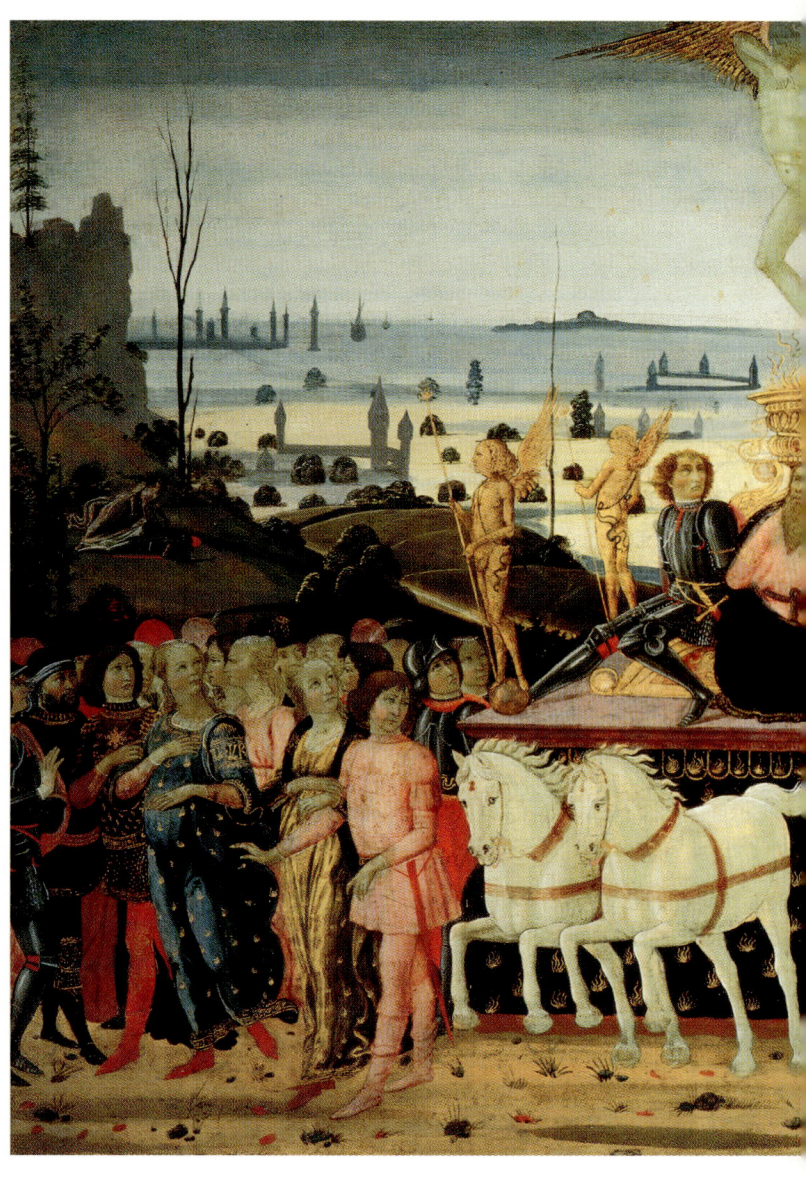

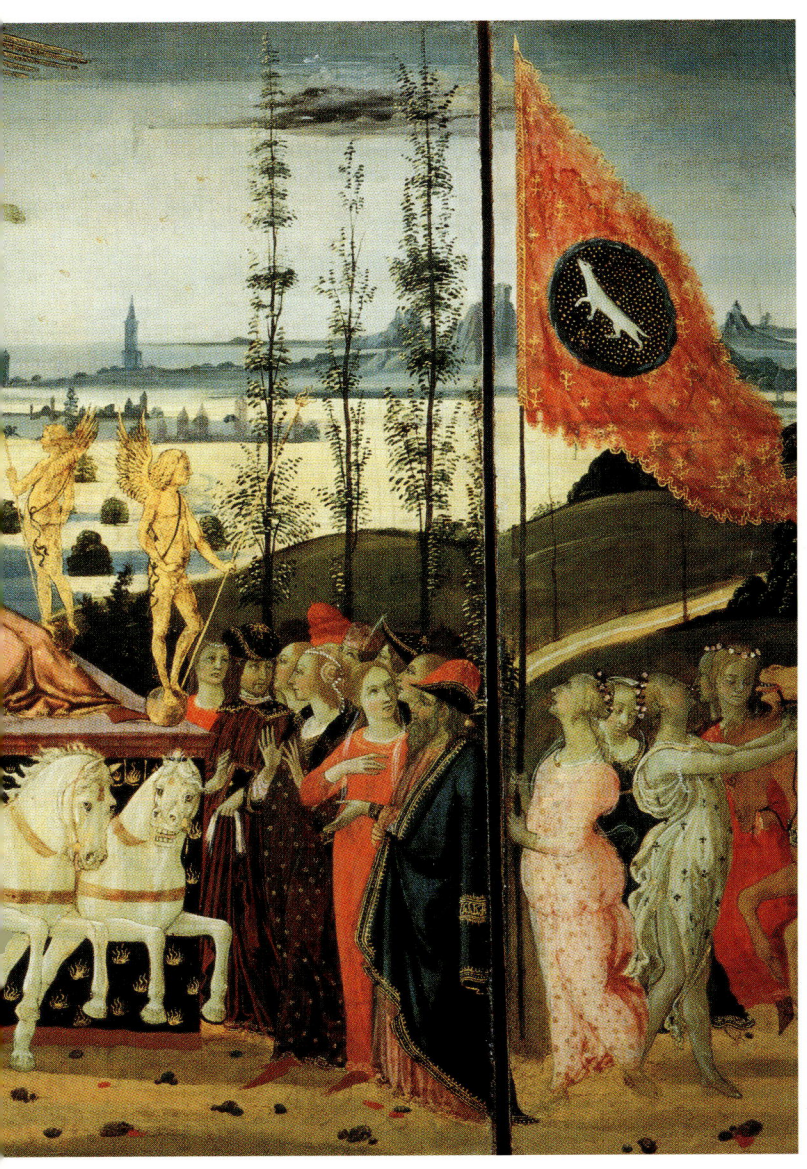

PLATE 3
Jacopo del Sellaio, *Triumph of Love*, Fiesole, Museo Bandini.
(Photograph by Nicolò Orsi Battaglini)

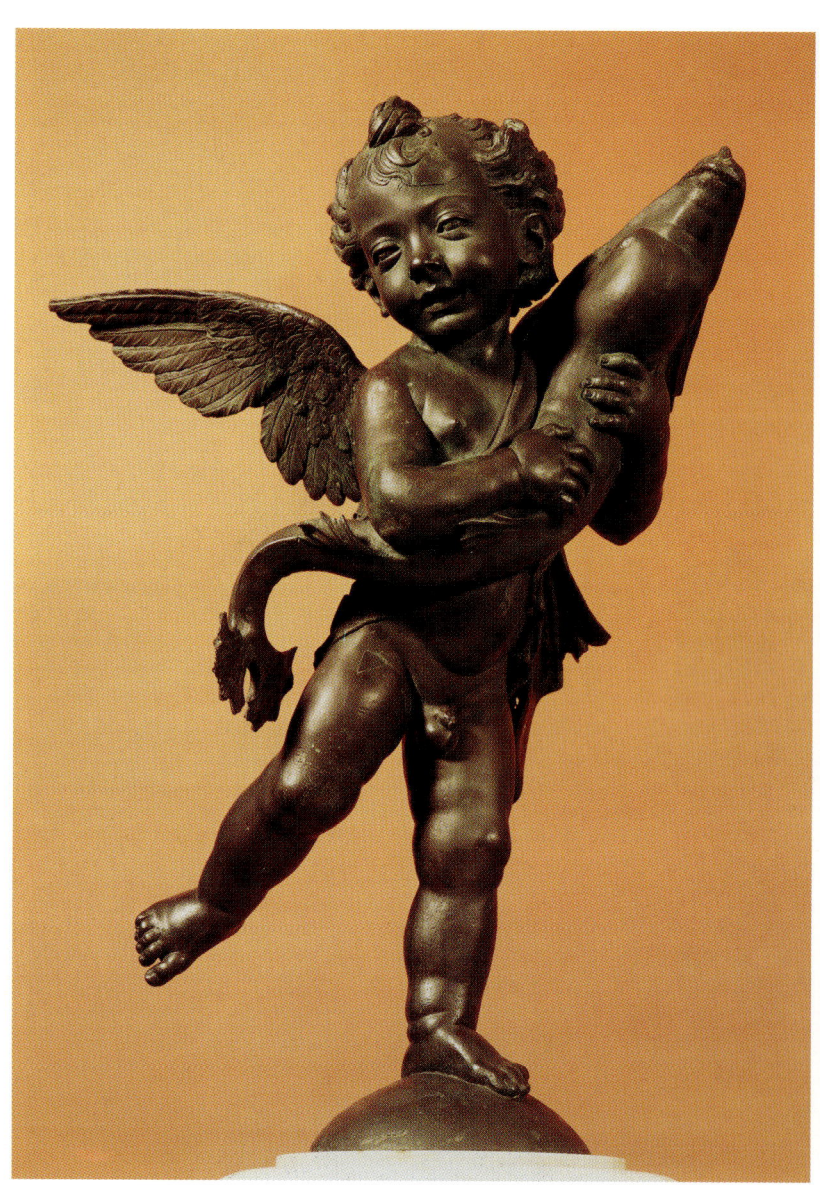

PLATE 4
Andrea del Verrocchio, *Putto with a Dolphin*, Florence, Palazzo Vecchio.
(Photograph: Scala/Art Resource)

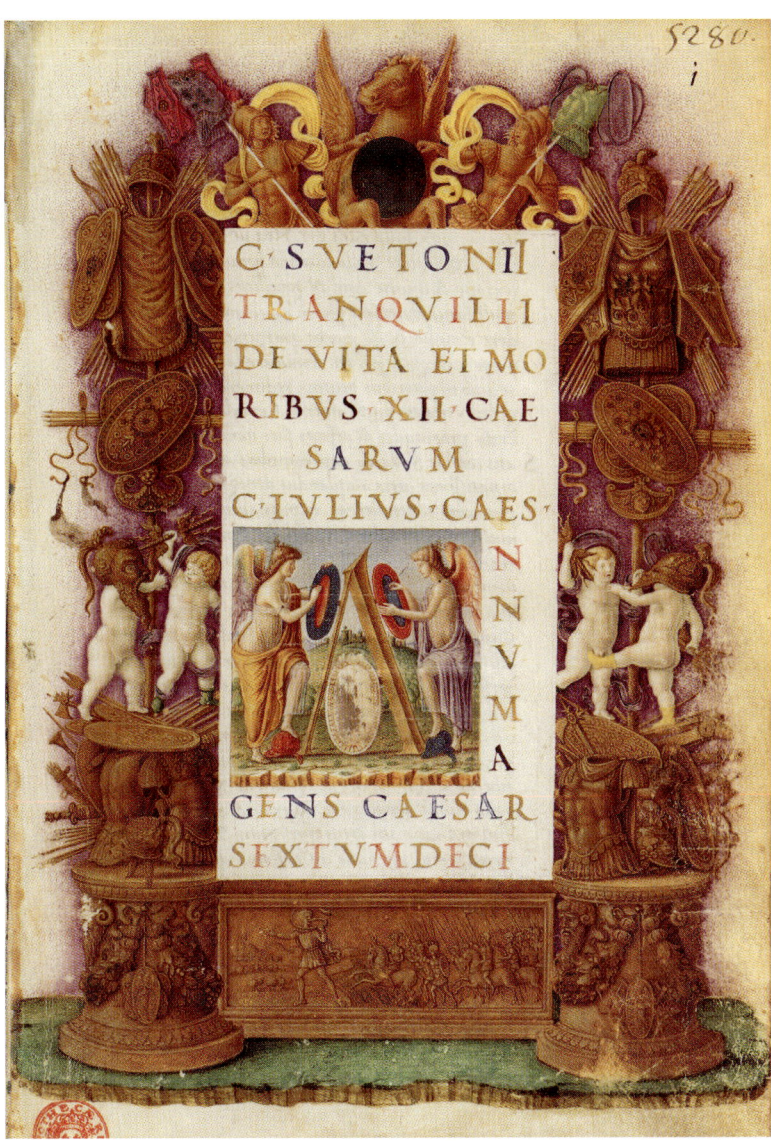

PLATE 5
Bartolomeo Sanvito, frontispiece to Suetonius, *Lives of the Caesars*, Paris,
Bibliothèque Nationale (ms. lat. 5814, fol. 1r.). Detail, *Larvate Putti Fighting*.
(Photograph: Cliché Bibliothèque Nationale de France, Paris)

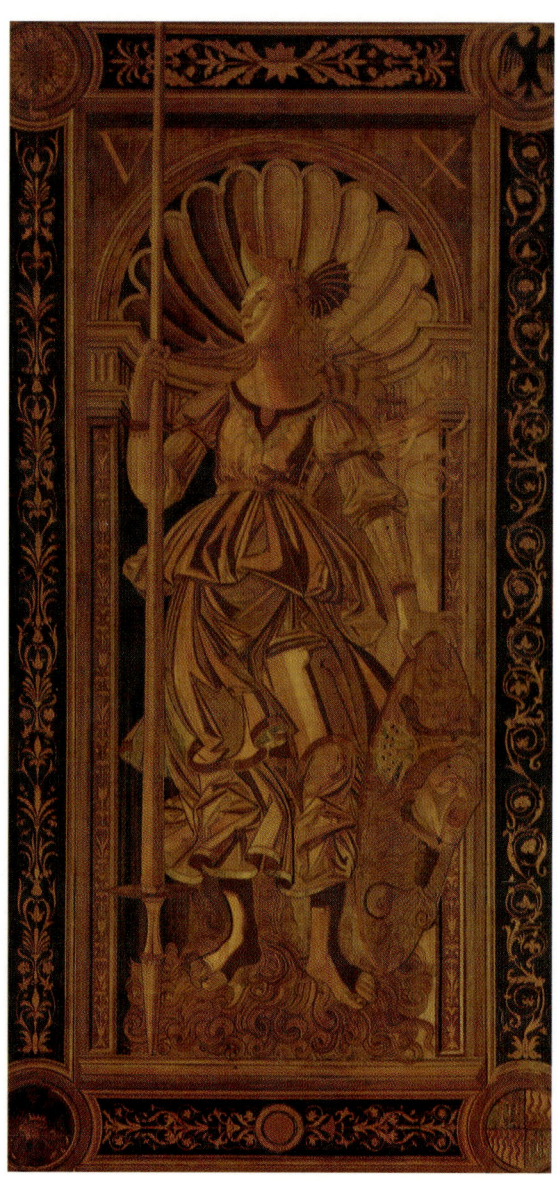

PLATE 6
Pallas with the Broncone, intarsia panel, Urbino, Palazzo Ducale.
(Photograph: Soprintendenza per I Beni artistici e Storiche per le Marche)

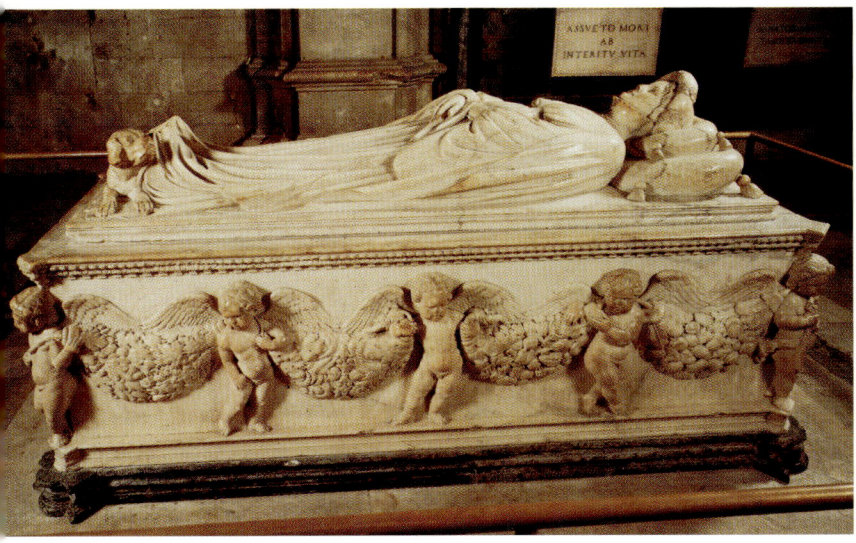

PLATE 7
Jacopo della Quercia, *Tomb of Ilaria del Carretto*, Lucca, S. Martino.
(Photograph: Scala/Art Resource)

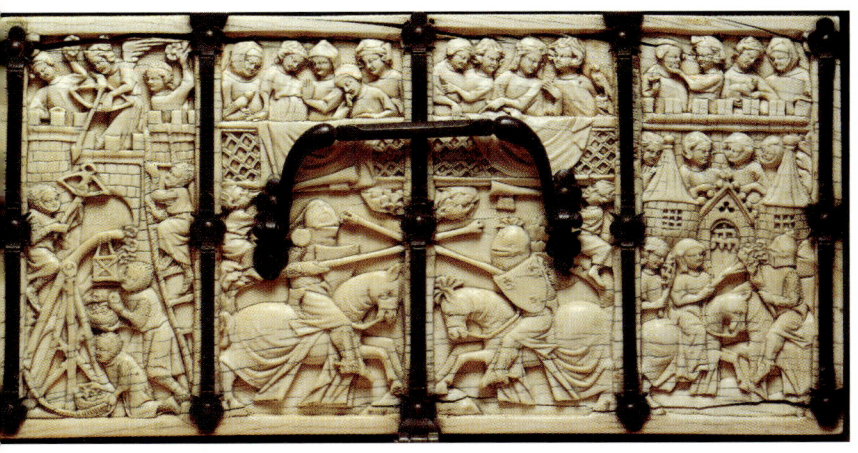

PLATE 8
A Joust before the Castle of Love, ivory casket, French, fourteenth century,
Baltimore, The Walters Art Gallery. (Photograph: The Walters Art Gallery)

they express sexual noxia, harmless, in Apuleius's words, to good men, but harmful to the susceptible or wicked, filling them with what Freud called hysterical anxieties and obsessive phobias, or what Politian named nympholeptic and panic terrors. They are by definition *terriculamenta*, the bugbears who provoke those *phantasmata panicorum* that disturb the sleep of one sunk in a torpid state of moral confusion and sensual self-indulgence. As we have seen, Politian defined such terrors in the *Miscellanea* as *lymphatici metus*, which are the terrors of the truly possessed (*lymphaticus* being synonymous, as Politian and Giraldi both note, with the Greek *nympholeptós*).[64] Lymphatic terrors turn the limbs to water, and are the terrors of those rapt, as by the nymphs, or by some god, or by a demon.

An extreme instance of nympholeptic possession is that of Hylas, whom the sight of the nymphs drew to his death in the water. In the *Nutricia* Politian wrote of *lymphatus Bacis* in reference to the Boeotian poet whom Pausanias and Cicero report was thought to have had the power of divination because of the frenzy roused in him by the nymphs.[65] Botticelli's Mars, on the other hand, is in the thrall of the coldly beautiful nymph—Venus herself—who lies alertly opposite him and directs the *panisci* in their work. She too is a demonic phantom, an image of Venus who, like the specter of Venus that led Paris astray in the *Historia destructionis Troiae*, is in reality a deceiving *lamia*. She is the object of Mars's hallucinatory panics, the nightmare phantasm who haunts his sleep. Far from representing benevolent harmony and bountiful marriages, Botticelli's Venus promises no true peace and release from strife at all, but only a confused image of idleness and self-indulgent pleasure that seem to turn back upon Mars and threaten him with harm. She is the spirit of that luxuriousness and seduction that has disarmed and unmanned *Mavors armipotens*, reducing the spirit of a once gloriously virile martial valor to ineffective and confused effeminacy and impotence.[66]

Grammatical investigation has forced a rethinking of the way in which we have perceived and experienced the relationships and actions of the figures within Botticelli's *Mars and Venus*, and renders problematic how we are to *see* and respond to the painting in its full psychological and emotional expressiveness. That there is high erotic content in the painting has generally been acknowledged, and this perception has been assisted by the understanding that the love of Mars and Venus is Botticelli's theme. Botticelli's erotic content has also been universally characterized as lighthearted and playful, something which is true, but also not so easy to reconcile with the terrors of the nightmare or with imagery that is perhaps better understood as more seriously sexual rather than merely erotic in its concerns. The pictorial and expressive import of Mars's jousting lance and its relation to the panic-inducing conch-shell seems a sexual reference too obvious to be overlooked, despite occasional demurrals on the grounds that such a reading is anachronistically Freudian, or perhaps overly determined by a modern obsession with sexual symbolism, the lance constituting in any event an "unprovable" sexual allusion. Yet psychological and sexual obsession (the primary sources of the phantasms of the nightmare in ancient dream theory), and in particular erotic obsession, are explicitly Botticelli's themes in the *Mars and Venus*. Politian was too skilled a reader of Aristophanes not to know that the Greeks employed the word *cogxe*, meaning the pink cavity of a conch-shell, in a rude way.[67] It was he, after all, who discovered what Catullus meant by Lesbia's sparrow, and when he read Lucian's account of Alexander watching his bride being disrobed while *eros* lifted the great warrior's spear like a heavy beam he would not have missed the double-entendre.[68] Insofar as the ithyphallic *panisci* playing with Mars's armor and obscenely waggling their tongues in Botticelli's painting are in part specifically motivated by this very passage in Lucian, and since the imagery of his painting is specifically determined by Politian's Greek philological learning, it seems to me misguided not to acknowledge the explicitly sexual signification of the lance and conch-shell.

 To perceive erotic wit in Botticelli's *Mars and Venus* is far from misguided, in other words, but at the same time such a perception is itself problematic. We should be wary of reading the eroticism of the painting in an automatic way, in the spirit of mere erotic conventionality. Humanist playfulness, like that of the pre-Hellenistic Greeks, has a sharper edge, and the wit expressed in the invention of the painting—cued by the initial decision to substitute *panisci* for the personifications of *eros* itself—adds a sharp pungency to its erotic content, a hard sting that follows the deceptively simple responses of a lighthearted pleasure such as are implied in Lucian's description of *erotes* playing in the armor of Alexander. Botticelli's *panisci* are not harmless to the susceptible, nor are the concepts they embody, and the painting is concerned with real emotions and anxieties.

In this respect, it is worth reconsidering just what the *panisci* are doing with Mars's jousting lance, which appears in so suggestive a relationship to the panic-inducing conch shell, and which they have hefted and are running against the tree on which the god's head is rested. As they poke the tree with the point of the lance, a swarm of wasps who have nested in a hole in the trunk emerge from their home and begin to buzz angrily around Mars's head, adding to the general panicky confusions and tumults disturbing his slumber. The *panisci* are literally "stirring up a hornet's nest," to quote the familiar saying that derives from the Latin adage *Irritare crabrones*, cited by Plautus in the *Amphitryone*. The Roman proverb itself derives from the Greek "To stir up a wasps' nest" (*sphekian erethisas*, as Erasmus has it in the *Adagia*), which in its turn is the source for the Italian *stuzzicare un vespaio*.[69] Erasmus adds that "The adage is applied by the poet [Plautus] to that spirit in women which, if roused in anger and you oppose them you only provoke all the more, nor do you escape without damage to yourself; for the hornet is a species of insect akin to the wasp, extremely tenacious and with a most pestilent sting."[70] So far as the Greek version of the proverb is concerned (and given the Greek foundation to the structure of Botticelli's invention it is this that is directly pertinent), the sexual reference is particularly explicit. The most famous Greek exemplification of the adage, which Erasmus also cites, appears in Aristophanes's *Lysistrata*, where the women of Athens, having pledged to withhold sexual favors from their men until they cease making war, warn their husbands and lovers not to seek honey in a wasps' nest—for if they try forcibly to plunder sweet honey where none exists they will only bring down a swarm of wasps round their heads (*è mè tis ósper sphekiài blítte me karethíze*).[71] We are therefore given to understand that for Botticelli's Mars there is no prospect of probing the honied rewards of Venus, but only the promise of a ferocious sting from the wasps provoked by the demon *panisci* at the bidding of the phantom *lamia* who fills his dreams in Venus's image.

SPIRITS OF THE NIGHTMARE

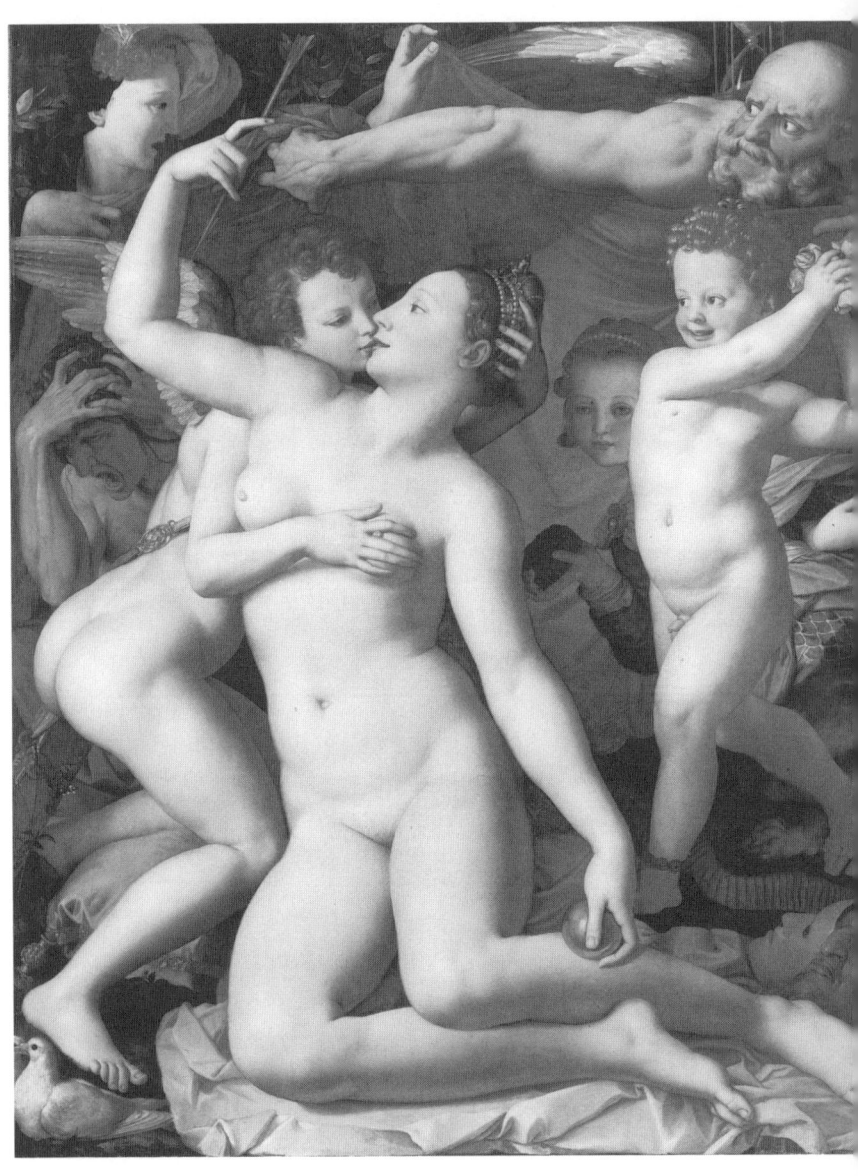

FIGURE 86
Bronzino, *Venus, Folly and Time*, London, National Gallery.
(Photograph © National Gallery)

A similar concept is expressed by appeal to a different, and more familiar visual metaphor in Bronzino's famous allegory of *Venus and Cupid* in London (Fig. 86). There a *lamia* is shown in attendance upon Venus, presenting a beautiful face to the viewer and seeming to offer the sweetness contained in the honeycomb she holds in her hand—but hidden under her dress is a reptilian body tapering to a monstrous tail armed with a terrible sting.[72]

Mars lies asleep in the shade of a tree at noon. He has removed his armor and dreams of Venus and love. But the dream he dreams is not truly of love. It is a dream of sensual desire, of sexual conquest and possession, which in turn possesses him. His dream is not a true vision but a nightmare, a nympholeptic phantasm of Venus who is only a *lamia*, a figment or demon bugbear of his own imagining that occupies and fills his every waking thought and desire, and which returns to haunt his sleep. He is further "bugged" by the phantom demons of the noonday, hobgoblin *panisci*, who seem to inhabit his own armor and to attack him from within it, turning the very instruments of his particular power, his martial armipotence, against him.[73] One panic bugbear lies sequestered in his cuirass, a second trumpets into his ear the reverberating sounds of terrified rout and tumultuous confusion, and two others lift his lance and advance in his direction. One of them is masked in Mars's own fearful helmet, the sight of which alone and empty can put whole armies to panicky flight, and together they direct Mars's lance against the god himself, idly thumping its point against the barren wasps' nest in the trunk of the tree against which he rests his head. The Greek invention for Botticelli's *Mars and Venus*, however sophisticated and witty in its philological foundations and pictorial disposition it may be, itself possesses a sharp pungency, *quasi vespa dimisso aculeo*. It is not concerned with merely straightforward or harmless erotic titillation, but with unfulfilled desire, a desire that returns to torment its author with turbulent and threatening phantasms, and it is an invention that treats of moral, spiritual, and psychological disaster. Mars is unmanned and helpless because of his obsession with a false image of love and beauty that bleeds him of all his strength and virility. The image fills and conquers his soul with childish anxieties and impotent

SPIRITS OF THE NIGHTMARE

panic fears, being only a phantasm that has in the end left him prey to the siren's promise of paradise here in earth, seeming to offer him a permanent state of sensual bliss. The promise is a delusion, as false as his own desire that wished it. Mars's dream is a nightmare that has left him in a state of moral confusion and inability to act, even in the fulfillment of his own false desire itself. We must now bend our efforts toward an understanding of what the false dream of love is that possesses him, and why he has been reduced to so timid and pitiful a condition.

CHAPTER FOUR

Politian's *Stanze per la Giostra di Giuliano de' Medici*

Julio's False Dream

THE DECADE in which Botticelli painted the *Mars and Venus* corresponds with a moment of extreme preoccupation with demons and witchcraft in Europe, and it is not at first an obvious decision whether we are to understand the *Satyrisci* who torment Mars in his picture as physical bodies or airy phantoms. On the one hand, we have seen that such *spiritelli* are only phantasms, the false semblances, or even projections of the empty terrors that afflict the soul; as Spenser wrote of such nightmarish delusions, the sleeper, disturbed by "troublous sights and dreames," suddenly "wakes with fearful frights, / As one aghast with feends or damned sprights" (*The Faerie Queene* 2.4). On the other hand, the classical and post-classical materials with which we have been dealing are in large part those also mined by writers on demonology and witchcraft. The ancient and patristic sources discussed in the last chapter provide the foundation to the argument of the *Malleus maleficarum*, which was published by order of Innocent VIII in the same decade that the *Mars and Venus* was painted.[1] Giovanni Francesco Pico's *Strix* was itself written in the context of inquisitorial witches' trials that took place in Mirandola in the 1520s, trials of the sort that Carlo Ginzburg has vividly described.[2] Leaving aside the practical desire of the authorities to put an end to socially aberrant and religiously blasphemous behavior, arising out of the old forms of popular superstition still deeply rooted in rural and peasant communities, the specific theological issue at bottom is this: are witches and vampires (*lamiae*), demon sprites and ghosts (*larvae*), creatures with corporeal substance who are capable of having sexual intercourse with human beings and reproducing their kind? Or are they airy spirits only, performing their evil and depraved deceptions by inhabiting the bodies of ordinary mortals, deluding them into wickedness? Enlightened resolution of this question (if such there be) is not helped by the fact that St. Augustine firmly espoused the former theory, and was followed in his belief by the Dominican authors of the *Malleus maleficarum*; and that Pope Innocent VIII, in his infamous bull of 5 December 1484, declared it a heresy to think otherwise. By either definition demons have real existence—the question is whether that existence is bodily or ethereal.

There is no doubt that Politian himself subscribed to the latter theory. This appears not only from his definition of the terrors of Pan as *phantasmata*, but also from his statements about witches in his *Lamia*, where he speaks of them as the sowers of false delusions, really as the bogeys of popular opinion that persecute and ridicule serious thinkers. The view of demons that emerges from Politian's writings is much more interesting than the suppositions of the witch-hunters, for it shows him concerned with far deeper social and individual psychological and pathological phenomena, and in a way not so remote from Freud or Jung as we might suppose.[3] For him panic terrors are a *phantasma*, and according to the ancient physicians the nightmare is a kind of sickness, *morbus*, resulting either from a disorder of the body or the soul.

Politian's deep interest in medicine and the symptoms of pathology has been extensively studied, and it has been shown in great detail how widely read he was in the medical literature.[4] The ancient physicians conceived the psychological (as opposed to the divinatory) dream as a movement of the soul, whether occasioned by simple indigestion, by disease, or by psychic disturbance. It is the soul that creates images which the reason may afterward interpret, diagnose for symptoms of illness, or psychoanalyze if you will. The personal status of the dreamer, his or her mental and physical health, determines the visions seen and experienced in *insomnium* and *incubus* (which by and large—in accordance with Artemidorus—were considered much the same), and consequently determines their interpretation.[5] All people dream about what has preoccupied them when awake, and the airy visions of the dream are accordingly shadows of real substances.[6] If the body or soul is disordered, the dreams will be nightmares, whether the result of the deliria produced by fever or an epileptic seizure (as in the citation from Euripides's *Medea* by Politian in his chapter on panic terrors), or whether provoked by the fantasies of an obsessed mind.[7]

So far as the deliria produced by physical disease are concerned, Perosa in an exemplary article has analyzed in close detail how Politian drew upon his medical knowledge for a new poetic invention, one without specific classical precedent, that of the goddess Fever (*Febris*) for his epicedion on the death of Albiera degli Albizzi.[8] Albiera, the young fiancée of Sigismondo della Stufa, had been suddenly struck down by illness after an open-air dance given in honor of Eleonora of Aragon in June of 1473, and she died a few days later. Perosa showed how Politian personified the fever that attacked Albiera, *Febris*, torch in one hand and snow in the other to induce the dying girl's alternating flushes and chills, and how in describing her particular illness he invented a new encompassing myth of this fell goddess Fever on the basis of "an imaginative technique derived from the classics, which he adapted to his own artistic sensibility." Politian did this by drawing on the one hand from ancient literary sources and myths (prominent among them, for example, Ovid's description of the Fury Tisiphone and her entourage), and on the other hand drawing from the specific symptoms of morbid pathology that are described in the medical texts. *Febris*, whom Politian conceived as one of the mythical children of Erebus and Night, not only is accompanied by familiar and broadly based literary personifications, such as *Luctus* and *Mors*, but also by quite unfamiliar and specifically pathological ones— *anhela Sitis* of the burning throat, *horridus Rigor*, the terrible sounds of *frequens Singultus*, and *inconstans Rubor*—all personifying the medical symptoms of Albiera's disease. The same is true of *ferox Anxietas*, *Insania* of the terrified face, *Insomnia* agitating the poor girl's fevered soul, and *Terrificus Pavor*, the overwhelming terror that deprives her of reason. The latter two, *Insomnia* and *Terrificus Pavor*, perplexed Perosa because he took them for personifications derived from ancient literature, which he combed in vain for precise parallels.⁹ As we saw in the last chapter, however, they are instead, like *Sitis* and *Singultus*, pathological symptoms described by the ancient physicians, who identified the panic terrors induced by *Pan Terrificus* not only with the nympholeptic experiences produced by being possessed by some demon or god, but also with the symptoms of fever and epileptic seizure. *Terrificus pavor* is produced by the nightmarish *phantasmata* of delirium (*Insomnia*), which seem to transport the soul beyond rational or bodily bounds and fill the patient with tremendous dread. Here is Politian's description of Fever and her train:

> Hic Febrim aethereas carpentem prospicit auras,
>   exerere Icarius dum parat ora Canis.
> Illam Erebo Nocteque satam comitantur euntem
>   luctusque et tenebris mors adoperta caput,
> et gemitus gravis et gemitu commixta querela
>   singultusque frequens anxietasque ferox,
> et tremor et macies, pavidoque insania vultu,
>   semper et ardenti pectore anhela sitis,
> horridus atque rigor trepidaeque insomnia mentis,
>   inconstansque rubor terrificusque pavor.¹⁰

([Nemesis] espied the chariot of Fever in the heavenly airs, at the time when the constellation Icarius prepared to bare the face of the Dog Star. She is the child of Erebus and Night, and those who accompany her are Affliction and Death, head covered in shadows, Deep Groaning, Complaint mixed with sighs, frequent Rattling, implacable Anxiety, Trembling and Emaciation, Madness with a terrified face, panting Thirst always burning in the throat, horrid Stiffness, and restless Dream of the fearful mind, together with inconstant Flushing and tremendous Dread.)

With regard to psychological disorder, on the other hand, we have already seen that the ancient physicians were interested in the fact that nightmares are often sexual in nature, and that the terrors of the nightmare commonly result from sexual preoccupation. It is no accident that the demons of the *incubus* are Pan and his band of Fauns and Satyrs, whose sexual proclivities need no documentation. Nightmare phantasms are especially associated, as we have learned from Macrobius, with the preoccupations and fears of lovers, and such deluding specters, or empty *ombre*, were well established as a topos in vernacular poetry long before they were philologically associated with Pan. Thus, Petrarch describes how he has been led astray by such *mentite larve*:

> Diceami il cor che per sé non saprebbe
> viver un giorno; e poi tra via m'apparve
> quel traditore in sì mentite larve
> che più saggio di me ingannato avrebbe.[11]

(My heart tells me that by itself it would not know how to live a single day; and then in my path there appeared to me that traitor masked in such deceiving *larve* that one wiser than myself would have been led astray.)

When in 1466 Luigi Pulci sent his remarkable *canzone* "Da poi che 'l Lauro" to Lorenzo de'Medici in Rome, informing him that his mistress and poetic *donna* Lucrezia Donati, only recently married to Niccolò Ardinghelli, was filled with misery and remorse and had become obsessed with the idea of divorce and withdrawal into the convent, he conveyed her obsessiveness to Lorenzo by writing that Lucrezia was in the thrall of an *ombra*, the phantom of her famously chaste ancestress Piccarda Donati, who had also sought refuge from an unwanted marriage in the convent.[12] Pulci had not at first been aware of the presence of Piccarda's *ombra*, in whose steps Lucrezia was compelled to tread, and when he did learn of the phantom's presence he was himself *tosto aombrato per subito parvenza*—immediately struck, his mind boggled by a sudden, larval terror—the very definition of panic terrors as later put forward by Politian:

> "Né già per me sarei
> condocta qui; ma scorgemi questa ombra."
> Allor fec'io come huom che tosto aombra
> per subita parvenza, et dixi: "Hor questa

>   sì bella et sì modesta
>   che è, se 'l Lauro tuo ti doni pace?"[13]

([She said:] "Nor have I been led here through myself, but this phantom leads me." Then I reacted like a man who all at once is spooked by a sudden terror, and I said: "Now who is this creature, so beautiful and so modest, if your Lauro gives you peace?")

Lorenzo's reply to Pulci's *canzone* was a sonnet, certainly intended for Lucrezia herself, in which he responds to Pulci's description of her obsession, and by echoing Pulci's very words, and goes on to observe that empty terrors often haunt the *alma spaventata* of lovers, among whom he includes himself:

>   Fortuna, come suol, pur mi dileggia
>   e di vane speranze ognor m'ingombra,
>   poi si muta in un punto e mostra ch'ombra
>   è quanto pe' mortal' si pensa o veggia.
>   Or benigna si fa e ora aspreggia,
>   or m'empie di pensier', e or mi sgombra,
>   e fa che l'alma spaventata aombra,
>   né par che del suo male ancor s'avveggia.
>   Teme, spera, rallegrasi e contrista
>   ben mille volte il dì nostra natura:
>   spesso il mal la fa lieta, il bene attrista.
>   Spera il suo danno, e del bene ha paura:
>   tanto ha il viver mortal corta la vista.
>   Alfin vano è ogni pensiero e cura.[14]

(Fortune, as is her custom, always derides me and every moment fills me with empty hopes, then changes in an instant and shows that everything thought or seen by mortals is but a phantom. Now she shows herself benign, now bitter, one moment she clutters my mind with thoughts, and the next empties me of them, and she boggles my terrified soul, which does not even seem capable of seeing its own harm. A good thousand times a day our nature fears, hopes, rejoices, and saddens, and is often made happy by the ill while taking sorrow from the good; so short is the sight of mortal existence that it hopes for its own harm, and fears its good. In the end every thought is empty and burdensome.)

We are now in a position to see how the profoundly humanist, Greek foundation to the invention of Botticelli's *Mars and Venus* naturally and without difficulty finds its vernacular expressive parallel in the poetry of Pulci and Lorenzo de'Medici. Even as Lucrezia Donati is obsessed by the *ombra* of the chaste Piccarda, who is only a misleading phantasm conjured up by her own confused desires, so Botticelli's Mars is possessed by the *ombra* of Venus. His *alma spaventata* is also *aombrata* by empty *larve*, idle preoccupations that burden his thoughts. The metaphor of the confused lover as "spooked" (*spaventata*) by empty fears, frightened by shadows like a suddenly shying horse, has a long pedigree. A good example is provided by Petrarch's sonnet 227, where the poet, transfixed by the sight of the breeze that wafts through Laura's hair and settles in her eyes, tells of the confused and contradictory meanderings of his mind between images of his beloved that are real and those that are only expressions of his own vexed and painful desires. The image of the wasps also resonates powerfully with that of Botticelli's *Mars and Venus*:

> tu stai nelli occhi ond' amorose vespe
> mi pungon sì che 'n fin qua il sento et ploro,
> et vacillando cerco il mio tesoro
> come animal che spesso adombre e 'ncespe;
> ch'or mel par ritrovar et or m'accorgo
> ch' i' ne son lunge, or mi sollievo or caggio,
> ch'or quel ch' i' bramo or quel ch' è vero scorgo.[15]

(You are in those eyes whence amorous wasps sting me so hard that even from here I feel it and weep, and uncertainly wandering I seek my treasure like an animal that is often spooked and stumbles; for one moment it seems to me I have found her, and the next I realize I am far away; now I take comfort, and now I am dejected, for in one moment I see what I desire, in the next what is real.)

Normally, of course, it is Love's dart that strikes from the amorous eyes of the poet's lady, not the hard stings of wasps, such as those that also afflict Botticelli's Mars. He too is anguished and confused (much more so in fact than is Petrarch), and the situation shown in the painting, despite the profound Hellenism of its invention, more closely resembles a familiar *koinos topos* of romance poetry than it does the classical fable of Mars's subjugation by Venus. A perception of Botticelli's conceit as something that finds its expression in the context of vernacular poetry, moreover, and therefore in the experiences of the present, is reinforced by the contemporaneity of Venus's *camicia da giorno* and Mars's sallet and jousting lance. The topos to which I refer, and in which Botticelli's invention is founded, is that of late-medieval and Renaissance literary dream visions. Such oneiric revelations were well established as literary topoi, the conventions of which ultimately derive from ancient models—Pamphilia's dream of Er in Plato's *Republic*, Cicero's *Somnium Scipionis*, and Macrobius's commentary to the *Dream of Scipio* providing familiar and extremely influential examples.[16] Dream visions provide the governing structure for many of the most famous and influential works of the later middle ages, among them Alain de Lille's *De planctu Naturae*, Guillaume de Lorris and Jean de Meung's *Roman de la rose*. Petrarch adopted the convention in the *Secretum* and the *Trionfi*, and Boccaccio was especially addicted to it, employing the dream vision in *Fiammetta*, *Filocolo*, the *Teseida*, the *Corbaccio*, the *Ninfale fiesolano*, and the *Amorosa visione*. Politian himself used the dream vision as the foundation for the unfinished second book of the *Stanze per la Giostra*, which we will shortly consider in close detail, and it continued to play a fundamental role in later literature, from the *Hypnerotomachia Polifili* (in which we experience the special disorientation of a dream within a dream) to Ariosto's *Orlando furioso*, Tasso's *Gerusalemme liberata*, and beyond.

Typically the dream vision occurs as a moral turning point, and is the means by which the hero, lost and confused in a state of sensual indulgence and moral bewilderment, is led to a higher position of enlightenment and understanding—although Boccaccio varied the convention in the *Amorosa visione* by seeming to leave the dreamer in a state of even deeper confusion, and Politian's dream of Julio in the *Stanze*, as we shall see, is presented as a false dream sent to lead the hero to his own destruction. The circumstances and topography of the hero's situation are highly conventionalized. The season is generally spring, and the hero, following his sensual appetites and immersed in a state of self-indulgent lethargy (preoccupied, in short, with the *phantasmata* of the sensory world), finds himself alone and separated from his companions and entering a beautiful meadow, a trackless waste, or perhaps a dark forest. He sinks into exhausted slumber by a spring, or in a wooded copse, and there appears to him a guide, who strikes him dumb with fright. The vision afflicts the hero with deep confusion—Tancred, for example, in Tasso's *Gerusalemme* is deeply concerned whether he has seen the real Clorinda or only a demon in her form. Even after the dream is over, the hero conventionally revives in a state of persistent doubt whether all he has seen and heard was real, and wondering whether the dream is true, or whether, like Guido delle Colonna's shepherd Paris, he has been enraptured by some demon who tempts him to his own destruction. A typical example appears in Spenser's account of Prince Arthur's dream in *The Faerie Queene*, and I quote it because of the uncanny similarity it bears to the imagery of Botticelli's *Mars and Venus*, which of course the poet could not have known. He tells how Arthur, after a day spent "ranging the forest wide on courser free," lies down upon the grass, using his helmet as a pillow; and how in sleep he thinks he sees a beautiful maiden, who comes and lies down beside him. Whether the dream he then had were true or not he was unable to say, but it seemed to him the maid requested his love:

> For-wearied with my sports, I did alight
> From loftie steed, and downe to sleepe me layd;
> The verdant gras my couch did goodly dight,
> And pillow was my helmet faire displayd:
> Whiles every sence the humour sweet embayd,
> And slombring soft my hart did steale away,
> Mee seemed, by my side a royall Mayd
> Her daintie limbes full softly down did lay:
> So faire a creature yet saw never sunny day.[17]

As it happens, Prince Arthur's dream is true, and the lady who appears so enticingly to him in his vision is Gloriana. The dream mirrors, however, another one that had occurred earlier in the poem. This dream was conjured by the magician Archimago, who had sent two "sprights" (or *spiritelli*), "the falsest two," to Morpheus so that he might fashion "a fit false dreame, that can delude the sleepers sent." One of them, returning, settles on the head of the sleeping Redcrosse knight:

> And made him dreame of loves and lustfull play,
> That nigh his manly hart did melt away,
> Bathed in wanton blis and wickèd ioy:
> Then seemed him his Lady by him lay . . .[18]

Two dreams, one true and one false. How is the dreamer to know? And how are we as witnesses to these dream visions to resolve the doubts that are so characteristic of the conventions of the form, and so essential to understanding the artist's allegory aright? So far as Spenser is concerned the answer is clear. The vision of love offered to Prince Arthur is as chaste as it is delightful, and its truth will be revealed "as when just time expired should appeare." The Redcrosse Knight's dream, on the other hand, is of immediate sensual satisfaction (and frustration), immersing him "in wanton blis and wicked ioy." The reader has also been party to the fell plotting of Archimago, whose wiles have conjured up the phantasm that will delude his victim. In the case of Botticelli's Mars the answer is also ready to hand, for we already know that he is tormented by nightmare *larvae* induced by the *lamia* Venus who possesses him, making him fitfully "dreame of loves and lustfull play."

Less easy to resolve, however, is the question of a parallel dream, one which, like the dream of the Redcrosse knight, is modeled on Ovid's story of Juno sending Iris to the cave of Somnus to form an empty dream in the shape of Ceyx to deceive Alcyone (*Metamorphoses* 11.592–632), and one which may itself have served as an additional model for Spenser. This is the dream of Julio, the figure for Giuliano de'Medici in Politian's *Stanze per la Giostra di Giuliano fratello del Magnifico Lorenzo de'Medici*. The problems of interpreting Politian's poem arise not only from the density and erudition of the poet's language and conceits, but also from the fact that his imaginative point of departure was an historical event. As Eugenio Donato has noted, despite the sense of formal purity and poetical abstraction projected by Politian's linguistic refinement and his mastery and virtually infinite citation of Latin and vernacular models, his characters do not have autonomous existence within the frame of the *Stanze* itself. They can only be understood (and the poem interpreted) in terms of the real people and events hidden behind and motivating their poetical names and actions.[19] The problem of interpretation is made yet more difficult by virtue of the fact that the point of departure for Politian's poem was a joust that took place early in 1475. As an event this too was an imaginative representation, a display of chivalric culture and civic idealism enacted in a ritual that was itself an expression of the collective public imagination, no less than that of the individual participants.[20] The leading contestant was Giuliano de'Medici, soon to be the victim of treachery and murder in the Pazzi Conspiracy of 1478 and the brother of Florence's leading citizen, Politian's patron Lorenzo the Magnificent, to whom the *Stanze* was dedicated. What is more, the symbolic structure of the poem arises in large part from the particular, personal chivalric and poetic symbolism that Giuliano had earlier adopted for the joust.

Giuliano had dedicated his knightly valor to the lady Simonetta Cattaneo Vespucci, and he entered the arena bearing a standard painted by Botticelli with an allegorical portrayal of her in the guise of Pallas. The standard, listed as still being in the Palazzo Medici in an inventory drawn up at the time of Lorenzo's death in 1492, is now lost. Politian's poem, together with accounts of the joust in contemporary chronicles and poems in both Latin and the vernacular, has naturally been used as evidence for reconstructing Botticelli's imagery and interpreting its possible symbolism as an expression of Giuliano's knightly idea. To a certain degree this is possible, but at the same time we must not lose sight of the fact that Politian's use of that symbolism in the *Stanze* was put to the service of his own poetic invention, and that he adapted the allegory of the standard as the poetic key for unlocking his own retrospective, and quite independent, interpretation of the meaning of the idea of chivalric and poetic love that

Giuliano had intended to express in the image painted on his ensign. Because the symbolism of the standard was adapted to Politian's poetic imagination, it is vain to suppose that his meaning corresponds to Giuliano's *tout court*. Before embarking upon an analysis of the *Stanze*, therefore, it is necessary to look into the joust itself, its context, and other accounts given of the standard's symbolism.

The joust took place on 29 January 1475 in the piazza of Santa Croce, which had been fitted round with banks of seats constructed, in the words of the humanist poet Naldo Naldi, *romani more theatri*.[21] The allusion to the spectacles staged in connection with Roman triumphs was apt, for the joust had been ordained, in accordance with law and custom, by the *Capitani di Parte Guelfa* in order to celebrate a treaty of peace concluded on 2 November 1474 between Florence and the rival powers of Italy. Preparations began immediately, as we know from a letter written that same month to Ludovico Gonzaga by Pietro del Tovaglia, the Marchese's observer in Florence, telling him his son Rodolfo's participation was desired, alerting him of the expenses to expect, and urging him to send some good horses ("perché qua si fa gran conto di chi manda assai cavagli degni da giostra").[22] As early as 11 December a kind of practice scrimmage was held for the testing of armor and equipment, as well as the skills of the young combatants. Lorenzo de'Medici organized the event, seeking support and participation from the principal cities and courts of Italy, but was not himself a contestant. The honor of being the leading participant fell to Giuliano, who was awarded the first prize at the end of the day's passages of arms.

Such chivalric spectacles were extremely popular, and many descriptions of them survive in prose and in poetry, so much so that they have been aptly characterized as virtually comprising a literary genre of their own.[23] To be sure, some descriptions are merely *ricordi* with no literary pretense, giving little more than a list of the combatants, their horses and armor, harnesses and caparisons studded with jewels, their even more munificently bejeweled costumes, splendidly liveried entourages, and their devices beautifully painted, often by the principal artists of the city, on ensigns carried before them into the arena by their standard-bearers. Some of them, however, appear in the form of humanist epistles addressed to friends but meant to be read by a wider audience. Some are vernacular poems written in more or less popularizing modes, and some are quite highly polished Latin verses. The importance of such descriptions goes well beyond the evidence they give of the magnificence and high pageantry of the tournaments per se, for in a fundamental way they are equally a part of the phenomenon of the celebrations themselves, being parallel expressions of the honor of the city. As Kristeller has written, the centrality of such festivals and tournaments to Renaissance culture was due not so much to "the luxury and magnificence of their display (however great that may have been), as to the contribution they made to the arts, to the enthusiasm with which both nobles and *popolani* took part in them, and to the interest they inspired in the learned and unlearned, both present and absent."[24] Within such spectacles was concentrated the collective aspirations and vitality of the city, and the special importance of the more literarily ambitious descriptions of them derives from their testing of the rival claims of Latin and the vernacular to portray and to interpret the civic myth of honor they represented. The interconnectedness of the triumphal games held to celebrate the conclusion of treaties of peace and the coinciding artistic expression of the city's honor and glory is nowhere more succinctly expressed than in the words written by Lorenzo de'Medici (or perhaps by Politian on his behalf), in the epistle prefacing the *Raccolta Aragonese*, the collection of poems he sent to Federico d'Aragona two years after Giuliano's *giostra*:

> L'onore è veramente quello che porge a ciascuna arte nutrimento; né da altra cosa quanto dalla gloria sono gli animi de'mortali alle preclare opere infiammati. A questo fine adunque a Roma i magnifici trionfi, in Grecia i famosi giuochi del monte Olimpo, appresso ad ambedue il poetico ed oratorio certame con tanto studio fu celebrato. Per questo solo il carro ed arco trionfale, i marmorei trofei, li ornatissimi teatri, le statue, le palme, le corone, le funebre laudazioni, per questo solo infiniti altri mirabilissimi ornamenti furono ordinati; né d'altronde veramente ebbono origine li leggiadri ed al-

teri fatti e col senno e con la spada, e tante mirabili eccellenzie de'valorosi antichi, li quali sanza alcun dubbio, come ben dice il nostro toscano poeta, non saranno mai sanza fama, "se l'universo pria non si dissolve."[25]

(Honor is truly that which offers nourishment to each art; nor are the souls of mortals inflamed to the making of illustrious works by anything so much as glory. To this end then the magnificent triumphs in Rome, the famous games of Mount Olympus in Greece, following both of which a poetic and oratorical competition was publicly celebrated with great care. For this alone the chariot and triumphal arch, the marble trophies, the most ornate theatrical spectacles, the statues, the palms, the crowns, the funeral laudations, for this alone infinite other most wonderful ornaments were ordained; nor truly was it from anything else that the happy and exalted achievements both of the intellect and the sword took their origin, and so many admirable excellences of the valorous ancients, who without any doubt, as our Tuscan poet well says, will never be without fame, "if the universe does not first fall apart.")

Lorenzo's words not only shed light on the motivations for composing literary descriptions of the tournaments and jousts, but also on the poetic competitions inspired by moments of public mourning. It is sufficient to recall again Politian's elegy on the death of Albiera degli Albizzi in 1473, which won him his initial employment in the house of Lorenzo the Magnificent; and the many poems written in Latin and the vernacular, including four sonnets by Lorenzo himself, lamenting the death in 1476 of Simonetta Cattaneo, the beauty to whom Giuliano had pledged his honor in the joust only a year before.[26] This joust naturally was no exception to the tradition of writing both formal and informal celebratory descriptions. An anonymous *ricordo* in the Biblioteca Magliabechiana contains an exceptionally detailed description of the magnificence of the day's pageantry, and there survives in Venice a more literarily ambitious Latin epistle (significantly describing itself as an *opusculum* rather than as an *epistola*) written by Filippo Corsini to Pietro Guicciardini, "ut ex illis annalibus sive commentis digna quandoque historia conscribi possit."[27] Naldo Naldi wrote an elegant elegy entitled *Hexametrum carmen de ludicro hastatorum equitum certamine ad Iulianum Medicen virum clarissimum certaminis victorem*, and the Riminese poet Giovanni Aurelio Augurelli sent to Bernardo Bembo, then the Venetian ambassador in Florence, no fewer than nineteen poems referring more or less directly to the joust.[28] But the eternally lasting fame of Giuliano's joust does not derive from these, and it depends very little upon the pageantry and actual events that occurred that day in 1475. It derives instead from the vernacular poem commemorating Giuliano's chivalry, Politian's *Stanze*.

The spectacle itself certainly rivaled, and possibly even surpassed in magnificence another joust, second only in fame to Giuliano's, that had taken place six years before, on 7 February 1469, in which the leading participant had been Lorenzo himself, who also had carried away the first prize. This earlier joust also had been ordained in order to celebrate a treaty of peace, the peace made with Venice that had brought with it the defeat of the anti-Medicean *fuorusciti*. Lorenzo's victory found its poet in Luigi Pulci, whose "La giostra di Lorenzo" was completed in late 1474, only scant months before Giuliano's joust, to which Pulci refers expectantly in the final stanza.[29] Although the peace celebrated in Lorenzo's joust, which removed the city from mortal peril and consolidated Medici power in Florence, was if anything greater in significance than the treaty occasioning Giuliano's, the secondary fame of his tournament is the direct consequence of the stature of Pulci's poetic achievement in relation to that of Politian. The former poem is retrospective, a richly descriptive account of Lorenzo's joust written in the popularizing modes of the earlier century with roots in the Trecento, while the latter belongs to the future, being written not as a description but as an imaginative fiction of Giuliano's love of glory written in a language that laid the foundations for the more purified and classically elevated poetic expression of the century to come. In the *Stanze*, as Politian himself was fully aware (he writes of himself, "e rinnuova in suo stil gli antichi tempi"), there is for the first time manifest a transforming linguistic *renovatio* that was to alter forever the course of Italian poetry. As a work of art, his poem, in keeping with Lorenzo's cultural understanding (and cultural policy) as put forward in the preface to the *Raccolta Aragonese*, permanently embodies the honor of the city, earning for it a far more enduring fame than the ephemeral events of the individual jousts themselves.[30]

With regard to the actual jousts, Machiavelli writes with approval of how they turned the thoughts of a restless people to affairs of honor, and, referring to Lorenzo's joust, he adds that it was then the custom for the leading young men of the city to appear in the same arena with the most famous knights of Italy.[31] Filippo Corsini also writes, referring to Giuliano's joust, that an important purpose of such martial games was to test the skill and mettle of the city's youths, seeing how well *nostri iuvenes* (whom he also calls *tirones adolescentes*) would perform with veterans in equestrian combat.[32] The youth who acquitted himself with the most honor was awarded the prize by the *Capitani di Parte Guelfa*. It was the custom for these well-born contestants to enter the field magnificently costumed in the full panoply of chivalric display, presenting themselves as *preux chevaliers* who had each dedicated his individual valor to a particular lady, and each of whom was preceded into the arena by a *vexilifer* bearing a standard upon which was painted an allegorical image and a motto representing the idea of chivalric love invested in the *dama* to whom each pledged his tournament. Luigi Pulci refers to twelve such standards in "La giostra di Lorenzo," and describes several of them in some detail, including the banner painted by Verrocchio for Lorenzo. In that earlier joust Lorenzo had vowed his honor to Lucrezia Donati, the adolescent wife of Niccolò Ardinghelli, who was the poetic *donna* of his sonnets as well as the *dama* of his tourney, and on his standard was painted the allegory of his devotion.[33] The costumes and standards carried by many of the participants in Giuliano's *giostra* were similarly described by the anonymous witness who wrote the Magliabechiana *ricordo*. The most elaborate of the banners, and surely the most beautiful, was painted by Botticelli and carried by a standard-bearer into the arena before Giuliano, whose virtue, as we have seen, had been dedicated to the famous beauty Simonetta Cattaneo, the wife of Marco Vespucci. It was partially described in Latin verses in one of the poems sent to Bernardo Bembo by Giovanni Aurelio

Augurelli (one of which, *Amica ad magnanimum Iulianum Medicem*, describes the joust in the words of Giuliano's lady). The poem was written in response to Bembo's request for an explanation of Giuliano's idea:

> In signis quare Medici sit, Bembe, requiris
> Post tergum vinctis pictus manibus amor
> Sub pedibusque tenens arcus fractamque pharetram;
> Pendeat ex humeris nullaque penna suis;
> Atque solo teneat fixos immotus ocellos,
> Immeritum veluti sentiat ille crucem.
> Horrida cui terreti Pallas supereminet hasta
> Et galea et saeva gorgone terribilis.
> Multi multa ferunt, eadem sententia nulla est:
> Pulchrius est pictus istud imaginibus.[34]

(You ask me, O Bembo, why Love is painted on the Medici ensign with his hands bound behind his back, his bow and broken quiver lying at his feet; and why no feather hangs from his shoulders; and why he stands motionless, his eyes fixed upon the ground as if to show he feels his martyrdom is unmerited. The frightful Pallas, the more dreadful for her sallet and the savage Gorgon shield, raises her lance over the terrified boy. Some give one explanation of it, and some another, but none comes up with the same meaning: this is the most beautiful of the painted images.)

The author of the *Anonimo Magliabechiano*, on the other hand, gives a prose description of the pageantry of the joust in minute and loving detail, culminating with Giuliano's arrival, riding a grey horse named Orso, into the piazza of Santa Croce. Giuliano entered the field escorted by two men-at-arms and nine mounted trumpeters bearing pennants made of Alexandrian taffetta. The fields of the pennants were filled with olive branches and flames, and at the center of each was emblazoned a compass and the Medici coat of arms. The trumpeters wore Medici livery with the device of the olive branch and flames embroidered in gold and silver, and the crests of their helmets displayed a golden falcon with wings spread. Giuliano's horse was in full armor, the lateral plates covered by a dark violet fabric studded with pearls, diamonds, balas rubies, and sapphires, and the chestplate covered with white taffeta upon which the head of Medusa was embroidered in large pearls—all of which, so the anonymous diarist reports, were lost in the ensuing passages of arms. Giuliano himself was resplendent in rich brocades adorned with even more valuable jewels, and he wore upon his head a silk garland (i.e, a *mazzocchio*) with two white wings, at the center of which was a jewel of immense value and fame—*una gioia nominata per tucto il mondo*—formed of a diamond, a balas ruby, and three enormous pearls. He was preceded by his standard-bearer, and the author of the *ricordo* describes the ensign painted by Botticelli in great detail:

> He carried in his hand a large lance painted blue, to which was attached a standard made of Alexandrian taffeta, sewn and fringed all around, at the top of which there was a sun. In the middle of this standard there was a large figure in the likeness of Pallas clad in a gold garment that extended half way down her legs. Beneath this she wore a white dress shaded with ground gold. She had on her legs a pair of blue stitched boots, and she held her feet over two flames of fire. From this fire there issued forth flames which burned olive branches placed in the middle of the lower part of the standard, in the midst of which there were branches without fire. She had on her head a burnished sallet in the antique style, and her hair was all unbound so that it blew in the wind. The said Pallas held a jousting lance in her right hand, and in her left the shield of Medusa. Behind this figure was a meadow adorned with variously colored flowers, out of which grew an olive tree with a large branch to which a God of Love was tied, his hands bound behind his back with golden cords. A bow, quiver, and broken arrows lay at his feet. A brief written in golden letters in the French style was attached to the olive branch to which the God of Love was bound, saying *la sans par*. The aforementioned Pallas gazed fixedly into the sun which was above her.[35]

Though a comprehensive interpretation of the meaning of Giuliano's device is perhaps not possible, especially given the loss of the image itself, nevertheless its general signification can be stated with some confidence. A partial derivation from the standard does in fact survive in an intarsia panel in Urbino, which shows Pallas with lance and shield standing on the Medici device of the *broncone*, which is partly in flames (Plate 6). The image of bound Love is also easily imaginable with the assistance of Baccio Baldini's fine-manner engraving, inspired by Petrarch's *Triumph of Chastity*, of Cupid tied to a tree, a quiver and broken arrows at his feet, being tormented by vindictively chaste women (Fig. 87).[36] Indeed, despite Augurelli's coyness in interpreting Giuliano's standard, no contemporary observer could have failed to recognize in the familiar figure of Cupid bound and despoiled of his arms an allusion to the *Triumph of Chastity*. Episodes from Petrarch's *Trionfi*, a poem universally beloved, were staples in popular art, the *Trionfi* being (as we have had a foretaste in Chapter 2) perhaps the most popular single source drawn upon for the imagery of festival floats, as well as paintings designed for domestic uses. A *desco da parto* of the *Triumph of Fame*, for example, painted for Lorenzo de'Medici's own birth, is merely an especially well known instance of the latter (Fig. 88).[37] It is in fact highly likely that Baldini's engraving of Cupid tied to a tree derives from Giuliano's banner, which showed Cupid bound to an olive, and it virtually quotes its Petrarchan origin by adding the virtuous women who despoil him of his arms. Normally Cupid is shown in representations of the *Triumph of Chastity* as the poem describes him, not as tied to a tree, but instead as bound at Chastity's feet on her triumphal chariot, as we see in Sellaio's painting in the Museo Bandini in Fiesole (Fig. 89). Nonetheless, Giuliano's (and Baldini's) allusion to Petrarch is unmistakable. Furthermore, the allegorical portrayal on Giuliano's standard of the lady Simonetta as Pallas wearing a white dress, protected by her Medusa shield, unmistakably alludes to Petrarch's allegorical description of the lady Laura as Chastity in the same poem.

In common with the description of Giuliano's Pallas by the *Anonimo*, Petrarch describes the figure of Chastity clad in a white gown and armed with the terrible shield on which Medusa's face had been frozen; and she appears with Cupid tied to a tree, despoiled of his feathers and with his broken arrows scattered round him:

> Ell'avea in dosso, il dì, candida gonna,
> lo scudo in man che mal vide Medusa.
> D'un bel diaspro er'ivi una colonna,
>   a la qual d'una in mezzo Lete infusa
> catena di diamante e di topazio,
> che s'usò fra le donne, oggi non s'usa,
>   legarlo vidi e farne quello strazio
> che bastò ben a mille altre vendette;
> ed io per me ne fui contento e sazio.
>   I' non poria le sacre e benedette
> vergini ch'ivi fur, chiudere in rima,
> non Calliope e Clio con l'altre sette;
>   ma alquante dirò che 'n su la cima
> son di vera onestate, infra le quali
> Lucrezia di man destra era la prima,
>   l'altra Penelopè: queste gli strali
> avean spezzato e la faretra a lato
> a quel protervo, e spennacchiato l'ali.[38]

(The goddess wore a white gown that day, with the shield in her hand that Medusa looked upon to her own harm. To a beautiful jasper column that was there, and with a chain of diamond and topaz that had once been dipped in Lethe, of a kind that was once worn by women but is used no more, I saw Cupid bound, and saw him then chastised enough to atone for a thousand other vengeances, and I was content and satisfied to see it. I could not number in rhyme all the holy and blessed virgins there, nor could Calliope and Clio with the remaining seven Muses, but I will at least say that in the fore were those of truest chastity, and among them was Lucretia first on the right, and on the other side Penelope. They had broken Cupid's arrows, torn the quiver from his flank, and plucked the feathers from his wings.)

Petrarch's metaphorical identification of Chastity with the virgin Pallas by virtue of her attribute of the Medusa shield is of course quite deliber-

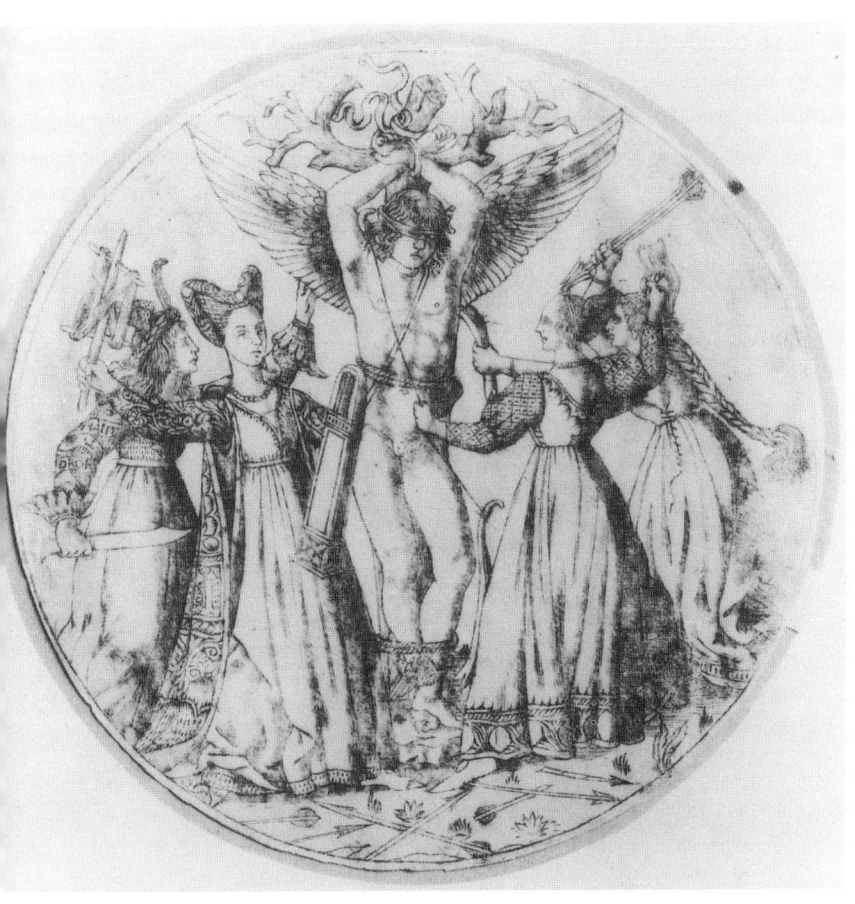

FIGURE 87
Baccio Baldini, *Cupid Chastized*, engraving, London, British Museum.
(Photograph by James T. Van Rensselaer)

ate, and it is no anomaly for Botticelli (or the inventor of the standard) to have elegantly returned the compliment by poetically figuring Pallas as Chastity triumphing over the bound and miserable Cupid. Having conquered Love and despoiled him of his weapons, the virgin goddess stands firmly on the Medici device of the *broncone* and fixes her gaze unwaveringly on the glory of the sun above her. Giuliano's standard testified to his

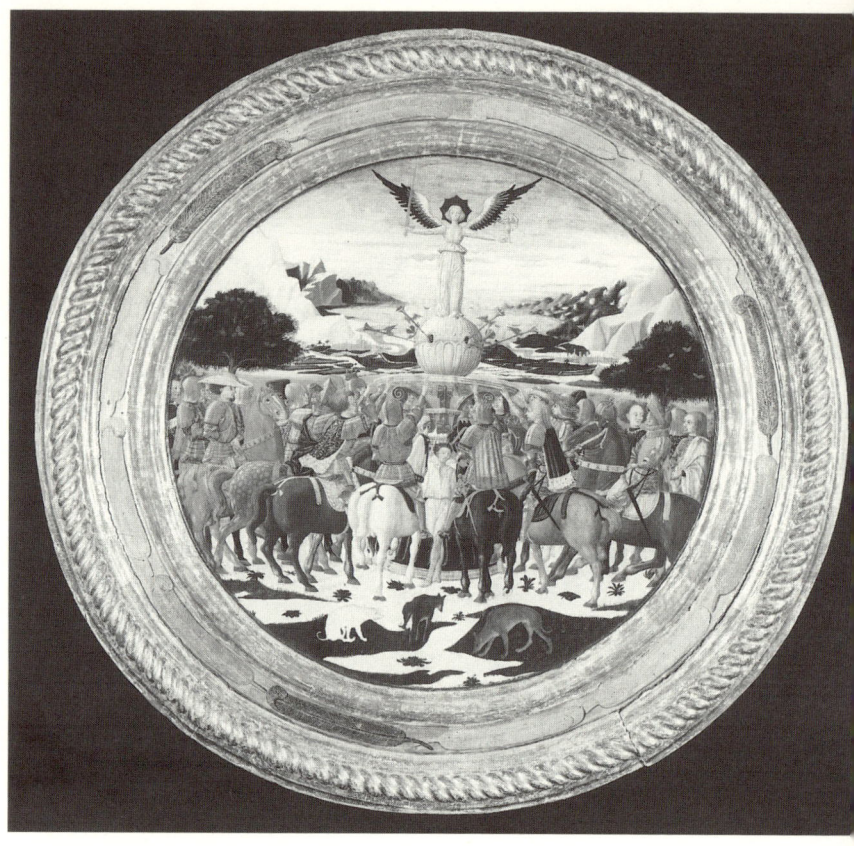

FIGURE 88

The Triumph of Fame, Florentine *Desco da parto*, New York, The Metropolitan Museum of Art, purchase in memory of Sir John Pope-Hennessy: Rogers Fund, The Annenberg Foundation, Drue Heinz Foundation, Annette de la Renta, Mr. and Mrs. Frank E. Richardson, and The Vincent Astor Foundation Gifts, Wrightsman and Gwynne Andrews Funds, special funds, and Gift of the children of Mrs. Harry Payne Whitney, Gift of Mr. and Mrs. Joshua Logan, and other gifts and bequests, by exchange (1995). (Photograph: The Metropolitan Museum of Art)

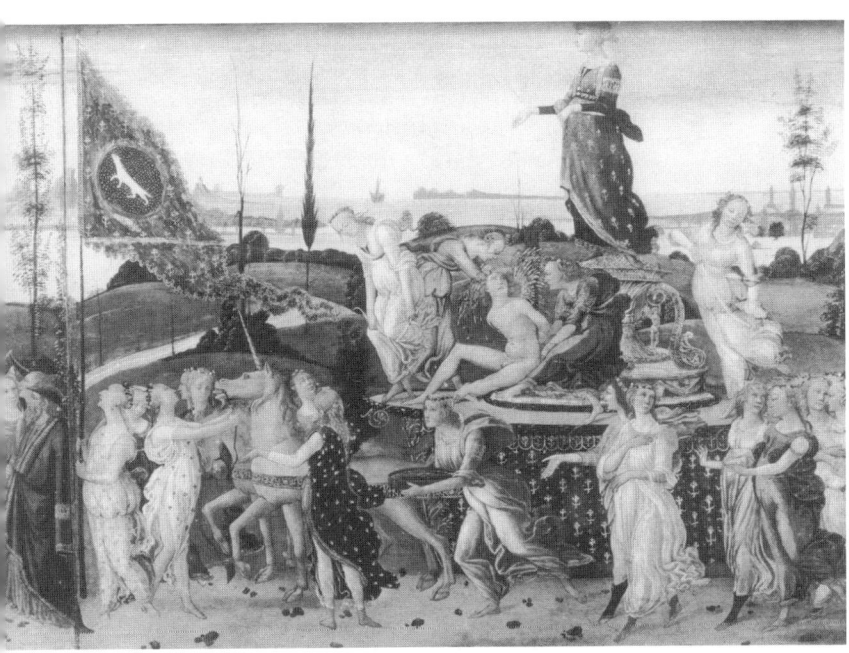

FIGURE 89
Jacopo del Sellaio, *The Triumph of Chastity*, Fiesole, Museo Bandini.
(Photograph: Alinari/Art Resource)

devotion to Chastity, whose portrayal as Pallas indicated his sapient conquering of carnal love and his desire to win glory in the field.

Politian, who in a letter to Hieronymus Donatus was later to complain that all his time was taken up in devising *argutiae* for *emblemata* and verses of ephemeral value, is an obvious candidate for having been the inventor of Giuliano's knightly allegory; and, even if he was not, there can be no doubt that he understood its meaning fully.[39] Indeed, the imagery of the ensign—which as an emblematic image of Giuliano himself records his particular idea of chivalric honor—plays a pivotal role in the unfinished second book of the *Stanze*. There Politian refers directly, and very accurately if we may judge by other descriptions of it, to Giuliano's standard when he describes the youthful Julio's dream, visited upon him at the behest of Venus before the ordination of the joust itself (2.28–32):

> Pargli veder feroce la sua donna,
> tutta nel volto rigida e proterva,
> legar Cupido alla verde colonna
> della felice pianta di Minerva,
> armata sopra alla candida gonna,
> che 'l casto petto col Gorgon conserva;
> e par che tutte gli spennecchi l'ali,
> e che rompa al meschin l'arco e li strali.
>
> Ahimè, quanto era mutato da quello
> Amor, che mo' tornò tutto gioioso!
> Non era sovra l'ale altero e snello,
> non del trionfo suo punto orgoglioso:
> anzi merzé chiamava el meschinello
> miseramente, e con volto pietoso
> gridando a Iulio: "Miserere mei,
> difendimi, o bel Iulio, da costei."
>
> E Iulio a lui dentro al fallace sonno
> parea risponder con mente confusa:
> "Come poss'io ciò far, dolce mio donno,
> ché nell'armi di Palla è tutta chiusa?
> Vedi i mie' spirti che soffrir non ponno
> la terribil sembianza di Medusa,
> e'l rabbioso fischiar delle ceraste,
> e'l volto e l'elmo e'l folgorar dell'aste."
>
> "Alza gli occhi, alza, Iulio, a quella fiamma
> che come un sol col suo splendor t'adombra:
> quivi è colei che l'alte mente infiamma,
> e che de' petti ogni viltà disgombra.
> Con essa, a guisa di semplice damma,

prenderai questa ch'or nel cor t'ingombra
tanta paura, e t'invilisce l'alma;
ché sol ti serba lei trionfal palma."

Così dicea Cupido, e già la Gloria
scendea giù folgorando ardente vampo:
con essa Poesia, con essa Istoria
volavon tutte accese del suo lampo.
Costei parea ch'ad acquistar vittoria
rapissi Iulio orribilmente in campo,
e che l'arme di Palla alla sua donna
spogliassi, e lei lasciassi in bianca gonna.

(He seems to see his lady, harsh and unbending in aspect, fiercely tie Cupid to the green trunk of Minerva's happy tree [the olive]; over her white gown she wears armor which protects her chaste bosom with its Gorgon breastplate; and she seems to pluck all the feathers from his wings, and she breaks the bow and arrows of the wretch. Alas, how changed he was from that Love who just now had joyfully returned! He was not haughtily and nimbly soaring, he was not at all gloating over his triumph: rather the little wretch was crying miserably for mercy, and called to Julio with a woeful countenance: "Have pity on me, defend me from her, fair Julio." And Julio within his false dream seemed to answer him with a confused mind: "How may I do this, my sweet lord, for she is all enclosed in the armor of Pallas? You see my spirits cannot endure the terrible features of Medusa, the angry hiss of her vipers, the face, the helmet and the flashing lance." "Raise, raise your eyes, Julio, to that flame which, like a sun, dazzles you with its brightness: there is she who inflames lofty minds and removes all baseness from the heart. With her you will capture, as you would a simple doe, this lady who now so burdens your heart with fear and makes base your soul; only a triumphal palm will win her for you." So Cupid was saying, and Glory was already descending, flashing about a fierce splendor: Poetry and History flew with her, kindled by her lightning. With dreadful force, she seemed to carry Julio off to the battlefield to gain victory, she seemed to strip the armor of Pallas from his lady and left her in her white gown.)[40]

Julio's dream vision as described by Politian is remarkably faithful in its details to the image that had been painted by Botticelli on the standard actually carried into the piazza of Santa Croce by Giuliano. Julio's lady appears to him in the guise of Pallas. She is dressed in a white gown, she wears a sallet (*ceraste*), and she bears the image of Medusa on her armor. The God of Love is bound to an olive tree (*la felice pianta di Minerva*), and Pallas has broken his bow and his arrows. Above her is a flame that appears like the sun, which in Politian's verse is interpreted as Glory, who descends to earth to claim the victory for Julio. And in the very last stanza of the poem this is the device, expressing his devotion to Love, Pallas, and Glory, that Julio vows to carry on his ensign into the field (2.46):

> "Con voi men vegno, Amor Minerva e Gloria
> ché 'l vostro foco tutto el cor m'avampa;
> da voi spero acquistar l'alta vittoria,
> ché tutto acceso son di vostra lampa;
> datemi aita sì ch'ogni memoria
> segnar si possa di mia eterna stampa,
> e facci umil colei ch'or ne disdegna:
> ch'io porterò di voi nel campo insegna."

("I accompany you, Love, Minerva, and Glory, for your fire inflames all my heart; from you I hope to gain the lofty victory, for I am all aflame with your light; give me such aid that every memory may be sealed with my eternal stamp, and make her humble who now disdains us: for yours is the standard I shall carry into the field.")

However, notwithstanding the close derivation of Politian's description of Julio's dream from the imagery actually painted on Giuliano's standard, how the imagery of the dream itself is to be interpreted is not obvious. Is Julio's dream a true allegorical dream (*somnium*), like Arthur's dream of

Gloriana in the *Faerie Queene*? Or is it a false dream (*insomnium*, or *visum*), like the Redcrosse Knight's dream of the false Una, whom "faire Venus seemde unto his bed to bring?" Moreover, the crux of any interpretation of the *Stanze* as a whole is Politian's explicit characterization of Julio's dream as untrue, of the young hero *dentro al fallace sonno* responding to Love's plea *con mente confusa* (2.30). The word "sonno" in the passage does not carry the meaning of "sleep" (for what might a "false sleep" mean?), but rather, as editors of the poem have universally noted, that of "sogno," a dream.[41] The same archaic use of the word also appears in Lorenzo de'Medici's *Comento sopra alcuni de'suoi sonetti*, where he writes of "sonni vani e bugiardi, come quelli che passano per la porta eburnea," that is, empty and lying dreams like those that issue from the ivory gate.[42]

Politian thus seems unambiguously to alert his readers that Julio, his spirit turbulent and confused, is caught up in a false, or mendacious dream. We have moreover been well prepared for this revelation, for in the preceding passages Politian tells of how Venus, exulting in Cupid's defeat of Julio and wishing to make their triumph complete, had sent Pasithea on a mission to Somnus so that he might cause some images to appear to Julio that will make him burn for the joust (2.22). Pasithea selects them from among various dreams whose faces are masked, "Sogni drento alle lor larve" (2.24), and these, in obedience to her bidding, then dispose themselves in new guises, "sotto nuove fogge" (2.25), so that in these shapes they might present to the sleeping Julio an image of "sua dolce fortuna" (2.27).

The dream, however, is anything but sweet. Julio is filled with terror, *tanta paura*, at the sight of his lady Simonetta, and he feels his soul made base and vile (2.31: *invilisce l'alma*). Glory seems to wrench him away *orribilmente*, transporting him terrified into the field (2.32). He is unable to interpret aright the confused signs and subterfuges, equivocating *ambagi*, that swarm around him (2.35), and he wakes in even greater confusion, crying out to Love that *se ver mi dice il sonno*—if his dream has indeed spoken the truth—then he will be Love's champion *against the lady Simonetta* (2.44):

> E s'io son, dolce Amor, s'io son pur degno
> essere il tuo campion contro a costei,
> contro a costei da cui con forza e 'ngegno,
> se ver mi dice il sonno, avinto sei,
> fa sì del tuo furor mio pensier pregno,
> che spirto di pietà nel cor li crei:
> mie virtù per se stessa ha l'ale corte,
> perché troppo è 'l valor di costei forte.

("And if I am, sweet Love, if I am indeed worthy to be your champion against her, against her by whose force and wit, if my dream tells me the truth, you have been bound, make my thought so full of your frenzy that a spirit of compassion may be produced in her heart: my virtue by itself has wings too short, because her valor is too great.")

But the reader already knows that Julio's dream is not true, that he is terrorized by the empty and misleading larval phantasms of *insomnium*.

And the dream is certainly confused. In Julio's *fallace sonno* he seems to see his lady become savage (*feroce*). With harsh and arrogant aspect (*nel volto rigida e proterva*), wearing her spotlessly white dress covered by Pallas's armor, she seems to bind Cupid to an olive tree, pluck his feathers, and despoil him of his weapons. The famous Petrarchan vision of the lady Laura as Chastity, which, as I have suggested, anyone attending Giuliano's actual joust might well have been expected to recognize, Julio himself is unable to read. The aspect of his lady fills him with terror and abases his very soul, and he turns away from her to attend instead to the bound Love, who cries out to him to take pity and to come to his defense, to defend him *from her*. What idea of chivalric or poetic love can it be that makes an enemy of the beloved, that requires Love to be defended from the very beloved to whom one's own honor is pledged? The painted allegorical image of Simonetta that the living Giuliano had carried into the Piazza of Santa Croce was conceived, in common with all such images, as a representation of his *mente*. It expressed, in the image of the beloved, Giuliano's own soul, his personal devotion to an idea of sapience secure in Pallas's armor and triumphant over carnal love, an idea Petrarch had personified in the image of Cupid bound in the triumphal chariot of Laura as Chastity, who carries the Medusa shield. In Giuliano's joust the lady Simonetta had been identified with the virgin Pallas, incarnating Giuliano's love of pure virtue armored by philosophy, to which his honor was pledged. In Julio's dream, however, the signs Politian derived from the allegory painted on the standard are hopelessly mixed. Although these images have a basis in reality, in the device on the ensign carried by Giuliano into the historical joust, in the *Stanze* they are uninterpretable by the dreaming Julio. For him they are equivocal and terrifying *ambagi* that create a nightmare of hopeless confusion. The dreaming Julio of the *Stanze* does not know, or even possess his own *mente*, which is completely captive to the vengeful Cupid. The very sight of his beloved fills him with fear, he cannot understand why she seems to turn so harshly against Love, and he piteously complains to Love that neither can he champion him, for his enfeebled spirits are unable to bear the terrible sight of Pallas's armor alone, the helmet, the flashing spear, or the shield with the semblance of Medusa's face ringed with hissing vipers.[43]

Love, who last was heard from in the *Stanze* maliciously crowing to Venus about his conquest of the once-proud Julio, all the while plunging his arrow into the breast of Mars and kissing him with venomed lips as the war god lies in effeminate luxury in Venus's lap, in reality has subdued not only Julio but also the very spirit of martial valor motivating the joust itself. He and his mother now desire Julio to take the field, not for his own glory or that of Mars but for their own—in Venus's words, for *nostra fama* and *la nostra gloria* (2.15). For this reason Venus sends Pasithea to seek out a false dream that will make Julio wish to show his valor in the field, a dream in which he seems to see Love not as we know him truly to be, triumphantly victorious over Julio, but instead as miserable and defeated at the hands of Julio's own beloved, Simonetta dressed in Pallas's armor. Thus mendaciously disguised, Love then directs Julio's loyalty *away from* Simonetta, and proposes that he follow instead a different lady, one who appears in the image of Glory like the sun. Love further tempts Julio by telling him that only by following this Glory will he be able to capture his beloved—the very Simonetta who has made his soul cowardly and base! The false image of Glory (who is really Venus, for we know the glory is hers and her son's) then snatches Julio away *orribilmente* to the field of battle, where she despoils Simonetta of Pallas's armor ("e che l'arme di Palla alla sua donna spogliassi") and fits Julio with it ("Poi Iulio di suo spoglie armava tutto"). The image, in contrast to Petrarch's *Trionfi*, is one of Chastity despoiled.

Within the mythology of Renaissance tournaments true Glory is no enemy to Chastity. On the contrary, as we have seen from Lorenzo de'Medici's preface to the *Raccolta Aragonese*, it is the love of glory that incites mortal souls to distinguished actions, for which reason the Romans celebrated their triumphs, the Greeks their Olympic Games—and the Florentines their *giostre*—in all of which the honor of the contestants and the city was invested, and was given permanent expression in parallel artistic competitions. The living Giuliano's desire for glory appeared in his dedicating his honor to an idea of love vested in Simonetta Cattaneo as the figure for Palladian wisdom and chastity, and this entailed no contradiction. In Politian's *Stanze*, on the other hand, the despoiling of Simonetta's chaste armor, which is a betrayal of the beloved in the name of a false idea of love, also entails a betrayal of the real Pallas and the true idea of philosophical love that Simonetta had represented as Giuliano's *donna* in the *giostra* of 1475. The defeat of Simonetta as the virgin Pallas in Julio's dream is one secured by Cupid and Venus, who has conjured up the dissimulating *larve* of Love, Pallas, and Glory, which all together roil and confuse his sleep. It is, in other words, not truly Glory who has disarmed Chastity, but Chastity's natural enemy Venus, who appears to Julio under the mask of Glory and assures the victory, and the glory, for herself and for Love.

Soon after, moreover, when Julio wakes from his dream and pledges to be Love's champion *against* Simonetta ("contro a costei da cui con forza e 'ngegno, se ver mi dice il sonno, avinto sei") and addresses prayers to goddesses whom he thinks are Pallas and Glory, the delusion under which he suffers is expressly indicated by the marginal rubrics and woodblock illustration printed on a crucial page (Fig. 90) in the first edition of the

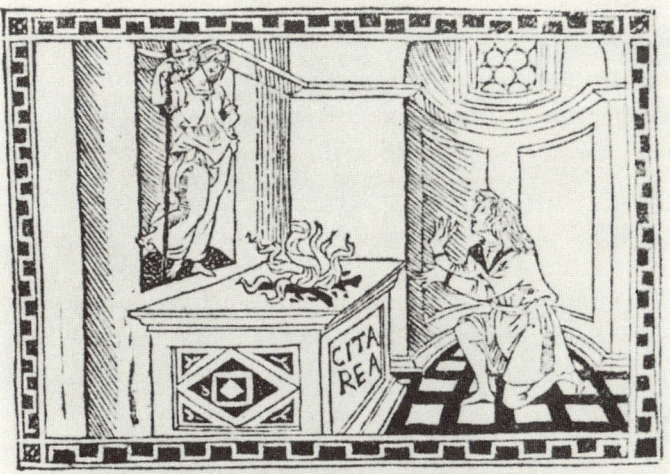

O sacrosancta Dea figlia di Gioue
  Per cui eltempio di Ian sapre & serra: Oratione
  Lacui potente dextra serba & muoue   di Iulio a
  Intero arbitro & di pace & di guerra: Pallade
  Vergine sancta che mirabil proue
  Mostri del tuo gran nume in cielo enterra:
  Che ualorosi cuori a uirtu infiammi:
  Socchorrimi hor Tritonia & uirtu dammi.

Sio uidi drento alle tua armi chiusa
  Lasembianza di lei che me a me fura
  Si uiddi eluolto horribil di Medusa
  Far lei contro ad amor troppo esser dura:
  Se poi mia mente dal tremor confusa
  Sotto iltuo schermo diuento sicura.
  Se amor con teco a grande opre michiama
  Mostrami elporto o Dea detterna phama.

Et tu che drento alla inffochata nube   Parole di
  Degnasti tua sembianza dimostrarmi: Iulio a Ve
  Et cognialtro pensier dal cor mirube   nere
  Fuor che damor/dalqual nō posso atarmi:

FIGURE 90
Julio at the Altar of Venus, woodcut illustration from Politian,
Stanze cominciate per la giostra di Giuliano de'Medici, Bologna, 1496.
(Photograph by James T. Van Rensselaer)

Stanze. This was published in Bologna in 1494 during Politian's lifetime under the editorship of his trusted friend Alessandro Sarti (Sarzio).[44] As Salvatore Settis has shown, this woodcut is the only one that was specifically designed for the *Stanze*, and hence it functions as a species of rubric explaining the text printed just beneath. It shows Julio in prayer in a kind of chapel, kneeling before the statue of a spear-carrying goddess set in a niche behind an altar, and it illustrates Stanza 2.41, the content of which an actual rubric printed in the margin "correctly" identifies as the "Oratione di Iulio a Pallade," Julio's prayer to Pallas.[45] This is consistent with the text, and seems reasonably consistent with the woodcut's portrayal of an armed woman dressed *alla ninfa*. (One thinks, for example, of Botticelli's *Pallas and the Centaur* [Fig. 91], in which Pallas is also dressed *alla ninfa* and wears a masquerade costume adorned with Medici rings, and which once was mistakenly identified as Giuliano's actual banner.) Moreover, as Settis pointed out, the burning branches on the altar evoke the *broncone* that appeared beneath Pallas's feet on that banner (cf. Plate 6). The altar, however, is not dedicated to Pallas but to CITAREA, and it is in fact to Venus, disguised as Pallas, that Julio prays in his delusion. Two stanzas later (2.43), when he turns his prayers to whom he thinks is Glory and so addresses, the marginal rubric informs the reader that these are instead the "Parole di Iulio a Venere" (Fig. 90). The dream whose spell still grips Julio has not told him the truth, and it is not truly Pallas and Glory he has seen in his vision and now seeks to address, but always and ever dissimulating Venus hidden behind their *larve*, the false masks of Pallas and Glory that disguise Venus.[46] It is she who has misled Julio with deceiving dreams of virtue and glory, and on her account that he enters the joust (that wretched subject, as Carducci wrote, for encomiastic poetry), leaving him a hostage to Fortune.

The possibility of a darkly ominous reading of the *Stanze* has always been acknowledged, and indeed was acknowledged, with the intent to refute it, by Isidoro del Lungo in his analysis of the problem of the poem's date, incorporated into Carducci's immortal essay prefacing his 1863 edition of the *Stanze*.[47] The necessity for such a dark reading is unambiguously announced by the rubric to 2.35 ("Sotto cotali ambagi al giovinetto /

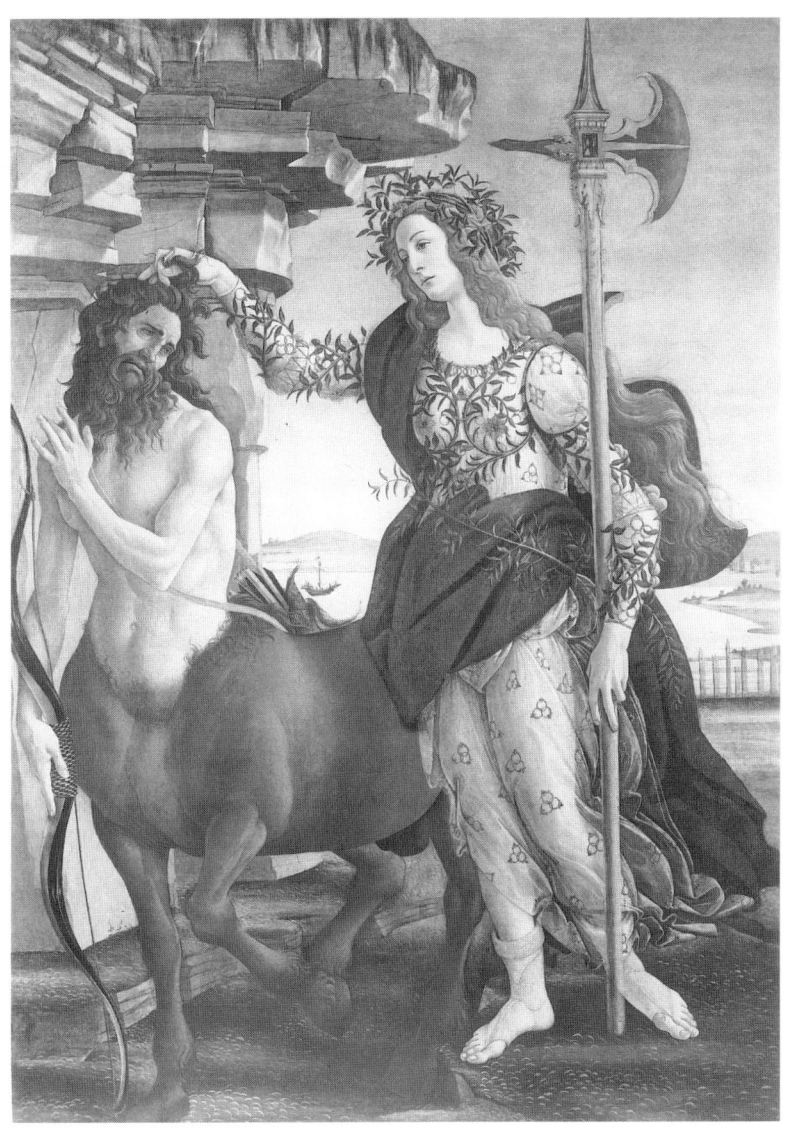

FIGURE 91
Sandro Botticelli, *Pallas and the Centaur*, Florence, Uffizi.
(Photograph: Alinari/Art Resource)

fu mostro de' suo' fati il leggier corso," etc.), which reads "Pronostico verissimo della morte di Iulio"—that is, a highly true prognostication of the death of Julio. This gives clear evidence of the way in which Politian's contemporaries were expected to understand the passage, and means that the poet intended the verses to be taken as a prophetic reference to the murder of Giuliano de'Medici by the participants in the Pazzi Conspiracy. Del Lungo's objection to such an interpretation of the *Stanze*, the only one that really counts, was immediately endorsed by other scholars and remains in force to this day: ". . . but a poem of love and jousts after the death of the hero would have been a misconception, and a vice in Politian that he did not possess: ingratitude."[48] Accordingly, Del Lungo argued that the verses must refer instead to the death of Simonetta, which by an extraordinary coincidence fell on 26 April 1476, two years to the day before Giuliano's murder on 26 April 1478. Politian's lines written of Julio's fate— "troppo felice, se nel suo diletto non mettea morte acerba il crudel morso" (2.35)—in del Lungo's view must have been written with reference, not to Giuliano's own death, but to the death of Simonetta, and with her the end of Giuliano's brief moment of intense happiness in love. He went on to argue that Politian began the *Stanze* soon after the joust in 1475, that the ominous change in the tone and content of the second book was owing to Simonetta's death in 1476, and that the poem was left unfinished either because of this tragedy, or because Politian could see no way to finish it after Giuliano's murder in 1478.

This view has remained virtually canonical, notwithstanding Giovanni Battista Picotti's excellently reasoned argument, first published in 1915, that the second book of the *Stanze* must have been written after Giuliano's death. Picotti's suggestion was at once challenged by Matteo Guerrieri, whose counter-arguments won all but universal approval.[49] The question then seemed to be settled definitively by Vincenzo Pernicone's edition of the *Stanze*, the most authoritative to appear to date, in which it was argued that, although the marginal rubrics to the first book were certainly written by Politian, those to the second (in which appeared the "Pronostico verissimo della morte di Iulio") must have been composed by an "incompetent editor," Sarti, who was responsible for the *editio princeps* of 1494.[50] Pernicone's view was based on the fact that the rubrics for Book 2 appear in only one early manuscript of the *Stanze*, in Pesaro, which clearly derives from this edition; and on the fact that the particular rubrics quoted above seem to be marred by errors introduced by Sarti—especially the rubric to 2.43 (see Fig. 90), identifying words the text clearly identifies as addressed to Glory by Julio as being the "Parole di Iulio a Venere."

However, recent technical study of the manuscript tradition by Guglielmo Gorni indicates that the second book of the *Stanze* could not have been written earlier than 1479, and was undoubtedly undertaken simultaneously with Politian's own revision of Book 1. The *terminus ante quem* for completion of the first draft of Book 1, moreover, is no earlier than September 1478, the likely date of the earliest surviving manuscript of the *Stanze*, which is comprised of an unrevised draft of only the first book copied out by Antonio Manetti, the biographer of Brunelleschi.[51] As Gorni pointed out, the Bologna edition of 1494 represents a more mature redaction of the text of Book 1, incorporating revisions which could not have been undertaken save by the author of the poem itself. Sarti, whom Vittorio Branca was later to call "the true Eckermann of Angelo," was no reviser and certainly no falsifier of the grammar and prosody of the century's greatest humanist scholar and poet—who was still living when the Bologna edition was published—but was himself a highly competent humanist editor in whom Politian expressed his complete faith and who, together with Andrea Magnani, had become more or less Politian's official editor after the latter's brief visit to Bologna in early June of 1491.[52]

In short order Sarti then saw through the press of Francesco (Platone) de'Benedetti Politian's *Nutricia* (22 June 1491), *Manto* (9 June 1492), *Rusticus* (15 June 1492), and *Ambra* (28 June 1492), followed by his *Epistola de obitu Laurentii Medicis* (25 July 1492), *S. Athanasius, stilus et character psalmorum* (27 August 1492), and *Herodianus, Historiae de imperio post Marcum* (31 August 1493).[53] The last Benedetti edition for which Sarti was responsible, which appreared just seven weeks before Politian's death on the night of 28–29 September 1494, was *Le cose volgari* (9 August 1494). This contains not only the first edition of the *Stanze*, but also several of the *Rime* together with the *Orfeo*, this last in an edition, in this case verifiable from the manuscripts, which Gorni characterized as "impeccable." With regard to the marginal rubrics to Book 2 of the *Stanze*, which Carducci and Picotti both believed had also been composed by Politian, Gorni added that "here too a drastic and complete rejection of B [the 1494 edition] would perhaps be courageous, and not altogether reassuring."[54] Gorni's establishment of 1479 as the *terminus post quem* for Politian's revision of the *Stanze*, together with his highly positive assessment of Sarti's capacities as an editor (later collaborating with Aldus Manutius and playing an important part, acknowledged by Manutius in a glowing preface, in putting together the excellent first edition of Politian's *Opera omnia*, published in 1498), has since received great support from the additional researches of Daniela Delcorno Branca.[55] Vittorio Branca has added that "a re-elaborative project for the *Stanze* posterior to 1479 is extremely probable," stating that in his view it is "unthinkable that a highly devoted admirer such as Sarti . . . would have printed [Politian's] writings unknown to him and against his will in an ambience and in a city so near and with such close ties to Florence."[56] Given Sarti's fidelity as an editor, the question of Politian's authorship of the rubrics to Book 2 now appears much less uncertain. At the least they would appear to be in a form known and acceptable to him, while the far stronger likelihood would be that Politian was himself the author of them, as he certainly was of the rubrics to Book 1.

As Picotti argued, however, the most important consideration so far as interpretation of the *Stanze* is concerned is that the two "erroneous" marginal rubrics indicating the deluded Julio's prayer to Venus disguised as Pallas and predicting his death seem merely to confirm what can be read in the poem itself. In the first instance, as we have seen, Politian explicitly alerts the reader to Julio's delusion by declaring his dream of love and glory to be false—"Iulio con mente confusa dentro al fallace sonno." It is a dream made up of deceiving images—"Sogni drento alle lor larve." And in the second instance, precisely because of the falsity of the dream of love Venus offers to Julio, in opposition to the chastely pure wisdom of Pallas represented in Simonetta—a specious dream of glory seducing him away from his faith in Simonetta and setting him against her in the very name of Love itself—Politian explicitly indicates that in consequence Julio has ceded his life to the caprices of Fortune. Julio dreams he wins the joust, but in the very moment of his glorious victory he uncomprehendingly sees Simonetta, whom Love had promised him as the prize only if he be faithless to her, snatched cruelly away, wrapped in a dark cloud. The moon and heavens seem to turn to blood, and the stars seem to fall from the skies. Simonetta then immediately reappears to him as Fortune, the fortune that will govern his life—"e prender lei di sua vita governo"—and ensure them both eternal fame, and in his confusion the world seems beautiful again. As Fortune she augurs for him a brief moment of happiness soon to be cut short by cruel death. Since Simonetta in Julio's vision is herself already dead, and since he is now at the mercy of the sovereign Fortune into which she has been transformed in death, the prophecy seems understandable only as referring to Giuliano's own murder in the unanticipated and cruel turn of fortune that produced the Pazzi Conspiracy.

Since Del Lungo, Simonetta's disappearance at the end of the *Stanze* has been understood as referring to her actual death in 1476. There can be no doubt of the truth of this interpretation, and so it is important to keep in mind that, if the poem were truly a mythological fable spun only around the historical event of Giuliano's joust in 1475, there would be, as Eugenio Donato observed in a shrewdly polemical article, no structural reason why Simonetta's death should even have been mentioned, since it would have no bearing on its theme at all.[57] Moreover, the *Stanze* cannot be read, like Politian's epicedion on the death of Albiera degli Albizzi, as a lamentation for Simonetta, except insofar as she is the mask for Julio's confused *mente*. For the poem is not at all about Simonetta, whose role is strictly subordinate to that of Giuliano as Julio, Politian's undoubted protagonist, whose fate is completely bound up in his love for her. Whether appearing as an ideal of chaste virtue to which he voluntarily pledges his life, or as a deaf and fickle Fortune that seizes control of it, she is inseparable from Giuliano's fate. The fact of Simonetta's death, a year after the joust, and with it her transformation into Fortune, must accordingly be read in relation to her meaning for the whole of Giuliano's life. This refers not only to his resplendent moment of glorious happiness at taking the prize in the joust, but also to the later history of his life, of which she as Fortune has taken possession, and for which she now stands.

The history of Giuliano's short life concluded with his murder, at age twenty-five, at the hands of the Pazzi conspirators on 26 April 1478, exactly the anniversary of Simonetta's death. To contemporary Florentines, acutely conscious of such coincidences, the connection must surely have seemed fated, and indeed the rubric—"pronostico verissimo della morte di Iulio"—in the margin beside the following verse in the 1494 edition of the *Stanze* (2.35) must have seemed to them only a restatement of what the verse actually says:

> Sotto cotali ambagi al giovinetto
> fu mostro de' suo' fati il leggier corso:
> troppo felice, se nel suo diletto
> non mettea morte acerba il crudel morso.
> Ma che puote a Fortuna esser disdetto,
> ch'a nostre cose allenta e stringe il morso?
> Né val perch'altri la lusinghi o morda,
> ch'a suo modo ne guida e sta pur sorda.

(In these confused signs the youth was shown the changing course of his fate: too happy, if early death were not placing its cruel bit on his delight. But what can be gainsaid to Fortune who slackens and pulls the reins of our affairs? The flattery and curses of others do not prevail, for she remains deaf and rules us as she pleases.)

For Simonetta's return as the Fortune who will govern Giuliano's life cannot have any positive meaning, as Donato has stressed.[58] The wisdom that is the gift of philosophy is the humanist's only safeguard against the vagaries of a cruel and randomly changeable Fortune. As Eugenio Garin has shown, Politian was preoccupied (and deeply frightened) by the contingency and uncertainty of events, of how the world seems governed only by Fortune, which reduces history to chaos and leads only to death and the final destruction of everything man strives to achieve.[59] And Biasin, in a fine analysis of Politian's account of the catastrophe of the actual Pazzi Conspiracy (in the *Coniurationis Pactianae commentarium*), has shown how it is organized, in a rhetorical tour de force, as a bitter diatribe against the blindness and brutality of Fortune.[60] Picotti long ago pointed out the paradox (were Del Lungo's interpretation to be believed) that Politian, in the verses in the *Stanze* immediately following those just quoted, indicts a diatribe against the folly of placing one's trust in Fortune, harsh and indifferent to human wishes or power, which the wise man resists "con fronte sicura." Politian writes that "blessed is he who rids his thoughts of Fortune, and wraps himself entirely inside his own virtue" (2.36: *Beato qual da lei suo' pensier solve, / e tutto drento alla virtù s'involve*). Such a one is not led by Fortune, but may himself govern the vagaries of chance (2.37: *Da sé sol pende, e 'n se stesso si fida, / né guidato è dal caso, anzi lui guida*). Of these lines Picotti acutely wrote, "What is said at length in Book Two of the *Stanze* about the power of Fortune and the necessity on the part of the wise man to resist her 'con fronte sicura' does not seem especially appropriate in the very place where he discourses upon the death of Simonetta; because, even putting aside the fact that this most gentle nymph should have been transformed into the deaf and capricious Fortune, how in the world could it then have been said to her lover, in the face of the loss of his beloved lady, that blessed is the man who pays no heed to Fortune, 'né guidato è dal caso, anzi lui guida?'"[61] How indeed? In the poem and in Politian's thought the principle represented by errant Fortune is abhorrent, and for Julio to find his life placed entirely under the governance of Fortune is a catastrophe. Now that he is in the hands of Fortune, Julio also learns but scarcely understands what his own fate will be: a brief moment of happiness, quickly to be cut short by death.

The end of the *Stanze* in fact sounds in ominous resonance to its beginning, where in the very first stanza Politian justifies his poem on the grounds that *fortuna o morte* might not obliterate great names and actions (1.1). The epic echo of this sentiment has particular poignancy insofar as Giuliano's joust stands only as the youthful prelude to a career of high expectations, a hope of achievement left unfulfilled, cut short by fortune and death. Nor is it at all obvious that the first book, however skillfully

Politian rehearses the familiar conventions of vernacular love poetry in the unweaving of his story, was ever conceived with the conventional happy ending in mind. Julio's *fallace sonno* in Book 2 echoes an earlier moment in the poem (1.34–55), when Love prepares his savage vengeance (*fera vendetta*) on him by spinning a beautiful doe out of thin air so that he might pursue in vain this empty image (*vana effigie*). Julio rises to the bait and for many a mile gives chase to *sua vana speranza*, his own empty hope, until he enters a flowered meadow, the deer vanishes, and in its place he beholds Simonetta seated on the grass.[62] He gazes upon her in wonder, stunned by her loveliness. But this is, as Politian's *comparazione* makes clear, only the reflected image of his desire, an empty *ombra* that infatuates him (1.39):

> Qual tigre, a cui dalla pietosa tana
> ha tolto il cacciator li suoi car figli;
> rabbiosa il segue per la selva ircana,
> che tosto crede insanguinar gli artigli;
> poi resta d'uno specchio all'ombra vana,
> all'ombra ch'e suoi nati par somigli;
> e mentre di tal vista s'innamora
> la sciocca, el predator la via divora.

(Even so a tigress, from whose rocky den the hunter has stolen her cherished young, follows him enraged through the Hyrcanian woods, thinking soon to bloody her claws; then is arrested by an empty shadow [*ombra vana*] reflected in a mirroring pool, by a shade [*ombra*] that seems to resemble her children; and while the fool is enamored of that sight, the hunter flies away.)

Moreover, Simonetta is herself described as masked, that is, not in normal dress but clad in a *painted* costume of the sort that were designed for ephemeral *mascherate* and depicted by Botticelli for Flora's dress in the *Primavera* and by Sellaio in his *Triumphs of Love and Chastity* (see Plate 3, Fig. 89): "White is her garment, though painted with roses, flowers, and grass" (1.43: *candida la vesta / ma pur di rose e fior dipinta e d'erba*).[63] The young girl upon whom Julio raptly gazes is only that, not truly a nymph but the *ombra* of one that has been conjured by Love. There follows Politian's celebrated description of Simonetta's beauty (1.43–48), until Julio at last finds courage to speak and tremblingly asks if she be nymph or goddess, so far does her beauty surpass human nature. After such poetry, as Donato wrote, Simonetta's answer (1.51–54) is surprisingly prosaic.[64] She uncovers the masquerade, telling Julio in no uncertain terms that *she is not what he takes her to be*: "Io non son qual tua mente invano auguria." She lives in Florence but comes from Liguria, she is married and lives nearby, she likes to walk in the meadow and often comes to enjoy the fresh air and flowers, she sometimes sits in the shade by a stream with one of her female friends, she goes to church with the other women to hear Mass on holidays, her beauty is nothing marvelous for she was born *in grembo a Venere*, and that since the hour is growing late she had better go home.[65] She then departs, never to appear as herself in the poem again, leaving Julio thunderstruck, like a man out of his senses (*forsennato*). The precedent for this passage in the first book of the *Aeneid* is especially significant.[66] There Venus appears to Aeneas in the *imago vana* of Diana, the while insisting to her son that she is only a simple Phoenician maiden, urging him to go to the palace of the unhappy Dido. She has just heard Jupiter's promise of the glories in store for Aeneas, who will wage a great war in Italy and refound the city of Lavinium, and his son Iulus, who will build Alba Longa and from whom will descend a Trojan Caesar, the great Julius. The *homericus adulescens* Politian, so named for his translation of several books of the *Iliad*, had hopes of writing an epic of his own, hopes postponed by events and by the disaster of the Pazzi Conspiracy and the wars that followed. The contrast of Iulus's fortune to Julio's is bitter, for the *Stanze* in the end is a lament for the thwarted hopes vested in him. So too is the contrast of the phantom Diana masking Venus in the *Aeneid* to the *imago vana* of Simonetta in the *Stanze* ("Se l'arco ha in mano, al fianco la faretra, / giurar potrai che sia Diana casta"). For, as Mario Martelli suggested, the *vana effigie* of the deer, "altera e bella," the enchantingly beautiful but fugitive vision of Simonetta, "nata in grembo di Venere," and the triumphant Venus herself are all manifestations of the same thing, and that is, I would suggest, a false and bewildering vision of beauty spun by Venus herself.[67]

There is no need to go into the remainder of Book I of the *Stanze*, save to take note of the fact that Love's vengeance upon Julio is unrelenting and nowhere mitigated in the slightest by any promise of mercy and amorous fulfillment. Julio, his virtue and his fortune now hostage to Love, returns home alone, and Love, having secured his triumph, returns home to the garden of Venus, to the description of which the rest of the book is given over. It is a place of paradisaical beauty, sexual luxuriousness and abandon, and filled with an appalling crew: false Hope and Vain Desire watering the whetstone upon which the *amorini* sharpen their arrows, its bloody axle turned by Charm and Intrigue; Tears and wan Pallor with fearful Affection; Gauntness, Anxiety, blind Error, Suspicion, Anguish, mad Frenzy, wretched Penitence, and Cruelty immersed in blood; silent Deception, simulated Laughter, Weeping, Grief, unrestrained License, and Desperation hanging herself.[68] In the midst of the garden is the palace of Venus, in which Cupid finds his mother with the vanquished Mars lying on his back in her lap, feeding his eyes upon her face while naked little Loves scatter roses over them.[69] The spirit of martial valor itself has been reduced to effeminate luxuriousness. Julio's joust now belongs to Venus and Cupid.

CHAPTER FIVE

The End of the Masquerade

VASARI AND Il Lasca both report that Lorenzo de'Medici reshaped the traditional Florentine civic celebrations attending feasts such as San Giovanni, Calendimaggio, and Carnevale, as well as occasions such as the official welcoming of a distinguished visitor, with the invention of new forms of poetic presentation and musical performance called masques, or public entertainments variously known as *mascherate, canti,* and *canti carnascialeschi*.[1] This does not mean that the wearing of fancy dress and masks in public festivals had not occurred earlier in Florence and Italy during the Trecento and Quattrocento.[2] It is only necessary to recall the ban enacted by the Consiglio Maggiore of Florence in 1447, two years before Lorenzo's birth, expressly forbidding celebrants of Carnevale to go about the city *cum facie coperta vel simulata cum aliqua tintura et seu ut vulgo dicitur cum mascheris*.[3] Lasca himself affirms that, "Before [Lorenzo's time] men celebrated Carnival by masking themselves and dressing as women, and they also used to go about at Calendimaggio cross-dressed [*travestiti*] as women and girls, singing *canzoni a ballo*."[4]

Although nothing about Lorenzo is without controversy, the prevailing view is that Lasca was right in saying that it was he who adapted and artistically refined the pre-existing traditions within polished and more sophisticated poetical and musical forms that were, in Lasca's words, "more beautiful, well made, and well ordered." Having found the traditional festival songs always the same, Lorenzo sought to vary "not only the *canti* but also their inventions and the way the words were composed."[5] In this way the *canzoni* lost their monotony and came to be written "with varied and different rhythms, and with music composed for them using new and diverse airs." Moreover, Lasca's account is supported by a letter of 1491 written by Lorenzo himself to Pietro Alamanni in Rome, promising to send him some *canti* with music composed by none other than the great Heinrich Isaac "in diverse manners, *et gravi et dolci et ropti et artificiosi*."[6] Lorenzo perhaps refers here to the music composed by Isaac for his own *rappresentazione di S. Giovanni e Paolo*, performed by the youthful Compagnia del Vangelista on 17 February 1491, but he could as well be referring to other *laude* or to secular *canti*, both of which Isaac set to music, which are really two sides to the same coin, and often sung to the same music.[7] This appears from frequent annotations in the musical and poetic manuscripts using the formula "Cantasi come." A well-known example is a manuscript annotation to one of Lorenzo's *laude*, "Quanto è grande la bellezza / di te Vergin santa e pia," directing that this should be "sung like the *Canzona di Bacco*" (that is, his famous *canto di carro*, "Quanto è bella giovinezza / che si fugge tuttavia").[8] In any event, it is clear that neither Lorenzo nor Lasca are referring to the repetitive forms of popular verse and music that had been transmitted in traditions passed down by the *canterini*, or street singers. They refer to poetry and music arising from a popular base to be sure, but also to forms of art that have been refined, and indeed professionalized.

The new *mascherate* with their freshly composed *canzoni* and music are characterized by an ennobling of the arts and the forms of traditional civic celebration in ways that coincide, as we have seen, with Lorenzo's cultural ambitions as stated in the letter with which he prefaced the collection of poems called the *Raccolta Aragonese*.[9] There Lorenzo praised the ancient Romans and their *trionfi*, with their richly decorated triumphal cars, their sculptures and trophies, their lavishly ornamented theaters, and their publicly sponsored oratorical and poetic competitions, as setting an exemplary precedent for the nourishment of the arts and for bringing honor to the city. "For this end alone," he wrote, the Romans "designed their *carri*, triumphal arches, theatrical displays and funeral laudations" (inevitably bringing to mind the poetic competitions among Florentine writers inspired by Albiera degli Albizzi's death in 1473, and Simonetta Vespucci's in 1476, to which Lorenzo himself contributed four sonnets). The ancient spectacles and *certamina* merited emulation as providing spurs to competing poets, orators, and artists, offering them all opportunities to acquire personal honor by encouraging a higher perfection in their individual performances. The result would be to attain a corresponding enrichment of the general culture—or what Lorenzo called the collective honor—of the city.

It is well to remember that Lasca's collection of *canti* was not limited to Carnival songs alone, but claimed in its title to be a collection of all the "Trionfi, Carri, Mascherate o Canti carnascialeschi" performed in Florence from the time of Lorenzo up to the year 1559. Many of the *canti* he collected take as their point of departure the tradesmen's songs sung by groups of masked singers walking the streets of Florence during Carnevale, which take as their themes the activities of the various *mestieri*, and are rich with obscene *double-entendres*. However, others are *canzoni di carro* composed around the literary and classical themes often represented on the *edifizi*, or parade floats, subjects of a type more often associated with the celebration of visits by distinguished foreigners or such feasts as *Calendimaggio*. Such *trionfi* were devised as quasi-theatrical displays centered upon the parade cars, accompanied by musicians, singers, and dancers who did not literally wear masks but were in costume—or a "disguisement" in the older English usage—to which Bishop Hall referred when he wrote of what he called the first English Court Masque, occurring the night of Epiphany in 1512, just twenty years after the death of Lorenzo de'Medici. That night "the king with a xi others were disguised, after the maner of Italie, called a maske, a thyng not sene before in Englande."[10]

It is also well known that Lasca was collecting poetry that was specially written, set to music (sometimes more than once, by different composers), and performed by experienced singers. This appears especially in Lasca's well-known report that Heinrich Isaac, "Master of the Choir of San Lorenzo and a musician highly esteemed in those days" (whose music for *canti* we have already seen Lorenzo de'Medici sending to Pietro Alamanni in 1491), wrote music in three voices (i.e., certainly for trained singers) for Lorenzo's *canzona de'confortini*, which Lasca calls the first to have been written by him.[11] Although evidence is scant regarding the authors of the earliest *canzoni*, it is significant that among the few written in

Lorenzo's lifetime for which authorship can be surely established, eleven are by Lorenzo himself, one by his brother-in-law Bernardo Rucellai, and one by either Politian or Agnolo Dovizi da Bibbiena.[12] Notwithstanding the *popolaresco* tone and address of most (but not all) of these *canzoni*, their forms are highly sophisticated, and certainly none of their authors is describable as *popolaresco*. Rather, as Lasca writes of the new *mascherate* invented by Lorenzo, "The inventions were noble, and accessible; the words clear and spirited; the music lively and expansive; the voices sonorous and united [again an indication of the professionalism of the singers]; the costumes [i.e., the disguisements] were rich and gay, appropriate to the invention, and made without stinting the cost; the parade apparatuses and furnishings adapted for them were built with mastery and painted beautifully; and the horses, when there was need of them, were very beautiful, and well caparisoned."[13]

Attestations from contemporary witnesses confirm Lasca's account of the changing standards for such spectacles. On 20 February 1490, for example, two years before the death of Lorenzo de'Medici, Filippo da Gagliano wrote to Niccolò Michelozzi that "We are waiting to enjoy this Carnevale, which would be colder than the north wind were it not for the [Compagnia della] Stella led by Mariottazio, which is staging a great mummer's parade tomorrow with seven *trionfi* of the seven planets, and a thousand beautiful things and inventions by the master's hand."[14] Four days later Piero Dovizi da Bibbiena also wrote to Michelozzi, saying, "We have done with the *maschere*, and are shut up here in a house filled with many beautiful ladies . . . I intend to send you by the first courier the *canzoni* composed by Lorenzo, which will seem marvelous to you, even though they are *carnascialeschi*, because the invention is new and beautiful."[15] On the basis of manuscript evidence, we know that two of the *canzoni* by Lorenzo accompanying the *trionfi* that year were the "Canzona de' sette pianeti" and the immortal "Canzona di Bacco" (neither of which are, properly speaking, *canti carnascialeschi*, but instead *canzoni di carro*, written to accompany parade floats, with no obscene plays on words nor any reference to the traditional *arti* and *mestieri*).[16] For the Feast of San Giovanni in the following year, 1491, the Compagnia della Stella again

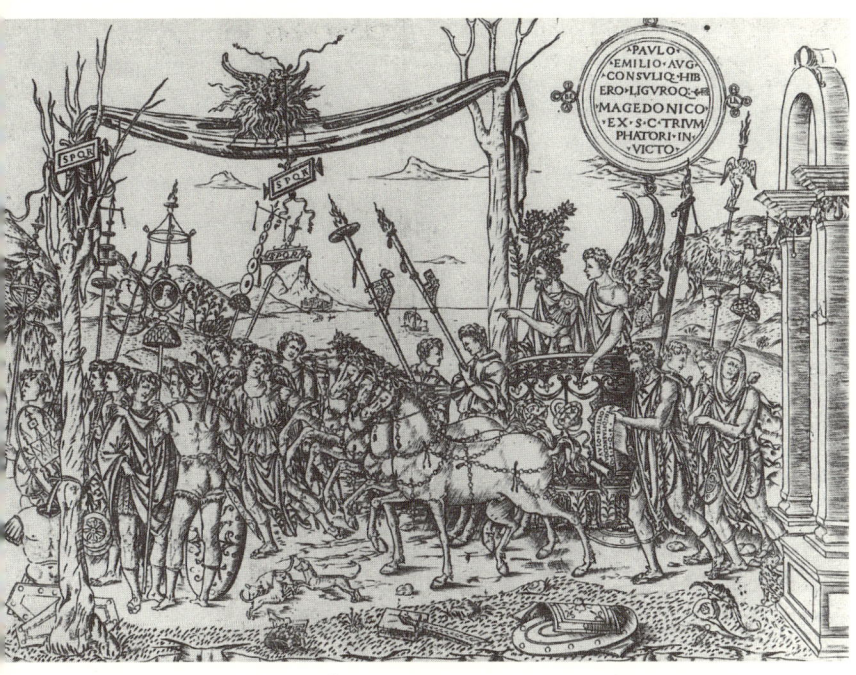

FIGURE 92
Anonymous, *The Triumph of Aemilius Paulus*, London, British Museum, engraving (Hind B.III.17). (Photograph © The British Museum)

managed the decoration of the cars representing the Triumph of Aemilius Paulus, based on Lorenzo's invention, and for which he officially supplied the horses and oxen. An engraving of this subject (Fig. 92), which must date close to 1491 and may record a design by Filippino Lippi for this *trionfo*, suggests something of its appearance, although it should be treated with caution because, like the *trionfo* itself, it too is an imaginative representation of a classical subject.[17] According to Vasari the inventions designed for this *mascherata* were "bellissimi," and he adds that Francesco Granacci, who was then a student in Lorenzo's sculpture garden at San Marco, had won praise for his paintings decorating the *carri*, even though he was still very young.[18] Moreover, we know that Lorenzo's "Canzona delle cicale" had been performed with a *carro* for Carnevale in 1489, the year before the *trionfi* of the Seven Planets;[19] and that for Carnevale of the year before that, in 1488, a "Canzona del carro" of the Nymphs and Poets was sung.[20] Even though the author of this last *canzone* is unknown, the title is enough to show that it was not a traditional carnival song, but instead was inspired by classical poetic themes that, like Lorenzo's "Canzona di Bacco" and "Canzona de'sette pianeti," were adapted for the imagery of the new *trionfi* and their *mascherate*.

Though incomplete, this is an impressive list of *mascherate*, and it includes every year from the resumption of Florentine civic celebrations in 1488, after a ten-year hiatus caused by the catastrophe of the Pazzi Conspiracy and the wars that followed, up to Lorenzo's death in April of 1492. Enough has been said to indicate that the level of artistic performance in the invention and decoration of the floats, and certainly in the composing of the *canzoni* and music that went with them (not to mention the performance and singing of that music), was extremely high. It included music composed not only by Isaac but also other professional composers, poetry written not only by Lorenzo de'Medici but also other skilled poets, and decoration painted not only by Filippino Lippi and Granacci but other artists as well. (One thinks too of the banners that had earlier been painted by Verrocchio and Pollaiuolo for Lorenzo's joust in 1469, and by Botticelli for Giuliano's in 1475.)

We know much less about the origin of Lorenzo's intervention in the planning of festival celebrations, and his transformation of them within the new forms of the *mascherata*. However, Politian's mention of Lorenzo's *laude* and *canti* (*carmina festis/excipienda choris*) in his *Nutricia* of 1486 certainly places his writing of festival *canzoni* before that date.[21] Indeed, Luigi Pulci, in a letter of 22 March 1466, sent with the canzone "Da poi che 'l Lauro" to Lorenzo in Rome, already refers to his seventeen-year-old patron's pleasure in masquerading in words put into the mouth of his lover Lucrezia Donati:[22]

> Quante fui esca et facie,
> quando e' faciea pur feste et nuovi advisi!
> Di che sovente già meco sorrisi

> allor che tutto trasformato apparve,
> et con sue certe larve
> credea ad me simular non esser desso.
> Ha, puro amante! hor non conosch'io appresso
> rose adamasche o mammole vihole?[23]

(How much was I the kindling and fire when he nonetheless gave parties and made new devices! I often laughed to myself when he appeared, completely transformed, and with certain of his masks [*larve*] thought to deceive me that he was not himself. Ha, a real lover! As though I should not know damask roses from common violets.)

And Pulci again refers back to the same period in his "La giostra di Lorenzo de'Medici," completed in 1474, in which he writes of the young Lorenzo consoling himself by writing poetry, inventing lovers' devices, and staging dances and nightime masquerades in order to entertain Lucrezia:

> E si dolea, ma con parole honeste;
> poi cominciò a tentar nuove arte e ingegni,
> e or cavagli, hor fantasie, hor veste
> mutar nuovi pensier', divise e segni,
> e hor far balli, e or nocturne feste
> (e che cosa è questo Amor non insegni?),
> e molte volte al suo bel sole apparve,
> per compiacergli, con mentite larve.[24]

(And he grieved, but with honorable words. Then he began to try new arts and things of wit, to spin new thoughts, sometimes with horses, sometimes with costumes, devices, and emblems, and sometimes staging dances and nighttime parties [for what is it Love does not teach?]. Many times he appeared to his beautiful sun in order to please her, in dissimulating masks.)

Although this is not evidence for Lorenzo's formal invention of the public *mascherata*, it does give some sense of its origins in the *feste* of his *brigata*. Such a party is described in a remarkable letter to Lorenzo written by Braccio Martelli in 1465, reporting of a visit to Lucrezia's villa and how she and members of the *brigata* listened to Lorenzo's love poems sung to music played by the lutenist Il Spagnuolo. They danced the *gioiosa*, the *chirintana*, and the *moresca*, and at one point one of the *brigata* emerged from a room *travestito* in one of Lucrezia's own dresses.[25] So far as *canti carnascialeschi* themselves are concerned, for internal reasons Lorenzo's "Canzona de'confortini" is securably datable before 1478 (the year of the Pazzi Conspiracy), and it very possibly dates as early as 1474 (ten years before Heinrich Isaac's arrival in Florence in 1484, only after which could he have set it to new music).[26] A letter from Piero Cennini to Pirrino Amerino describing the Feast of San Giovanni in 1475 is highly suggestive because of its description of boys on stilts hidden beneath effigies of giants painted on paper, or dressed as *spiritelli* roaming the city together with fauns and centaurs:

> The sprites were of more than one kind: one type was outfitted with a bow and quiver in the manner of a nymph, or brandishing a spear; another was dressed as a species of angel wearing on his head a shining skull-cap as a halo, with wings suspended from both shoulders; another was completely nude, with wings at the shoulders and winged sandals attached to his feet. The fauns were hairy and had goats' feet, the centaurs seemed to be half horses, and painted paper [*charta picta*] completed what otherwise would be lacking in these animated effigies.[27]

The classical imagery Cennini describes irresistibly calls to mind images like Baccio Baldini's engraving of the triumph of Bacchus and Ariadne in a car drawn by centaurs and accompanied by fauns and nymphs, dating to around 1475 (Fig. 93). In its turn the engraving is reminiscent of Lorenzo de'Medici's "Canzona di Bacco" (though it does not correspond to any of the cars described by Cennini), so much so that it prompts the speculation whether Lorenzo's *canzone* might not have been written in the mid-1470s, notwithstanding the claim made in two manuscripts that both the "Canzona di Bacco" and the "'Canzona de' sette pianeti' andarono in

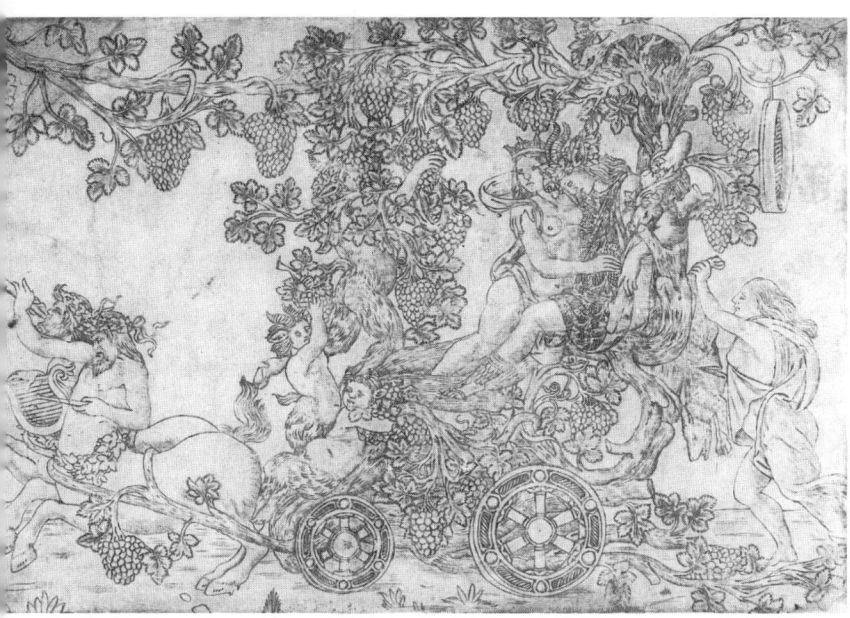

FIGURE 93
Baccio Baldini, *The Triumph of Bacchus and Ariadne*, London, British Museum, engraving (Hind A.II.26). Detail. (Photograph © The British Museum)

maschera nel 14[90]:—[28] Bacchus is not one of the seven planets, however, and so one may well wonder whether Lorenzo actually composed this *canzona* for a *trionfo* devoted to one of the planets, or whether he first wrote it as a *canzona di carro* for some earlier Triumph of Bacchus, and that it was again sung at the later date.

Speculation aside, Baldini's engraving is useful as a guide to assessing the value of artistic images as representations of actuality, in this case civic *mascherate*. His *trionfo*, for example, does not entirely aim to represent a parade float as it actually appeared, not only because the gods' nudity is real and not feigned, but also because the centaurs and fauns are "real," and not masked paraders whose costumes have been supplemented by painted paper cutouts. At the same time, the form of Bacchus's car is hardly ancient but clearly takes as its point of departure parade *edifizi* the artist had actually seen and experienced at first hand. The value of the engraving as a work of art—that is as itself an imaginative representation but one based in popular experience—derives from what it tells us about the place that the imagery of such civic rituals held in the public imagination, popular as well as aristocratic (to which Richard Trexler and Pierre Francastel have been especially alert, although a lively historical discussion continues about the social and political inferences to be drawn from Lorenzo's interventions in the major urban feasts).[29] If we now turn, however, to a particular set of artistic representations of triumphs ubiquitous in manuscript illuminations, tapestries, *deschi da parto*, cassoni, engravings, and domestic paintings of the Quattrocento—namely illustrations to Petrarch's *Trionfi*—which all depict one or another of those Triumphs in ways that certainly reflect the imagery of the actual *edifizi* built for Florentine festivals, something significant emerges about the kinds of dress worn for these celebrations, and about their evolution into "disguisements," the quasi-theatrical costumes specifically designed for *mascherate*.

We may begin with a miniature of the Triumph of Love from a manuscript of Petrarch's *Trionfi e canzoniere* (Fig. 94), dating from the 1440s, that shows a relatively simple *carro* carrying a nude *spiritello d'Amore* (shown as a living infant, though in real *edifizi* he would often have been made of painted wood or papier maché), shooting flaming arrows. Fashionably dressed men and women walk in attendance upon Love's chariot, and although they present themselves as subjects to Love, they are not portrayed as the literary and historical lovers named by Petrarch. They are instead young Florentines promenading in their best and most up-to-date clothes. The same appears from a *desco da parto* in the Galleria Sabauda in Turin, dating from the 1450s (see Fig. 58), in which we see a more elaborated version of Love's chariot. The *carro* is decorated with rich brocades and fur hangings, and it is followed by a cortège of noble young ladies and youths even more elegantly dressed than before, in clothes that now unmistakably represent the new French courtly fashions. Especially noticeable are the tall *hennins* worn by the women, hats in the French style with twin peaks (*a corna* or *a sella*, as they were called by the Italians), as well as their richly embroidered gowns (*cioppe*) and cloaks (*giornee*), not to

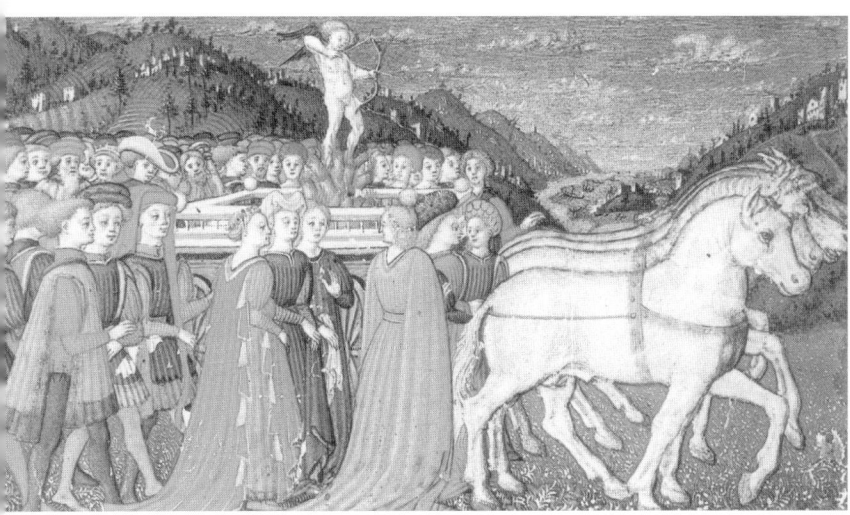

FIGURE 94
The Triumph of Love, frontispiece to Petrarch, *Trionfi*, Florence,
Biblioteca Nazionale (Cod. Palatina 192, fol. 1r).
(Photograph by James T. Van Rensselaer)

mention the fur-lined hats worn by the men, which are set with pearls that spell out lovers' mottos in the chivalric French manner. A nascent theatrical element is introduced by the two women (who again appear in another *desco da parto* in the Victoria and Albert Museum; see Fig. 59), who are also in contemporary dress but who act the roles of the courtesan Phyllis riding on Aristotle's back and Delilah shearing Samson's hair. It would be easy to imagine both figures in actual parades played by real persons, either women or *uomini travestiti*, whose aspect is supplemented, as Cennini put it, by *charta picta*, that is, painted-paper cutouts of Aristotle and Samson. This proto-theatrical element is soon to be developed substantially, as we find in Baccio Baldini's engraving of the *Triumph of Love* from the mid-1470s (see Fig. 60), in which there again appear women in fashionable French dress wearing the twin-peaked *hennin*, but the men instead are shown in a species of costume. Some of them wear extravagantly ornamented pseudo-armor, with wings on their helmets, and some

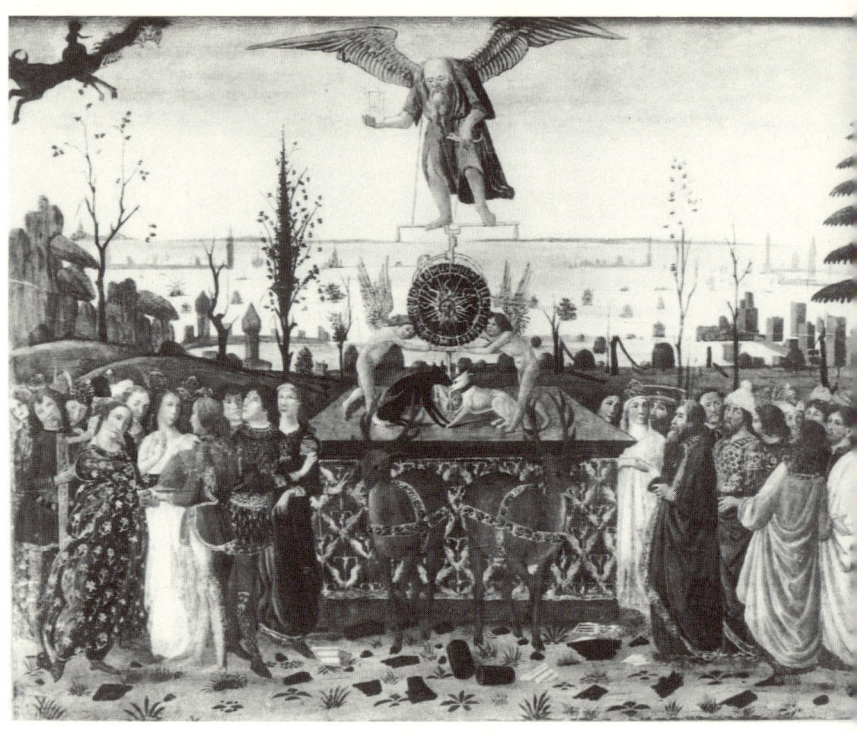

FIGURE 95
Jacopo del Sellaio, *The Triumph of Time*, Fiesole, Museo Bandini.
(Photograph: Alinari/Art Resource)

are dressed as ancient, bearded sages wearing oriental turbans and exotic Byzantine hats, and hence they not only stand for, but also masquerade as those ancient and Biblical worthies whom Petrarch had named as victims to the power of Love. Also noteworthy are the cornucopias that decorate the four corners of Love's chariot, which belch flames from their mouths in a manner that certainly evokes real civic displays accompanied by fireworks such as those designed by Lo Cecca, to which we have earlier referred, as well as Bartolomeo Benci's *carro* with the Triumph of Love, which was rigged with the fireworks that Lappacini saw set off before Marietta Strozzi's window. And by the 1480s we find in Jacopo del Sel-

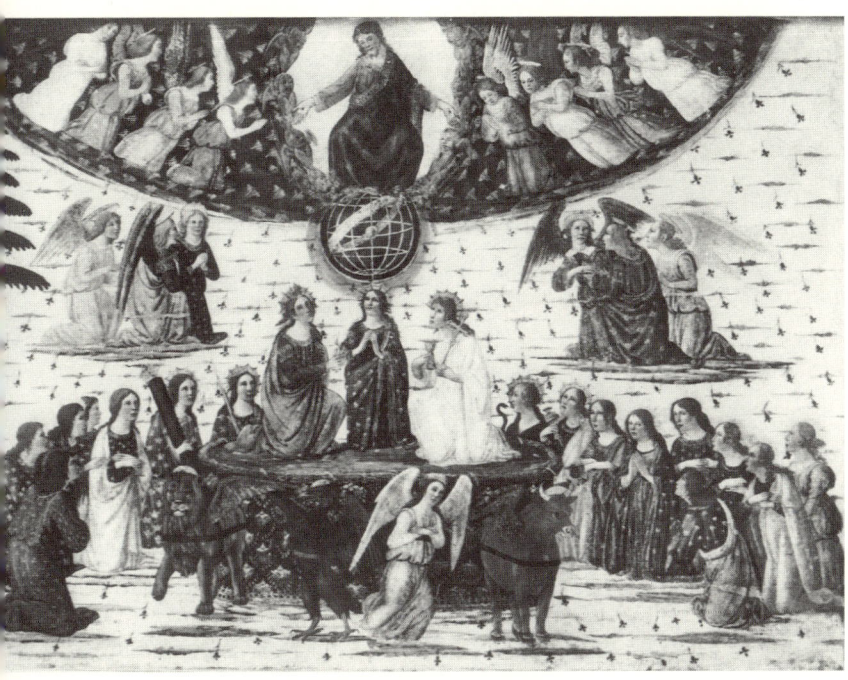

FIGURE 96
Jacopo del Sellaio, *The Triumph of Eternity*, Fiesole, Museo Bandini.
(Photograph: Alinari / Art Resource)

laio's *Triumphs of Love, Chastity, Time,* and *Eternity,* now in the Museo Bandini in Fiesole (Figs. 95, 96; see also Plate 3, Fig. 89), that the prototheatrical *trionfi* depicted by Baldini have now been transformed into true *mascherate*.

Sellaio's paintings have been cut into four separate panels, but originally represented a continuous parade in an imaginary landscape, as can be seen by the overlappings from one picture to another. The parade is made up of four *carri*, and in the *Triumph of Love* there appear at the corners of Love's *edifizio* four gilded *spiritelli* with flaming darts. Musicians accompany the *carri*, playing lutes and horns (Fig. 95), and some of the men and women are shown dancing to the music of the *canzoni a ballo* (see

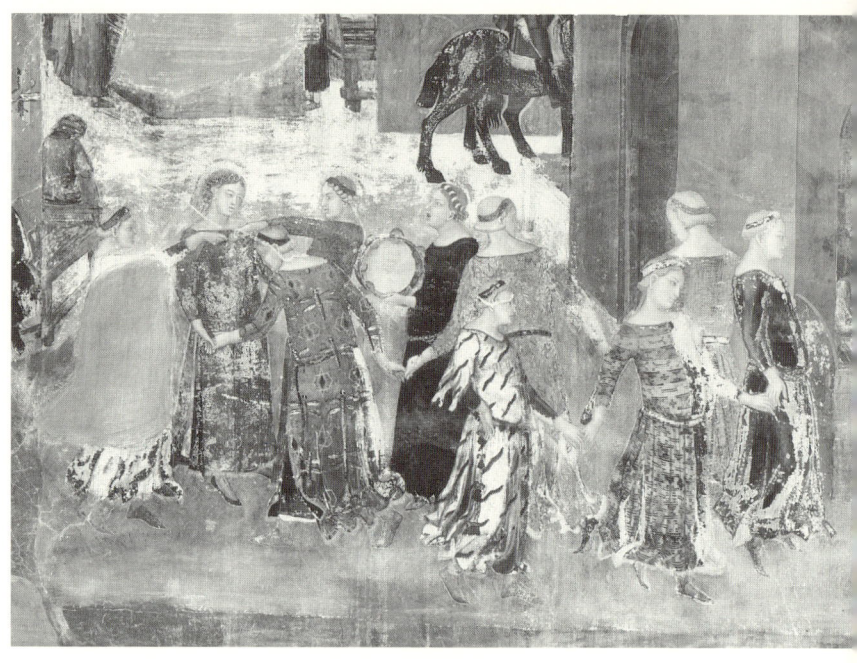

FIGURE 97
Ambrogio Lorenzetti, *The Effects of Good Government in the City*, Siena, Palazzo Pubblico. Detail, *Dancing Maidens*. (Photograph: Scala/Art Resource)

Fig. 89). Of special interest are the womens' costumes, which are *camicie da giorno* that are gaily gilded and painted with pseudo-lettering, with flowers, and with tongues of flame (see Fig. 89). The patterns are not woven, like the brocaded dresses worn by fashionable young Florentine women, but are painted as disguisements, that is, ephemeral costumes that have been specifically designed for a *mascherata*.[30] Even so, like everything else relevant to Lorenzo de'Medici's invention of the *mascherata*, these costumed maidens descend from the traditions of Tuscan folklore. A familiar example appears in Ambrogio Lorenzetti's vignette of the dancing women in his fresco of *The Effects of Good Government in the City* in the Sala della Pace of the Palazzo Pubblico in Siena (Fig. 97). The fresco shows the activities of a well-regulated city at peace, and the women wear dresses painted with dragonflies and other insects as they dance in one of the city's festivals. Such festivals could only be celebrated in times of peace, and for this reason the women virtually personify the conditions of peace fostered by the city's governing fathers. Sellaio's nymphs, on the other hand, are not simple maidens, or *contadine*. They are rather actors in a larger and unified fiction organized round the Petrarchan themes stated in the triumphal *carri*, to which the music, the dance, the poetry and painted decoration all make a contribution. Nor are they dressed in the latest French fashion, but are habited in costume, *alla ninfa*. They play a role, and dance to the music and singing of those *canzoni a ballo* composed for a true *mascherata*.

I wish to call special attention to one of these costumes, which we have already briefly mentioned, namely the white dress worn by one of the dancing women at the left of the *Triumph of Chastity* (Fig. 98), which is painted with a lovely pattern of blue cornflowers (*fiordilisi*). Although it is not precisely identical, the costume is in all fundamental respects the twin to the white dress painted with blue cornflowers worn by the figure of Flora in Botticelli's *Birth of Venus* (Fig. 99). Botticelli's Flora, in other words, is also disguised as for a masque (though she plays a part in an independent literary invention specifically created for the painting, which can hardly be taken as a representation of an actual spectacle), this time on the theme of Venus and the Spring. Moreover, the same masking is evident in the painted costume worn by Flora in the *Primavera* (Fig. 100), which also takes the Laurentian *mascherata* as the point of departure for its own independent (and profoundly classical) invention.[31] In this painted masque of the Spring, dating to about 1477, Mercury is also in costume. He wears a red cloak painted with flaming tongues (like some of the nymphs in Sellaio's *Trionfi*), and carries a richly jeweled parade sword suspended from his belt. And so too is Venus in a disguisement. She wears a costume made from a *camicia da giorno* painted with gold rays at the breast, and with huge pearls hanging suspended from the hem of her robe (much like the pearls described by chroniclers decorating the lavish

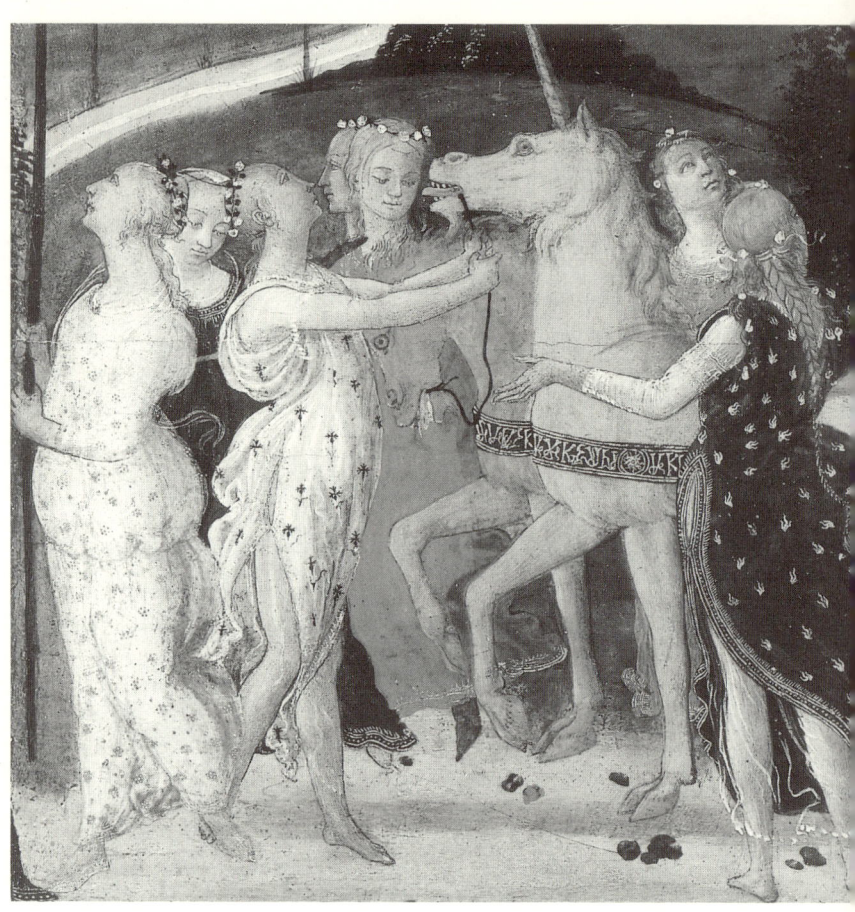

FIGURE 98
Jacopo del Sellaio, *The Triumph of Chastity*, Fiesole, Museo Bandini. Detail, *Nymphs*. (Photograph by James T. Van Rensselaer)

outfits worn at the feasts and jousts). Her costume, like the others, is not made for everyday use but is ephemeral, a quasi-theatrical dress designed for a *mascherata*. Botticelli's *Primavera*, in other words, expresses its classical subject within the vernacular poetic idioms of the *mascherata*, and in this masque of the Spring Flora again appears in her white dress painted

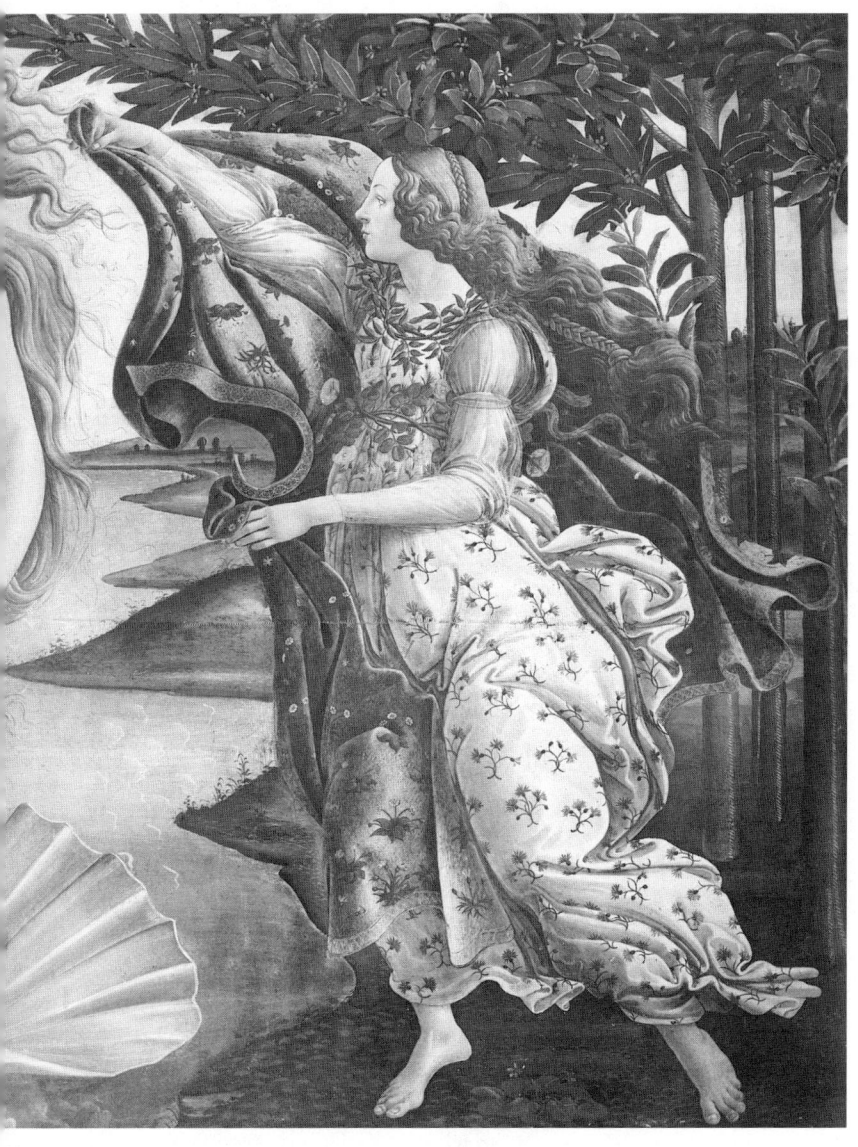

FIGURE 99
Sandro Botticelli, *The Birth of Venus*, Florence, Uffizi. Detail, *Flora*.
(Photograph: Alinari/Art Resource)

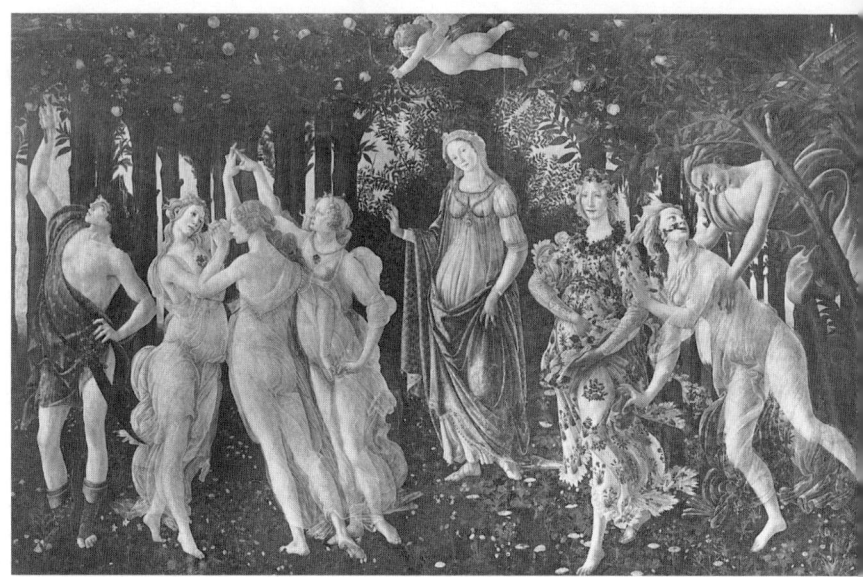

FIGURE 100
Sandro Botticelli, *Primavera*, Florence, Uffizi.
(Photograph: Alinari/Art Resource)

with flowers. Its decoration is more elaborate than that for the painted costume she later wears in the *Birth of Venus*, or for that adorning the costume of Sellaio's nymph in the *Triumph of Chastity*. Her dress is painted with white and red roses, carnations and cornflowers, and she is wreathed with violets, daisies, forget-me-nots, and lilies of the valley—in brief, with all the springtime colors of the flowers that she strews over the *prato variopinto*.[32]

Finally, it has long been known, ever since Warburg in fact, that Flora as depicted in Botticelli's *Primavera* (and to a lesser extent Flora in his *Birth of Venus*) bears a close resemblance to Politian's description of Simonetta Cattaneo Vespucci, the lady to whom Giuliano de'Medici had dedicated the joust he won in 1475, who is twice described in the *Stanze per la giostra di Giuliano de'Medici* as masked, that is, as wearing a shining white dress painted with flowers:

> Candida è ella, e candida la vesta
> Ma pur di rose e fior dipinta e d'erba³³

(She is shining white, and shining white is her dress, though painted with roses, flowers, and greenery.)

And again:

> Ell'era assisa sovra la verdura,
> Allegra, e ghirlandetta avea contesta
> Di quanti fior creassi mai natura,
> De'quai tutta dipinta era sua vesta.³⁴

(She was seated upon the grass, and, lighthearted, had woven a garland out of as many flowers as nature had ever created, the flowers with which her dress was painted.)

On this basis Warburg suggested that Flora in the *Primavera* is in some sense a portrait of Simonetta, who had died in 1476, not so very long before the completion of the picture. If so, and I believe it is, then this is a portrait in a rather complex sense, not only because Simonetta's portrayal is posthumous, but also because she is in disguise. And the same is true of Politian's equally posthumous portrait of her in the *Stanze*, where she is again described in a disguisement, wearing a painted masquerade dress. What is more, as we have already seen, in this, the only appearance of Simonetta in the poem, following upon Politian's celebrated description of her beauty, when she is asked by the delirious Julio what kind of goddess she is, she discovers the masquerade, telling him that she is not what he takes her to be.

The problem of portraiture in Florentine Quattrocento art is one of the knottier and hotly contested (though with more heat than light) areas of art-historical research. It is not made any easier by introducing the concept of the masquerade, whereby real people are shown in disguise. Yet the phenomenon of role-playing is real, and becomes an especially pressing critical issue when we consider the art produced during the lifetime of Lorenzo the Magnificent. Among many possible examples, I will illus-

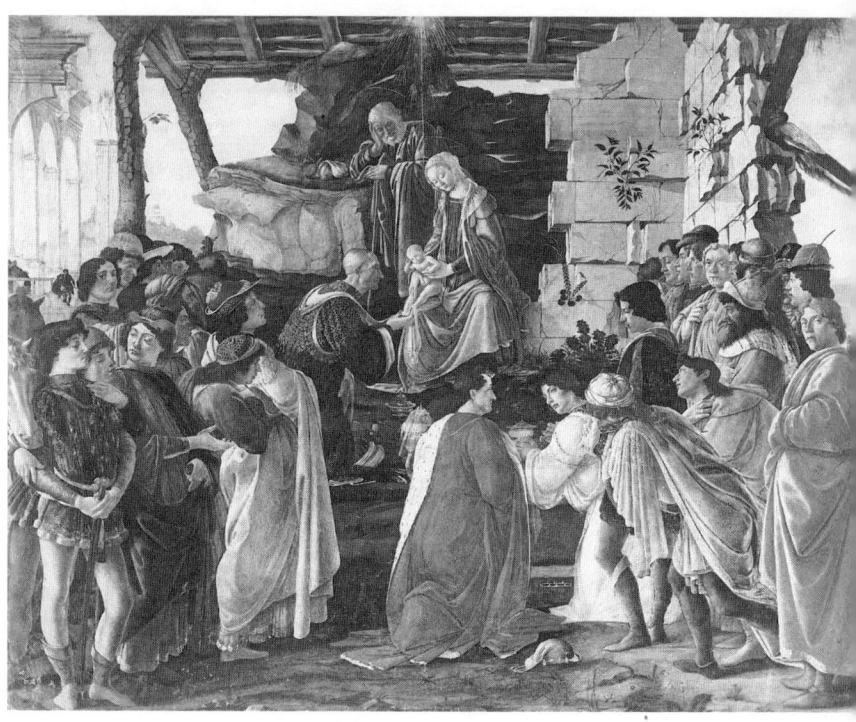

FIGURE 101
Sandro Botticelli, *Adoration of the Magi*, Florence, Uffizi.
(Photograph: Alinari / Art Resource)

trate the problem by briefly adducing only one other well-known painting, also by Botticelli, the *Adoration of the Magi* he painted for Guasparre del Lama around 1476 (Fig. 101). There are two classes of portrait in this painting. The first, as reported by Vasari, himself an expert on Medici iconography, is represented by the portraits of Cosimo de'Medici and his sons Giovanni and Piero, all of them posthumous (like Simonetta-Flora in the *Primavera*). Furthermore, each is in disguisement, masquerading as one of the Magi. It is the fact of their death that allows them this role as actors within a timeless religious drama, for they are done with the contingencies of the present and have themselves entered into the perma-

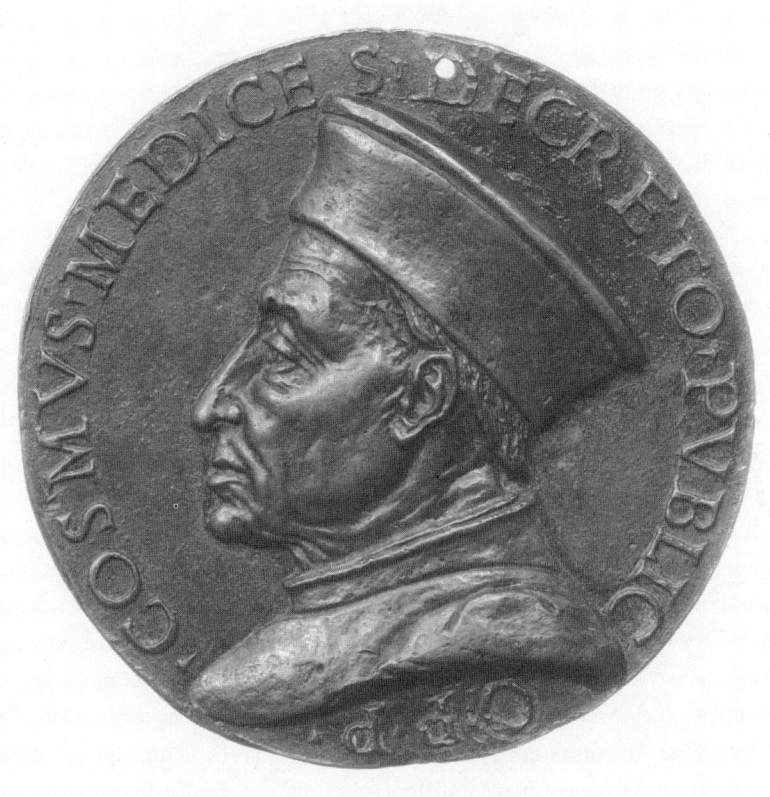

FIGURE 102
Cosimo de'Medici, medal, obverse, Samuel H. Kress Collection, Washington, National Gallery of Art. (Photograph © Board of Trustees, National Gallery of Art)

nence of history, of which they are now part, and to the sum total of which, not least by their particular devotion to the feast of the Magi, they have contributed a measure of added pious and cultural perfection. Especially interesting is the portrait of Cosimo, which differs enough from his image on the well-known medal struck after his death in 1464 (Fig. 102) to have caused some scholars to challenge Vasari's identification of him.[35] However, close examination shows that Botticelli in fact followed very closely the outline of Cosimo's profile on the medal, but at the same time carefully deleted all the marks of old age in a man who had died in his seventies. Cosimo's sunken eyes, wrinkles, and wattles, all carefully limned on the medal, were erased by Botticelli in signification of Cosimo's now eternally ageless existence. What we see is not Cosimo as he was, but an ageless idea of him, the perfected mask of an idea he represents that is to be handed down to posterity. The second class of portrait in the *Adoration of the Magi* is that of the living, who stand as witnesses to this eternalized masque but who, because their characters are still in flux, subject to the unknowable contingencies of fortune, are as yet unfinished and can not yet assume their parts in it. Among the living witnesses we see Lorenzo, his brother Giuliano, and Botticelli himself. Giuliano is at the left, shown as the youth he then was, superciliously proud, eyes looking haughtily down his long nose, with a sensuous mouth that curves downward and then rises at the corners in a kind of smirk. The same features are recorded in a bust of the living Giuliano often attributed to Verrocchio in the National Gallery of Art in Washington (Fig. 103).[36] Both portraits are usefully compared to Botticelli's posthumous portrait of him, also in the National Gallery (Fig. 104). Here, as in the portrait of Cosimo in the *Adoration of the Magi*, Giuliano's most salient identifying features—his aquiline nose, haughtily downcast eyes, and double-curving mouth—are not only abstracted, but also exaggerated, creating an image, not of Giuliano as he was, but of an eternalized idea of him, his perfected mask.

To return to Simonetta, she appears in Politian's *Stanze*, not as Flora, but masked as a nymph pledged to Diana, which happens to be one of the senhals—or masks—used by Lorenzo de' Medici in his earliest poetry to cover his poetic lady, Lucrezia Donati (after 1470 her familiar mask changed to that of the Sun). In 1466 Luigi Pulci also referred to her under the senhal Diana in "Da poi che 'Lauro," a *canzone* he sent as a letter to Lorenzo in Rome, telling him in a form of poetic cipher of Lucrezia's actual misery in his absence.[37] It is in fact a characteristic of the poetry written by Lorenzo and his clients, whether composed in the vernacular

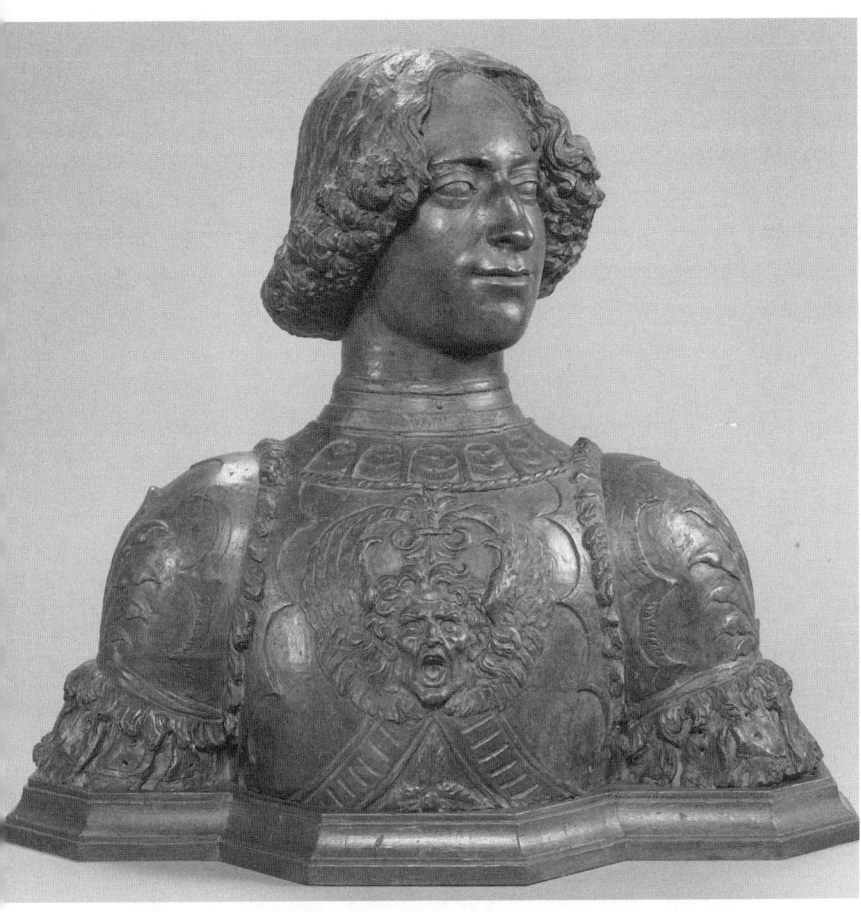

FIGURE 103
Andrea del Verrocchio, attr., *Giuliano de'Medici*, Washington, National Gallery of Art, Andrew W. Mellon Collection. (Photograph © Board of Trustees, National Gallery of Art)

by such poets as the Pulci brothers, or in Latin by the likes of Naldo Naldi or Ugolino Verino (and I suggest that the same is true of painting, Botticelli's especially), that it continually refers to actual people and real events, interpreting and rationalizing the unpredictable turns of these events as they unfold in the light of poetic concepts of love—fictional masks—that

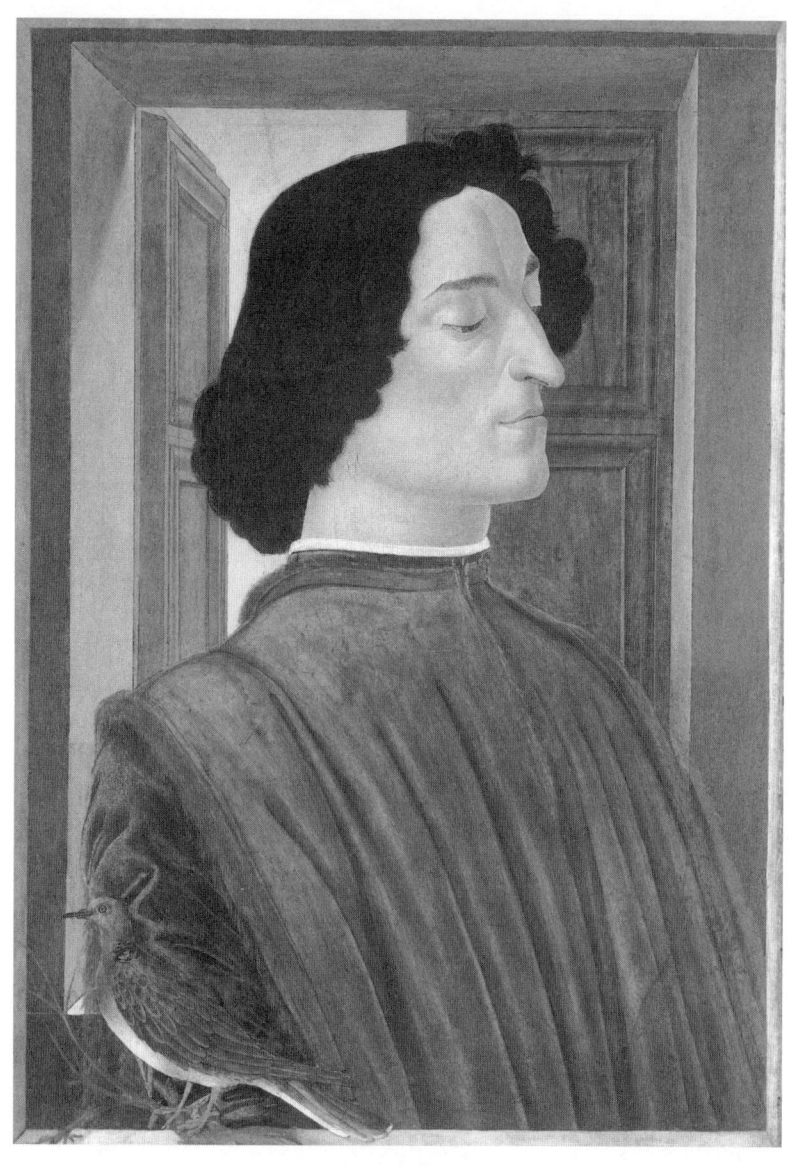

FIGURE 104
Sandro Botticelli, *Giuliano de'Medici*, Washington, National Gallery of Art, Samuel H. Kress Collection. (Photograph © Board of Trustees, National Gallery of Art)

are to some degree linked to evolving cultural and political ideals identifiable with the genius and honor of Florence. On a popular level such topicality of reference (and language) can be found, as we have seen, in *canzoni* written for festival *trionfi* (or in Luigi Pulci's *frottole*, like the enchanting "Le Galee per Quaracchi"). On a more patrician level it also informs the poems lamenting the deaths of such beauties as Albiera degli Albizzi and Simonetta herself, as well as those gathered in Lorenzo de' Medici's *Canzoniere*, in which many of the poems refer to specific alterations in the progress of a very real love affair. One example is the sestina "Fuggo i bei raggi del mio ardente Sole" of 1466, which is about Lorenzo's love for Lucrezia Donati masked as Diana, and which he sent her by way of Braccio Martelli and the *brigata*, who helped interpret it to her and for themselves.[38] On the deepest level, works like Politian's *Stanze* and Lorenzo's unfinished *Comento* to his own sonnets artfully mask larger (and differing, and changing) interpretations of contemporary events.

Thus far in this chapter we have traced an evolution, subtle but distinct in outline, in the forms of Florentine civic celebration, including new poems by literarily sophisticated and able poets, set to music written by professional composers, and sung in parts by trained singers. Concomitantly, we have also seen a corresponding growth in sophistication, and lavishness, in the invention and presentation of particular themes, both traditional as in the case of Petrarch's *Trionfi*, and new (and with classical components) as in the Triumph of the Seven Planets or the Triumph of Aemilius Paulus. These themes, with their accompanying music and *canzoni a ballo*, were unified around the imagery displayed on the triumphal cars (decorated by the best artists), accompanied by figures whose attire changes gradually from fashionable dress to a kind of theatrical disguise. All of these, taken together, define the new *mascherata* in recognizable terms, and directly prefigure its later development in the spectacles and *intermezzi* of the Florentine grand-dukes, in French *ballets du cour*, and in English masques. However, with Lorenzo's poetry, Politian's *Stanze*, and Botticelli's *Primavera* and *Mars and Venus*, we have moved, and almost imperceptibly so, into the realm of a high art that takes the Laurentian masque as its point of departure, and hence establishes masking itself as its hermeneutic crux. It is an art on the one hand sophisticated in the extreme, with internal references to a thousand poetic and artistic models (so characteristic of Politian). And on the other hand it is an art rooted in the popular imagination and the common experiences of the present.

Both Botticelli and Politian (who was certainly the advisor for the invention of the *Mars and Venus*, and almost certainly so for the *Primavera*) have been repeatedly interpreted as artists whose aim was to transform the contingencies of historical experience—subsuming, as Carducci would have it, the "wretched pretext" afforded the poet by Giuliano's joust (or the painter by a mere Calendimaggio celebration)—into a world of pure myth, each expressing a humanist "sogno primaverile" defined entirely within the refined lineaments of a pure art. Both poet and painter have often been characterized as being "endowed with an exquisite sentiment for form, and a complete indifference to any kind of content."[39] And for both the experiences of the present have seemed to be completely absorbed within an abstractly ideal poetic and mythical universe that acquires contemporary meaning only by incidental iconographical allusions to Medicean themes and devices, contributing in turn to what historians have called the "myth" of Lorenzo de'Medici. However, as was pointed out by Donato in a shrewdly polemical article, this solution remains on the whole awkward and unsuccessful.[40] As regards the *Stanze*, the figures of Julio, Lauro, and the nymph Simonetta do not have exclusively poetic existences. They can only be understood in terms of historical persons and events that are scarcely concealed by their poetic disguisements. Simonetta is not the poetically ideal equivalent of Beatrice and Laura, as indeed we have heard her carefully explaining to the delirious Julio. She does not, like Beatrice in the *Vita nuova* or Laura in Petrarch's *Canzoniere*, exist only within the self-sufficient framework of a poetic argument that she structures and is herself defined by. Although Politian brings to bear all his poetic skills, deploying his virtually infinite repertory of literary models in order to stress her idealization, even so Simonetta's historical reality is always present in the *Stanze*, and indeed is insisted upon, as are the realities of Giuliano and Lorenzo. This is why, as we saw in the last chapter, it makes all the difference in the world for interpreting the poem if we date its inception to 1475, the year of Giuliano's joust—or to 1476, when the twenty-three-year-old Simonetta died on April 26—or to 1478, when the 25-year-old Giuliano was murdered on April 26, exactly the second anniversary of her death. Any attempt to understand the poetry of the *Stanze* must take this tension between art and history into account, and the same is true of Lorenzo's poetry, or Pulci's, or Naldo Naldi's. It is also true of the Masque of the Spring enacted in Botticelli's *Primavera*, as well as the *sacra rappresentazione* with the masked figures of Cosimo and his two sons shown in his *Adoration of the Magi*. And it is especially true of the Masque of the Joust depicted in his *Mars and Venus*.

I say the "Masque of the Joust" not only because of the clearly contemporary costumes and armaments shown in the *Mars and Venus* but also, and more fundamentally, because Politian was beyond any doubt the author of the Greek invention for the painting, which closely parallels (but does not illustrate) the argument he invented for his *Stanze*. Botticelli's *Satyrisci* appear playing in fifteenth-century armor, masking themselves beneath the god's sallet and cuirass, and using his jousting lance to tilt against wasps. Because the concept of the panicky and empty nightmare terrors they embody cannot have any positive meaning by definition, it follows that they, by masking themselves within Mars's own armor, are conceptually akin to the false dreams hidden behind deceiving masks (*sogni drento alle lor larve*) that assail and confuse the sleeping Julio in the second book of the *Stanze*. There Julio is himself the victim of Venus's wiles, and hence the counterpart to Mars as described at the end of the first book—Mars who is the spirit and very personification of martial valor, Mars who has been enfeebled by Cupid's dart and venomous kisses, and Mars who languishes in Venus's lap, lost in effeminate luxuriousness, his mind far from any thoughts of military glory. All this being so, it is impossible to avoid, as a methodological imperative, raising the question of whether Botticelli's Mars and Venus, who are also inventions by Politian, are not also posthumous masks for Simonetta Cattaneo Vespucci and Giuliano de'Medici, in the same way that Julio and his nymph in the *Stanze* are thinly veiled interpretive masks for the same historical figures. In both works of art an errant and confused dream of love and courtly glory can be seen to have sapped true martial alertness. It had been such a spirit of neglect, paradoxically produced by an excess of peacetime *otium*, that had exposed Florence to the deadly and completely unexpected treachery of the Pazzi Conspiracy, and the wars that followed.

Moreover, such an interpretation of the situation in Florence, as expressed in allegorical form in two great works of art, agrees with the view of Machiavelli, who had come of age in the time of the Pazzi wars. Although, as we have seen, in one context he had praised the jousts and civic celebrations as a useful means of keeping the minds of the citizens diverted from thoughts of sedition, he also reports in his *Istorie fiorentine* that many "buoni cittadini" had become concerned about the courtly refinements and manners that had softened the youth of the city, leaving them indifferent to any dangers that threatened from without or within. Such evils, he wrote, often arise in times of peace when the young men, enjoying greater freedom than usual, consume their time and substance in wanton behavior (*lascivie*), in idleness and games, thinking only of fine costumes and pleasing the ladies with their sharp speech and wit. Such manners had already become well established in Florence at the time of the visit of the Duke of Milan with all his court in 1471, but "if the Duke found the city of Florence filled with *cortiginiani delicatezze e costumi*, contrary to every well-ordered *civiltà*, he left it much more so."[41] In such a way the Florentines had become lulled into complacency and left vulnerable to the onslaughts of treason and fortune.

At this point we must return to Del Lungo's fundamental objection to reading the *Stanze* as referring to Giuliano's murder in 1478 (despite the fatal rubric to *Stanze* 2.35, "Pronostico verissimo della morte di Iulio"), which would apply with equal force to Botticelli's *Mars and Venus*, dating to the first half of the 1480s, and which, as I suggested earlier, is the only one that really counts. The objection is that "a poem of love and jousts after the death of the hero would have been a misconception, and in Politian a vice that he did not possess—ingratitude."[42] For this reason Del Lungo proposed an alternative reading, that the ominous change in the tone and content of the second book was occasioned by Simonetta's death in 1476. However, as Donato pointed out, if the poem were really only about Giuliano's joust the year before, then there would really have been no reason to introduce the subject of Simonetta's death in the first place. And I would repeat that the *Stanze* cannot be read, like Politian's earlier epicedion for Albiera degli Albizzi, as a lamentation for her, except insofar as Simonetta is the mask for Giuliano's confused *mente*. Giuliano's unfinished life, which had encompassed only a single memorable public display, and this of merely adolescent virtue, namely acquitting himself well in the joust ("equestre certamen," in the words of Filippo Corsini, a show of "nostrorum adolescentium virtus"), is truly the subject of the unfinished *Stanze*, and Simonetta is the mask for his unhappy fortune.[43]

Whether this means, as Del Lungo's objection would imply, that Politian (who published the *Stanze* only in 1494) had indeed turned against his former patron and was hence tainted with the vice of ingratitude, is most unlikely. After the trauma of the Pazzi Conspiracy the nature of Lorenzo de'Medici's management of the affairs of the city changed markedly (and of necessity), and it was from that moment that he increasingly began to assume many of the characteristics of an autocratic leader. What is more, his own changing ideal of the city and its ethos is explicitly stated in his own literary production, and notably in his *Comento sopra alcuni de' suoi sonetti*, in which Lorenzo interprets his sonnets as expressions of a love evolving through the flux of fortune and changing events, the meaning of which could not be fully understood at the time, but only grasped in retrospective contemplation. It is well known, for example, that the first four sonnets interpreted by Lorenzo in the *Comento* had been written on the occasion of Simonetta's death in 1476 (and included in the *Raccolta Aragonese* he sent to Naples later in the same year), when he and all the other poets in the city vied with one another in lamenting her loss in verse. But it has not been generally appreciated that their incorporation within the broader argument of the *Comento* is also a part of Lorenzo's revised interpretation of their meaning in the light of subsequent events.[44] Simonetta is there masked as Lorenzo's own first love, a poetic role she had never played, and she appears as Venus, the morning star, and the brightest light of heaven. This former ideal of his youth is dead (and it is impossible to avoid the allusion to Lorenzo's murdered brother, whose fortune had been identified with Simonetta in the joust), immediately to be eclipsed by a yet brighter star, the Sun. The Sun, as we have seen, is the mask for Lucrezia Donati, who had from the beginning always been the lady of Lorenzo's poetry. In so doing he remained true to the lady Lucrezia as his poetic love, even as he altered the idea of love she stood for into a new concept, more abstractly philosophical, indeed Neoplatonic in character. In the *Comento* Lorenzo took the youthfully erotic ideal of love that Lucrezia had originally represented, and reidentified this idea with Simonetta, masked as Venus, in order to signify a beauty both literally dead and dead to him. In poetic terms, to claim Simonetta as his first love was no more than to state his love for the lost Giuliano, with whom the ideals of Lorenzo's own youth had died, and to identify that youth with an exquisite, carefree delight in the sheer beauty of life that had gone tragically wrong. No such idea of carefree youth was possible after the realities of treachery, murder, and war had settled in around Florence. And when the clouds cleared a decade later, and once again *mascherate* with their spectacularly produced triumphal cars, costumes, music, dancing, and *canzoni* were sponsored by Lorenzo in Florence, the reality hidden by the new masks had doubtless changed into something more closely resembling what Machiavelli later suggested. As productions that became more and more stage-managed by Lorenzo, they took on the character not only of manifestations of the collective honor of the city, as he had claimed them to be, but also inevitably identified that honor with the person of Lorenzo himself. As such, the old civic rituals began to assume the coloration of the *panem et circenses* by which an increasingly remote leader sought to keep the people diverted, and which is especially characteristic of the *mascherate* and spectacles sponsored by Leo X upon his return to Florence in 1512, as well as by the Medici grand-dukes in the later sixteenth century.

As a response to Del Lungo's scruple concerning Politian's putative ingratitude in his portrayal of the enamored Giuliano in the *Stanze*, it is of course of the greatest significance that Lorenzo himself, in the aftermath of the Pazzi Conspiracy, turned his back on the same idea of youthful erotic love to which his own early poetry had itself been dedicated, and substituted for it a more austere, Neoplatonic concept of abstract and virtuous beauty. In so doing he acknowledged that his first love, which through Simonetta he identified with Venus as the star of the morning, beautiful though it may have been, had also been doomed. However, in returning to Politian's *Stanze* and Botticelli's *Mars and Venus*, it should be kept in mind that all interpretations of ongoing history (and especially artistic ones) are contingent, and that every work of art has its own meaning. In the case of Laurentian Florence, and especially in that art arising close to the person of Lorenzo, this entailed the artist's own response to experiences common to all (which is why the question of dating is so crucial). The ominous consequences of the idea of youthful love, consecrated to an all-powerful Venus, and masked in the inventions by Politian for both the *Stanze* and the *Mars and Venus*, is not identical in its psychological and moral shading to the idea of youthful love masked by Simonetta as Venus in Lorenzo's *Comento*. Lorenzo, unlike Politian, terrified by human helplessness in the face of the capriciousness and brutality of Fortune, was an adroit master in adapting to events in unpredictable flux, and he regretfully but firmly consigns Simonetta (and with her Giuliano) to an irrecoverable past. Nor certainly is the meaning of either, as a work of art, identical to the optimistic expression embodied in Botticelli's earlier (and surely pre-conspiracy) *Primavera*, in which Lorenzo's first idea of perennially youthful and fecund love presided over by Venus is celebrated and made permanently manifest in an earthly paradise of imperishable and eternally renewing beauty.[45] Nevertheless, in works produced both before and after the Pazzi Conspiracy by all three artists—Lorenzo, Politian, and Botticelli—Simonetta and Venus broadly masked the same idea, namely the innocence, intensity, and pure beauty of youthful love and desire. The meaning of that idea changed over time as it was overtaken by history and altered by events that each interpreted differently. But for each of them, Youth itself had died with Giuliano, and with Lorenzo's hairsbreadth's escape from the assassin's blade. What was left was the empty mask.

Lorenzo de'Medici died in 1492, and a quarter of a century later plans were made for his body to be permanently interred, together with those of his murdered brother and their namesakes, Lorenzo's son Giuliano, the

Duke of Nemours, and his grandson Lorenzo, the Duke of Urbino, in a majestic memorial chapel to be built in the Medici family church of San Lorenzo. This is of course the Medici Chapel in the New Sacristy, commissioned from Michelangelo in 1519 and left magnificently incomplete when the artist departed Florence forever in 1533. Although Lorenzo's son Giovanni still lived, and was seated on the papal throne as Leo X, the occasion that brought about the commission was the extinction of the principal branch of the Medici, which had descended from Cosimo Vecchio through his grandson Lorenzo the Magnificent, and which came to an end with the death in 1519 of the younger Lorenzo, its last male descendant. Cardinal Giulio de'Medici, the bastard son of the murdered Giuliano, was charged with overseeing the project, which ended when, as Clement VII, he entered into what the Florentines, and Michelangelo among them, saw as an unholy pact with the emperor, whose armies laid siege to the city on his behalf and established the Medici duchy that forever ended the ancient liberties of Florence. In both its beginning and its ending, the project was inevitably freighted with the deepest emotions about the history of the city and its leading family.

This was especially true for Michelangelo himself, who had lived in the house of the Magnificent as a familiar, had learned his art as a sculptor there, and who was himself a poet. An early plan for the tombs of the Magnifici shows Michelangelo's original scheme to display a sculptural relief showing the Garden of the Hesperides over Giuliano's tomb, a poetic allusion to the garden of eternally renewing youth and the springtime of life that is also evoked in the *Primavera*, as well as in Lorenzo's motto *Le tems revient* (not to mention the Medici arms with the orange *palle*); and a second relief showing Orpheus above Lorenzo's tomb, in reference to his stature as a poet.[46] And in the scheme of the chapel itself Michelangelo evolved his poetic conceit for memorializing the extinct Medici line with an extended meditation on the final end to earthly ambition and glory, centered upon the metaphor of the mask, or *larva*.

Thus, next to the figure of Night on the tomb of Duke Giuliano in the Medici Chapel Michelangelo sculptured a Satyr-mask, through the eyeholes of which appears a pair of startled eyes (Fig. 105), an image irresist-

THE END OF THE MASQUERADE

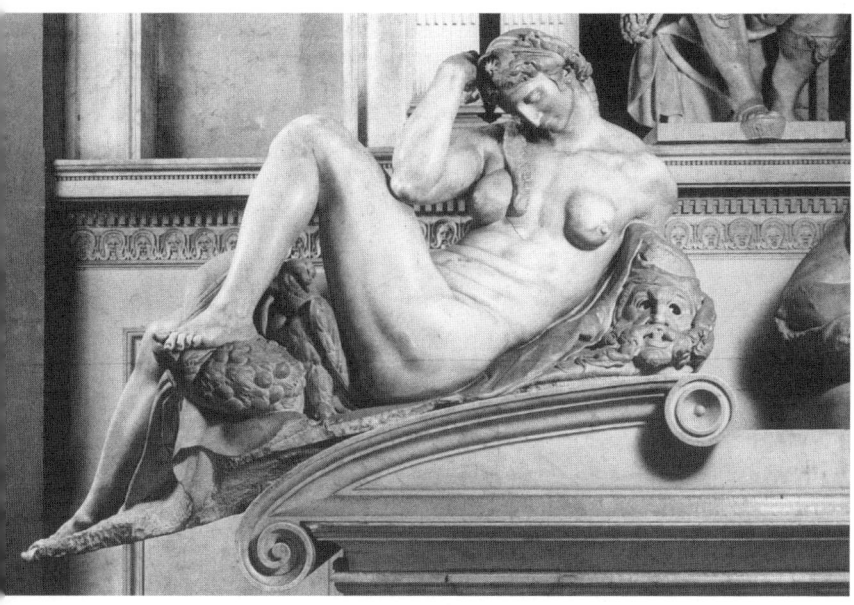

FIGURE 105
Michelangelo, *Night*, Florence, San Lorenzo, New Sacristy (Medici Chapel).
(Photograph by James T. Van Rensselaer)

ably recalling Politian's reference in the *Stanze* to *sogni dentro alle lor larve*, or dreams hidden behind their deceiving masks.[47] As surely as the conch-blowing *paniscus* in Botticelli's *Mars and Venus* denotes the *ombre* of the nightmares disturbing Mars's *alma spaventata*, so Michelangelo's *larva* also denotes the turbulent nightmares, or ghostly cares crowding in and filling Night's troubled sleep. A variant copy of Michelangelo's *Night* attributed to Michele Tosini (Michele di Ridolfo del Ghirlandaio) clearly interprets these nightmares as erotic, for standing next to the sleeping giantess appears *eros* hiding his face behind a Satyr-mask (Fig. 106).[48] Given the parallel derivation of Tosini's conception from Michelangelo's allegory of Venus and Cupid, copied by Pontormo in his *Venus and Cupid* in the Accademia and several times varied upon by Bronzino, most famously in his London *Allegory of Venus and Cupid*, and also given the closeness of Michelangelo's

THE END OF THE MASQUERADE

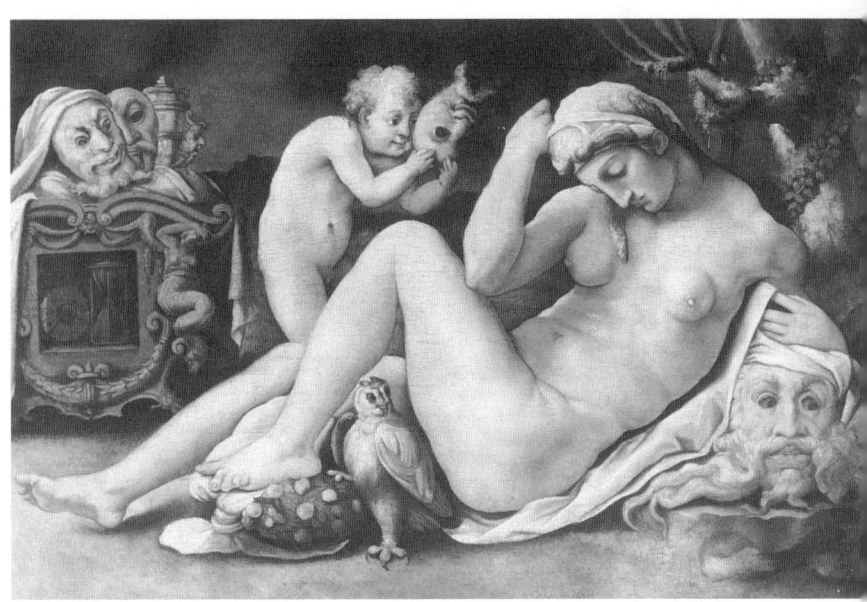

FIGURE 106
Michele Tosini, *Night with a Larvate Eros*, Brescia, Art Market.
(Photograph by Mario Brogiolo)

conception of *Night* to his famous, and highly erotic cartoon of *Leda*, such an interpretation on Tosini's part is hardly surprising. Nevertheless, it is precisely the absence of *eros* in the Medici Chapel which suggests that for Michelangelo the dreams of Night are, while certainly not free of anguished sexual emotion, more broadly teeming with the phantasms of generically sensual obsessions, with terrestrial desires and ambitions that are forever doomed to frustration.[49] Indeed, the whole of the chapel itself is literally haunted, *aombrata*, the frieze carved round its walls (Fig. 107), and architectural details such as the decorations on the capitals (Fig. 108), being filled with hundreds of mocking masks, or *larve*.[50] The duke Lorenzo rests a heavy arm upon a cash-box, the mask on its side denoting the empty *larva* of earthly riches, while his armor and that of the duke Giuliano display the larvate insignia of military prowess and ambition (Fig. 109),

THE END OF THE MASQUERADE

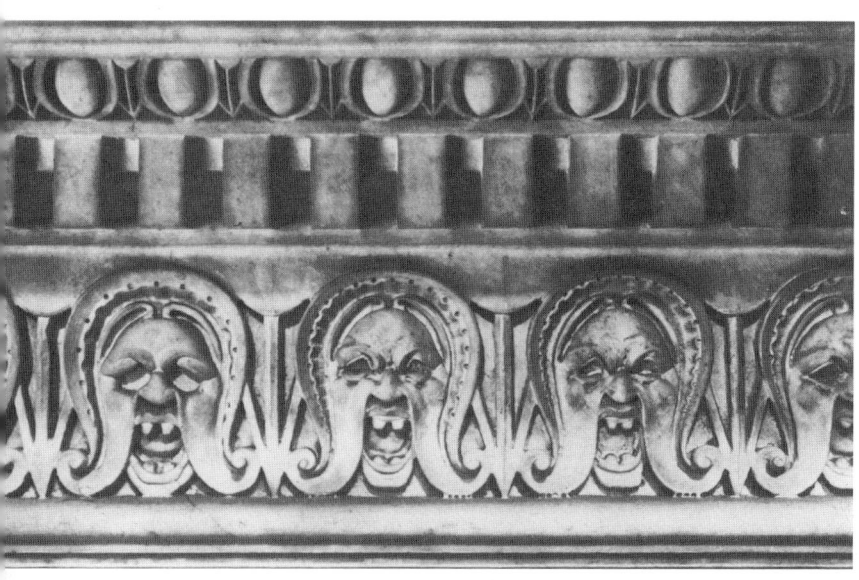

FIGURE 107
Larvate Frieze, Florence, San Lorenzo, New Sacristy (Medici Chapel).
(Photograph by James T. Van Rensselaer)

never to be fulfilled. What are these phantasms of unsatiated desire that crowd the chapel? What are the *ombre* that possess Night's thoughts?

Here we are helped by Michelangelo himself, who on a drawing containing different designs for the column bases of the Medici Chapel, the profile of one of which is ingeniously transformed by the artist's fantasy into an abstraction of the theme of the mask that is endlessly developed throughout the New Sacristy, wrote the following remarkable sentences regarding the tomb of Duke Giuliano (Fig. 110):

> El dì e la nocte parlano e dichono noi abiamo chol nostro veloce chorso chondocto alla morte el ducha giuliano è ben giusto che e' ne facci vendecta chome fa e la vendecta è questa che avendo noi morto a ctolta la luce a noi e chogli ochi chiusi a serrato e nostri che non risplendono più sopra la terra che avrebbe di noi dunche facta mentre vivea

THE END OF THE MASQUERADE

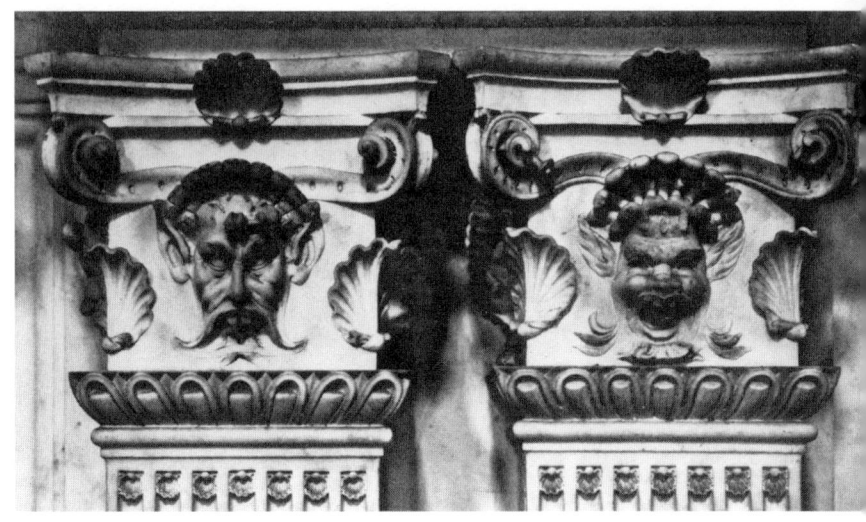

FIGURE 108
Larvate Capitals, Florence, San Lorenzo, New Sacristy (Medici Chapel). (Photograph by James T. Van Rensselaer)

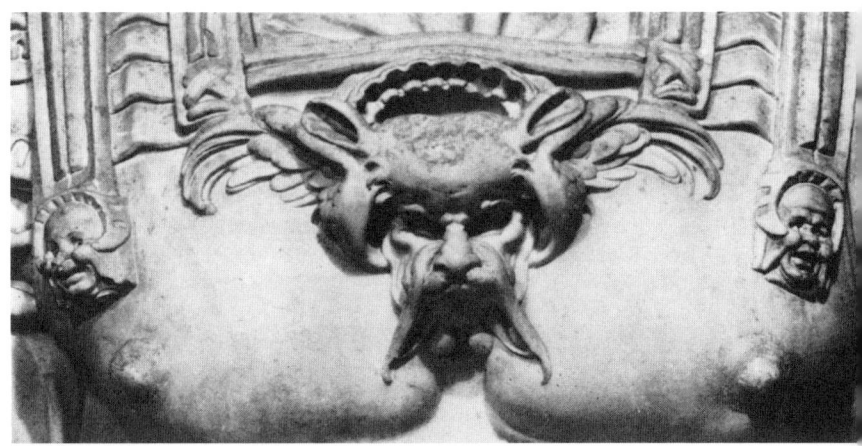

FIGURE 109
Michelangelo, *Giuliano de'Medici*, Florence, San Lorenzo, New Sacristy (Medici Chapel). Detail, *Breastplate*. (Photograph by James T. Van Rensselaer)

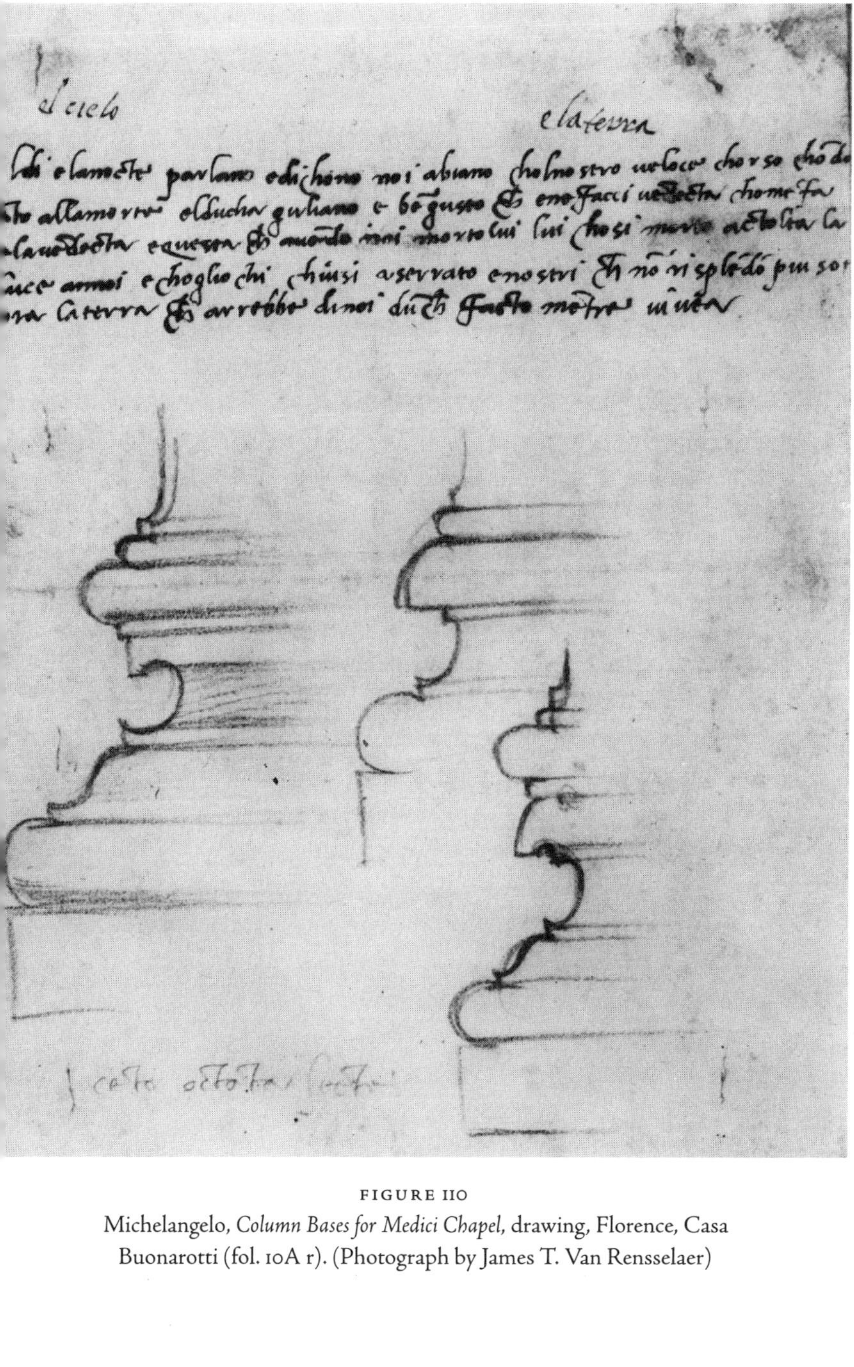

FIGURE 110
Michelangelo, *Column Bases for Medici Chapel*, drawing, Florence, Casa Buonarotti (fol. 10A r). (Photograph by James T. Van Rensselaer)

(Day and Night are speaking and saying, we have with our swift course led the Duke Giuliano to his death. It is quite just that he should take revenge on us as he does, and the revenge is this: that we, having killed him, he thus dead has taken the light from us and with his closed eyes has shut ours so that they may no more shine forth over the earth. What would he have done with us, then, had he lived?)

This passage has never been satisfactorily interpreted, and indeed has played very little part in the principal interpretations of the chapel. Steinmann characterized it as very odd, and other scholars have dismissed it as unclear and disjointed.[51] Their inability to grasp its meaning, however, derives from what is only an assumption, which is that it is Day and Night as general personifications that are shown on the tomb of Duke Giuliano. If this were so, what in the world could Michelangelo have meant in writing that Giuliano's closed eyes have blinded Day and Night in revenge for his death? What bizarre threat of vengeance against Nature itself is implied in "What would he have done with us, then, had he lived?"

However, the passage makes it plain that Michelangelo was not thinking of Day and Night in general, but of the particular days and nights allotted to Duke Giuliano. *His* days and *his* nights have conspired against him, and it is *they* who have brought him to an untimely death. For killing him prematurely, taking the light from his eyes, they are compelled as punishment—themselves now blinded in consequence of his death, and themselves never again to look out over the face of the earth—nevertheless to live out their own existence, all the days and nights that should have remained to Giuliano. As Creighton Gilbert noticed, all the statues in the Medici Chapel, uniquely so in Michelangelo's work, are in fact shown as blind-eyed.[52] Beneath Lorenzo Dawn rises, blind, to a helpless awakening, groaning with the weight of an epic corporeality that will not melt, and beneath Giuliano Day strains every muscle in conflicted and frozen motion, one arm pinned behind his back, his upper torso swung backward and lower legs forward in a mighty effort, an exaggerated *contrapposto* that leaves him locked in helpless immobility (Fig. 111). Having stopped time

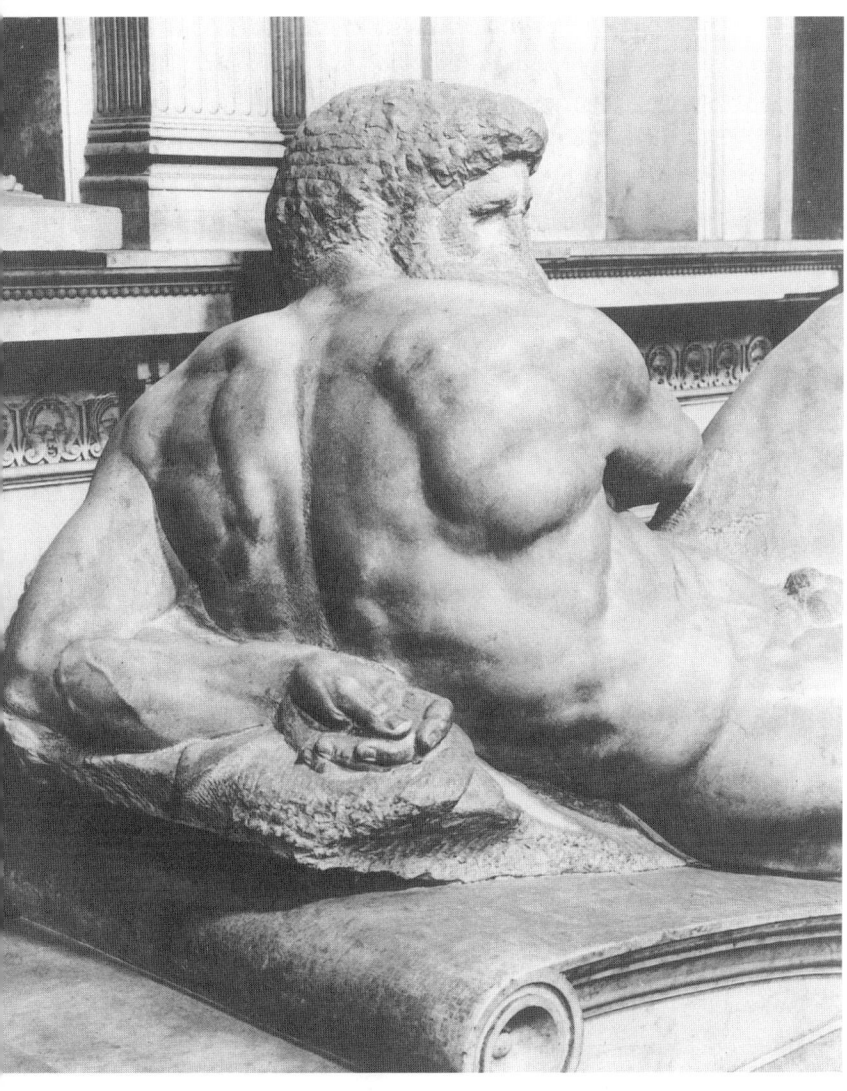

FIGURE III
Michelangelo, *Day*, Florence, San Lorenzo, New Sacristy (Medici Chapel).
(Photograph by James T. Van Rensselaer)

for the dukes, their days and evenings, nights and new dawnings, the personifications of these days and nights have in consequence disabled themselves, and they are left as mourners for them, and for their own empty existence. Their strength is helpless, nullified together with Giuliano's and Lorenzo's power to use them. Their punishment is that they cannot themselves die, but are left to think in vain of what use the dukes might have made of them. Day is knotted in Promethean impotency, and Night's dreams are filled with empty phantasms of what earthly triumphs the dukes might have attained had they been allowed to live out their allotted time. Their inability to function Michelangelo directly expressed in the paradox—wholly typical of his thought and poetry—that they, having taken the light from the dukes' eyes by killing them, are themselves blinded and powerless in token of the dukes' punishment and vengeance upon them. The dukes have died untimely, and the days and nights of the balance of the Biblical span of life allotted them can neither act nor themselves die. The *larve* that torment Night and her companions are the empty *ombre* of earthly ambition and mortal hopes that are forevermore thwarted and vain.

Time is stopped for the Dukes, and can go neither backward nor forward, and this thought was developed by Michelangelo in a second drawing (Fig. 112). It shows a plan for the paired tombs of Lorenzo de'Medici and his brother Giuliano, one never executed in the Medici Chapel but that is integral to its meaning. For, as we have seen, it is the extinction of Lorenzo de'Medici's line that is commemorated and mourned in the New Sacristy of San Lorenzo, in which the Magnificent lies buried together with his murdered brother and his son and grandson.[53] The drawing shows the tombs side by side, with between them the Madonna and Child flanked on either side by Saints Cosmas and Damian. Beneath the Madonna is faintly sketched a figure with arms outstretched, identified and explained by Michelangelo in the brief note that appears at the bottom of the sheet:

> La fama tiene gli epitaffi a giacere perchè son morti, e 'l loro operare fermo non va né innanzi né indietro

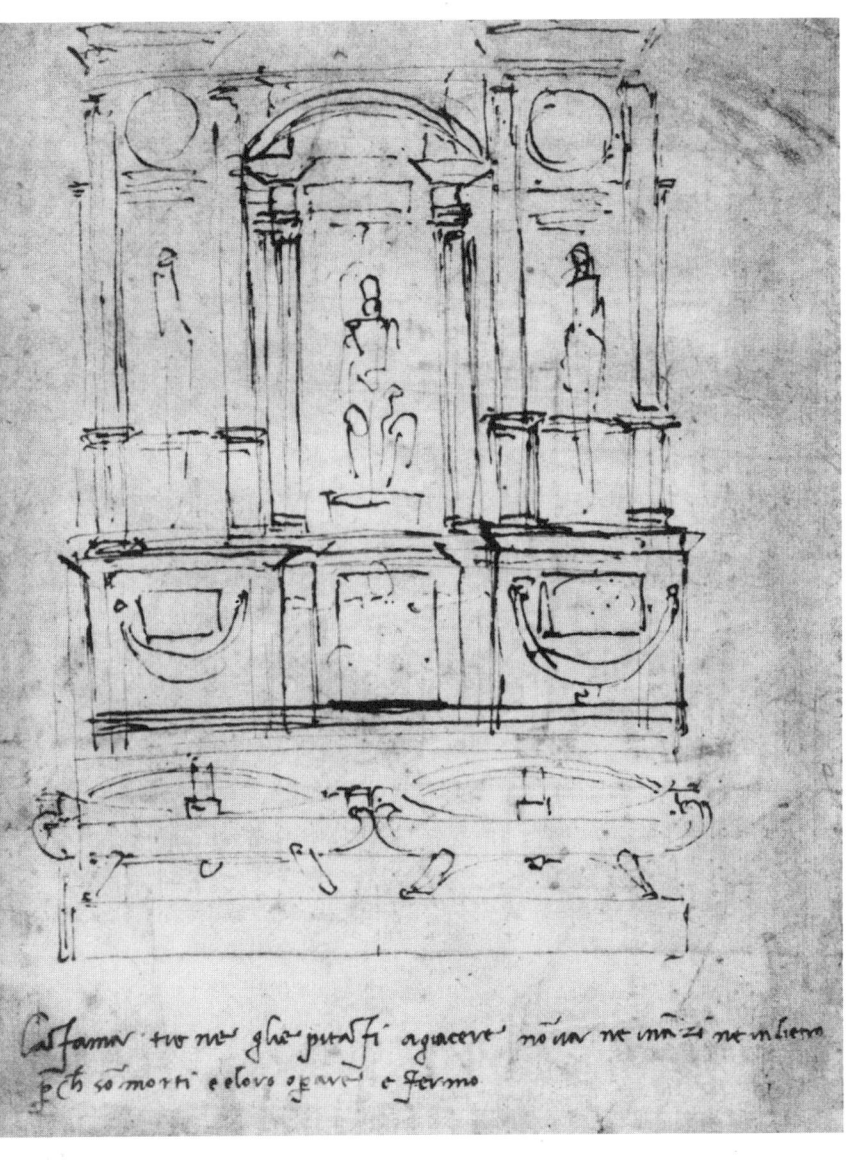

FIGURE 112
Michelangelo, *Study for the Tombs of the Magnifici*, drawing, London, British Museum (fol. W. 28v). (Photograph by James T. Van Rensselaer)

(Fame, reclining, holds the epitaphs, because they are dead and their work is stopped; it goes neither forward nor backward.)

The fame of Lorenzo's house, the days and nights allotted his line are stopped, frozen forever in time, and Fame itself is left to mourn, with no further function, save to lie down forever and to display the epitaphs. Startled by death in the midst of the other *larve* of their earthly existence, the heirs of Lorenzo now sit in eternal contemplation of Christ. Their fame, and his, lies interred in this chapel, for by definition Fame also is of the earth and temporal, as are the quickly expended days and nights allotted to Lorenzo and his descendents. The hope and dream of permanent and eternally increasing fame, even for great houses, is the greatest *larva* of all. Eternity has triumphed over Fame.

The young Lorenzo had been wise enough to know, as he wrote in one of his early sonnets, that everything seen or wished for by mortals is but an *ombra*. He had also been wise enough to know that what mortals see and wish for defines their lives, and entails ethical, political, and intellectual commitment to a personal idea of love in the world, a permanent idea for which his poetry, and the poetry and art he sponsored, stands as the representation. In the letter prefacing the *Raccolta Aragonese* he wrote of his desire to renew and elevate the forms of vernacular expression in art, and in his own poetry there can be traced a gradual refinement of language and content deriving from a progressive assimilation of ancient ideas and forms of speech. In consequence, to use Lorenzo's own metaphor, the hitherto roughly cultivated gardens of literature and art began to put forth new and ever more perfect flowers. The new art fortified by the new learning, both of them based in the mastery of ancient forms and models, was the only secure guide to an idea of perfectibility attainable here on earth. Such art provides the antidote to those empty *ombre* and hobgoblin fantasies to which mankind is eternally prey—whether appearing as Giuliano de'Medici's dream of martial glory, as Mars's wish to escape from strife and descend into luxuriant idleness, or as a multitude of infantile panics induced by such empty desires as the hope to cheat fortune and death through riches, honors, family, and the pursuit of time-bound fame.

The New Sacristy is not the empty repository of Lorenzo's dream, however, nor is it only the commemoration of the dead fame of his house, about the ambitions of which there is every reason to believe that Michelangelo harbored deep misgivings. It is, as a work of art, the direct consequence and an expression of that dream. Michelangelo there paid his own homage to the man in whose house he had lived as a familiar and where he had first found his own, new art. It is the homage of one Florentine poet to another—rendered not to a false and vain phantom, the *larva* of perpetually increasing Medicean fame and glory, but to Lorenzo's true dream, or *visio* of human perfectibility expressed in poetry and learning, and given its permanent embodiment in the idea captured in an eternally living art.

NOTES

Chapter One

1. Gotthold Ephraim Lessing, *Selected Prose Works of G. E. Lessing*, ed. Edward Bell (London, 1913), 175–226.
2. Pietro Santi Bartoli and Giovan Pietro Bellori, *Admiranda romanarum antiquitatem ac veteris sculpturae vestigia* (Rome, 1691), fig. 67.
3. Lessing, *Selected Prose Works*, 183.
4. Ernst Gombrich, *Symbolic Images: Studies in the Art of the Renaissance* (London, 1972), 1–5. For a fuller account of the Shaftesbury monument, see Richard Dorment, *Alfred Gilbert* (New Haven, 1985).
5. See Stephen Murray, *Notre Dame, Cathedral of Amiens: The Power of Change in Gothic* (Cambridge and New York, 1996).
6. Murray, *Cathedral of Amiens*, 115–16 and 207; and see K. Basford, *The Green Man* (Ipswich, 1978).
7. For festivals of the spring, see André Varagnac, *Civilisation traditionelle et genres de vie* (Paris, 1948); and Charles Dempsey, *The Portrayal of Love: Botticelli's Primavera and Humanist Culture at the Time of Lorenzo the Magnificent* (Princeton, 1992), 74–77.
8. Samo Štefanac, "Niccolò di Giovanni Fiorentino e la Cappella del Beato Giovanni Orsini a Traù: il progetto, l'architettura, la decorazione scultorea," in *Quattrocento Adriatico: Fifteenth-Century Art of the Adriatic Rim* (Villa Spelman Colloquia, no. 5), ed. Charles Dempsey (Bologna, 1996), 123–41, esp. 128. See also Hans Semper, *Donatello, seine Zeit und Schule* (Vienna, 1875), 318–20.
9. Antonio Averlino detto il Filarete, *Trattato di architettura*, ed. Anna Maria Finoli and Liliana Grassi, vol. 2 (Milan, 1972), 699: "El davanzale d'esse, cioè la cornice, e 'l fregio che è di sotto è fatto a spiritegli e a teste e altri varii intagli. . . . Ha tre porti: una da una testa, e l'altra da l'altra, e una nel mezzo, la quale è dignissima di marmo intagliata con varii intaglie di figure, fogliami e spiritegli e feste, e l'armi divise, con la testa dello illustratissimo Francesco Sforza e quella della illustratissima Madonna Bianca, e altre varie figure."
10. *Giovanni Rucellai ed il suo zibaldone I: "Il zibaldone quaresimale,"* Studies of the Warburg Institute, no. 24, ed. Alessandro Perosa, (London, 1960), 21–22: "Cominciono due spalliere di bossi di qua e di là della detta pergola. . . . E di sopra dette spalliere una festa con molte arme della chasa." And further: ". . . vasi, urciuoli, coro doppio, cioè che mostra da ogni parte gioganti, huomini, donne,

marzocchi con bandiere del comune, bertuccie, dragoni, cientauri, chamelli, diamanti, spiritelli coll'archo," etc. During his visit to Rome Giovanni also admired in Sta. Costanza the mosaics "con figure piccole in perfectione et con fogliami et alberi et molti spiritegli che navicano in diverse maniere" (p. 74). See also *Giovanni Rucellai ed il suo zibaldone II: A Florentine Patrician and his Palace*, Studies of the Warburg Institute, no. 24 (London, 1981), 70.

11. See the editor's note to Filarete, *Trattato di architettura*, 699, and see the UTET *Grande Dizionario della lingua italiana*, s.v. "festa."

12. Petar Kolendić, "Dokumenti o Andriji Alešiju u Trogiru," in *Arhiv za arbanašku starinu jezik i arheologiju* 2 (1924; Belgrade, 1925): 70–78. The document was again edited and republished in the appendix to Dempsey, *Quattrocento Adriatico*, 225–30. The relevant citation is as follows: "... e tra uno e l'altro di dicti pilastri die esser a similitudine d'una portella, de la qual jusir de un spiritello de longeza de pie 3 tenendo in mano una fiasella per uno, che serano per numero XVII bene lavoradi et relevadi segondo la faza sotto de Christo et como appar nel disegno; et in la dita spaliera, la quale recenze el pilastro da tre bade, in logo di spiritelli die esser 3 feste romane, zoè una per cadauna de le dite façe, come appar nel disegno."

13. See Robert Turcan, *Les sarcophages romains a représentations Dionysiaques: Essai de chronologie et d'histoire religieuse*, Bibliothèque des Écoles françaises d'Athènes et de Rome, fascicule deux-cent-dixième (Paris, 1966).

14. James Beck, *Jacopo della Quercia*, vol. 1 (New York, 1991), 55–67 and 142–48 (cat. 2).

15. Adolfo Venturi, *La scultura del Quattrocento*, vol. 6 of *Storia dell'arte italiana* (Milan, 1908), 70–71.

16. V. Herzner, "Regesti Donatelliani," *Rivista dell'Istituto Nazionale d'Archeologia e Storia dell'Arte*, n.s., 2 (1979): 169–228: "libbre 12 di cera ... per fare le forme di cierti fanciulini ignudi." The sampling of Latin terms is taken from the inventories of Paul II's famous gem collection, published in *Il tesoro di Lorenzo il Magnifico, I: Le gemme*, ed. Nicole Dacos, Antonio Giuliano, and Ulrico Pannuti (Florence, 1973), 87–118.

17. See, for example, for Siena, Vecchietta's estimation in 1471 of two sculptures, "uno spiritello di bronzo, et uno ignudo di piombo," by Urbano di Pietro da Cortona, *Documenti per la storia dell'arte senese*, ed. Gaetano Milanesi, vol. 2 (Siena, 1854), no. 245, p. 347; for Bologna, Giovanni Sabadino degli Arienti's account in 1487 in his *Hymeneo Bentivoglio* of "spiritelli che pareano vivi" decorating a room in Palazzo Bentivoglio (C. James, "The Palazzo Bentivoglio in 1487," *Mitteilungen des Kunsthistorischen Institutes in Florenz* 41 (1997): 188–96, esp. 189 and 195; and, for Ferrara, an inventory of 1496 listing "una medaya de corno, cum uno spiritelli facta de sua mano" (Ann H. Allison, "The Bronzes of Pier Jacopo Alari-

Bonacolsi, called Antico," *Jahrbuch der Kunsthistorischen Sammlungen in Wien* 53–54 (1993–94): 37–310, esp. 272.

18. Herzner, "Regesti Donatelliani," no. 103, in which it is specified that the circular parapet will be "diviso in sei spatii, ne'quali s'abbi a 'ntaglare spiritelli che tengono in mezzo l'arme del Comune di Prato . . . o altro cosa se piacera." Donatello in fact divided the balustrade into seven sections decorated with music-playing and dancing *spiritelli* (which are not necessarily the same as angels). The document also specifies that the capital of the rectangular pier supporting the pulpit will be adorned with "due spiritelli" (in fact there are three).

19. Doris Carl, "La casa vecchia dei Medici e il suo giardino," in *Il Palazzo Medici-Riccardi di Firenze* (Florence, 1995), 38–43, esp. 42. The entry she quotes from the Quaderno di spese dell'orto di Cosimo e Lorenzo de'Medici reads: "Adì 26 di marzo paghai Antonio dipintore per oro andò alo spiritello sopra il pozo . . ."

20. Giovanni Poggi, *Il Duomo di Firenze: I documenti sulla decorazione della chiesa e del campanile tratti dall'Archivio dell'Opera*, ed. with notes by Margaret Haines, vol. 1 (Florence, 1988), no. 1315: "et omne compensum in predictis spiritellis."

21. Francesco Malaguzzi-Valeri, "La miniatura in Bologna dal XIII al XVIII secolo," *Archivio storico italiano*, 5th ser., 18 (1896): 242–315, esp. 310–13.

22. *Zibaldone*, as quoted in note 10 above.

23. Julius von Schlosser, "Über einige antiken Ghibertis," *Jahrbuch der kunsthistorischen Sammlungen des Allerhöchsten Kaiserhauses* 24 (1904): 125–59, esp. 152–55.

24. Herzner, "Regesti Donatelliani," no. 124. The letter is dated 10 December 1430: "Qua si dicie che gliè il champo a Lucha e che sono ante chastela, s'io fusi chostà andr'io tra Pisa e Lucha a tore due sipolture antiche che vi sono ispiritegli alluna, allaltro è la storia di Baccho. Donato l'a lodate per cose buone, sarebbe agievole averle." In another letter (no. 106) Fora writes that the sarcophagus, which today is in the Camposanto at Pisa, is "al monte a S. Giuliano a una chiesa si chiama Vichopelaglio." See further Carlo Chiarlo, "Donato l'a lodate per chose buone: Il reimpiego dei sarcofagi di Lucca a Firenze," in *Colloquio sul reimpiego dei sarcofagi romani nel Medioevo* (Pisa, 5–12 settembre 1982), ed. Bernard Andreae and Salvatore Settis (Marburg, 1983).

25. Carlo Gasparri, ed., *Le gemme Farnese* (Naples, 1994), 13 and 140 (cat. 30), and fig. 8.

26. Marco Spallanzani and Giovanna Gaeta Bertelà, eds., *Libro d'inventario dei beni di Lorenzo il Magnifico* (Florence, 1992), 38 (c. 20): "Uno chanmeo leghato in oro, intagliato in chavo, suvi una fighura gnuda chon uno albero alle spalle, uno bambino alla ruota, una fighura allato al braccio ritto, uno spiritello in sul timone che getta fuocho, tirata da dua fighure fra nude e vestite di veli, rosso, intagliato di bronchoni."

27. Spallanzani and Bertelà, *Libro d'inventario*, 36 (c. 18v): "Uno chammeo

leghato in oro, suvi 2 spiritegli, una cholonna nel mezzo, allato all'uno uno ghallo e una palma in mano, dall'altro uno altro ghallo, campo rosso e rovescio fogliami intagliati;" p. 39 (c. 20v): "Uno chammeo legato in oro, entrovi una fighura d'uno vecchio che siede chol capo chinato e in sulle mani uno spiritello al quale un'altra fighura d'uno altro vecchio, pure sedente, porge una asta, da rovescio niellato di foglie e una testa;" p. 39 (c. 20v): "Uno chammeo leghato in oro, entrovi uno carro, suvi dua fighure, tirato da dua lioni, in s'uno de'quali siede uno spiritello, da rovescio punzonato con cervio;" and p. 46 (c. 24v): "Uno oriuolo a uso di tabernacolo chon quori e strafori di rame dorato, che chorre sanza contrapeso, chon arme e spiritegli smaltati nella faccia dove mostra l'ore."

28. John Pope-Hennessy, *Donatello Sculptor* (New York, 1993), 86–87, and Artur Rosenauer, *Donatello* (Milan, 1993), 77 and 101–2 (cat. 15).

29. Wilhelm Bode, "Versuche der Ausbildung des Genre und der Putto in der florentiner Plastik des Quattrocento," in *Florentiner Bildhauer der Renaissance*, 4th ed. (Berlin, 1921), 230–31; translation mine. The attribution of the invention of the putto to Donatello has often been repeated; see, aside from Eugène Muntz, *Les artistes celèbres: Donatello* (Paris, 1889), more recent discussions by J. Kunstmann, *The Transformation of Eros* (Philadelphia, 1965), 21; and S. A. Struthers, "Donatello's Putti: Their Genesis, Importance and Influence on Quattrocento Sculpture and Painting" (Ph.D. diss., Ohio State University, 1992).

30. For these and other examples of pre-Donatellan putti, see the illuminating discussion by Erwin Panofsky, *Renaissance and Renascences in Western Art* (New York, 1972), 101–5. See also Hans Wentzel, "Antiken-Imitationen des 12. und 13. Jahrhunderts in Italien," *Zeitschrift für Kunstwissenschaft* 9(1955): 29–72; and Annarosa Garzelli, *Sculture toscane nel Dugento e nel Trecento* (Florence, 1969). For the sculptures at Pistoia, see also Venturi, *Storia dell'arte italiana*, vol. 4, 399–400.

31. For the Aragazzi tomb, see Ronald Lightbown, *Donatello and Michelozzo: An Artistic Partnership and its Patrons in the Early Renaissance*, vol. 1 (London, 1980), 128–229. Lightbown is careful throughout to name Michelozzo's putti as *spiritelli* on the basis of the nomenclature for them used in the documents. He cites in particular the documents for the Fulgosio tomb in Padua, first published by Vittorio Lazzarini, "Il Mausoleo di Raffaello Fulgosio nella Basilica del Santo," *Archivio Veneto-Tridentino* 4(1923): 147–53. For the Sacrestia delle Messe, see Margaret Haines, *The "Sacrestia delle Messe" of the Florentine Cathedral* (Florence, 1983), esp. 207–10 and 299, doc. 155 (the 1468 commission, referring to "la grilanda la quale à stare sopra agli armari della sagrestia con spiritelli").

32. See Venturi, *Storia dell'arte italiana*, vol. 4, 738–57; and George Goldner, *Niccolò and Pietro Lamberti* (New York, 1978); see also M. Bergstein, "Two Early Renaissance Putti: Niccolò di Pietro Lamberti and Nanni di Banco," *Zeitschrift für Kunstgeschichte* 1 (1989): 82–88.

33. The quotation is from Eric Maclagen, *Italian Sculpture of the Renaissance*,

The Charles Eliot Norton Lectures for the Years 1927–1928 (Cambridge, Mass., 1935), 65.

34. Vasari-Milanesi, 2.397: "... per paura dell'altezza, tenendosi abbracciati l'un l'altro, si assicurino."

35. For Pontormo's following of Donatello's invention, see Carlo Falciani, *Pontormo: Disegni degli Uffizi* (exhibition catalogue, Gabinetto Disegni e Stampe degli Uffizi, Florence, 1996), no. 79, 118–19, cat. 8.10, and fig. 72; and Elizabeth Cropper, *Pontormo: Portrait of a Halberdier*, Getty Museum Studies on Art (Los Angeles, 1997), 85–86.

36. Vasari-Milanesi, 2.397: "... grande ingegno e arte mostrò [Donatello] nella figura della Vergine, la quale impaurita dall'improvviso apparire dell'Angelo, muove timidamente con dolcezza la persona a una onestissima reverenza, con bellissima grazia rivolgendosi a chi la saluta."

37. In this way the Virgin seems instantaneously to embody at least three if not all the five states of response to the Angel Annunciate enumerated by Michael Baxandall, *Painting and Experience in Fifteenth-century Italy: A Primer in the Social History of Pictorial Style* (New York, 1972), 51–56. These would include *conturbatio*, her being frightened and troubled by the appearance of the archangel, *cogitatio*, her immediate understanding of his words, "Fear not, Mary," and *humilitatio*, her making a reverence to him and responding with the words "Behold the Handmaiden of the Lord."

38. Benvenuto Cellini, *La vita*, ed. Luigi Bellotto (Parma, 1996), 2.18, p. 519.

39. Pope-Hennessy, *Donatello Sculptor*, 219 and figs. 231–36; Rosenauer, *Donatello*, 232–40, cat. 48.

40. The literature is vast, but suffice it to mention C. R. S. Harris, *The Heart and the Vascular System in Ancient Greek Medicine* (Oxford, 1973); Giorgio Agamben, *Stanze: La parola e il fantasma nella cultura occidentale* (Turin, 1977), 105ff.; Robert Klein, "Spirito peregrino," in *La forme e l'intelligible* (Paris, 1970), 31–64 (translated into English in Robert Klein, *Form and Meaning: Writings on the Renaissance and Modern Art* [New York, 1979], 62–85); and G. Vitale, "Ricerche intorno all'elemento filosofico nei poeti del dolce stil novo," *Giornale dantesco* 18 (1910): 168–74.

41. Quoted from Jennifer Montagu, *The Expression of the Passions: The Origin and Influence of Charles Le Brun's Conférence sur l'expression général et particulière* (New Haven, 1994), 52. The original is from René Bary, *Methode pour bien prononcer un discours, et pour le bien animer: Ouvrage tres-utile à tous ceux qui parlent en public, & particulierement aux prédicateurs, & aux avocats* (Paris, 1679), 102–3: "Quand la Crainte est excité par la presence de la chose formidable, elle a la voix faible & hesitante, parce que la crainte ayant attiré les esprits de la circonference au centre, sur-charge le coeur, & que le coeur sur-chargé estant sur le point d'estre étouffé, celuy qui parle est tellement allarmé, qu'il reste comme interdit."

42. Dante, *Vita nuova*, 38.3: "tu vedi che questo è uno spiramento d'Amore, che

ne reca li disiri d'amore dinanzi, ed è mosso da così gentil parte come'è quella de li occhi de la donna che tanto pietosa ci s'hae mostrata."

43. Dante, *Vita nuova*, 2.4: "In quello punto dico veracemente che lo spirito della vita, lo quale dimora ne la secretissima camera de lo cuore, cominciò a tremare sì fortemente, che apparia ne li menimi polsi orribilmente; e tremando disse queste parole: "Ecce deus fortior me, qui veniens dominabitur michi." In quello punto lo spirito animale, lo quale dimora ne l'alta camera ne la quale tutti li spiriti sensitivi portano le loro percezioni, si cominciò a maravigliare molto, e parlando spezialmente a li spiriti del viso, sì disse queste parole: "Apparuit iam beatitudo vestra." In quello punto lo spirito naturale, lo quale dimora in quella parte ove si ministra lo nutrimento nostro, cominciò a piangere, e piangendo disse queste parole: "Heu miser, quia frequenter impeditus ero deinceps!"

44. Lorenzo de'Medici, *Opere*, ed. Tiziano Zanato (Turin, 1992), 614 (comment to sonnet 5): "E però diventavo tutto pallido, perché el cuore, essendo già acceso e avendo il dubbio che di sopra abbiamo detto, non poteva fare che sommamente non temessi. Di questo suo timore nasceva in lui affano, e però i spiriti vitali, correndo per soccorrere al cuore, lasciavano la faccia mia sanza colore, pallida e smorta; e insieme con li spiriti, come ha ordinato la natura, assai copia di sangue intorno al cuore conveniva. Questo generava in quel luogo caldo assai più che l'usato; né nasceva quasi una suffocazione di quelli spiriti e sangue.... Ma poi, rimirando la faccia sua, parendomi vi fussi tanti segni di pietà, il cuore poneva da parte la paura e ripigliava qualche ardire; e per questo li spiriti vitali ritornavano al luogo onde prima erono partiti, e con loro tornava il valore e colore prima perduto." As Zanato notes, such physiological description of the effects of love, based in the precedents of Dante and the poetry of the *stil novo*, is widely diffused. He cites, for example, Cristoforo Landino's commentary to the *Divine Comedy*: "Il cuore . . . è rocca e sedia principale della vita; adunque a quello rivoca il sangue, in che massimamente consiste la vita, onde le parti esteriori private di sangue perdono il colore et diventano pallide, et perdono il caldo il quale è nel sangue: et rimase fredde triemano. Adunque per questo dinota la paura." See also Marsilio Ficino, *De vita*, 2.18, 177.

45. For the "spirito sensibile che riceve lo suono," see Dante, *Convivio*, 2.13; and for the "vocale spirto," see *Purgatorio*, 21.88.

46. Vasari-Milanesi, 2.405.

47. Giovan Pietro Bellori, *Le vite de' pittori, scultori e architetti moderni*, ed. Evelina Borea (Turin, 1976), 448: "Giace l'infermo in abbandono de gli spiriti e delle forze.... L'istesso effetto si palesa nelle membra estreme, e particolarmente ne' piedi, che primi sono a morire."

48. For the Orsini Chapel, see Kolendić, "Dokumenti," and Štefanac, "Niccolò di Giovanni Fiorentino." And see Anne Markham Schulz, *Niccolò di Giovanni and Venetian Sculpture of the Early Renaissance* (New York, 1978); Ivan Fisković, "'Ne-

beski Jeruzalem' u Kapeli Blaženog Ivana Trogirskog," in *Prijateljev Zbornik: Zbornik radova posvećenih sedamdesetogodišnjici života Kruna Prijatelja*, vol. 1, ed. Josko Belamarić (Split, 1992), 481–531 (with an English summary); and Charles Dempsey, "Niccolò di Giovanni's *Spiritelli* in the Chapel of the Blessed Giovanni Orsini in the Cathedral of Trogir" in *Razprave iz Europske Umetnosti za Ksenijo Rozman*, ed. Barbara Jaki (Ljubljana, 1999), 43–55.

49. Haines, *Sacrestia delle Messe*, cited in note 31 above.

50. Corrado Ricci, *Il Tempio Malatestiano*, reprinted with an appendix by P. G. Pasini (Rimini, 1974), 45ff. and figs. 545, 548, and 549. Agostino di Duccio's sculptures in the Tempio Malatestiano are of course especially noteworthy and important for the highly inventive and extensive use of the Donatellesque *spiritello* throughout, and especially in the Cappella dei Giuochi Infantili.

51. Tommaso's list has been published several times, originally by Carel von Fabriczy, "Andrea Verrocchio ai servigi dei Medici," *Archivio storico dell'arte* 1 (1895): 163–66, and again by Charles Seymour Jr., *The Sculpture of Verrocchio* (Greenwich, Conn., 1971), 174, Appendix 1, B, item 3.

52. Piero Adorno, *Il Verrocchio: Nuove proposte nella civiltà artistica del tempo di Lorenzo il Magnifico* (Florence, 1991), 153. See also Andrew Butterfield, *The Sculptures of Andrea del Verrocchio* (New Haven, 1997), 22–23, 126–35, and cat. 20.

53. William Shakespeare, *Othello*, 2.3.285.

54. Antonio Natale, "*Exemplum salutis publicae*," in *Donatello e il restauro della Giuditta*, ed. Loretta Dolcini (Florence, 1988), 19–32.

55. Francesco Colonna, *Hypnerotomachia Polifili* (Venice, 1499; Garland Reprint, New York, 1988), fol. 88 recto.

56. Horst W. Janson, *The Sculpture of Donatello*, vol. 2 (Princeton, 1957), 143–47, where he argues that the so-called *Attis-Amorino* is in fact a genius of wine. As the *spiritello del vino* he would more specifically personify the alcoholic spirits produced by the process of fermentation.

57. Janson, *Donatello*, 145. As Janson points out, Reymond observed that the chaps worn by Donatello's *spiritello* are virtually identical with those worn by the workmen in Benozzo Gozzoli's frescoes in the Camposanto in Pisa; see in particular the two workmen to the right center of the *Building of the Tower of Babel*. See also Pope-Hennessy, *Donatello Sculptor*, 156, and Rosenauer, *Donatello*, cat. 42, 191–92.

58. James Draper, *Bertoldo di Giovanni, Sculptor of the Medici Household: Critical Reappraisal and Catalogue raisonné* (New York, 1992), 27–28 and 107–11, cat. 7.

Chapter Two

1. Robert Turcan, *Les sarcophages romains a représentations Dionysiaques: Essai de chronologie et d'histoire religieuse* (Paris, 1966), 418–25. See also Roger Stuveras, *Le putto dans l'art romain*, Collection Latomus 99 (Brussels, 1969).

2. Turcan, *Sarcophages*, 533, who also cites Cyprian, and adds that, "Pour les chrétiens comme pour les fidèles de Bacchus, le foulage évoquait un sacrifice suivi de résurrection: il appartient au fonds commun d'images où ces générations ont puisé l'espérance et la foi."

3. Elizabeth S. Malbon, *The Iconography of the Sarcophagus of Junius Bassus* (Princeton, 1990), 91–103; and see Anton de Waal, *Der Sarkophag des Junius Bassus in den Grotten von Sankt Peter: Eine archäologische Studie* (Rome, 1900).

4. Jean Bonnet, *Lorenzo Lotto* (Paris, 1996), 89–95, and, for a detailed study, Francesca Cortesi Bosco, *Gli affreschi dell'Oratorio Suardi: Lorenzo Lotto nella crisi della Riforma* (Bergamo, 1980).

5. See the exemplary discussion by Anthony Colantuono, "The Tender Infant: Invenzione and Figura in the Art of Poussin" (Ph.D. diss., Johns Hopkins University, 1986), 75–90. As Colantuono observes, Juvenal in the fourteenth Satire cites the phrase "parcendum est teneris" as a *sententia*, meaning "Let the children be spared." He adds that Pontanus, in his commentary to the second *Georgic*, recalls Juvenal's maxim by writing that "This can refer directly to men, in proverbial form warning parents and teachers to treat children with care, not making heavy demands on the young and weak," and hence directs the reader's attention to Virgil's use of personification.

6. Colantuono, "The Tender Infant," 58–75 (chapter 1: "*Scherzi e baccanali*: The Poetics of Poussin's *Children's Bacchanals*"). See also Anthony Colantuono, "Titian's Tender Infants: On the Imitation of Venetian Painting in Baroque Rome," *I Tatti Studies* 3 (1989): 207–34.

7. Charles Seymour Jr., *The Sculpture of Verrocchio* (Greenwich, Conn., 1971), 174, Appendix 1, no. 1, item 3.

8. Seymour, *Verrocchio*, 174, Appendix 1, no. 1, item 10.

9. Published by Giovanni Poggi, "La giostra medicea del 1475 e la 'Pallade' del Botticelli," *L'Arte* 5 (1902): 71–77, esp. 77.

10. David Allan Brown, "Verrocchio and Leonardo: Studies for the *Giostra*," in *Florentine Drawing at the time of Lorenzo the Magnificent*, ed. Elizabeth Cropper (Bologna, [1994]), 99–109. See also the entry on the drawing by Gianvittorio Dillon in *Il disegno fiorentino del tempo di Lorenzo il Magnifico*, ed. Annamaria Petrioli Tofani (exhibition catalogue, Gabinetto Disegni e Stampe, Uffizi, Florence, Milan, 1992), no. 7.5, 150–51.

11. Luigi Pulci, *La giostra di Lorenzo de'Medici*, 51–52, in *Opere minori*, ed. Paolo Orvieto (Milan, 1986), 81–82. For the anonymous eyewitness account, see Paolo Fanfani, "Ricordo d'una giostra fatta a Firenze a dì 7 febbraio 1468 sulla piazza di Santa Croce," *Borghini* 2 (1864): 474–83 and 530–42, esp. 483 for the description of Salvestro's helm with the "donna ignuda con un velo atraverso." The passage from Pulci's poem, translated in the text above, reads:

> Intanto un gran rumor si fu levato,
> e tutto il popolo gridava: "Ci vela:"
> ecco apparir Salvestro Benci armato,
> e come gentil cor che 'l ver non cela,
> nello stendardo suo leggiadro e bello
> non avea dama, anzi uno spiritello.
>
> Ma il suo cimier è pur d'una fanciulla,
> ché interpretar no llo saprei altrimenti,
> se non che 'l mio Salvestro ci trastulla
> a questo modo, e fa impazzar le genti . . .

12. Published by Rossella Bessi, "Lo spettacolo e la scrittura," in *Le tems revient, 'L tempo si rinuova: Feste e spettacoli nella Firenze di Lorenzo il Magnifico*, ed. Paola Ventrone (exhibition catalogue, Palazzo Medici-Riccardi, Florence, 1992), 103–17, esp. 108–9; and see 152–53, no. 2.4. The poem:

> El triunfo era fatto in questa forma:
>   aveva quattro facce, che ognuna
>   all'insù digradava con gran norma,
> Et posa in quattro rote, che ciascuna
>   era il bilico grande a rrotar via,
>   et ruotan tutte, che ne movesse una.
> Ora ti vo' contar la leggiadria
>   di sua conposizion per ogni faccia,
>   et quanto lustro, snello et degno sia.
> Ciascuna faccia è dappiè cinque braccia
>   et è ornata di tanto ornamento
>   che 'npossibil mi par che mai si faccia.
> Molti lavori v'è d'oro et d'ariento,
>   con tanti smalti e vetri cristallini,
>   che come a specchio vi si specchia drento.
> Razzeggia, come il sol, tutti i confini,
>   et in su la sommità d'i quattro canti
>   son quattro spiritelli peregrini,
> Et nel mezzo di lor son tre diamanti
>   che 'n sulle punte han d'oro una gran palla,
>   et son d'oro i diamanti tutti quanti.
> Li spiritelli ognun festante galla
>   et ha ciascuno in mano una lumera,
>   et sono innudi, con l'ale alla spalla.

> La fiaccola di scaglie d'argento era
> et for gittavan fiamma con gran foco,
> intendi ben, di foco et fiamma vera.
> Et è il trionfo intorno in ciascun loco
> ripien di tanto foco e tanta fiamma
> che il più alto elemento parrià poco.
> Colui il quale a ccui Venere è mamma
> in sul caccume della palla stava,
> ritto, senza piegar solo una dramma:
> La benda agli occhi et l'arco in man portava,
> turcasso al fianco, et rappresenta crudo
> et sanza umanità sua piedi usava,
> Con due grandi ale et tutto 'l corpo nudo.

13. See Charles Dempsey, "Portraits and Masks in the Art of Lorenzo de'Medici, Botticelli, and Politian's *Stanze per la giostra*," *Renaissance Quarterly* 52 (1999): 1–42; and see Chapter 5 below.

14. For Lapaccini's poem see Antonio Lanza, ed., *Lirici toscani del Quattrocento*, vol. 2 (Rome, 1975), 1–16; and for the anonymous *notizia* see Isidoro Del Lungo, *La donna fiorentina del buon tempo antico*, 2nd ed. (Florence, 1926), 208–10.

15. Del Lungo, *La donna fiorentina*, 208. Such proclamations by the Signoria were by no means unusual; see Richard Trexler, *Public Life in Renaissance Florence* (New York, 1980), 227.

16. Del Lungo, *La donna fiorentina*, 208: ". . . co' molti ispiritegli d'amore con archi in mano."

17. Ibid., 208–9. Lapaccini describes the destruction of the Triumph in the following terms:

> io vidi Amore assunto al degno trono
> co' l'arco in mano e la faretra al fianco
> e quelli stral che mai mi diêr perdono.
> Non sazio di mirar, né punto stanco
> ero in quel punto ch'io senti' romore,
> che mi fé quasi il senso venir manco;
> e raddoppiar senti' il tuono e 'l calore,
> perché il carro ch'io dissi tanto addorno
> vid'io volgere in fiamma a gran furore.
> Tutti i leggiadri amanti il circundorno
> e, perch'i più non vidi Amore in cima,
> penso ch'alla sua spera e' fé ritorno.
> Cosa non vid'io mai tanto sublima . . .

(I saw Love raised up to his worthy throne, with bow in hand and the quiver at his side, and those arrows that never show me pity. Neither satiated with wonder nor at all tired, I was at a point where I heard such a noise as made me almost lose my senses; and I heard the noise and felt the heat redouble, because I saw the chariot which I have described as so lovely go up in flames in a great fury. All the pretty lovers surrounded it, and, because I could no longer see Love at the summit, I thought that he had made his return to his own sphere. Never did I see anything so sublime . . .)

18. Vasari-Milanesi, 3.202; and see Piero Cennini's letter to Pirrino Amerino describing boys appearing as *spiritelli* in the Feast of S. Giovanni in 1475, published by G. Mancini, "Il bel S. Giovanni e le feste patronali di Firenze descritte nel 1475 da Piero Cennini," *Rivista d'arte* 6 (1909): 185–227.

19. Paolo Fazion, "*Nuptiae Bentivolorum*: La città in festa nel commento di Filippo Beroaldo," in *Bentivolorum magnificentia: Principe e cultura a Bologna nel rinascimento*, ed. B. Basile (Rome, 1984), 115–33, esp. 131. The ingenuity of the Catherine's Wheel designed for this occasion recalls that of the fireworks designed for Bartolomeo Benci's *armeggeria* more than twenty years earlier:

Florentinus quidam machinator egregius et mechanicae artis scientissimus machinam solertissimo artificio fabricaverat, quam girandolam vulgus appellat, quae nostra lingua orbis flammeus dici potest: utar enim hoc vocabulo quo adinvenero melius. Erat haec machina funibus suspensa sub papillione Bentivoli fori ingentis magnitudinis in rotunditatem circumacta. . . . Ignis intra machinam furtim inclusus arte mechanica alebatur per fomites incendiorum discurrentes quibus tota moles erat refertissima debebatque hora sub vesperum stata cum crepitu bomboque maximo flagrantes radios eiaculari. Machinator praedixerat post primam horam nocturnam futuram flammarum eiaculationem. Iam sublato tentorio reductisque velis avidissime praestolabatur populus numerosus condictum tempus conflagrationis.

See also G. Cazzola, "'Bentivoli machinatores:' Aspetti politici e momenti teatrali di una festa quattrocentesca bolognese," *Biblioteca teatrale* 23–24 (1979): 14–38; and C. James, "The Palazzo Bentivoglio in 1487," *Mitteilungen des Kunsthistorischen Institutes in Florenz* 41 (1997): 188–96.

20. Vasari-Milanesi, 3.202.

21. Trexler, *Public Life*, 224–25. See also Lapaccini (as cited in note 14), vv. 49–54:

"O donna, a cui Fortuna è tanta pia,
o gloria, o fama, o triunfante onore
del sangue Strozza, o ben che si disia!"

> diss'io ripien d'un amoroso ardore,
> e mai non volsi gli occhi in altro loco
> ch'a rimirar di questa il suo splendore.

22. Giovanni Villani, *Cronica di Giovanni Villani*, ed. G. Dragomanni (Florence, 1844), 7.89.

23. See Raimond Van Marle, *Iconographie de l'art profane au Moyen-age et à la Renaissance*, vol. 2 (The Hague, 1931), 423.

24. Van Marle, *Iconographie*, vol. 2, 421–26 and figs. 449 (ivory formerly in the Salting collection), 450 (ivory in the Bargello in Florence), and 451 (ivory in the Bargello in Florence). For the iconography see Roger S. Loomis, "The Allegorical Siege in the Art of the Middle Ages," *American Journal of Archaeology* 3 (1914): 255. See also Richard H. Randall, *The Golden Age of Ivory: Gothic Carvings in North American Collections* (New York, 1993), 125, no. 189.

25. Van Marle, *Iconographie*, vol. 1, 142, fig. 128 (ivory from Ravenna), and plate opposite 144 (ivory from the Oppenheim collection, Cologne). See also *Images in Ivory: Precious Objects of the Gothic Age*, ed. Peter Barnet (exhibition catalogue, Detroit Institute of Arts, Princeton, 1997), 230f. and 245–48 (nos. 57 and 64).

26. Politian (Angelo Ambrogini), *Stanze*, 2.16; and Vincenzo Cartari, *Imagini de gli dei delli antichi* (Padua, 1614), 444–50.

27. Politian, *Stanze*, 1.123 (*i piccioletti Amori*), 2.16 (*Esortazione di Venere a' fratelli di Cupido*), 2.20 (*gli Amori* and *Gli spirite' d'amor*), and 2.21 (*Gli ardenti spiritelli*).

28. See the quotations from the inventory cited in Chapter 1, notes 25 and 26.

29. Dante, *Vita nuova*, 38.8–22.

30. Dante, *Convivio, Trattato secondo, Canzone prima*, 40–48.

31. Dante, *Convivio, Trattato secondo*, 10 [11], 3–4: "Dice adunque, continuandosi a l'ultime sue parole: Non è vero che tu sie morta; ma la cagione per che morta ti pare essere, sì è uno smarrimento nel quale se' caduta vilmente per questa donna che è apparita:—e qui è da notare che, sì come dice Boezio ne la sua Consolazione, 'ogni subito movimento di cose non avviene sanza alcuno discorrimento d'animo'—; e questo vuol dire lo riprendere di questo pensiero. Lo quale si chiama 'spiritello d'amore' a dare a intendere che lo consentimento mio piegava inver di lui; e così si può questo intendere maggiormente, e conoscere la sua vittoria, quando dice già 'anima nostra,' facendosi familiare di quella."

32. Dante, *Convivio, Trattato secondo*, 15 [16], 10: "Poi, nel quarto verso, dove dice: *uno spiritel d'amore*, s'intende uno pensiero che nasce del mio studio. Onde è da sapere che per amore, in questa allegoria, sempre s'intende esso studio, lo quale è applicazione de l'animo innamorato de la cosa a quella cosa. . . . E così, in fine di questo secondo trattato, dico e affermo che la donna di cu' io innamorai appresso lo primo amore fu la bellissima e onestissima figlia de lo imperadore de lo universo, a quale Pittagora pose nome Filosofia."

33. Dante, *Convivio*, *Trattato secondo*, 10 [11], 4 (quoted in note 31).

34. Boccaccio, *Fiammetta*, 5 (p. 1134 in the Ricciardi edition of Boccaccio, *Opere*). In a similar vein, as we saw in Chapter 1, the vital spirits personified in Niccolò di Giovanni Fiorentino's Chapel of the Blessed Giovanni Orsini in Trogir are conceived as reviving after a long period of dormancy.

35. Florence, Biblioteca Medicea Laurenziana, Plut. 82.10, c. 3; see *All'ombra del lauro: Documenti librari della cultura in età Laurenziana*, ed. Anna Lenzuni (exhibition catalogue, Florence, Biblioteca Medicea Laurenziana, Milan, 1992), 131–32, no. 3.13.

36. Florence, Biblioteca Medicea Laurenziana, Plut. 68.23, in *All'ombra del lauro*, 116–18, no. 2.100.

37. Charles Dempsey, "Lorenzo's Ombra," in *Lorenzo il Magnifico e il suo mondo* (Convegno internazionale di studi, Firenze, 9–13 giugno 1992), ed. Gian Carlo Garfagnini (Florence, 1994), 341–55. See also Michael L. Evans, "Bartolomeo Sanvito and an Antique Motif," *The British Library Journal* 11 (1985): 123–30, and Jonathan J. G. Alexander, *Italian Renaissance Illuminations* (New York, 1977).

38. Lucian, *How to Write History*, 23.

39. Synesius, *De insomniis*, in *Patrologia greca*, 66.1290.

40. Giorgio Agamben, *Stanze: La parola e il fantasma nella cultura occidentale* (Turin, 1977), 28–35 ("I fantasmi di Eros"); and see 105–20 ("'Spiritus phantasticus'") and 121–29 ("Spiriti d'amore"). See also the exemplary study by Robert Klein, "Spirito peregrino," in *La forme et l'intelligible*, ed. André Chastel (Paris, 1970), 31–64 (translated into English in *Form and Meaning: Writings on the Renaissance and Modern Art* [New York, 1979], 62–85).

41. Agamben, *Stanze*, 123–24; and for the topos of the war of the spirits, see Klein, "Spirito peregrino," 75.

42. *Andrea Mantegna*, ed. Jane Martineau (exhibition catalogue, London, 1992), 457–58, no. 149. For Raphael's Alexandrianism in the Farnesina, undoubtedly inspired by Andrea Navagero (whose poetry was based in imitation of the Planudean Anthology), and its revival in the seventeenth century, see Charles Dempsey, *Annibale Carracci: The Farnese Gallery, Rome* (New York, 1995), 23–24.

43. Iacopo Sannazaro, *Arcadia*, 11.35–38: "E subito ordinò i premi a coloro che lottare volessono, offrendo di dare al vincitore un bel vaso di legno di acero, ove per mano del padoano Mantegna, artefice sovra tutti gli altri accorto e ingegnosissimo, eran dipinte molte cose: . . . si vedean duo fanciulli pur nudi, i quali, avendosi posti duo volti orribili di mascare, cacciavano per le bocche di quelli le picciole mani per porre spavento a duo altri che davanti gli stavano; de' quali l'uno fuggendo si volgea indietro e per paura gridava, l'altro caduto già in terra piangeva e, non possendosi altrimenti aiutare, stendeva la mano per graffiarlo." The relationship between the drawing and this passage was first pointed out by Paul Kristeller, *Andrea Mantegna* (London, 1901), 461, and given more extensive anal-

ysis by Otto Kurz, "Sannazaro and Mantegna," in *Studi in onore di Riccardo Filangieri* (Naples, 1959), 277–83.

44. See Waldemar Deonna, "Éros jouant avec un masque de Silène," *Revue archéologique*, 3d ser., 5 (1916): 74–97. Important sculptural examples in Rome include sarcophagi in the Mattei and Albani collections, as well as reliefs in the Albani collection and in the Capitoline Museum. The Albani sarcophagus, which shows an *eros* behind a colossal Silenus-mask who terrifies a companion by thrusting a hand through the mouth of the mask, was earlier drawn for the Codex Pighianus and was acquired by the Albani from the collection of Vincenzo Giustiniani, who had it engraved for the *Galleria Giustiniana*, vol. 2, 128 (see Fig. 55). It is certainly fundamental for Mantegna as well as for Poussin and Duquesnoy's reinterpretation of the motif. For masked *erotes* on ancient gems, see O. Nemerov, *Antichnye Kamei v sobranii Ermitazha Katalog* (Leningrad, 1988), nos. 62 and 66; Marie-Louise Vollenweider, *Deliciae Leonis: Antike geschnittene Steine und Ringe aus der Privatsammlung* (Mainz, 1984), no. 99 (with extensive further references); Vollenweider, *Die Steinschneidekunst und ihre Künstler in spätrepublikanischer und augusteischer Zeit* (Baden-Baden, 1966), no. 24; and Adolf Furtwängler, *Beschreibung der geschnittenen Steine im Antiquarium* (Berlin, 1896), nos. 11125 and 11169.

45. Roberto Canneta, in *Rilievi e plachette dal XV al XVIII secolo* (exhibition catalogue, Palazzo Venezia, Rome, 1982), 14; and G. Pucci, "Antichità e manifatture: un itinerario," in *Dalla tradizione all'archeologia*, vol. 3 of *Memoria dell'antico nell'arte italiana*, ed. Salvatore Settis (Turin, 1986), 251–92, esp. 290–92. There are many surviving casts from this matrix (some three dozen according to Douglas Lewis, Curator of Sculpture and Decorative Arts at the National Gallery of Art in Washington, to whom I am grateful for assistance). One is reproduced in John Pope-Hennessy, *Renaissance Bronzes from the Samuel H. Kress Foundation* (London, 1965), fig. 303, and another, in the Bargello, is shown in Leo Planiscig, *Andrea Riccio* (Vienna, 1927), fig. 357.

46. John Pope-Hennessy, "The Italian Plaquette," *Proceedings of the British Academy* 50 (1964): 63–85; and see Francesco Rossi, "Le gemme antiche e le origini della placchetta," in *Italian Plaquettes*, ed. Alison Luchs (Washington D.C., 1989), 55–68, and Nicole Dacos, "Le rôle des plaquettes dans la diffusion des gemmes antiques: Le cas de la collection Médicis," in *Italian Plaquettes*, 71–89.

47. Eckhard Leuschner, *Persona, Larva, Maske: Ikonologische Studien zum 16. bis 18. Jahrhundert*, Europäische Hochschulschriften, Reihe 28, Kunstgeschichte (Frankfurt am Main, 1997).

48. Angelo Poliziano, *Detti piacevoli*, ed. Tiziano Zanato (Rome, 1983), 45 (no. 6). Afranius's joke is recorded in the grammarian Nonius's *De compendia doctrina*, 325, 25; and see *Scaenicae romanorum fragmenta tertiis curis*, vol. 2, ed. Otto Ribbeck

(Leipzig, 1898), (*Comicorum fragmenta*), 236. Nonius received at least five editions before 1480, the *editio princeps* being published in the care of Pomponius Laetus in 1471; for which, see Nonius, *De compendia doctrina*, ed. Louis Quicherat (Paris, 1872), xiv.

49. Erasmus, *Adagiorum chiliades*, Chil. 3, Cent. 7, Prov. 3 (*Panicus casus*), in *Opera omnia*, vol. 2 (Leiden, 1703); and see Politian, *Miscellanea*, 28, in *Opera*, vol. 1 (Lyon, 1536), 563–66, as well as the further discussion of panic terrors in the next chapter.

50. Erasmus, *Adagiorum chiliades*, Chil. 2, Cent. 3, Prov. 53 ("Metum inanem metuisti"): ". . . nam *mormolykeion* Graecis persona est, larvae aut malo genio similis, qua pueros territant quidam."

51. Erasmus, *Adagiorum chiliades*, Chil. 2, Cent. 3, Prov. 53 ("Metum inanem metuisti").

52. Angelo Poliziano, *Commento inedito alle Selve di Stazio*, ed. Lucia Cesarini Martinelli (Florence, 1978), 147, quoting Apuleius, *De deo Socratis*, 13–14.

53. Benedetto Varchi, *Opere*, vol. 2 (Trieste, 1858–59), 577: ". . . che ancora con varie larve, ciò è faccie e forme, il che significa con nuovi e varii sospetti, ritorna ogni ora, più, e va sempre crescendo con maggiore inquietitudine. Ed essendo anco questa parte chiara per sé, non diremo altro, se non che come sapete, LARVE in lingua latina significa, oltre quello che noi diciamo maschere, l'anime dannate de' rei, che noi volgarmente chiamiamo spiriti. Ma qui vuol dire sotto varie figure ed apparizioni, come dicono, appariscono quelle, ed é tolto dal Petrarca quando disse nel sonetto *Fuggendo la prigione, ove Amor m'ebbe* [Son. 60]:

> . . . e poi tra via m'apparve
> Quel traditor in sì mentite larve,
> Chi più saggio di me 'ngannato arebbe."

54. Leuschner, *Persona, Larva, Maske*, 353, cat. 3. And see Max Seidel, "Studien zur Antikenrezeption Nicola Pisanos," *Mitteilungen des Kunsthistorishen Institutes Florenz* 19 (1975): 307–82.

55. Plato, *Phaedo*, 77E.

56. For the Della Torre tomb, see Leo Planiscig, *Andrea Riccio* (Vienna, 1927), 371–412 and 495 (and figs. 471, 485–89, 491–92). The motif of one putto frightening another with a mask was also adopted by Riccio in the ornamentation of his famous Paschal candlestick for the Sánto in Padua (Planiscig's figs. 354 and 370).

57. Aristophanes, *Achanians*, 582; and *Pax*, 474.

58. Politian, *Le stanze per la giostra*, 2.21 and 2.24.

59. Pierre de Ronsard, "Les Daimons," in *Oeuvres complètes*, ed. G. Cohen (Paris, 1950), 2.167–74.

Chapter Three

1. Paul Oskar Kristeller, *Renaissance Thought: The Classic, Scholastic and Humanist Strains* (New York, 1961), esp. chap. 1, "The Humanist Movement."
2. Eugenio Garin, *La cultura filosofica del rinascimento italiano* (Florence, 1961), 329.
3. See Leon Battista Alberti, *On the Art of Building in Ten Books*, trans. Joseph Ryckwert, Neil Leach, and Robert Tavernor (Cambridge, 1988).
4. Angelo Poliziano, *Le Selve e la Strega: Prolusioni nello Studio Fiorentino*, ed. Isidoro Del Lungo (Florence, 1926), 184–229 (text and translation of the *Lamia*). See also *Lamia: Praelectio in priora Aristotelis analytica*, ed. Ari Wesseling (Leiden, 1986).
5. *Lamia*, 186 (Del Lungo), 4 (Wesseling).
6. *Lamia*, 220, 222 (Del Lungo), 16–17 (Wesseling).
7. A. E. Housman, *Selected Prose*, ed. John Carter (Cambridge, 1961), 168.
8. Politian, *Panepistemon* in *Omnia opera Angeli Politiani et alia quaedam lectu digna* [unpaginated] (Basilea, 1553); and see Charles Dempsey, *The Portrayal of Love: Botticelli's Primavera and Humanist Culture at the Time of Lorenzo the Magnificent* (Princeton, 1992), 26. The question of a humanist dialectic has greatly engaged much recent historical research, for which suffice it to cite, with earlier references, Nancy Struever, "Lorenzo Valla's Grammar of Subject and Object: An Ethical Inquiry," *I Tatti Studies* 2 (1987): 239–67 (see 241: . . . "Valla affirms rhetoric as the master science, the embedding discipline, which undertakes the complete task of linguistic inquiry. . . . Valla insists on the logical priority of grammatical study, and the late, derived, auxiliary nature of dialectical inquiry.").
9. Ronald Lightbown, *Sandro Botticelli*, vol. 2 (Berkeley, 1978), 55–57, no. B41. For Botticelli's rendering of contemporary (and not antique) costumes, see Dempsey, *Portrayal of Love*, 65–78, as well as Chapter 5 below.
10. Vasari-Milanesi, 6.121f. See further *Giorgio Vasari*, ed. Laura Corti, Margaret Daly Davis, Charles Davis, and Julian Kliemann (exhibition catalogue, Florence, 1981), nos. 8, 20, and p. 265, and fig. 320.
11. Erika Simon, "Nonnos und das Elfenbeinkästchen aus Veroli," *Jahrbuch des Deutschen Archäologischen Instituts* 79 (1964): 279–336; and Lydie Hadermann-Misguich, "L'image antique, byzantine et moderne du putto au masque," in *Rayonnement Grec: Hommages à Charles Delvoye*, ed. Lydie Hadermann-Misguich (Brussels, 1982), 516–18.
12. Giovanni Rosini, *Storia della pittura italiana esposta coi monumenti*, vol. 3 (Pisa, 1839–47), 152, note 13. Botticelli's allusion to Politian was then picked up by Adolph Gaspary, *Geschichte der Italienischen Literatur*, vol. 2 (Strasburg, 1885–88), 232–34, from which it passed to Aby Warburg in his celebrated dissertation of

1893 (Sandro Botticellis "Geburt der Venus" und "Frühlung," republished in *Gesammelte Schriften: Die Erneuerung der heidischen Antike* Leipzig, 1932, vol. 1, 5–68 and 307–28), and thence into the art-historical literature (summarized in Dempsey, *Portrayal of Love*).

13. Erwin Panofsky, *The Iconography of Correggio's Camera di San Paolo* (London, 1961), 39–45.

14. *Commentariorum in Aratum reliquiae*, ed. Ernst Maass (Berlin, 1898), 397.

15. *Commentariorum in Aratum*, 237.

16. Vladimir Juřen, "'Pan Terrificus' de Politien," *Bibliothèque d'Humanisme et Renaissance* 33 (1971): 641–45.

17. Politian, *Miscellaneorum centuria una*, in *Opera*, vol. 1 (Lyons, 1536), 563–66.

18. Politian, *Miscellaneorum centuria una*, 563–66.

19. Erasmus, *Adagiorum chiliades*, Chil. 3, Cent. 7, Prov. 3 (*Panicus casus*), Chil. 2, Cent. 10, Prov. 19 (*Multa in bellis inania*), and Chil. 2, Cent. 3, Prov. 80 (*Metum inanem metuisti*), cols. 884, 689, and 515 respectively in Erasmus, *Opera omnia*, vol. 2 (Leiden, 1703). And for the emblem *In subitum terrorem*, see Andrea Alciati, *Emblemata cum commentariis . . . et notis L. Pignorii Patavini* (1621; Garland Reprints, New York, 1976), 529–32.

20. Lightbown, *Botticelli*, vol. 1, 93, for example, insists on the essential playfulness of the painting, suggesting that the shell-trumpet is a kind of shepherd's horn rather than an attribute of the power of Pan and his cohorts to induce panic terrors. The most extensive attempt to explain away the evidence of Panofsky and Juřen's philologically impeccable observations with regard to the *paniscus* trumpeting on the conch shell (and also to challenge the identity of Botticelli's protagonists as Mars and Venus) was written by Paul Holberton, "Botticelli's *Hypnerotomachia* in the National Gallery, London: A Problem of the Use of Classical Sources in Art," *Illinois Classical Studies* 9, no. 2 (1984): 149–82. Although I am in sympathy with Holberton's instinct that Botticelli's painting is to be understood as responding to the conventions of vernacular poetry, this most certainly does not require, as he seems to think, denying the classical foundation to his subject matter.

21. C. N. Plunkett, *Sandro Botticelli* (London, 1900), 44f. For Alexander and Roxana, see also A. Lagi De Caro, "Alessandro e Rossane come Ares ed Afrodite in un dipinto della casa *Regio VI, Insula Occidentalis, n. 42,*" *Studia pompeiana & classica in honor of Wilhelmina F. Jashemski*, ed. R. I. Curtis (New Rochelle, New York), vol. 1, 75–83.

22. Lucian, *Herodotus or Aëtion*, 5.

23. Juřen, "Pan Terrificus," 642.

24. The *Trésor de la langue française* gives Rabelais's *Gargantua* of 1534 as the earliest appearance of *panique*, but Littré cites a usage already at the end of the fif-

teenth century. The *OED* has as the first usage of "panic" a 1603 translation of Plutarch's *Moralia*, a prominent source cited in the humanist literature for *panikós* (see note 34 below). And for *panisch*, see the Grimm dictionary (*Deutsches Wörterbuch*).

25. Hyginus, *Poetica astronomica*, 2.28.

26. Cicero, *Epistulae ad familiares*, 16.23.

27. *Scholia graeca in Euripidis tragoedias ex codicibus aucta et emendata*, ed. G. Dindorfius (Oxford, 1863), *Scholia in Medeam* 1172 (*panikà deìmata*), 72.

28. Synesius, *De providentia*, in *Patrologia greca*, vol. 66, col. 1260.

29. *Nicetai Choniatae Orationes et Epistolae* (Corpus Fontium Historiae Byzantinae III), ed. Ioannes Aloysius van Dieten (Berlin, 1972), 82 (Orat. 8). In the apparatus van Dieten cites Pausanias, 10, 23, 7, apropos Brennus, for *phobos panikos*, as well as the *Suda*, Pi 201. See also Politian, *Miscellanea*, cap. 28.

30. Valerius Flaccus, *Argonautica*, 3.43–57.

31. Panofsky, *Correggio's Camera di San Paolo*, 41. And see the examples collected in Alciati, *Emblematum liber*, 529–32, as well as in Daremberg-Saglio, *Dictionnaire des antiquités grecques et romaines*, vol. 4, 1, 298–300, and Wilhelm Heinrich Roscher, *Ausführliches Lexicon der griechischen und römischen Mythologie*, Leipzig, 1884–94, vol. 3, 1, col. 1388ff.

32. Dionysus of Halicarnassus, 5.16, 3.

33. Alciati, *Emblematum liber*, 529–32.

34. Livy, *Roman History*, 2.7.

35. Plutarch, *Numa*, 15.6.

36. Plutarch, *Moralia*, 17 (*De defectu oraculum*).

37. Lilio Gregorio Giraldi, *De deis gentium* (1548; Garland Reprint, New York, 1976), 608. Giraldi follows Politian (*Miscellanea* 28) in attributing to these creatures those "terriculamentis . . . à graecis *nympholeptoi*, & à Latinis lymphati nuncupati."

38. Pierre de Ronsard, *Les Daimons*, in *Oeuvres complètes*, ed. Gustave Cohen (Paris, 1950), 167–74. See further Hélène Moreau, "Les Daimons ou de la fantaisie," in *Autours des "Hymnes" de Ronsard*, ed. Maurice Lazard (Paris, 1984), 215–42.

39. Reposianus, *De concubitu Martis et Veneris*, 15f. Franz Wickhoff, "Die Hochzeitsbilder Sandro Botticellis," *Jahrbuch der preusszischer Kunstsammlungen in Wien* 27 (1906): 206–7, proposed that Botticelli's *Mars and Venus* was derived from this poem, to which it does indeed bear some marked similarities. However, this idea has been discounted because the unique surviving example of the poem appears in the Codex Salmasius, a collection of poems and epitaphs from the Latin Anthology, which cannot be traced earlier than the seventeenth century. Nevertheless, the question cannot be considered entirely closed, in that Politian does cite scattered materials from the Latin Anthology in his commentary to *Statius* (which, however, can also be found in other sources).

40. Politian in the *Panepistemon* discusses dreams under Divination: "Insomnia phantasma occurit, quod visum Cicero appellat, et Ephialtes, qui Latine Incubus dicitur."

41. I have used the following editions: Artemidor von Daldis, *Traumbuch*, trans. Friedrich S. Krauss (Basel and Stuttgart, 1965), and Macrobius, *Commentary on the Dream of Scipio*, trans. William Harris Stahl (New York, 1952). The literature is vast, and of necessity repetitive, but the following are reliable guides: Francis Xavier Newman, "Somnium: Medieval Theories of Dreaming and the Form of Vision Poetry" (Ph.D. diss., Princeton, 1962); A. C. Spearing, *Medieval Dream Poetry* (Cambridge, 1976); F. Hallyn, "Le songe de Kepler," *Bibliothèque d'Humanisme et Renaissance* 42 (1980): 329–47; and the formidable collection of essays published in *Le songe à la Renaissance* (Colloque International de Cannes 29–31 Mai 1987), ed. Françoise Charpentier (Nice, 1989), to which is appended, on pp. 255–71, a useful "Bibliographie sommaire d'ouvrages sur le songe publiés en France et en Italie jusqu'en 1600," compiled by R. Cooper.

42. Macrobius, 3.2–3 (p. 88 in the Stahl edition). Nightmares may be caused by physical disorders, such as indigestion; or by mental disorders, preoccupations, and anxieties that cause the dreamer to experience vexations similar to those that preoccupy him when awake. Examples of such dreams are given by Chaucer in the *Parlement of Fowles*, in which the poet describes his own dream after reading Cicero's *In somnium Scipionis* and lists everyday psychological dreams that are merely reflections of what has most preoccupied different sleepers during the day:

> The wearie hunter sleeping in his bedde,
> To wood ayen his mind goeth anone;
> The judge dreameth how his plees be spedde;
> The carter dremeth how his cartes gone;
> The rich of gold, the knight fights with his fone;
> The sicke mette he drinketh of the tonne;
> The lover mette he hath his lady wonne.

For a general but intelligent discussion, drawing parallels but also distinguishing between ancient and Freudian dream theories, see Marco Hagge, *Il sogno e la scrittura* (Florence, 1986).

43. Guido de Columnis, *Historia destructionis Troiae*, ed. N. E. Griffin (Cambridge, Mass., 1936), 61ff. As Margaret R. Scherer, *The Legends of Troy in Art and Literature* (New York, 1963), 15–18, notes, medieval romances customarily interpreted the judgment of Paris as a dream, something that appears as early as the second century in Dio Chrysostom's suggestion that Paris was deluded "like a soul which in its sleep follows its phantasies and imaginings and spins out some long and coherent dream;" and then firmly basing themselves upon the forthright assertion in Dares's slightly later *Excidio Troiae historia* that Paris was dreaming.

44. Giovanni Francesco Pico della Mirandola, *La strega, o vero, De gli inganni de demoni* (Bologna, 1524), a translation of *Strix, sive, De ludificatione daemonum* on p. 32.

45. Macrobius, 3.3–6 (pp. 87–88 in the Stahl edition).

46. Giraldi, *De deis gentium*, 622. And see the indispensable study by Wilhelm Heinrich Roscher, *Ephialtes: Eine pathologische-mythologische Abhandlung über die Alpträume des klassischen Altertums* (Leipzig, 1900). (Translated into English as *Pan and the Nightmare* [Zürich, 1972], with an important introduction by James Hillman.)

47. Roger Caillois, "Les démons de midi," *Revue de l'histoire des religions* 58, nos. 115–16 (1937): 142–73, 53–82, and 143–86; and Nicholas J. Perella, *Midday in Italian Literature: Variations on an Archetypal Theme* (Princeton, 1979). The Swiss-born painter Arnold Böcklin devoted a number of paintings to the theme of Pan as the noonday demon inspiring panic terror in shepherds; see E. Tumasonis, "The Piper among the Ruins: The God Pan in the Works of Arnold Böcklin," *RACAR—Revue d'art canadienne: Canadian Art Review* 17, no. 1 (1990): 54–63.

48. The most famous artistic representation of the incubus (or rather succubus) who presses down upon the diaphragm and produces erotic sensations, is, of course, Fuseli's *The Nightmare*, for which see Nicolas Powell, *Fuseli: The Nightmare* (London, 1973). Here the demon is not imagined as a Pan or Satyr, but rather as a kind of kobold, or hobgoblin, which is a northern European, folklore version of the same thing. For the erotic incubus as a Pan or Satyr stealing up on a sleeping Nymph, one might adduce Rembrandt's so-called *Jupiter and Antiope* of 1659 (Bartsch, 203), as well as Correggio's equally misnamed *Jupiter and Antiope* in the Louvre. Other examples are legion, and suffice it here only to mention Titian's so-called *Pardo Venus*, also in the Louvre.

49. Giraldi, *De deis gentium*, 608.

50. St. Augustine, *Civitas Dei*, 15.23: ". . . Sylvanos et Panes, quos vulgo incubos vocant, improbos saepe extitisse mulieribus et earum appetisse ac peregisse concubitum . . ." One again thinks of the Carracci, certainly Agostino's *lascivie*, but also Annibale's highly erotic *Nymph and Satyr*.

51. Isidore of Seville, *Isidori Hispalensis episcopi etymologiarum sive originum libri XX*, ed. W. M. Lindsay (Oxford, 1911), 8.11: "Larvae ex hominibus factos daemones aiunt, qui meriti mali fuerint. . . . Pilosi, qui Graece Panitae, Latine Incubi appellantur, sive Inui ab ineundo passim cum animalibus. Unde et Incubi dicuntur ab incumbendo, hoc est stuprando." And see St. Jerome, *In Esaiam*, 13.21.22: "*Pilosi saltabunt ibi*, vel incubones, vel satyros, vel sylvestres quosdam homines, quos nonnulli fatuos ficarios vocant, aut daemonum genera intelligunt." For the identification of *Incubi* with Satyrs and Pans, see also Annibale Caro's program for a fresco cycle, in *Lettere familiari*, 3.743.18, discussed by Clare Robertson, "Annibal Caro as Iconographer: Sources and Method," *Journal of the Warburg and*

Courtauld Institutes 45 (1982): 160–81, esp. 165 n. 28: ". . . incubi, che sono alcuni demoni . . . la forma de' quali è la medesima che de' Fauni e de' Silvani."

52. For *fauni* (or *fatui*) *ficarii*, see Roscher, *Pan and the Nightmare* (as cited in note 46), 55–56.

53. See note 51 above.

54. Roscher, *Pan and the Nightmare* (as cited in note 44), 54.

55. Angelo Poliziano, *Commento inedito alle Selve di Stazio*, ed. Lucia Cesarini Martinelli (Florence, 1978), 450–51, wherein Politian quotes St. Jerome, *Vita Pauli*, 8.

56. Vasari-Milanesi, 4.140.

57. Daniel Arasse, "Piero di Cosimo, L'excentrique des origines," in *L'exces: Nouvelle revue de Psychanalyse* 43 (1991): 125–48, following Paul Barolsky, *Infinite Jest: Wit and Humor in Italian Renaissance Art* (Columbia, 1978), 44–46. Barolsky aptly cites Politian's Catullan *In puellam suam* in this regard ("Puella delicatior lepuscolo et cunicolo"). It is also to his great credit that he is the first to insist upon the comic elements in Botticelli's *Mars and Venus* (6–7, 38–45, and 113–14).

58. However, that later tradition is by no means uniform. The theme of Mars and Venus may be treated in a comic vein, as it was by Rosso Fiorentino, or as an allegory of peace, as it was by Rubens, or as an exploration of human sexuality and emasculation, as it was by Poussin (and by Politian in the *Stanze*, for which see the next chapter). See Elizabeth Cropper and Charles Dempsey, *Nicolas Poussin: Friendship and the Love of Painting* (Princeton, 1996), 216–49.

59. For the question of Botticelli's treatment of classical gods in contemporary costume in the *Primavera*, see Dempsey, *The Portrayal of Love*, 65–70, and see further Chapter 5 below.

60. Cropper and Dempsey, *Nicolas Poussin*, 219. Ovid's story of the adulterous love-making of Mars and Venus and their entrapment in Vulcan's net derives from a different tradition, one not easily reconcilable with the well-known allegorization of their union by the Romans as being emblematic of peace and marriage (for which, see Lagi di Caro, "Alessandro e Rossane," as cited in note 21). Ovid's story is almost invariably treated in a broadly comico-erotic vein. (Wtewael was especially fond of the theme, for which see Anne W. Lowenthal, *Mars and Venus Surprised by Vulcan*, Getty Museum Studies on Art [Malibu, 1995].) Very rarely, however, the Lucretian and Ovidian stories could be brought together, as they were by Reposianus (for which see note 37).

61. Dempsey, *The Portrayal of Love*, 30, 46–47.

62. Lagi di Caro, "Alessandro e Rossane" (see note 21 above).

63. Ernst Gombrich, "Botticelli's Mythologies: A Study in the Neoplatonic Symbolism of his Circle," in *Symbolic Images: Studies in the Art of the Renaissance* (London, 1972): 31–81.

64. See further Roberto Calasso, "Le folie qui vient des Nymphes," *RES* 25

(1994): 125–33, and for nympholepsy, panolepsy, theolepsy, etc., see Philippe Borgeaud, *The Cult of Pan in Ancient Greece*, trans. Kathleen Atlass and James Redfield (Chicago, 1979). The Roman grammarians tried to establish an etymological identity between the two words by deriving *lympha* (clear water) from *nympha* (Nymph); see, for example, Festus, *De verborum significatu*, ed. A. Thewrewk de Ponor (Budapest, 1889), 1.86: "Lymphe dictae sunt a nymphis. Vulgo autem memoriae proditum est, quicumque speciem quandam e fonte, id est effigiem nymphae, viderint, furendi non fecisse finem: quos Graeci *nympholéptous* vocant, Latini *lymphaticos* appellant."

65. *Nutricia*, 226. The passage is initiated by a specific reference to panic terrors (211: "Moxque lycaonias Pan carmine terruit umbras"), inducing the *enthusiasmos*, or poetic furor that possesses Bacis; for which the *locus classicus* is Plato's telling of Socrates's delirium, and subsequent propitiation of Pan, in the *Phaedrus*.

66. For Politian's characterization of an emasculated Mars in the *Stanze* see A. Bartlett Giammatti, *The Earthly Paradise and Renaissance Epic* (Princeton, 1966), 129–34, as well as Chapter 4 below; and for Poussin's treatment of the same theme (though not in a political context), see Cropper and Dempsey, *Nicolas Poussin*, 216–60.

67. Jeffrey Henderson, *The Maculate Muse: Obscene Language in Attic Comedy* (New Haven, 1975), 142; and see William S. Heckscher, "The Anadyomene in the Medieval Tradition (Pelagia-Cleopatra-Aphrodite): A Prelude to Botticelli's *Birth of Venus*," in *Art and Literature: Studies in Relationship*, ed. Egon Verheyen (Baden-Baden, 1994), 127–64, esp. 151–52.

68. For Politian's interpretation of Catullus's sparrow, still controversial, see *Miscellanea* 6; and see further Julia Haig Gaisser, *Catullus and His Renaissance Readers* (Oxford, 1993), 75–78 and 236–54.

69. Erasmus, *Adagiorum chiliades*, Chil. 1, Cent. 1, Prov. 60 (*Irritare crabrones*). See also Benedetto Varchi, *Ercol.*, 81: "Quando un si sta ne' suoi panni senza dar noja a persona, e un altro comincia per qualche cagione a morderlo e offenderlo di parole, se colui è uomo da non su lasciare malmenare e bistrattare, ma per rendergli, come si dice i coltellini, si usa dire: egli stuzzica il formicajo, e le pecchie, o sì veramente il vespajo, che i Latini dicevano *irritare crabrones*." One also finds Carlo Sigonio writing to Onofrio Panvinio: "di gratia impariamo a vivere et non stuccichiamo i vespai" (William McCuaig, *Carlo Sigonio: The Changing World of the Renaissance* [Princeton, 1989], 17). The proverb has additional relevance for late Quattrocento Florence, since a *vespaio* also refers to a head ornament worn by women that displays pearls scattered through the hair so that they seem like wasps gathered around their nest. A spectacular example is shown in the so-called *Simonetta Vespucci* attributed to Botticelli's school in the Staedel Museum in Frankfurt. See Luigi Pulci's enchanting *frottola*, *Le galee per Quaracchi*, for mention

of a *vespaio* carried with other female vanities to the villa of Bernardo Rucellai at Quaracchi; and see Dempsey, *The Portrayal of Love*, 68.

70. Erasmus, *Adagiorum chiliades*, Chil. 1, Cent. 1, Prov. 60.

71. Aristophanes, *Lysistrata*, 475.

72. For the identification of this figure as a *lamia*, which is absolutely correct, see Graham Smith, "Jealousy, Pleasure and Pain in Agnolo Bronzino's 'Allegory of Venus and Cupid,'" *Pantheon* 39 (1981): 150–65. See also Giraldi, *De deis gentium*, 614, who gives a standard account of the nature and appearance of *lamiae*, which he notes are of the same genus as *mormolykeia*: "Facies est mulieris, & formosae quidem, ubera & pectora longè pulcherrima, quae neque melius pictor possit effingere. . . . reliqua pars dura, & infrangibilis, ob squammas confertae, inferiora sunt serpentis," etc. Much material, naturally, is gathered in Heinrich Kramer and Jacob Sprenger, *Malleus maleficarum*, trans. Montague Summers (New York, 1971).

73. For Pan and his followers as demons of the noonday, see Giorgio Agamben, *Stanze: La parola e il fantasma nella cultura occidentale* (Turin, 1977), 1–14 ("Il demone meridiano"), as well as note 45 above. And for the Lucretian paradox of Mars who is *armipotens* and *impotens*, see Cropper and Dempsey, *Nicolas Poussin*, 217–19.

Chapter Four

1. See the introduction to Heinrich Kramer and Jacob Sprenger, *The Malleus Maleficarum*, trans. Montague Summers (New York, 1971).

2. Carlo Ginzburg, *The Night Battles: Witchcraft and Agrarian Cults in the Sixteenth and Seventeenth Centuries* (New York, 1986); and see Carlo Ginzburg, *Ecstasies: Deciphering the Witch's Sabbath* (New York, 1992). See also Richard Kieckhefer, *European Witch Trials: Their Foundations in Popular and Learned Culture, 1300–1500* (Berkeley, 1976); Walter Stephens, "The Quest for Satan: Witch-hunting and Religious Doubt," in *Stregoneria e streghe nell'Europa moderna* (Convegno internazionale di studi, Pisa, 24–26 marzo 1994) (Pisa, 1995), 49–71; and Walter Stephens, "De dignitate strigis: La copula mundi nel pensiero dei due Pico e di Torquato Tasso," in *Giovanni e Francesco Pico: L'opera e la fortuna di due studenti ferraresi*, ed. Patrizia Castelli (Florence, 1998), 325–49.

3. Giorgio Agamben, *Stanze: La parola e il fantasma nella cultura occidentale* (Turin, 1977); and Marco Hagge, *Il sogno e la scrittura*, Florence, 1986.

4. See, with further bibliography, Alessandro Perosa, "Codici di Galeno postillati dal Poliziano," in *Umanesimo e Rinascimento: Studi offerti a Paul Oskar Kristeller* (Florence, 1980), 75–109; *A. Politiani Sylva in scabiem*, ed. Alessandro Perosa (Rome, 1954); and Alessandro Perosa, "Febris: A Poetic Myth Created by Poliziano," *Journal of the Warburg and Courtauld Institutes* 9 (1946): 74–95, esp. 93.

5. See also Macrobius, *Commentarium in somnium Scipionis* 3.2, as well as the material discussed in Chapter 3 above.

6. Macrobius, *Somnium Scipionis*, 3.3.

7. Politian, *Miscellanea*, 28 (*Panici terrores*), cites the scholiast to Euripides attributing Medea's epileptic seizure to a kind of panic (or panolepsy). And see Philippe Borgeaud, *The Cult of Pan in Ancient Greece* (Chicago, 1979). It is significant, as we shall see, that in his lament for Albiera, Politian names *Terrificus Pavor* as one of the symptoms of her fevered delirium.

8. Perosa, "Febris" (as cited in note 4).

9. Perosa, "Febris," 92–93.

10. Angelo Poliziano, "In Albieram Albitiam, puellam formosissimam, morientem: Ad Sismundum Stupham eius sponsum," vv. 95–106, in *Michele Marullo, Poliziano, Iacopo Sannazzaro: Poesie Latine*, Classici Ricciardi 14, ed. Francesco Arnaldi and Lucia Gualdo Rosa (Turin, 1976), 89–104.

11. Petrarch, *Rime sparse*, 89 ("Fuggendo la pregione ove Amor m'ebbe"), in *Petrarch's Lyric Poems: The Rime sparse and Other Lyrics*, ed. and trans. Robert M. Durling (Cambridge, Mass., 1976), 193.

12. Charles Dempsey, *The Portrayal of Love: Botticelli's Primavera and Humanist Culture at the Time of Lorenzo the Magnificent* (Princeton, 1992), 85–90.

13. Luigi Pulci, "Da poi che 'l Lauro," vv. 121–33, in Luigi Pulci, *Opere minori*, ed. Paolo Orvieto (Milan, 1986), 44–50. For the word *aombra*, to "boggle" or "spook," which is all but synonymous with "to panic," see the following note.

14. Lorenzo de'Medici, *Canzoniere*, ed. Paolo Orvieto (Milan, 1984), no. 24, 53–55. As Orvieto notes, *aombra* (like the English "to boggle") is an equine metaphor deriving its meaning from a horse that has been "spooked" by an *ombra* into bolting. See, for example, the interesting (and sad) inscription on the tomb of the unfortunate Carlo Petracchi in the cloister of S. Michele in Carmignano:

> O Morte
> In quante guise fai strazio degli uomini!
> Carlo Petracchi
> presso a San Donato
> da destriero per subita ombra infrenabile
> stramazzato di cocchio
> e nello spedale della vicina Firenze
> fra le braccia degli amici
> dopo cinque giorni spirato qui
> nella notte dei IV Giugno MDCCCLXI

Panic terrors, as we saw in the last chapter, also refer to the empty shadows that provoke stampedes.

15. Petrarch, *Rime sparse*, 227 (p. 383 in the Durling edition).

16. Francis X. Newman, "Somnium: Medieval Theories of Dreaming and the Form of Vision Poetry," (Ph.D. diss., Princeton University, 1962); and see the discussion, together with further citations, in Chapter 3 above. See also the fine introduction to Giovanni Boccaccio, *The Corbaccio*, ed. and trans. Anthony K. Cassell (Urbana, 1975), xi–xxvii.

17. Edmund Spenser, *The Faerie Queene*, 1.9.13–14 (in *The Works of Edmund Spenser: A Variorum Edition*, ed. Edwin Greenlaw et al. [Baltimore, 1932], 113).

18. *The Faerie Queene*, 1.1.47 (p. 16 in Greenlaw edition).

19. Eugenio Donato, "Death and History in Politian's *Stanze*," *MLN* 80 (1965): 27–40.

20. See Pierre Francastel, "La fête mythologique au Quattrocento: Expression littéraire et visualisation plastique," in *Oeuvres II: La réalité figurative: Éléments structurels de sociologie et de l'art* Paris, 1965), 229–52; Richard Trexler, *Public Life in Renaissance Florence* (New York, 1980); and Dempsey, *The Portrayal of Love*, 73–80. Much useful material about jousts is gathered in *Le tems revient,'l tempo si rinuova: Feste e spettacoli nella Firenze di Lorenzo il Magnifico*, ed. Paola Ventrone (exhibition catalogue, Milan, 1992).

21. Cited by Ruggero M. Ruggieri, "Letterati, poeti e pittori intorno alla giostra di Giuliano de'Medici," *Rinascimento* 10 (1959): 165–96, esp. 166.

22. Ruggieri, "Letterati," 165.

23. Paul Oskar Kristeller, "Un documento sconosciuto sulla giostra di Giuliano de'Medici," in *Studies in Renaissance Thought and Letters* (Storia e letteratura, Raccolata di studi e testi 54) (Rome, 1956), 437–50.

24. Kristeller, "Un documento sconosciuto," 438.

25. *Prosatori volgari del Quattrocento*, ed. Claudio Varese (La letteratura italiana: Storia e testi 14) (Milan and Naples, n.d.), 987.

26. For poems mourning the death of Albiera degli Albizzi, see Federico Patetta, "Una raccolta manoscritta di versi e prose in morte d'Albiera degli Albizzi," *Atti della R. Accademia della Scienza di Torino* 53 (1917–18): 310–25. For poets lamenting the death of Simonetta Cattaneo Vespucci, which included, besides Lorenzo, Politian, Bernardo Pulci, Naldo Naldi, Pietro Dovizi da Bibiena, et al., see André Rochon, *La jeunesse de Laurent de Médicis (1449–1478)* (Paris, 1963), 246.

27. For Corsini's letter see Kristeller, "Un documento sconosciuto," 445–48; and for the Magliabechiana manuscript and other *testimonia*, see Isidoro Del Lungo, "La giostra di Giuliano," in *Florentia: Uomini e cose del Quattrocento* (Florence, 1897), 391–412; Giovanni Pozzi, "La giostra medicea del 1475 e la 'Pallade' del Botticelli," *L'Arte* 5 (1902): 71–77; and especially Ruggieri, "Letterati" (see note 21), and Salvatore Settis, "Citarea 'su una impresa di bronconi,'" *Journal of the Warburg and Courtauld Institutes* 34 (1971): 135–77.

28. For Naldi, see Ruggieri, "Letterati," 166; and Alice Hulubei, "Naldo Naldi: Étude sur la joûte de Julien et sur les bucoliques dediés a Laurent de Médicis,"

Humanisme et Renaissance 3 (1936): 169–77. For Augurelli (as well as Naldi), see the comprehensive note in Settis, "Citarea," 138.

29. Luigi Pulci, *La giostra di Lorenzo de'Medici* (as cited in note 13), 53–120. See further Guido Carocci, *La giostra di Lorenzo de'Medici messa in rima da Luigi Pulci* (Bologna, 1899); and Dempsey, *The Portrayal of Love*, 80–85.

30. A point already stressed by Carducci in his famous essay prefacing the 1863 edition of the *Stanze* and Politian's other vernacular poems, as well as by Garin and other modern scholars.

31. Niccolò Machiavelli, *Istorie fiorentine*, 7.12. This passage is often read in a negative sense, as an example of Lorenzo's use of *panem et circenses* to divert the minds of the people from the affairs of state. However, he is referring to a moment of civic discord ("ribollendo adunque questi umori per la città"), when the minds of an idle citizenry are easily turned to sedition. In order to give the idle something to do ("per torre via adunque questo ozio, e dare che pensare agli uomini qualche cosa, che levassero i pensieri dello stato"), it was decided to create some *nuova allegrezza*, that is the joust and a representation of the journey of the Magi. Machiavelli's only note of disapproval, as I read the passage, is that the diversion didn't work for long. "Celebrati questi spettaculi," he concludes, "ritornorono ne' cittadini i medesemi pensieri," that is, seditious schemes.

32. Kristeller, "Un documento sconosciuto," 445.

33. Luigi Pulci, *La giostra* (as cited in note 13), 53–120; and see Carocci, *La giostra di Lorenzo*, and Dempsey, *The Portrayal of Love*, 79–83.

34. The text is taken from Ida Maïer, *Ange Politien: La Formation d'un poète humaniste (1469–1480)* (Geneva, 1966), 307.

35. Pozzi, "La giostra medicea del 1475," 72–73 (quoting the Anonimo Magliabecchiano), and see also Ruggieri, "Letterati," 168–70. Naldi also describes the banner, his account and that of the anonymous chronicler mutually confirming each other (Hulubei, "Naldo Naldi," 176):

> Cuius ut esse queas victricia dicere signa
> Pallada conspicies spectantem in lumina solis:
> Atque hastam manibus: scutumque insigne gerente
> Gorgonis anguiferae: pedibus quae diva pudicis
> Calcat: iter faciens tremulas castissima flammas
> Hic tu non tenerum quicquam: neque molle videbis:
> Sed Veneris natum manibus post terga revinctis
> Haerentem trunco teretis nisi fallor olivae,
> Viribus effractum victricis in omnia divae:

36. For the Urbino intarsia, which has long been associated with the imagery described on Botticelli's standard by contemporary witnesses, see Settis, "Cit-

area," 140; and for the engraving, see Arthur M. Hind, *Early Italian Engraving*, vol. 1 (London, 1938–48), 47, no. A.I.56. For Baccio Baldini, see Jay A. Levenson, Konrad Oberhuber, and Jacquelyn L. Sheehan, *Early Italian Engravings from the National Gallery of Art* (exhibition catalogue, Washington, D.C., 1973), 13–39.

37. See John Pope-Hennessy and Keith Christiansen, "Secular Painting in Fifteenth-century Tuscany: Birth Trays, Cassone Panels, and Portraits," *Metropolitan Museum Bulletin* (summer 1980).

38. *Triumphus Pudicitie*, 118–35, in Francesco Petrarca, *Triumphi*, ed. Marco Ariani (Milan, 1988), 214–18. The connection between the imagery of Giuliano's standard and these verses has long been established: Ruggero M. Ruggieri, "Spiriti e forme epico-cavalleresche nella *Giostra* del Poliziano," *Lettere italiane* 11 (1959): 1–24; and see Settis, "Citarea," 146.

39. See Politian's letter to Hieronymus Donatus in *Angeli Politiani opera*, vol. 1 (Lyons, 1533) (*Epistolarum libros XII: Miscellaneorum Centuriam*) 56–60.

40. I have here and throughout followed the translations in *The Stanze of Angelo Poliziano*, trans. David Quint (Amherst, Mass., 1979).

41. See, for example, Angelo Poliziano, *Poesie italiane*, ed. Saverio Orlando (Milan, 1976), 98, in which the phrase "fallace sonno" is glossed as "sogno ingannatore." See also Ghino Ghinassi, *Il volgare letterario nel Quattrocento e le Stanze del Poliziano* (Florence, 1957), 168.

42. Lorenzo de'Medici, *Commento sopra alcuni de'suoi sonetti*, in *Opere*, ed. L. Cavalli (Naples, 1969), 335–473, esp. 411.

43. We are again reminded of Lamachus's empty armor and Braccio Martelli's jest about Renato de'Pazzi's fear of an empty helmet (Angelo Poliziano, *Detti piacevoli*, ed. Tiziano Zanato [Rome, 1983], 45 [no. 6]), discussed at length with other *larve* in Chapters 2 and 3 above.

44. *Cose volgare del Politiano. In fine. Qui finischono le stanze composte da messer Angelo Politiano facte per la giostra de Giuliano fratello del Magnifico Lorenzo di Medici de Fiorenzi insieme con la festa de Orpheo et altre gentileze stampate curiosamente a Bologna per Platone delli Benedicti impressore accuratissimo del Anno M.cccc.lxxxx.iii a di nove di Agosto*. For the editor, Alessandro Sarti (Sarzio), see Julia Hill Cotton, "Alessandro Sarti e il Poliziano," *La bibliofilia* 64 (1962): 225–46; Daniela Delcorno Branca, *Sulla tradizione delle Rime del Poliziano* (Florence, 1979), 22–25; and Vittore Branca, *Poliziano e l'umanesimo della parola* (Turin, 1983), 3–12.

45. Settis, "Citarea," 153–55.

46. Ever since Warburg's famous dissertation on Botticelli's *Birth of Venus* and *Primavera*, there have been many attempts to interpret the meaning of this woodcut, and the history of this scholarship has been admirably treated, with full references, by Settis, "Citarea." I am here, of course, arguing that the woodcut functions as an additional rubric (cued by the dedication of the altar to Cythera),

and at this juncture I part company with the earlier interpreters of the image, including Settis.

47. Angelo Poliziano, *Le Stanze, l'Orfeo e le Rime di Messer Angelo Ambrogini Poliziano*, ed. Giosue Carducci (Florence, 1863). Del Lungo's important intervention appears on xxix–xxxiv.

48. Poliziano, *Le Stanze*, ed. Carducci, xxxiii.

49. Giovanni Battista Picotti, "Sulla data dell' *Orfeo* e delle *Stanze* di Agnolo Poliziano," *Rendiconti della R. Accademia dei Lincei* 23 (1915): 319–57, republished in Giovanni Battista Picotti, *Ricerche umanistiche* (Florence, 1955), 87–120; and Matteo Guerrieri, *L'ipotesi di G. B. Picotti sulla data di composizione delle "Stanze per la giostra" di Agnolo Poliziano* (Galantina, 1920). The arguments are summarized, and Guerrieri's given powerful support, in Arnaldo Momigliano's influential edition of the *Stanze, Orfeo,* and *Rime* (Turin, 1921).

50. Angelo Poliziano, *Stanze cominciate per la giostra di Giuliano de'Medici: Edizione critica*, ed. Vincenzo Pernicone (Turin, 1954), lxix–lxxi.

51. Guglielmo Gorni, "Novità su testo e tradizione delle 'Stanze' di Poliziano," *Studi di filologia italiana* 33 (1975): 241–64; and Guglielmo Gorni, "Le gloriose pompe (e i fieri ludi) della filologia italiana," *Rivista di letteratura italiana* 4 (1986): 391–412.

52. See Branca, *Poliziano e l'umanesimo della parola*, 3–7, and Delcorna Branca, *Sulla tradizione delle Rime del Poliziano*, 22–25, from which I quote the following assessment of Sarti written by Politian in the letter to Andrea Magnani apropos his *Herodianus*:

> Ad haec vero facile procuranda [a scrupulous fidelity of the printed text to the original] obeundaque magis idoneum habere magisque ex usu tuo neminem possis quam Alexandrum Sartium civem tuum literatum hominem nostrique studiosum tum (quod ego in hac re primum puto) neutiquam in amici negocio dormitantem.

See also the important study by Julia Hill Cotton, "Alessandro Sarti e il Poliziano," as well as the preface by Aldus to the first edition of Politian's *Opera omnia*.

53. Cotton, "Alessandro Sarti," 225–26, Gorni, "Novità," 263.

54. Gorni, "Novità," 264.

55. Delcorno Branca, *Sulla tradizione delle Rime di Poliziano*, 22–25.

56. Branca, *Poliziano e l'umanesimo della parola*, 3–12; and see Delcorno Branca, *Sulla tradizione delle rime di Poliziano*, 22–25.

57. For Del Lungo's arguments, see Carducci's 1863 edition of the *Stanze*, xxix–xxxiv (as cited in note 47 above); and see Donato, "Death and History in Politian's *Stanze*," (as cited in note 19 above). Donato's argument that all is not right in the world portrayed in the *Stanze* has found echoes in Quint's introduction to his

translation of the poem, and especially in James T. Chiampi, "Poliziano's 'Confessions:' The *Stanze* as Epic of Concupiscence," *Forum italicum* 23, nos. 1–2 (1989): 58–79.

58. Donato, "Death and History" (as cited in note 19 above), 27–30. See also Julia Hill (née Cotton), "Death and Politian," *Durham University Journal* 46, no. 3 (1954): 96–105.

59. Eugenio Garin, "L'ambiente del Poliziano," in *Il Poliziano e il suo tempo* (Florence, 1957), 17–39.

60. Gian-Paolo Biasin, "Messer Iacopo giù per Arno se ne va . . . ," *MLN* 79 (1964): 1–13.

61. Picotti, "Sulla data," 114 n. 2.

62. The theme of the hunt of the stag, according to which the hunter himself becomes the prey of love, is a well-known topos of romance literature; see Marcelle Thiébaux, *The Stag of Love: The Chase in Medieval Literature* (Ithaca, 1974). However, like all such topoi it is susceptible to ambiguous or dual interpretation, depending on whether the idea of love that ensnares the hunter is true or false. In the case of the *Stanze* the enchantment spun by Cupid is especially hallucinatory, and only as the poem comes to the end of the first book and commences the second does it become clear that Julio has been hopelessly deceived, and that his idea of love is false.

63. For masquerade costumes, see the next chapter, as well as Dempsey, *The Portrayal of Love*, 65–80.

64. Donato, "Death and History," 30–32.

65. Mario Martelli, *Angelo Poliziano: Storia e metastoria* (Lecce, 1995), 102–4, observes that, "In grembo a Venere non può voler dire altro se non 'nel seno, nel ventre di;' e *nascere nel grembo di* nient'altro può significare se non 'nascere da.'" On this basis he improbably (and rather literal-mindedly) argues that this means Simonetta is Love, since everybody knows that Amor is the carnal child of Venus, and hence represents a Neoplatonic concept of the rational soul born from the angelic mind. However, the metaphor certainly does suggest that Simonetta here completely drops her disguise, telling Julio that the beauty he sees in her is in an absolutely physical sense the creature of Venus.

66. Virgil, *Aeneid*, 1.257ff., esp. 314ff. I am grateful to David Quint for pointing out to me Politian's dependence on this passage.

67. Mario Martelli, *Angelo Poliziano*, 101–5. I do not follow Martelli's further argument that the triad of the deer, Simonetta, and Venus signifies a Neoplatonic ascent of the divine soul to the angelic mind, symbolized by Venus. See also Branca, *Poliziano e l'umanesimo della parola*, 44–46.

68. *Stanze*, 1.72–76.

69. The image, as has always been noticed, derives from the opening invocation

of Lucretius's *De rerum natura*, in which the paradox of *Mavors armipotens* and *impotens* is also a theme; see Elizabeth Cropper and Charles Dempsey, *Nicolas Poussin: Friendship and the Love of Painting* (Princeton, 1996), 218–60.

Chapter Five

1. *Tutti i Trionfi, Carri, Mascherate o Canti carnascialeschi andati per Firenze dal tempo del Magnifico Lorenzo de'Medici fino all'anno 1559*, 2nd ed., ed. Il Lasca (Francesco Grazzini) (Cosmopoli, 1750), xxxix–xliv; and Giorgio Vasari, *Le vite de'più eccellenti pittori scultori ed architettori*, vol. 5, ed. Gaetano Milanesi (Florence, 1906), 340.

2. Giovanni Ciappelli, *Carnevale e Quaresima: Comportamenti sociali e cultura a Firenze nel Rinascimento*, Temi e Testi 37, Edizioni di Storia e Letteratura (Rome, 1997). I will keep my references to the vast bibliography to the essential minimum necessary for my particular argument, referring the reader to the bibliographies compiled in Ciappelli's excellent study and in Nicole Carew-Reid, *Les fêtes florentines au temps de Lorenzo il Magnifico*, Quaderni di "Rinascimento" 23, Istituto Nazionale di Studi sul Rinascimento (Florence, 1995). Both list the important recent contributions by Paola Ventrone and Nerida Newbigin, among others, and, naturally, Richard Trexler's pioneering *Public Life in Renaissance Florence* (New York, 1980), upon which all later interpretations, whether in agreement or in opposition, greatly depend.

3. Ciappelli, *Carnevale e Quaresima*, 188.

4. Lasca, *Mascherate o Canti carnascialeschi*, xxxix–xliv.

5. Ibid.

6. *Le tems revient / 'l tempo si rinuova: Feste e spettacoli nella Firenze di Lorenzo il Magnifico*, ed. Paola Ventrone (exhibition catalogue for the Comitato Nazionale per le celebrazioni del V centenario della morte di Lorenzo il Magnifico, Milan, 1992), 237, no. 7.5; and see Paola Ventrone, "Note sul carnevale fiorentino de età laurenziana," in *Atti del XIII convegno del Centro Studi sul teatro medioevale e rinascimentale*, (Viterbo, 1990), 321–66, esp. 343.

7. Federico Ghisi, "Le musiche di Isaac per il 'S. Giovanni e Paolo' di Lorenzo di Medici," *La Rassegna musicale* (1943): 264–73.

8. Cf. Lorenzo de'Medici, *Opere*, ed. Tiziano Zanato (Turin, 1992), 401–7 (introduction to the *Laude*). See also *Trionfi e canti carnascialeschi toscani del Rinascimento*, ed. Riccardo Bruscagli (Rome, 1986).

9. For the preface to the *Raccolta Aragonese*, which is generally attributed to Politian writing in Lorenzo's name, see *Prosatori volgari del Quattrocento*, vol. 14 of *La letteratura italiana: Storia e testi*, ed. Claudio Varese (Milan, n.d.), 987–91. There is, however, no reason to think it was not written by Lorenzo himself. For Lorenzo's *Comento* see *Opere*, 555–773.

10. Quoted from *The Man and His Work*, vol. 2 of *Ben Jonson*, ed. Brinsley Nicholson and Charles H. Herford (Oxford, 1925), 251.

11. Lasca, *Mascherate o Canti carnascialeschi*, xxxix–xliv.

12. Ciappelli, *Carnevale e Quaresima*, 199–200, and 199 n. 17, for other anonymous *canzoni* datable before 1486 on the basis of manuscript evidence.

13. Lasca, *Mascherate o Canti carnascialeschi*, xxxix–xliv.

14. Lorenzo de'Medici, *Opere*, 357. See further Mario Martelli, "Una vacanza letteraria di Lorenzo: Il Carnevale del 1490," in Martelli, *Studi Laurenziani* (Florence, 1965), 37–49; and for a lengthy account of the *mascherata* of the Seven Planets, see Paola Ventrone, "Note sul Carnevale fiorentino di età Laurenziana," in *Il Carnevale: Dalla tradizione arcaica alla traduzione colta del Rinascimento* (Atti del Convegno di Studi, Roma 31 maggio–4 giugno 1989), ed. Maria Chiabò and Federico Doglio (Rome, 1990), 321–66, esp. 355–66 (with close attention to Naldo Naldi's poem, *Elegia in septem stellas errantes sub humana specie per urbem florentinam curribus a Laurentio Medice patriae patre duci iussas more triumphantium*).

15. Quoted in Lorenzo de'Medici, *Opere*, 357, and in Martelli, "Una vacanza letteraria," 38.

16. Lorenzo de'Medici, *Opere*, 357.

17. I thank Jonathan Nelson, who will discuss the engraving in greater detail in his forthcoming book on Filippino Lippi, for sharing his thoughts about it with me. Arthur M. Hind, *Early Italian Engraving: A Critical Catalogue with Complete Reproduction of all the Prints Described*, vol. 1 (London, 1938), no. 17, 144–45, already noticed "the most evident influence of Filippino Lippi." A drawing by Filippino of an enthroned woman on a triumphal *carro* may also be connected with the "mascherata di 7 trionfi di 7 pianeti." See further Catherine Whistler, "Drawings from the Weiler Collection," *The Ashmolean* 30 (1996) 15–17; and George Goldner and Carmen C. Bambach, *The Drawings of Filippino Lippi and his Circle* (exhibition catalogue, New York, 1997), no. 56, 218–19.

18. Vasari-Milanesi, 5.340.

19. Lorenzo de'Medici, *Opere*, 357.

20. Ciappelli, *Carnevale e Quaresima*, 201; and see *Canzone del Carro delle Ninfe coi Poeti, cantata in Firenze nel Carnevale del MCDLXXXVIII*, ed. A. Brandi (Arezzo, 1880).

21. Politian, *Nutricia*, vv. 764–65.

22. For a discussion of Pulci's poem see Charles Dempsey, *The Portrayal of Love: Botticelli's Primavera and Humanist Culture at the Time of Lorenzo the Magnificent* (Princeton, 1992), 85–90. See also Mario Martelli, *Letteratura fiorentina del Quattrocento: Il filtro degli anni sessanta* (Florence, 1996), 189–95.

23. Luigi Pulci, *Da poi che 'Lauro*, vv. 64–71, in *Opere minore*, ed. Paolo Orvieto (Milan, 1986), 46–47. Note the the pun on "mask" in *rose adamasche*.

24. Luigi Pulci, *La giostra di Lorenzo de'Medici*, octave 17, in *Opere minore* (edition cited in note 23), 68. See also the discussion in Dempsey, *The Portrayal of Love*, 79–81.

25. Dempsey, *The Portrayal of Love*, 89–95. For the complete Italian text of Martelli's letter, see Isidoro Del Lungo, *Gli amori del Lorenzo il Magnifico* (Bologna, 1924), 33–37.

26. For the date of the *Canzona de' confortini* see Zanato's commentary in Lorenzo de'Medici, *Opere*, 358–59; and for Isaac's arrival in Florence, see Frank A. D'Accone, "Heinrich Isaac in Florence: New and Unpublished Documents," *The Musical Quarterly* 69 (1963): 464–83.

27. Girolamo Mancini, "Il bel s. Giovanni e le feste patronali di Firenze descritte nel 1475 da Piero Cennini," *Rivista d'arte* 6 (1909): 185–227, esp. 224.

28. Lorenzo de'Medici, *Opere*, 357.

29. Trexler, *Public Life*, and Pierre Francastel, *La réalité figurative: Éléments structurels de sociologie et de l'Art*, vol. 2 of *Oeuvres* (Paris, 1965).

30. For a further discussion of such costumes, see Dempsey, *The Portrayal of Love*, 65–72.

31. Ibid., for a discussion of the costumes in the *Primavera* and for the argument that Botticelli's classical subject is expressed in the forms of vernacular poetic traditions as well as the popular experiences of Florentine festivals.

32. For the flowers, see Mirella Levi D'Ancona, *Botticelli's Primavera: A Botanical Interpretation including Astrology, Alchemy, and the Medici* (Florence, 1983) (and see my review in *Renaissance Quarterly* 37 [1981]: 98–102).

33. Politian, *Stanze*, 1.43.

34. Politian, *Stanze*, 1.47.

35. See Rab Hatfield, *Botticelli's Uffizi "Adoration"* (Princeton, 1976), 74, who accepts Vasari's testimony. And see his figs. 27 and 29, for the comparison of Cosimo's features as portrayed by Botticelli and as they appear on the medal.

36. Andrew Butterfield, *The Sculptures of Verrocchio* (New Haven, 1997), 239–40, advances strong reasons for doubting the attribution to Verrocchio. His arguments that the evidence that the bust was "gessoed, polychromed, gilded, and decorated with metal attachments" makes it seem likely that it "would have been made for a festival decoration of some kind" carry much less conviction. Such decoration is common in Renaissance sculpture of all kinds and purposes. I also doubt his suggestion that the portrait may be posthumous.

37. See Dempsey, *The Portrayal of Love*, 85–96.

38. Ibid., 99.

39. The quotation is from Francesco De Sanctis's highly influential essay on Politian in *Storia della letteratura italiana* (Bari, 1958), 358. See also Bernard Berenson's equally influential *The Florentine Painters of the Renaissance* (New York, 1903), 73: "The mere subject, and even representation in general, was so indifferent to

Botticelli, that he appears almost as if haunted by the idea of communicating the unembodied values of touch and movement."

40. Eugenio Donato, "Death and History in Politian's *Stanze*," *MLN* 80 (1965): 27–40. For an excellent critique of recent work on the *Stanze*, see also Emilio Bigi, "Impegno civile e allegorie neoplatoniche nelle 'Stanze,'" in *Poliziano e il suo tempo: Atti del VI Convegno Internazionale (Chianciano-Montepulciano 18–21 luglio 1994)*, ed. Luisa Secchi Tarughi (Florence, 1996), 45–54. And see, for an extension of Donato's criticism, James T. Chiampi, "Poliziano's 'Confessions:' The *Stanze* as Epic of Concupiscence," *Forum Italicum* 23, nos. 1–2 (1989): 58–79.

41. Niccolò Machiavelli, *Istorie fiorentine*, 28.

42. See *Le Stanze, l'Orfeo e le Rime di Messer Angelo Ambrogini Poliziano*, ed. Giosue Carducci (Florence, 1863), xxix–xxxiv, esp. xxxiii.

43. For Corsini's characterization of the joust, see Paul Oskar Kristeller, "Un documento sconosciuto sulla giostra di Giuliano de'Medici," in *Studies in Renaissance Thought and Letters* (Rome, 1956), 437–50, esp. 445.

44. See Dempsey, *The Portrayal of Love*, 125–30.

45. Dempsey, *The Portrayal of Love*, 140–66. For stylistic reasons I hold to the traditional view that the *Primavera* dates to around 1477, which means that it, unlike Politian's *Stanze* and Lorenzo's *Comento*, was conceived and very likely painted before the Pazzi Conspiracy. Recent attempts to date it later are driven by the theory that the painting was made for Lorenzo di Pierfrancesco de'Medici, the younger cousin and ward of the Magnificent. This is, however, only a theory, to which I hope to return in another place. Ronald Lightbown's suggestion in his *Botticelli, Life and Work* (London, 1978), that the painting might date to 1483 (when Lorenzo di Pierfrancesco was married) seems late on grounds of style, though it is perhaps debatable. Horst Bredekamp's radical redating of it to the 1490s in his *Botticelli, Primavera: Florenz als Garten der Venus* (Frankfurt am Main, 1988), is impossible to defend.

46. Paul Joannides, "A Newly Unveiled Drawing by Michelangelo and the Early Iconography of the Magnifici Tombs," *Master Drawings* 29, no. 3 (1991): 255–62.

47. Angelo Poliziano, *Stanze cominciate per la giostra del Magnifico Giuliano di Piero de'Medici*, 2.24. For a convenient summary of interpretations of *Night* and her mask, see Giorgio Vasari, *La vita di Michelangelo nelle redazioni del 1550 e del 1568*, ed. and comm. Paola Barocchi, vol. 3 (Milan, 1962), 1040–41. Among English-speaking scholars the mask is often interpreted as Fraud, which is the meaning given to masks by Ripa, based upon Panofsky's famous exposition of their meaning; suffice it to observe, however, that the meaning of *fraus* is a narrower derivation from the meaning inherent in the deceiving and frightening *larva*. Romance-language scholars, on the other hand, have been more sensitive to the darkly primitive connotations of the mask: see, among the examples cited by Barocchi,

1042–43, Brion ("Ce masque du cauchemar . . . Jamais le génie de Michelangelo n'a inventé quelque chose de plus hideux et de plus terrifiant"); or Papini ("una maschera allucinante . . . indubbiamente simbolo della Terrore").

48. The painting is attributed to Tosini by Federico Zeri, and so far as I know has been published only in a catalogue of the Galleria d'Arte Armondi, *Antologia di maestri antichi* (Brescia, March 1992), no. 11. It is clearly connected thematically to a group of specifically erotic paintings depicting Venus and Cupid (and masks) that are related to the Accademia *Venus and Cupid* traditionally, and rightly, ascribed to Pontormo on the basis of Vasari's famous account of a *Venus* Pontormo painted after a cartoon by Michelangelo (Vasari-Milanesi, 6.277–79 and 291–93; and see *Mostra del Pontormo e del primo manierismo fiorentino*, ed. Mario Salmi [Florence, 1956], 44–45, no. 70, and plate 63). The most famous of them (and the most independent of Michelangelo's model) is of course Bronzino's *Venus and Cupid* in the National Gallery in London. Tosini's inversion of the mask held by *eros* derives from another lost invention by Michelangelo preserved in three drawings, the best of which is in the Uffizi and ascribed to Battista Franco (see John Paoletti, "Michelangelo's Masks," *Art Bulletin* 74 (1992): 423–40, figs. 13 and 14).

49. This is clearly the theme of Michelangelo's famous drawing entitled the *Dream of Human Life*, in which a nude youth is roused from his position on a box filled with masks and is diverted by a trumpeting angel away from the generically obsessive, terrestrial nightmare *phantasmata* of the seven deadly sins swirling around him. See Ludwig Goldscheider, *Michelangelo Drawings* (London, 1951), 49–50 (no. 93), and fig. 93; and for the vexed question of the attribution of the drawing, see Alexander Perrig, *Michelangelo's Drawings: The Science of Attribution* (New Haven, 1991), 33.

50. For various interpretations of the friezes with their masks, see Vasari-Milanesi, 3.824–25. Of special importance are Charles de Tolnay's observation that the motif derives from ancient funeral imagery (*Michelangelo, III: The Medici Chapel* [Princeton, 1948], 165f.); Groote's perception that they refer to the *le favole del mondo*, or the dreams of earthly existence (*Die Deutung der Medici Grabdenkmäler Michelangelos* [Strassburg, 1927], 43); and Schottmüller's association of them with the terrestrial demons of primitive antiquity (in the context of an argument that the masks in fact represent no more than Michelangelo's artistic fantasy): "Denn das Tier ist in elementarer Vorstellung dem Menschen artverwandt oder von höherer Ordnung; und nur dem Primitiven und dem Genie ist die Erde bevölkert mit menschlichen und tierischen Dämonen" (*Jahrbuch der Kunsthistorischen Sammlungen in Wien* 2 [1928]: 232). For humanists such as Poliziano, and for Michelangelo, such ancient apotropaic demons—ancient ghosts, or *larve*—function not literally (for Michelangelo was no pagan), but metaphorically, standing for the empty bogeys, or childishly panicked dreams of mortal desire.

However, as everybody knows, the mask motifs designed by Michelangelo for the Medici Chapel instantly became ubiquitous in Tuscan architectural, sculptural, and funerary decoration, and in particular one of the sculptors who helped to carve the mask-frieze, the prodigiously talented Silvio Cosini, was accused of dabbling in black magic because of his compelling, and even obsessive, images of demons in the form of *larve*; see Carlo Del Bravo, "Silvio e la magia," *Artista: Critica dell'arte in Toscana* 4 (1992): 8–19.

51. See Ernst Steinmann, *Das Geheimnis der Medicigraeber Michel Angelos* (Leipzig, 1907), 36–42. Erica Tietze-Conrat, "The Church Program of Michelangelo's Medici Chapel," *Art Bulletin* 36 (1954): 222–24, dismissed the problem of the passage written on the drawing by asserting in effect that Michelangelo didn't know what he meant when he wrote it in the first place, a suggestion that might best be left in oblivion were it not surprisingly often restated. Among the serious attempts to interpret the inscription, one of the best is Creighton Gilbert, "Texts and Contexts of the Medici Chapel," *Art Quarterly* 34 (1971): 391–408.

52. Gilbert, "Texts and Contexts," 391–408.

53. See Frederick Hartt, "The Meaning of Michelangelo's Medici Chapel," *Essays in Honor of Georg Swarzenski* (Chicago, 1951), 145–55.

INDEX

Adorno, Piero, 54
Agamben, Giorgio, 95
Agathius, 90; *De bello gothorum*, 90, 92
Agostino di Duccio, 24, 50, 53; Chapel of the Infant Games, 24; Chapel of the Planets, 50, 51, 53
Alain de Lille, 154; *De planctu Naturae*, 154
Alamanni, Pietro, 190, 191
Alberti, Leon Battista, 109; *De architectura*, 109
Albertus Magnus, 94
Albizzi, Albiera degli, x, 149, 190, 213
Alciati, Andrea, 117, 118, 125; *Emblematum liber*, 117, 118
Aldrovandi, Ulisse, xiii
Aldus Manutius, 117, 182
Alessandro morente, xiii
Alessi, Andrea, 8, 13; baptistry, Trogir, 8, 11; Chapel of the Blessed Giovanni Orsini, 8, 10, 13
Alexander and Roxana, 119, 120, 138, 140, 142
Ambrogini, Angelo. *See* Politian
Amerino, Pirrino, 196
Amiens, cathedral at, 6, 7
Amor, 1, 3, 4, 13, 15, 16, 81, 82, 85
Amores, 61, 86
Amorino, 4, 12, 13, 72
Angel, 41
Angel-*pneuma*, 41
Apelles, 119
Apuleius, 103, 141; *De deo Socratis*, 103
Aratus, 115, 117, 119, 121, 122; *Phaenomena*, 116

Ardinghelli, Niccolò, 151, 162
Aretino, Pietro, xiii
Ariosto, Ludovico, 154; *Orlando furioso*, 154
Aristophanes, 104, 142, 143; *Achanians*, 104; *Lysistrata*, 143
Aristotle, 41, 109, 110; *Prior Analytics*, 109
Armeggeria, 77–79, 81, 82, 85, 86
Artemidorus, 126, 129, 148; *Oneirocritica*, 129
Attavante, 90; frontispiece to *Enneads*, 90, 91
Augurelli, Giovanni Aurelio, 161–63, 165; *Amica ad magnanimum Iulianum Medicem*, 163; *In signis quare Medici sit*, 163
Augustine, Saint, 136, 148; *City of God*, 136
Aulus Gellius, 121; *Attic Nights*, 121
Averlino, Antonio. *See* Filarete

Bacchoi, xii, 64, 66, 70
Baldini, Baccio, 76, 82–84, 165, 167, 196, 199; *Cupid Chastized*, 165, 167; *The Planet Venus*, 82–84; *Triumph of Bacchus and Ariadne*, 196, 197; *Triumph of Love*, 76, 79, 199
Barbaro, Ermolao, the Elder, 8
Barker, Alexander, 112
Bartoli, Pietro, 1, 3, 4; *Admiranda romanarum antiquitatum*, 1, 2
Bary, René, 41, 43, 44; *Méthode pur bien prononcer un discours*, 41, 43
Basilius Athanaeus, 103

Bellori, Giovan Pietro, 3, 49
Bembo, Bernardo, 161, 162
Bembo, Pietro, x, xi
Benci, Bartolomeo, 77–82, 85, 86, 200
Benci, Salvestro, 73
Benedetti, Francesco (Platone) de', 181
Bentivoglio, Annibale, 81
Beroaldo, Filippo, 81
Bertoldo di Giovanni, 60; *Bacchic Procession*, 60
Bessi, Rossella, 73
Biasin, Gian-Paolo, 184, 185
Boccaccio, Giovanni, x, 89, 154; *Amorosa visione*, 154; *Corbaccio*, 154; *Fiammetta*, 89, 90, 154; *Filocolo*, 154; *Ninfale fiesolano*, 154; *Teseida*, 154
Bode, Wilhelm, 20, 22, 26, 28, 34
Boethius, 88, 89, 94; *De consolatione philosophiae*, 88
Botticelli, Sandro, x, xi, 71, 100, 111–46 passim, 147, 153–56, 162, 167, 172, 178, 179, 186, 194, 203–16, 219; *Adoration of the Magi*, 208–10, 215; *Birth of Venus*, xi, 76, 115, 140, 203–6; *Calumny of Apelles*, 119; *Mars and Venus*, xv, 100, 106, 107, 111–46 passim, 147, 153–56, 213–16, 221; *Pallas and the Centaur*, 178, 179; *Portrait of Giuliano de' Medici*, 210, 212; *Primavera*, x, 140, 186, 203, 204, 206–8, 213–15, 219, 220; standard for joust of Giuliano de' Medici, 71, 157, 162–67, 172, 194
Bracciolini, Poggio, 140
Branca, Vittorio, 181, 182
Brandt, Sebastian, 129, 132; *Narrenschiff*, 129, 132
Bronzino, Agnolo, 144, 145, 221; *Allegory of Venus and Cupid*, 144, 145, 221
Brown, David, 72
Brunelleschi, Filippo, 181

Buffalmacco, 32; *Triumph of Death*, 32, 34
Bugbears (bogeys, *terriculamenta*), 103, 104, 109, 126, 128, 129, 141, 145, 148. *See also* Hobgoblins

Calabria, Maria di, tomb of, 12
Calendimaggio, 189, 191, 214
Cameos, 16
Canti, 189–91, 194; *carnascialeschi*, 189, 191, 192, 196
Canzoni, 191, 192, 194, 196, 210, 213, 218; *a ballo*, 189, 201, 213; *di carro*, 191, 192, 194, 197
Carducci, Giosue, 178, 182, 214
Carl, Doris, 13
Carnevale, 189, 191–94
Carracci, Annibale, 134, 135; *Temptation of St. Anthony*, 134, 135
Cartari, Vincenzo, 86
Casa, Giovanni della, 103; sonnet on *Cura*, 103
Castle of Love, 82, 85, 86
Cattaneo, Simonetta, 140. *See also* Vespucci, Simonetta Cataneo
Cavalcanti, Guido, 94, 95
Cecca, Lo, 81, 200
Cellini, Benvenuto, 40
Cennini, Piero, 196, 199
Cicero, 122, 128, 129, 141, 154; *Epistulae ad familiares*, 122; *Somnium Scipionis*, 154
Cimabue, 28; upper church, Assisi, 28
Città di Castello, Duomo in, 28, 29, 34
Clement of Alexandria, 64
Colantuono, Anthony, xiv
Colonna, Francesco, 56, 57, 64; *Hypnerotomachia Polifili*, 56–58, 63, 64, 154
Colonne, Guido delle, 131, 155; *Historiae destructionis Troiae*, 131, 141

INDEX

Compagnia della Stella, 192, 193
Compagnia del Vangelista, 190
Correggio, Antonio, 115–17; *Pan with the Conch-shell*, 115–17
Corsini, Filippo, 160–62
Costumes, 76, 178, 198–208, 218
Cranach, Lucas, 129, 133; *Judgement of Paris*, 129, 133
Crivelli, Taddeo, 14, 90; *Bible of Borso d'Este*, 17; choir books for San Petronio, 14, 90
Cupidi, 61

Dante, x, 43, 44, 87–90, 94, 95, 105; *Convivio*, 88, 89; *Vita nuova*, 43, 44, 87, 214
Delcorno Branca, Daniela, 182
Del Lungo, Isidoro, 178, 180, 183, 185, 216–18
Desco da parto (painted birth-tray), 198; *Triumph of Fame*, 165, 168; *Triumph of Love*, Galleria Sabauda, 76, 77, 198; *Triumph of Love*, Victoria and Albert Museum, 76, 78, 199
Dionysus of Halicarnassus, 125
Donatello, x, xiii, xiv, 8, 13–16, 18–20, 26, 28, 32–35, 37–42, 45–50, 54–60, 63, 64, 69; *Attis-Amorino*, 58–60; baptismal font, Siena, 13, 18–20, 32, 45; Cantoria, Duomo in Florence, 14, 15, 46, 47; *Cavalcanti Altar*, 22, 35, 37–41, 45, 56; *Judith and Holofernes*, 48–50, 54–58, 63, 64; *Music-making Angel-Spiritelli*, 41, 42, 45; Prato pulpit, 13, 14, 15, 45, 46; *St. Daniel*, 25; *St. Louis tabernacle*, 32
Donati, Lucrezia, 151–53, 162, 194–96, 210, 213, 218
Donati, Piccarda, 151–53
Donato, Eugenio, 157, 183, 184, 187, 214, 216

Donatus, Hieronymus, 169
Dovizi da Bibiena, Agnolo, 192
Dovizi da Bibiena, Piero, 192
Dreams: allegorical (*óneiros, somnium*), 129, 172; common (*enúpnion, insomnium*), 129, 135, 136, 148–50, 173, 174; false (*phantásma, visum*), 129, 135, 136, 173; as literary topos, 129, 154–56; oracular (*chrematismós, oraculum*), 129; prophetic (*órama, visio*), 129, 135
Duquesnoy, François, 67, 68, 99; *Infant Bacchanal with Larvate Putto and Goat*, 67, 68
Durazza, Maria di, tomb of, 12

Edifizio. See *Trionfo*
Eleanora of Aragon, 149
Emerson, Ralph Waldo, 105
Ephialtae (nightmare demons), 126, 129, 136. See also *Incubi*
Erasmus, 102, 103, 117, 143; *Adagia*, 102, 103, 117, 143
Eratosthenes, 116, 117, 121, 124, 126
Eros, 4, 13, 71, 72, 86, 94, 102, 105, 112, 138, 142, 221, 222
Erotes, 13, 61, 64, 86, 99, 119, 120, 138–40, 143
Este, Lucrezia d', 81
Ethos, xi, xiii
Euripides, 122, 149; *Medea*, 122, 149

Fantasia, 94
Faunus, 118, 125, 137
Feasts: Calendimaggio, 189, 191, 214; Carnevale, 189, 191–94; San Giovanni, 189, 192, 196
Febris (Fever), 149, 150
Federico d'Aragona, 159
Festa, 6, 8, 13, 38; corona, 6, 8, 13; romana, 8, 12, 28, 35, 50, 51

INDEX

271

Filarete, 8, 9, 13; Medici Bank, 8–10
Folletto, 58
Follies, 94
Fortune, 152, 173, 178, 183–85, 219
Francastel, Pierre, x, 198
Fuochi fatui, 41

Gagliano, Filippo da, 192
Galen, 41
Garin, Eugenio, x, xiv, 107, 184
Genius, 1, 3, 4, 6, 13, 14, 40, 66; of Death, 3; of Love, 3; of Wine, 69
Ghiberti, Lorenzo, x; *Commentarii*, x
Gilbert, Albert, 4; Shaftesbury monument, 4, 5
Gilbert, Creighton, 226
Gilio, Giovanni Andrea, xiii
Ginzburg, Carlo, 147
Giotto, x, xi
Giraldi, Lilio Gregorio, 126, 135, 136; *De deis gentium*, 126, 135
Giuliano da Maiano, 28, 33, 50; *Spiritelli*, 50
Giustiniani, Vincenzo, 67
Gombrich, Ernst, 4
Gonzaga, Ludovico, 158
Gorni, Guglielmo, 181, 182
Grammaticus, 110, 111
Granacci, Francesco, 193, 194
Grazzini, Francesco, 189–92
Green Man, 6, 7
Guerrieri, Matteo, 180
Guicciardini, Pietro, 160
Guidi, Jacopo di Piero, 36; *Porta della Mandorla*, 36

Harvey, William, 41
Hobgoblins, xii, xiv, 20, 105, 112, 128, 145, 230. See also Bugbears
Housman, A. E., 111

Humanism, 107–12
Hyginus, 121, 122
Hyphialtae (nightmare demons), 126, 136. See also *Succubi*

Incubi, 126, 129, 135, 136, 137, 148, 151
Innocent VIII (pope), 147, 148
Insomnium. See Dreams
Inuus, 137
Isaac, Heinrich, 190, 191, 194, 196
Isidore of Seville, 137
Ivories, French, 82, 85; *Battle for the Castle of Love*, 82; *Joust before the Castle of Love*, 85

Janson, Horst, 58
Jerome, Saint, 137; commentary to Isaiah, 137; *Life of Paul the Hermit*, 137
Jousts. See Medici, Giuliano de': joust of; Medici, Lorenzo: joust of
Juřen, Vladimir, 117, 121

Klotz, Christian Adolf, 1, 3, 4
Kobolds, xii, 20
Kristeller, Paul Oskar, 107–9, 159

Lama, Guasparre del, 208
Lamberti, Niccolò di Pietro, 32, 33; Porta della Mandorla, 33, 34; *Tomb of Nofri Strozzi*, 32, 35
Lamia, 109, 135, 141, 143, 145, 147, 156
Laokoon, xiii
Lapaccini, Filippo di Lorenzo, 78, 80, 200; "Report of the Festival . . . organized by Bartolomeo Benci," 78–81
Larva, xiv, xv, 1, 58, 100, 102, 103, 105, 112, 121, 126, 127, 147, 151, 153, 156, 173, 174, 178, 182, 215, 220–22, 228, 230, 231. See also *Mormolykeion*
Lasca, 189–92

Laude, 190
Le Brun, Charles, 41; *Conférence* on the Passions, 41
Leonardo da Vinci, 72
Leo X (pope), 218, 220
Lessing, Gotthold Ephraim, 1–4, 40; *Antiquarian Letters*, 1; *How the Ancients Represented Death*, 1–4; *Laokoon*, 1
Letto di Policleto, xiv
Leuschner, Eckhard, 99
Lippi, Filippino, 193, 194
Livy, 125
Longhi, Roberto, xii
Lorenzetti, Ambrogio, 202, 203; *Good Government in the City*, 202, 203
Lorenzetti, Pietro, 28, 32; *Last Supper*, 32
Lorris, Guillaume de, 154; *Roman de la rose*, 82, 154
Lotto, Lorenzo, 64, 72, 74; *Christ the Vine*, 64–66; *Sleeping Nymph*, 72, 74
Lucian, 94, 119, 120, 138–40, 142; *Calumny*, 119; *Herodotus, or Aëtion*, 119, 138
Lucius Afranius, 101
Lucretius, 140; *De rerum natura*, 140
Lymphaticus, 122, 126, 128, 141, 150

Machiavelli, Niccolò, 107, 162, 216, 218; *Istorie fiorentine*, 216
Macrobius, 129, 135, 136, 151, 154; commentary to Cicero's *Somnium Scipionis*, 129, 135, 154
Maffei, Sonia, xiii
Magnani, Andrea, 181
Maius (May branch), 6
Malleus maleficarum, 147, 148
Manetti, Antonio, 181
Mannerism, ix
Mantegna, Andrea, x, xi, 96, 98, 99; *Larvate Erotes* (copy), 96, 98; *Triumph of Caesar*, x, xi
Mariottazio, 192
Martelli, Braccio, 101, 102, 196, 213
Martelli, Mario, 187
Martini, Simone, x, xi
Mascherata (masque, masquerade), xv, 76, 186, 189–98, 200–208, 213, 215, 218
Master of the Die, 67, 68, 100, 102, 112; *Procession of Putti with Goat and Masked Infant*, 100, 102; *Tender Sprites attacking a Goat*, 57, 68
Medici, Cosimo, 13, 75, 208–10, 215, 220
Medici, Giovanni di Cosimo, 208
Medici, Giovanni di Lorenzo, 218, 220
Medici, Giuliano, 71, 72, 156–65, 169, 172, 174–80, 185, 206, 210, 214–20, 228, 230; joust of, 71, 72, 157–67, 185, 188, 206, 214, 215, 217
Medici, Giuliano (duke of Nemours), 219, 220
Medici, Giulio, 220
Medici, Lorenzo, xii, xv, 16, 44, 45, 71–73, 75, 86, 90, 99, 109, 151–53, 156–62, 165, 173, 176, 189–97, 207, 210, 213–15, 217–20, 228–31; *Canzona de' confortini*, 191, 196; *Canzona delle cicale*, 193; *Canzona de' sette pianeti*, 192, 194, 196, 197; *Canzona di Bacco* ("Quanto è bella giovinezza"), 190, 192, 194, 196; *Canzoniere*, 213; *Comento sopra alcuni de' suoi sonetti*, 44, 45, 173, 213, 217–19; "Fuggo i bei raggi del mio ardente Sole," 213; joust of, 162, 194; "Quanto è grande la bellezza" (lauda), 190; *Raccolta Aragonese*, xii, 159, 160, 162, 176, 190, 217, 230; *Rappresentazione di SS. Giovanni e Paolo*, 190

Medici, Lorenzo (duke of Urbino), 220
Medici, Piero di Cosimo, 208
Medici Bank, 8–10
Medici *casa vecchia* (*orticino del pozzo*), 13
Medici Chapel, New Sacristy, San Lorenzo, 220–31
Medici family, 70, 220
Medici Palace, 13, 16, 86
Medici Villa, 14, 54, 70
Meung, Jean de, 154; *Roman de la rose*, 82, 154
Michelangelo, x, 220–31; *Dawn*, 226; *Day*, 223, 226–28; drawing for column bases, 223, 225, 226; drawing for tombs of the Magnifici with Fame, 228–30; drawing for Tombs of the Magnifici with Hesperides, 220; Duke Giuliano, 220, 222–24, 226, 228; Duke Lorenzo, 222, 228; larvate capitals, 222, 224; larvate frieze, 222, 223; *Leda*, 222; Medici Chapel, New Sacristy, San Lorenzo, 220–31; *Night*, 220–23, 226, 228; *Venus and Cupid*, 221
Michelozzi, Niccolò, 192
Michelozzo, 22, 28, 51; Prato pulpit (*see* Donatello); tomb of Bartolomeo Aragazzi, 22, 28, 51
Modena, Duomo in, 26
Monreale, cloister of, 26
Morelli, Giovanni di Papi, 71, 72
Mormolykeion, 102–4, 112, 114, 121. See also *Larva*
Mormon, 104
Müntz, Eugène, 20

Naldi, Naldo, 158, 161, 211, 215; *Carmen de ludicro hastatorum equitum certamine ad Iulianum Medicen*, 161

Nanni di Viterbo (Il Fora), 15, 55
Niccolò di Giovanni Fiorentino, 8, 13, 50, 52; baptistry, Trogir, 8, 11; Chapel of the Blessed Giovanni Orsini, 8, 10, 11, 13, 50–52
Nicetas Choniates, 123; *Orationes*, 123
Nightmares, 107, 128, 129, 136, 140, 142, 145, 146, 148–51, 156, 215, 221
Nonius Marcellus, 101
Nympholeptós, 122, 126, 128, 141, 150
Nymphs, xii, xiii, 126, 136, 178, 203

Oraculum. See Dreams
Oscillum, 67, 100
Ovid, 149, 156; *Metamorphoses*, 149, 156

Pallas with the broncone, 165
Pamphili, Camillo, 3
Pan Belliger, 123, 124
Pan Ephialtes, 136
"Panic terrors," 102, 105, 112, 114, 116–29, 141, 147–52, 215
Pan Inuus, 137
Paniscus (Pan-putto, Pan-sprite), 100, 117, 119, 120, 124, 126–28, 135, 137–43, 145, 150, 221
Panofsky, Erwin, ix, xi, 28, 115–17, 125; *Renaissance and Renascences*, ix, xi
Pan Terrificus, 121, 150
Patavin, Roland, 82
Pathos, xi, xiii
Pathosformel, xiii, xiv
Paul II (pope), 99
Pausanias, 141
Pazzi, Renato de', 101, 102, 114, 123, 128
Pazzi Conspiracy, 157, 180, 183–85, 187, 194, 196, 216–19
Pensiero (*d'amore*), 87–90, 94, 103
Pernicone, Vincenzo, 180, 181
Perosa, Alessandro, 149

Perugia: Palazzo dei Priori in, 26, 27; San Domenico in, 26
Petrarch, x, xi, 82, 151, 153, 154, 160, 165, 166, 174–76, 198–200, 203, 213, 214; *Rime*, 151, 153; *Secretum*, 154; *Trionfi*, 82, 154, 176, 198, 213; *Triumph of Chastity*, 165, 166
Phantasm (phantasma, phantasmatum), 95, 123, 125, 128, 129, 135–37, 141, 145, 147, 148, 150, 151, 153, 155, 174, 223, 228
Pico della Mirandola, Giovanni Francesco, 135, 147; *Praenotiones*, 135; *Strix*, 135, 147
Picotti, Giovanni Battista, 180, 182, 185
Picus, 125
Pierino da Vinci, 112, 113; *Puer mingens*, 112, 113
Piero di Cosimo, 138, 139; *Mars and Venus*, 138, 139
Pisano, Nicola, 103, 104; *Last Judgment* (baptismal font, Pisa), 103, 104
Pistoia, baptistry in, 28, 30, 34
Pius II (pope), 75, 78
Plato, 103, 154; *Phaedrus*, 103; *Republic*, 154
Plautus, 143; *Amphitryone*, 143
Plutarch, 125, 126; *Moralia*, 126; *Numa*, 125
Pneuma. See Spirits
Pneumatic School of Medicine, 41
Politian, x, xiv, xv, 60, 61, 101–3, 105, 109–11, 115, 117, 119–24, 127–29, 136, 137, 139, 141, 142, 147–51, 154, 156–59, 169–88, 192, 194, 207, 210, 213–19, 221; *Ambra*, 181; *Coniurationis Pactianae commentarium*, 185; *Le cose volgari*, 181; *Detti piacevoli*, 101; epicedion on death of Albiera degli Albizzi, x, 149, 150, 160, 183; *Epistola de obitu Laurentii Medicis*, 181; *Herodianus, historiae de imperio post Marcum*, 181; introduction to Alberti, *De architectura*, 109; *Julio at the Altar of Venus* for, 176–78; *Lamia*, 109–11, 148; *Manto*, 181; *Miscellanea*, 102, 117, 120, 121, 141; *Nutricia*, 141, 181, 194; *Opera omnia*, 182; *Orfeo*, 181, 182; *Panepistemon*, 111, 129, 136; *Rime*, 181; *Rusticus*, 181; *S. Athanasius, stilus et character psalmorum*, 181; *Stanze per la giostra di Giuliano de' Medici*, x, xv, 60, 61, 86, 105, 115, 147, 154, 156–58, 169–88, 206, 207, 210, 213, 214–19, 221
Pollaiuolo, Antonio, 194; standard for joust of Lorenzo de' Medici, 194
Pontormo, Jacopo da, 38, 40, 221; *Venus and Cupid*, 221; *Vertumnus and Pomona*, 38, 40
Pope-Hennessy, John, 18
Poussin, Nicolas, 49, 67, 69, 99; *Extreme Unction*, 49, 50; *Infant Bacchanal with Chariot and Masks*, 69, 70; *Infant Bacchanal with Goat and Larvate Putto*, 69
Primaticcio, xii, xiv
Pulci, Luigi, 72, 73, 151–53, 161, 162, 194, 195, 210, 213, 215; "Da poi che 'Lauro," 151, 152, 194, 210; "Le galee per Quaracchi," 213; "La giostra di Lorenzo de' Medici," 72, 73, 161, 162, 195
Pulci, 211
Putti, xii, xiii, xiv, 4, 10, 13, 14, 20, 22, 26, 28, 32, 47, 50, 63, 64, 86, 90, 94, 96, 99; *moderno*, 67; *reggifestone*, 28, 50, 54, 64; *reggistemma*, 28, 32, 90; *Satyriscus*, 60

Quaracchi, 8, 213
Quercia, Jacopo della, 10, 12, 20, 33, 35,

51, 64; baptismal font, Siena, 20; tomb of Ilaria del Carretto, 10, 12, 20, 28, 33, 35, 51, 63, 64

Raphael, x, xi, 67, 119, 120, 129; *Dream of the Knight*, 129, 131; *Marriage of Alexander and Roxana*, 119, 120; *St. Cecilia*, 129, 130
Renaissance, ix, xi, 107, 108
Reymond, Marcel, 35, 58
Riccio, Andrea, 104, 105; *Funeral of Gerolamo della Torre*, 104, 105
Ristoro d'Arezzo, 15; *Libro della composizione del Mondo*, 15
Rome: Santa Costanza in, 15, 28
Santa Maria Maggiore in, 28, 31
Ronsard, Pierre de, 105, 106, 126; "Les Daimons," 106, 126
Rosenauer, Artur, 18
Rosini, Giovanni, 115
Rosselino, Antonio, 21; tomb of the Cardinal of Portugal, 21
Rosso Fiorentino, xii, xiv
Rucellai, Bernardo, 192
Rucellai, Giovanni, 8, 15, 28; *Zibaldone*, 8

Sannazzaro, Iacopo, 96; *Arcadia*, 96, 99
Sanvito, Bartolomeo, 90, 93–97, 99, 100, 104, 112; frontispiece to Eusebius, *Ecclesiastical History*, 96, 97; frontispiece to Suetonius, *Lives of the Caesars*, 90, 93–96, 104, 112
Sarcophagi, Roman: Bacchic (Dionysiac), 16, 17, 55, 58, 63, 64, 66, 67, 70, 71, 99; "garland," 10; Good Shepherd, 64, 65; Junius Bassus, 64; Meleager, xiv; Prometheus, 3; season, 64
Sarti (Sarzio), Alessandro, 178, 180–82

Satyriscus (satyr-putto, satyr-sprite), 60, 112, 114, 121, 126, 215
Satyrs, xii, 26, 116, 126, 136, 137
Sellaio, Jacopo del, 76, 81, 165, 169, 186, 200, 201, 203, 204, 206; *Triumph of Chastity*, 76, 165, 169, 186, 201, 203, 204, 206; *Triumph of Eternity*, 201; *Triumph of Love*, 76, 81, 186, 201; *Triumph of Time*, 200, 201
Settis, Salvatore, xiii, 178
Sforza, Galeazzo Maria, 75, 78
Shakespeare, William, xiv; *Othello*, 55
Siena, Duomo in, 26
Signorelli, Luca, 124–26; *Realm of Pan*, 124–26
Silenus-mask (satyr-mask), xiv, 94, 96, 99, 102, 220, 221
Somnium. See Dreams
Sostratos, 16, 18
Spenser, Edmund, 103, 147, 155, 156; *The Faerie Queene*, 147, 155, 156
Spirits (*pneuma, spirito, spiritus*), 15, 41, 43, 49, 50, 66, 94; angel, 41; animal, 43–45, 50; natural, 43, 44, 50, 54, 64; nightmare, 107, 139, 140; sensitive (*spiriti sensitivi*), 43–46; of sound (*spiriti del suono*), 43, 46, 47, 63; of sight (*spiriti del viso*), 43–45, 63, 95; *spirito fantastico* (*spiritus phantasticus*), 94, 95, 128; *Spirito sensibile*, 46; vital, 43–45, 50; *vocale spirto*, 46; water, 54, 70
Spiritello, xii–xv, 6, 8, 10, 13–16, 18, 20, 28, 33, 40, 41, 45, 47, 49–51, 55–61, 63, 66, 69–73, 75, 76, 86, 89, 90, 94, 95, 100, 102, 104, 105, 112, 114, 147, 196, 201; *spiritello d'amore*, 43, 63, 70, 80, 81, 86–90, 94–96, 102, 103, 105, 138, 139, 198; *Spiritello del vino*, 55–60
Squarcione, Francesco, x
Statius, 137; *Sylvae*, 137

Steinmann, Ernst, 226
Strozzi, Lorenzo di Messer Palla, 79
Strozzi, Marietta degli, 78–82, 85, 86, 200
Strozzi, Matteo, 15
Stufa, Sigismondo della, 149
Succubi, 126, 136. See also *Incubi*
Sylvanus, 125
Synesius, 94, 122; *De insomniis*, 94; *De providentia*, 122

Tasso, Torquato, 154, 155; *Gerusalemme liberata*, 154, 155
Tener (teneri), 66–69
Tennyson, Alfred, Lord, 89; "In memoriam," 89
Theon of Alexandria, 116, 117
Torriti, Jacopo, 28; apse mosaic, Santa Maria Maggiore, 28, 31
Tosini, Michele di Ridolfo del Ghirlandaio, 221, 222; *Night with a Larvate Eros*, 221, 222
Tovaglia, Pietro del, 158
Trexler, Richard, 81, 198
Trionfo (carro, edifizio, parade car), 75, 76, 80, 82, 190–94, 197–201, 203, 213, 218
Triumph of Aemilius Paulus, 193, 213
Triumph of Chastity, 165, 166
Triumph of Eternity, 201
Triumph of Fame, 165, 168
Triumph of Love, 76, 77, 79, 81, 186, 198, 199, 201
Triumph of Time, 200, 201

Valerius Flaccus, 100, 123, 128; *Argonautica*, 123
Vallaresso, Maffeo (bishop of Zara), 8
Valois, Marie de, tomb of, 12
Varchi, Benedetto, 103; *Opere*, 103
Vasari, Giorgio, x, 38, 41, 45, 49, 81, 112, 139, 189, 193, 208, 210; *Vite*, x
Venturi, Adolfo, 12, 13
Verino, Ugolino, 211
Veroli casket, 112, 114
Verrocchio, Andrea del, 14, 51, 70, 71, 73, 162, 210; bust of Giuliano de' Medici, 210, 211; *Nymph and Spiritello*), 72, 73; *Putto with a Dolphin*, 14, 51, 54, 70; standard for joust of Giuliano de' Medici, 71; standard for joust of Lorenzo de' Medici, 162, 194
Vespucci, Marco, 162
Vespucci, Simonetta Cattaneo, 157, 160, 162, 165, 173–76, 180, 182–88, 190, 206–8, 210, 215–19
Vespucci family, 140
Villani, Giovanni, 81; *Chronicle*, 81
Vindemia, 64
Virgil, 66, 67, 99, 135; *Aeneid*, 135, 187; *Georgics*, 66, 67, 99
Visio. See Dreams
Visum. See Dreams

Warburg, Aby, x, xiii, 206, 207
Wasps, 127, 128, 140, 143, 145, 153, 154, 215
Witchcraft, 147, 148